# CHINA'S GLOBAL ENERGY EXPANSION

Should Chinese energy investments be excluded from the liberal economic system based on geopolitical assessments only? This book explores the potential regulatory control by the Chinese government over foreign energy investments to achieve their perceived strategic objectives.

Host states in which Chinese energy companies make investments have increasingly opposed Chinese energy investments in their national security reviews, based on concerns that these investments have strategic objectives. The book analyses China's investment-related law, regulations, and energy policies to examine how overseas energy investment-making is governed. The book also explores the role of the Chinese government in energy investment promotion and protection.

Uniquely, the examination of China's potential regulatory control provides an objective criterion, rather than geopolitical considerations, for host states to assess the nature of Chinese energy investments.

The book helps readers to open the 'black box' of Chinese energy investments from a regulatory perspective. It is a useful resource for researchers as well as practising lawyers assisting their Chinese clients through national security reviews, or when trying to determine whether China's SOEs can bring cases before investor-state arbitration tribunals.

**Global Energy Law and Policy: Volume 8**

**Global Energy Law and Policy**



Energy policy and energy law are undergoing rapid global transformation, characterised by the push in favour of decarbonisation. The 2015 Sustainable Development Goals and the 2015 Paris Agreement on international climate action have forged a consensus for a pathway to a universal just transition towards a low-carbon economy for all states and all societies.

This series publishes conceptual works that help academics, legal practitioners and decision-makers to make sense of these transformational changes. The perspective of the series is global. It welcomes contributions on international law, regional law (for example, from the EU, US and ASEAN regions), and the domestic law of all states with emphasis on comparative works that identify horizontal trends, and including transnational law. The series' scope is comprehensive, embracing both public and commercial law on energy in all forms and sources and throughout the energy life-cycle from extraction, production, operation, consumption and waste management/decommissioning. The series is a forum for innovative interdisciplinary work that uses the insights of cognate disciplines to achieve a better understanding of energy law and policy in the 21st century.

**Recent titles in this series:**

*Decarbonisation and the Energy Industry*
edited by Tade Oyewumni, Penelope Crossley, Frédéric Gilles Sourgens and Kim Talus

*The Global Energy Transition: Law, Policy and Economics for Energy in the 21st Century*
edited by Peter D Cameron, Xiaoyi Mu and Volker Roeben

*The Law and Governance of Mining and Minerals: A Global Perspective*
by Ana Elizabeth Bastida

*National Climate Change Acts: The Emergence, Form and Nature of National Framework Climate Legislation*
edited by Thomas L Muinzer

*Governing the Extractive Sector: Regulating the Foreign Conduct of International Mining Firms*
by Jeffrey Bone

*Stability and Legitimate Expectations in International Energy Investments*
by Rahmi Kopar

*Land Law and the Extractive Industries: Challenges and Opportunities in Africa*
by Victoria R Nalule

*China's Global Energy Expansion: A Regulatory Assessment*
By Xiaohan Gong

# China's Global Energy Expansion

*A Regulatory Assessment*

Xiaohan Gong

•HART•
OXFORD • LONDON • NEW YORK • NEW DELHI • SYDNEY

HART PUBLISHING

Bloomsbury Publishing Plc

Kemp House, Chawley Park, Cumnor Hill, Oxford, OX2 9PH, UK

1385 Broadway, New York, NY 10018, USA

29 Earlsfort Terrace, Dublin 2, Ireland



First published in Great Britain 2024



A catalogue record for this book is available from the British Library.

A catalogue record for this book is available from the Library of Congress.

Library of Congress Control Number: 2024940206

ISBN: HB: 978-1-50996-619-6
ePDF: 978-1-50996-621-9
ePub: 978-1-50996-620-2

Typeset by Compuscript Ltd, Shannon

*This book is dedicated to Mom, Dad and Longkun.*

## CONTENTS

# 1

# Introduction

## I. Security Considerations and Energy Investment Promotion

States can capitalise on foreign competition to guarantee their economic growth.[1] The international law on foreign investments is thus established to promote capital flows freely at the global level and to enable market forces to play a role in allocating capital,[2] by restricting government interference with inward investments.[3] In the energy sector, investments in the exploration of fossil fuels, the generation of renewable energy power, infrastructure and clean-energy technologies are perceived to be important in guaranteeing energy supply.[4] For the purpose of energy security, multilateral legal regimes have been taking action to deter host states from imposing penalties on energy companies without relying on pre-established regulations.[5]

However, security considerations surrounding commercial activities conducted by sovereign investors have played an increasingly critical role in the current international economic order.[6] The perception of security threats posed by sovereign

[1] R Dolzer and C Schreuer, *Principles of International Investment Law*, 2nd edn (Oxford, Oxford University Press, 2012) 23–24.

[2] M Sornarajah, *The International Law on Foreign Investment*, 4th edn (Cambridge, Cambridge University Press, 2017) 3; KJ Vandevelde, 'Sustainable Liberalism and the International Investment Regime' (1998) 19 *Michigan Journal of International Law* 373, 373.

[3] Sornarajah (n 2).

[4] International Energy Agency (IEA), *Energy Supply Security: Emergency Response of IEA Countries* (OECD Publishing, 2014) 13. See, eg, J Karl, 'FDI in the Energy Sector: Recent Trends and Policy Issues' in ED Brabandere and T Gazzini (eds), *Foreign Investment in the Energy Sector: Balancing Private and Public Interests* (Leiden, Brill, 2014) 7–28.

[5] P Cameron, *International Energy Investment Law: The Pursuit of Stability*, 1st edn (Oxford, Oxford University Press, 2010).

[6] JB Heath, 'The New National Security Challenge to the Economic Order' (2020) 129 *Yale Law Journal* 1020; A Roberts, HC Moraes and V Ferguson, 'Toward a Geoeconomic Order in International Trade and Investment' (2019) 22 *Journal of International Economic Law* 655, 657; JE Mendenhall, 'Assessing Security Risks Posed by State-Owned Enterprises in the Context of International Investment Agreements' (2016) 31 *ICSID Review* 36; A DeLuca, 'The EU and Member States: FDI Portfolios Investments, Golden Powers and SWFs' in F Bassan (ed), *Research Handbook on Sovereign Wealth Funds and International Investment* (Cheltenham, Edward Elgar, 2015) 178–205; WB Hamida, 'Sovereign FDI and International Investment Agreements: Questions Relating to the Qualification of Sovereign Entities and the Admission of their Investments under Investment Agreements' (2010) 9 *The Law and Practice of International Courts and Tribunals* 17; E Whitsitt and T Weiler, 'Sovereign

investors could become even more urgent in the energy sector, because this sector is important for a state's social stability, economic development and foreign policy interests.[7] Due to national security concerns, an increasing proportion of host states in which companies make investments have taken government measures that could affect free capital flows.[8]

Host states' national security concerns may be explained by the phenomenon that industrialising economies in which the state plays a dominant role, such as China, have become the main capital exporters.[9] For example, the national oil companies (NOCs) in China and other industrialising economies compete with privately-owned oil and gas companies in global fields.[10] The power companies in these industrialising economies also expand their shares of the foreign energy markets.[11] Host states, usually developed states, assert sovereign control over the incoming investments made by investors in those industrialising economies, and ban such investments to eradicate perceived threats to national security.[12] This perception can undermine regulatory stability and thus lead to anxiety by sovereign investors.[13] Accordingly, the free-capital flows in the global energy sector, guarded by international energy investment law, have been challenged by security considerations which derive from arbitrary assessments based on the competition for power between host states and home states.

Nevertheless, investments made by state-owned investors in the energy sector do not always present national security threats, and these investors should not be subject to discrimination from private entities, or be automatically deprived of the right to make, operate and exit outbound investments.[14] Therefore, energy investments made by state-owned investors deserve rigorous analysis to determine whether the state plays a dominant role in these investments in various scenarios, such as the decision to protect their investments under investment treaties.[15]

Wealth Funds and Bilateral Investment Treaties' New Models: Issues, New Trends and State Practice' in F Bassan (ed), *Research Handbook on Sovereign Wealth Funds and International Investment Law* (Cheltenham, Edward Elgar, 2015) 273–318, 275.

[7] T Waelde, 'Treaties and Regulatory Risk in Infrastructure Investment' (2000) 34 *Journal of World Trade* 1, 1.

[8] Heath (n 6) 1050.

[9] Cameron (n 5) para 1.38; MA Carrai, 'The Rise of Screening Mechanisms in the Global North: Weaponizing the Law against China' s Weaponized Investments?' (2020) 8 *The Chinese Journal of Comparative Law* 351.

[10] United Nation, *World Investment Report 2012: Towards a New Generation of Investment Policies* (United Nation, New York and Geneva, 2012) 5.

[11] See, eg, P Pareja-Alcaraz, 'Chinese Investments in Southern Europe's Energy Sectors: Similarities and Divergences in China's Strategies in Greece, Italy, Portugal and Spain' (2017) 101 *Energy Policy* 700.

[12] Sornarajah (n 2) 5.

[13] Heath (n 6) 1042.

[14] Whitsitt and Weiler (n 6) 317.

[15] On scholars' call for proper assessments of investments made by state-owned investors, see, eg, Mendenhall (n 6) 37; M Ussama, 'Sovereign Wealth Funds and Investor-State Dispute Settlement: Examining Questions of ICSID's Jurisdiction and the Impact of Investment-Treaty Arbitration' (2021) 7(1) *Washington College Law Journals & Law Reviews* 11, 51.

State-owned investors are crucial players in financing global energy investments,[16] in addition to international energy companies. Having nuanced regulatory assessment of state-owned investors will enhance their confidence and incentivise them to make energy investments, thus contributing to global energy security.

## II. The Need to Assess China's Overseas Energy Investments

Against this context, investments made by Chinese companies have been viewed as a challenge to the international economic system and a threat to the national security of host states.[17] Host states' severe reactions to China's overseas energy investments illustrate the phenomenon of coping with the emergence of security considerations in the liberal economic system. In other words, there is a clash between development of the international law on foreign energy investments and the increasing number of geopolitical assessments of China's overseas energy investments. China is unique because of the particularly prominent role of the Chinese Government and the Party in national economic development.[18] The perceived dominance of the state in China's economy makes host states wary of possible ulterior motives behind its investments.[19] The close and complex relationship between China's state-owned enterprises (SOEs) and the Government can be a 'geopolitical challenge' to host states, because they believe the SOEs remain the tools of the Chinese Government.[20] These states are also suspicious of the political connections between privately-owned enterprises (POEs) and the Chinese Government. For instance, Sweden has banned Huawei's sensitive telecom business based on the perceived close connections between Huawei and the Chinese Government.[21] Therefore, host states have strengthened their regulatory powers regarding China's energy investments because of suspicions of the motives

[16] OECD, 'State-Owned Enterprises and the Low-Carbon Transition' (2018) OECD Environment Working Papers, 18 April 2018. (last accessed 5 January 2020).

[17] J Ganesh, 'China Sows Discord in the "Special Relationship"' *Financial Times* (5 June 2019) at www.ft.com/content/4d4df67c-86df-11e9-97ea-05ac2431f453. See also M Wu, 'The "China, Inc." Challenge to Global Trade Governance' (2016) 57 *Harvard International Law Journal* 261; J Kynge et al, 'West Begins to Close Door on Chinese Investment' *Financial Times* (1 August 2018) at www.ft.com/content/2003d460-94bf-11e8-b747-fb1e803ee64e.

[18] S Meunier, 'China's Investment Political Challenges in Europe and US' in J Chaisse (ed), *China's International Investment Strategy* (Oxford, Oxford University Press, 2019) 345–59, 349–52.

[19] ibid.

[20] J Li, *The Clash of Capitalisms? Chinese Companies in the United States* (Cambridge, Cambridge University Press, 2018) 200.

[21] The criticism of Chinese foreign investments extends to privately-owned but potentially state-directed companies such as Huawei. See, eg, C Balding and D Clarke, 'Who Owns Huawei?' (2019) at ssrn.com/abstract=3372669.

behind them.[22] For example, they require Chinese companies to disclose their source of finance, to examine the possible existence of state control in inward investments.[23]

Because of the 'geopolitical sensitivity' of the energy sector, host states are particularly cautious with regard to China's energy investments. This 'geopolitical sensitivity' may arise from the possibility that energy projects will help the Chinese Government to minimise supply vulnerabilities, exert a strategic influence on other states or maintain internal political stability.[24] China's energy companies, regardless of their ownership, have to convince host states that they are commercially oriented and do not control energy resources for the benefit of the Chinese Government.[25]

Considering the growing national security concerns of the state's influence on energy investments made by China's SOEs and POEs, this book aims to question whether there are official channels for exerting state influence on overseas energy investments. In other words, are China's domestic regulatory framework and international legal arrangements designed to limit or facilitate state influence on the making of investments?

The role of the Chinese Government in global energy expansion has so far mainly been discussed in the field of international relations.[26] Accommodating the

[22] Li (n 20) 193. On the geopolitics/geoeconomics of Chinese foreign-energy investments, see, eg, R Blackwill and J Harris, *War by Other Means: Geoeconomics and Statecraft* (Cambridge, MA, Harvard University Press, 2016) 93–151; W Norris, *Chinese Economic Statecraft* (Ithaca, NY, Cornell University Press, 2016). See, eg, Treasury of the Commonwealth of Australia, 'Foreign Investment Reforms' (2020) at treasury.gov.au/sites/default/files/2020-06/p2020-87595_0.pdf; Regulation (EU) 2019/452 of the European Parliament and of the Council of 19 March 2019 Establishing a Framework for the Screening of Foreign Direct Investments into the Union [2019] OJ L79I/1; CIFUS, The Foreign Investment Risk Review Modernization Act of 2018 at www.congress.gov/115/bills/hr5841/BILLS-115hr5841eh.pdf. See also M McLaughlin, 'State-Owned Enterprises and Threats to National Security Under Investment Treaties' (2020) 19 *Chinese Journal of International Law* 283.

[23] A Collier, *China Buys the World: Analyzing China's Overseas Investments* (Singapore, Springer, 2018).

[24] FitchRatings, 'China's One Belt, One Road Initiative Brings Risks' (25 January 2017) at www.fitchratings.com/site/pr/1018144. See, eg, Ø Tunsjø, *Security and Profit in China's Energy Policy* (New York, Columbia University Press, 2013) 151–76; T Marketos, *China's Energy Geopolitics* (London, Routledge, 2009); M Laruelle and S Peyrouse, *The Chinese Question in Central Asia* (London, Hurst Publishers, 2012); H Zhao, 'Central Asia in Chinese Strategic Thinking' in T Fingar (ed), *The New Great Game* (Stanford, CA, Stanford University Press, 2016) 171–86.

[25] H Zhang, 'China's Privately-owned Companies Face Financing Risks in Overseas Investments and Control them' [《中国民营企业"走出去"面临的融资风险及其控制》] (2017) 7 *Practice in Foreign Trade* 81, 83.

[26] See, eg, K Woodard, *The International Energy Relations of China* (Stanford, CA, Stanford University Press, 1980); R Ebel, *Energy and Geopolitics in China: Mixing Oil and Politics* (Washing, DC, Centre for Strategic & International Studies, 2009); R Bedeski and N Swanström (eds), *Eurasia's Ascent in Energy and Geopolitics: Rivalry or Partnership for China, Russia and Central Asia?* (London, Routledge, 2012); B Cole, *China's Quest for Great Power: Ships, Oil, and Foreign Policy* (Annapolis, MD, Naval Institute Press, 2016); DG Victor and L Yueh, 'The New Energy Order' (2010) 89 *Foreign Affairs* 61, 62; R Dannreuther, 'China and Global Oil: Vulnerability and Opportunity' (2011) 87 *International Affairs* 1345, 1346; Marketos (n 24). See, however, M Du, 'When China's National Champions Go Global' (2014) 48 *Journal of World Trade* 1127; Li (n 20); L Trakman, 'Geopolitics, China, and Investor-State Arbitration' in L Toohey, C Picker and J Greenacre (eds), *China in the International Economic Order* (Cambridge, Cambridge University Press, 2015) 268–92. Special Issue: China's External Energy

participation of China's energy companies in the international energy market is often perceived as a challenge to the liberal energy order, in which energy companies are free from political interference and make investments for profit.[27] China's investments in foreign energy production and transmission networks are viewed as part of the Government's efforts to quench the thirst for energy security.[28] In addition to the objective of managing energy import dependence, for Marketos and others, the direct state involvement in overseas energy investments enables the Government to seek geostrategic interests in global energy expansion.[29] Apart from state control over investment decision-making, these scholars also perceive the Chinese Government as having actively sought access to foreign energy markets and protected foreign energy interests.[30] Maintaining a good diplomatic relationship between China and host states ensures that the host state not only admits China's energy investments but also protects them.[31] Financial aid plays a more important role in helping Chinese energy companies to secure deals.[32] In the long term, it has been argued that the state involvement in China's overseas energy investments would distort development of the international energy market.[33]

Nevertheless, the role of the Chinese Government in global energy expansion has rarely been discussed in energy law literature.[34] Energy law originates from

Security – Energy Trade and Investment Along the 'Belt and Road', (2019) 20 *Journal of World Investment and Trade*. This special issue examines legal aspects of China's energy investments in the Belt Road Initiative (BRI).

[27] See, eg, A Goldthau, 'Energy Diplomacy in Trade and Investment of Oil and Gas' in A Goldthau and JM Witte (eds), *Global Energy Governance: The New Rules of the Game* (Berlin, Global Public Policy Institute; Brookings Institution Press 2010) 25–47; A Goldthau and N Sitter, *A Liberal Actor in a Realist World: The European Union Regulatory State and the Global Political Economy of Energy* (Oxford, Oxford University Press, 2015) 5.

[28] Marketos (n 24) 103–08.

[29] ibid; SB Cáceres, *The Hungry Dragon: How China's Quest for Resources is Reshaping the World* (London, Taylor & Francis Group, 2013) 18–56; D Holtbrügge and SC Berning, 'The National Government's Role in Chinese Outward FDI' in C Julian, Z Ahmed and J Xu (eds), *Research Handbook on the Globalization of Chinese Firms* (Cheltenham, Edward Elgar Publishing, 2014) 94–134.

[30] See, eg, P Bustelo, 'China and the Geopolitics of Oil in the Asian Pacific Region' (2005) Elcano Royal Institute Working Paper 38/2005, 20 (last accessed 20 January 2020); H Lee and D Shalmon, *Searching for Oil: China's Oil Initiatives in the Middle East* (Belfer Center for Science and International Affairs, January 2007) 9.

[31] See, eg, K Yu, 'Energy Cooperation Under the Belt and Road Initiative: Implications for Global Energy Governance' (2019) 20 *Journal of World Investment & Trade* 243, 249.

[32] B Gransow, 'Chinese Infrastructure Investment in Latin America – an Assessment of Strategies, Actors and Risks' (2015) 20 *Journal of Chinese Political Science* 267; E Downs, *Inside China Inc: China Development Bank's Cross-Border Energy Deals* (Brookings, March 2011).

[33] H Zhao, 'China's Overseas Energy Investments: Myth and Reality' (2009) 19 *Contemporary International Relations* 89, 89; I Bremmer, 'The Return of State Capitalism' (2008) 50 *Survival: Global Politics and Strategy* 55, 56; Norris (n 22).

[34] However, Chinese scholars have discussed the protection of overseas energy projects. For example, see W Shan (ed), *International Law Protection of China's Outward Energy Investment* [《中国对外能源投资的国际法保护》] (Beijing, Tsinghua University Press, 2014); Z Bai, 'Dispute Settlement Mechanisms Under the Energy Charter Treaty' [《能源宪章条约的争端解决机制研究》] (2011) 3 *Foreign Affairs Review* 88. More recently, a special issue of the *Journal of World Investment and Trade* (n 26) introduced legal aspects of Chinese energy trade and investments in the BRI. In addition, China's national energy laws and policies have been discussed before for the purposes of domestic renewable energy development and internal measures of energy security (see, eg, J Liu, 'China's

laws at the international, national and local level.[35] The study of the energy law also requires the discussion of energy policy.[36] The existing energy law literature tends to focus on the energy law and policies of the European Union (EU) or the United States (US).[37] Given the importance of China in financing global energy investments,[38] it is necessary to conduct a regulatory assessment of the official channels that can be used by the Chinese Government to influence China's global energy expansion. By examining the role of the Chinese Government in the global energy expansion from a regulatory perspective, this book will contribute to the energy law literature regarding the legal aspects of China's external energy security, with a focus on investment-making. More specifically, this book aims to provide a regulatory analysis of how domestic regulatory requirements relevant to outbound energy investments govern the investing behaviour of energy companies. The book also attempts to examine whether China's international legal arrangements are conducive to the Government's influence on the promotion and protection of energy investments.

In addition to contributing to the energy law literature, this research into the role of the Chinese Government in overseas energy investments also has policy implications. This research provides a case study of how to stimulate energy investments in the context of increasing security considerations. Host states may refer to the regulatory assessment of China's overseas energy investments in the screening mechanism for inward investments.

## III. The Legal Dimension of Governing Global Energy Investments

The regulatory assessment of the role of the state in China's global energy expansion is conducted in the light of the legal dimension of governing global energy investments. Although the international relations literature throws valuable light on the phenomenon of strategic energy investments, it does not establish clear criteria to distinguish commercial investments from strategic investments. The criteria are important for assessing the role of the Chinese Government in overseas energy investments. Therefore, this book turns to the legal dimension of global

Renewable Energy Law and Policy: A Critical Review' (2019) 99 *Renewable and Sustainable Energy Reviews* 212). See also the discussion of China's energy policy from the perspective of international relations in P Andrews-Speed, *Energy Policy and Regulation in the People's Republic of China* (London, Kluwer Law International, 2004).

[35] RJ Heffron, *Energy Law: An Introduction* (Singapore, Springer, 2015) 3–4.

[36] ibid.

[37] S Haghighi, *Energy Security: The External Legal Relations of the European Union with Major Oil-and Gas-Supplying Countries* (Oxford, Hart Publishing, 2007); A Belyi, 'EU External Energy Policies: A Paradox of Integration' in J Orbie (ed), *Europe's Global Role: External Policies of the European Union* (Surrey, Ashgate, 2008) 203–16.

[38] IEA, *World Energy Outlook 2017* (OECD Publshing, 2017).

energy investments to delineate these criteria. The legal dimension includes the approach to promoting and protecting energy investments under international energy investment law, and the governance of investments made by state-owned entities.

Law has become a significant factor in guaranteeing energy security, as various countries have adopted instruments to regulate the development, transport and distribution of natural resources.[39] When addressing energy security within the investment cycle, legal instruments play an important role in ensuring the effective functioning of energy supply chains, from production and transmission to distribution, through guaranteeing capital flows.[40] International energy investment law promotes and protects investments by imposing obligations on host states.[41] By performing treaty obligations and complying with their commitments as regards market access, host states grant investors access to foreign energy markets.[42] After energy investments are made, pre-established rights in investment treaties will help investors to settle disputes with host states.[43]

As increasing energy investments are made by Sovereign Wealth Funds (SWFs) and SOEs, it is necessary to regulate sovereign investors to ensure the commercial orientation of these investments.[44] Customary international law and decisions made by investor–state arbitration tribunals offer guidelines on whether acts of investment should be attributed to state-owned investors or the state.[45] The international soft rules governing SOEs and SWFs, such as the OECD Guidelines on Corporate Governance of SOEs and the Santiago principles, have also recommended how sovereign investors should conduct commercial activities.[46] To make commercial investments, sovereign investors need to invest abroad in accordance with commercial interests, to disclose their economic and political mandates, and to be independent from government influence.[47]

[39] B Barton et al, 'Introduction' in B Barton et al (eds), *Energy Security Managing Risk in A Dynamic Legal and Regulatory Environment* (Oxford, Oxford University Press, 2004) 1–13, 8; K Talus, *Introduction to EU Energy Law* (Oxford, Oxford University Press, 2016) 2–4.

[40] A Konoplyanik, 'Energy Security and International Energy Market Development' in Barton et al (eds) (n 39) 47–84, 47.

[41] Cameron (n 5).

[42] Waelde (n 7).

[43] See, eg, T Waelde, 'International Law of Foreign Investment: Towards Regulation by Multilateral Treaties' (1999) *Business Law International* 1, 50; Cameron (n 5).

[44] See, eg, LS Poulsen, 'Investment Treaties and Globalization of State Capitalism: Opportunities and Constraints for Host States' in R Echandi and P Sauvé (eds), *Prospects in International Investment Law and Policy: World Trade Forum* (Cambridge, Cambridge University Press, 2013) 73–90.

[45] United Nation's Convention on Jurisdictional Immunities of States and Their Property, adopted 2 December 2004; International Law Commission, Articles on Responsibility of States for Internationally Wrongful Acts (2001). See, eg, *Ceskoslovenska Obchodni Banka v Slovakia*, ICSID Case ARB/97/4, Decision on Objections to Jurisdiction, 24 May 1999, para 20.

[46] International Working Group of Sovereign Wealth Funds (IWG), 'Sovereign Wealth Funds – Generally Accepted Principles and Practices' (October 2008) at www.ifswf.org/sites/default/files/santiagoprinciples_0_0.pdf; Organization for Economic Cooperation and Development (OECD), *OECD Guidelines on Corporate Governance of State-Owned Enterprises* (OECD Publishing, 2015).

[47] IWG (n 46); OECD (n 46); United Nations Convention on Jurisdictional Immunities of States and Their Property (n 45); International Law Commission (n 45). See, eg, *CSOB v Slovakia* (n 45) para 20;

## IV. Methodology

Given the criteria for distinguishing commercial investments from strategic investments, this book discusses whether the Chinese Government can rely on the regulations governing outbound energy investments to influence China's global energy expansion. Institutional measures of states, such as policies, regulations and laws, reflect the Government's expectation.[48] The regulatory analysis will present a nuanced and detailed picture of how the Chinese Government interacts with energy companies within the legal framework.

More specifically, the book assesses whether it is probable that energy companies will pursue corporate development when complying with the investment approval procedure, energy policy guidance and corporate rules on the governance structure of energy companies. The National Development and Reform Commission (NDRC) and the Ministry of Commerce (MOFCOM) are responsible for managing overseas investments. The Chinese Government drafts five-year plans for national economic and social development, energy-sector-specific five-year plans based on those of macro-economic development and other energy-related policy documents to disclose government prospects for developing the energy industry. The PRC Company Law and the Party rules governing the Party branches regulate the decision-making of both energy SOEs and POEs. The corporate governance of SOEs also needs to take into account the role of the state shareholder, namely, the State-Owned Assets Supervision and Administration (SASAC).

In addition to the impact of the domestic institutional context on the investment-making of energy companies, this book also discusses whether it is possible for the Chinese Government to achieve strategic objectives in its global energy expansion by looking at investment treaties and international non-binding arrangements for investment promotion and protection. In response to the approach to promoting investments through imposing obligations on host states in international energy investment law, the analysis focuses on whether China's regulatory efforts to facilitate domestic energy companies' access to foreign energy markets are official channels that maintain its influence over global energy expansion or that assist energy companies to obtain the right to make investments in host states. Also, in response to the guidance on marginalising the role of home states behind the mechanism of investor–state arbitration in international energy investment law, the analysis focuses on the rationales behind China's regulatory efforts to

*CDC Group PLC v Seychelles*, ICSID Case ARB/02/14, Award, 17 December 2003, para 17. Similarly, see International Court of Justice, *Certain Iranian Assets* (Jurisdiction), Judgment of 13 February 2019, para 87. See also M Feldman, 'The Standing of State-Owned Entities under Investment Treaties' in K Sauvant (ed), *Yearbook on International Investment Law and Policy 2010–2011* (Oxford, Oxford University Press, 2012) 615–38.

[48] K Hobér, 'State Responsibility and Attribution' in P Muchlinski, F Ortino and C Schreuer (eds), *The Oxford Handbook of International Investment Law* (Oxford, Oxford University Press, 2008) 549–83, 556; S Hu, 'State Enterprises in International Investment Disputes: Focus on Actor or Action?' (2020) 51 *Georgetown Journal of International Law* 323, 351.

shield overseas energy investments from political risks, examining whether these regulatory efforts can help the Chinese Government to maintain its influence over global energy expansion or to enable energy companies to resolve disputes with host states in the legal realm.

The study of China's specific foreign energy projects, by relying on literature in the field of international relations, complements the regulatory assessment. Based on the literature on China's external energy security and overseas energy investments, this book analyses the interaction between state interests and commercial interests in different types of energy investments. These analyses help in our examination of how the Chinese Government implemented energy policies and investment-related regulations in different types of energy investments in practice. Furthermore, given the 'geopolitical sensitivity' of the energy sector, investment promotion and investment protection cannot be isolated from the geopolitical landscape either.[49] Before investments are made, it is currently difficult for energy companies to seek compensation from host states through legal agendas if their investments are perceived as tools for locking global energy resources or exerting strategic influence by host states. After investments are made, security threats resulting from domestic or transboundary military confrontations add difficulty to the protection of energy investments through legal agendas. The literature on China's foreign energy investments helps in examination of how energy companies manage difficulty before and after investments are made.

This book also makes use of interviews with practising lawyers to allow us to understand how energy policies and investment law are carried out. Semi-structured interviews were conducted with 15 practising lawyers working in international or national law firms, and with two in-house lawyers employed by SOEs operating in overseas markets, in February and August 2020, March and November 2022, and March 2023. All the interviewees have extensive and first-hand experience of advising, or directly working with, Chinese companies in the making of outbound energy investments. Appendix 5 to this book listed typical interview questions. The conducting of the interviews for the purpose of writing the book has been carried out in accordance with approved research ethics.

## V. Structure of the Book

This book is divided into 10 chapters. To determine the importance of overseas energy investments for China's external energy security, chapter two gives a broad picture of China's strategy by looking at energy policies. What are the external threats to China's energy security in the eyes of energy policymakers? What measures does the Government consider necessary to manage these threats?

[49] Sornarajah (n 2); A Anghie, 'Imperialism and International Legal Theory' in A Orford and F Hoffmann (eds), *The Oxford Handbook of the Theory of International Law* (Oxford, Oxford University Press, 2016) 156–71.

Chapter three establishes the criteria for distinguishing strategic investments from commercial investments based on international soft rules governing SOEs and SWFs, customary international law, decisions made by investor–state arbitration tribunals, and the legal scholarship.

Chapter four argues that energy policies remain an official channel for influencing the global expansion of energy companies. The Chinese Government supports foreign energy projects that at least help to achieve energy policy objectives, including securing the energy supply and the export of energy equipment, services and technologies.

Chapter five discusses the way in which NDRC and MOFCOM have reduced regulatory control over energy companies (regardless of ownership) and simultaneously helped to carry out policy guidance (ie, protecting energy and diplomatic interests). This chapter also reveals how these regulations are implemented in practice.

Chapter six assesses how the state shareholder and Party branches help the Chinese Government to exert influence over the investment-making of energy SOEs, even though SOE reform and energy market reform are designed to enhance the autonomy of energy SOEs. This chapter also shows that Party branches maintain avenues for influencing the investment decision-making of energy POEs.

Chapter seven provides case studies examining whether different types of energy company can pursue their business interests in China's foreign energy projects, based on the international relations literature. These case studies demonstrate that energy companies, whether in the oil and gas sectors or the power sector, have occasionally failed to comply with regulatory requirements due to the pursuit of corporate development. Another finding is that, by checking the timelines of some energy projects, energy companies realised their projects to pursue business interests even before those projects were endorsed in energy policies.

Chapter eight establishes how the Chinese Government assists energy companies to mitigate pre-investment risks, especially the risk relating to denial of access to host states' markets based on the national security concerns of those states. Regarding domestic measures, MOFCOM needs to provide energy companies with as much information on the investment environment as possible. This chapter also gives examples of how energy companies dealt with national security reviews, based on the international relations literature, to see whether these companies seek remedies offered by the Government. As for international arrangements, China has been increasingly inclined to grant greater protection to companies at the *ex ante* stage during the negotiation of investment treaties. China also aims at coordinating energy-development policies with host states to pursue common development, to alleviate host states' concerns regarding national security threats posed by China's energy investments.

Chapter nine discusses the protection of China's overseas energy investments. The Ministry of Foreign Affairs (MFA) and MOFCOM help energy companies deal with security threats. China has also collaborated with its energy cooperation partners to prevent attacks from damaging energy projects. Simultaneously, China has aligned with the legal agenda to help domestic investors to manage the risk of regulatory instability, by embracing wider access to investor–state arbitration and devising flexible mechanisms for the settlement of investor–state disputes to cater for the development of underdeveloped states. The flexible mechanisms of investor–state dispute settlement might be a way for China to reform international investment law.

Chapter ten offers conclusions and suggests the implications. This research highlights that the Chinese Government has reformed the investment approval system, promoted energy SOE reform, and is willing to address energy companies' access to foreign energy markets and investment protection through legal agendas. Nevertheless, it is still possible for the Government to influence investment-making by identifying a project as a sensitive investment, guiding investments by policies or relying on the influence exerted by SASAC and Party branches on the governance structure of energy companies. This conclusion helps readers to understand how the reforms of the domestic regulatory framework have in principle granted energy companies investment autonomy. Internationally, it is expected to be a stronger legal framework for promoting investments. Otherwise, China will continue its efforts to coordinate energy policies. While the mitigation of security threats still requires state involvement, the Chinese Government is not as willing to settle disputes between energy companies and host states as discussed in the international relations literature, because of the diplomatic pressure.

# 2

# China's External Energy Strategy

## I. Introduction

This chapter aims to determine the importance of overseas energy investments to China's energy security, by looking at its external energy strategy. This strategy manifests itself in China's energy policies, which are robust governance tools of the Government.[1] The five-year energy plans are the most important policy documents that map out China's energy strategy.[2] These policies provide 'structural guidance' for foreign energy activities, for example overseas investments. This chapter reviews the contents of China's macro-economic plans, five-year plans, the mid- and long-term energy plans and foreign investment plans to understand the Government's expectation of overseas energy investments. It was not until 2000, when oil imports doubled, that the term 'energy security' garnered much attention, and therefore this chapter pays more attention to energy policies formulated since 2000.[3]

Section II introduces common strategies for managing import dependence. Section III explains why the external dimension of China's energy security is important. Section IV discusses threats to energy security as seen by China's energy policymakers. This discussion lays the foundation for understanding how overseas energy investments can contribute to external energy security in the view of the policymakers. Section V maps out China's external energy strategy. Sections VI and VII explain how overseas energy investments help to implement the strategy. Section VIII sums up and discusses the implications.

## II. Managing Supply Vulnerabilities

Security of supply requires 'an adequate match between supply and demand at a cost deemed affordable to a country's economy'.[4] In other words, importing

[1] AG Hu, 'The Five-Year Plan: A New Tool for Energy Saving and Emissions Reduction in China' (2016) 7 *Advances in Climate Change Research* 222, 223.

[2] X Yuan and J Zuo, 'Transition to Low Carbon Energy Policies in China – from the Five-Year Plan Perspective' (2011) 39 *Energy Policy* 3855, 3855.

[3] E Downs, *Energy Security Series: China* (The Brookings Foreign Policy Studies, 2006) 13 at www.brookings.edu/research/reports/2006/12/china.

[4] M Meidan, 'Perceptions and Misperceptions of Energy Supply Security in Europe and the "China Factor"' in A Marquina (ed), *Energy Security: Visions from Asia and Europe* (London, Palgrave Macmillan, 2008) 34–53, 47.

states can draw on foreign oil and gas, and transport them through cross-border infrastructure.[5] However, price shocks and physical interruptions, rising from geopolitical tensions,[6] are major threats to external oil and gas supplies.[7] To manage import dependence, the United Nations Development Programme (UNDP) has suggested that importing states should diversify oil and gas suppliers, and build strategic reserves.[8]

Diversification is defined as the way for import-dependent states not to have to rely on one resource or one supplier, instead distributing their dependency among various resources and suppliers.[9] Diversification will enable these states to swiftly change from one resource to another,[10] and to replace insecure suppliers or routes with secure ones.[11] Supply disruption caused by one supplier will result in only a minor reduction in the total supply.[12] Therefore, diversification is important for guaranteeing stable supplies of oil and gas.[13] As investments in oil and gas exploration and transportation infrastructure are part of the diversification strategy,[14] the World Bank has suggested that governments eliminate barriers to energy investments, provide financial support for energy investments, improve the efficiency of energy SOEs and enhance transparency within the energy sector.[15]

Apart from diversifying as regards suppliers, resilience to supply disruption is another important strategy.[16] Oil and gas stocks are able to respond to short-term price shocks, sudden surges in demand or supply disruption.[17] The stocks could be held by companies or state utilities.[18] The size of these stocks determines their contribution to reliable energy supplies during a given period.

[5] H Khatib, 'Energy Security' in MM Brown, N Desai and G Doucet (eds), *World Energy Assessment: Energy and the Challenges of Sustainability* (UNDP, 2000) 112–31.

[6] E Bompard et al, 'National Energy Security Assessment in A Geopolitical Perspective' (2017) 130 *Energy* 144, 146.

[7] P Andrews-Speed, 'Energy Security in East Asia: a European View', paper presented at the Symposium on Pacific Energy Cooperation 2003 (12–13 February 2003) 2; JH Keppler, *International Relations and Security of Energy Supply: Risks to Continuity and Geopolitical Risks* (European Parliament's Committee on Foreign Affairs, 2007) 21.

[8] Khatib (n 5) 112; G Bahgat, *Energy Security: An Interdisciplinary Approach* (New York, Wiley, 2011) 3.

[9] D Yergin, 'Ensuring Energy Security' (2006) 85 *Foreign Affairs* 69, 76; V Vivoda, 'Diversification of Oil Import Sources and Energy Security: A Key Strategy or an Elusive Objective?' (2009) 37 *Energy Policy* 4615, 4616; S Haghighi, *Energy Security: The External Legal Relations of the European Union with Major Oil-and Gas-Supplying Countries* (Oxford, Hart Publishing, 2007) 18.

[10] Haghighi (n 9) 11.

[11] L Hughes, 'The Four 'R's of Energy Security' (2009) 37 *Energy Policy* 2459, 2460.

[12] Vivoda (n 9).

[13] H Zhao and H Wu, 'China's Energy Foreign Policy towards the Caspian Region: The Case of Kazakhstan' in M Amineh and Y Guang (eds), *Secure Oil and Alternative Energy* (Leiden, Brill, 2012) 167–95, 177.

[14] Vivoda (n 9) 4620; The World Bank Group, *Energy Security Issues* (5 December 2005) 1.

[15] The World Bank Group (n 14) 6 and 9.

[16] Yergin (n 9) 76.

[17] The World Bank Group (n 14) 12; Ø Tunsjø, *Security and Profit in China's Energy Policy* (New York, Columbia University Press, 2013) 61.

[18] Khatib (n 5) 121.

## III. China's Import Dependence

China became the largest international energy consumer in 2011.[19] The International Energy Agency (IEA) reported in 2017 that China had been the largest importer of fossil fuels.[20] Domestic oil and gas production cannot meet demand.[21] The major oil fields, including Daqing, Shengli and Liaohe, are almost depleted.[22] China's oil production in 2017 accounted for only one-third of domestic demand.[23] Moreover, there are no major new reserves to replace declining production. In the gas sector, domestic energy companies have been struggling to boost shale gas production.[24] Therefore, China has been forced to turn to importing oil and gas. China's oil demand has been increasing since 1995, and China became the largest oil importer in 2014.[25] The Middle East, Africa, Russia and the Central Asian states were once the most important crude oil suppliers to China.[26] As for gas, China has been a net gas importer since 2007 and was the third-largest liquified natural gas (LNG) consumer in 2012.[27] Russia, Turkmenistan, Qatar and North America are key sources of the LNG supply to China.[28] China is projected to be the biggest LNG importer by 2024.[29]

## IV. Challenges to China's External Energy Security

China's import dependency makes the external dimension of China's supply situation important. Fast-growing domestic demands and reliance on foreign oil and gas supplies since the 1990s have meant that China has been faced with the risk of

[19] Energy Information Administration (EIA), 'China' (International energy data and analysis, 14 May 2015) at www.eia.gov/international/content/analysis/countries_long/China/archive/pdf/china_2011.pdf; S Yilmaz and O Daksueva, 'The Energy Nexus in China–Russia Strategic Partnership' (2019) 19 *International Relations of the Asia-Pacific* 63, 70.

[20] IEA, *World Energy Outlook* (OECD Publishing, 2017) 486.

[21] 'The Impact of Chinese Energy Demand on World Energy Markets', *Openlink* at openlink.com/en/insights/articles/the-impact-of-chinese-energy-demand-on-world-energy-markets/.

[22] R Weitz, 'China's Energy Security Strategy' *World Politics Review* (9 November 2010) at www.worldpoliticsreview.com/articles/6989/chinas-energy-security-strategy.

[23] Openlink (n 21).

[24] D Ma, *Rebalancing China's Energy Strategy* (Paulson Papers on Energy and Environment, January 2015) 15. Regarding the difficulty on shale gas development in China, see, eg, A Chen, 'Analysis: Chinese majors to struggle to extend shale gas boom beyond 2025' *Reuters* (26 January 2021) at www.reuters.com/article/us-china-shalegas-idUSKBN29V0ZE; B Spegele and J Scheck, 'Energy-Hungry China Struggles to Join Shale-Gas Revolution' *The Wall Street Journal* (5 September 2013) at www.wsj.com/articles/energyhungry-china-struggles-to-join-shalegas-revolution-1378350220.

[25] K Ferriggi, *Security of Oil Supply in China* (Clingendael International Energy Programme, 2020).

[26] C Tian, 'China's 2016 Oil Import/Export' [《2016年中国石油进出口状况分析》] (2017) 25 *International Petroleum Economics* 15, 19.

[27] EIA (n 19).

[28] IEA (n 20) 594.

[29] IEA, *Gas 2019: Analysis and forecast to 2024* (IEA, June 2019) 9–11.

supply insecurity.[30] Accordingly, stability in the supply of oil and gas has become a priority in the five-year plans or long-term energy planning.[31] For example, *China's Energy Policy 2012* stressed 'a grave challenge to energy security', as China's reliance on international oil supplies increased by 25 per cent.[32] Similar to energy policymakers in other importing states, China's energy policymakers perceive physical supply disruptions and price shocks as major threats to the state's external energy supply.[33] These policymakers have further realised that China's vulnerability to foreign energy supply essentially lies in the difficulty of exerting influence on the global energy market, including global energy transition.[34] Continuously nurturing domestic energy companies is thus an important dimension of China's external energy strategy.

With *The 10th Energy Development Five-Year-Plan* (2001), energy policymakers came to realise that oil supplies to China were significantly affected by the sharp volatility of the international oil market resulting from sudden global conflicts.[35] Volatile oil prices posed threats to social and economic development, according to several five-year energy development plans.[36] In the short term, high oil prices would directly force China to pay more for imports.[37] In the long term, oil market volatility can result in economic losses, such as declining industrial output and increasing production costs in the domestic energy industry (eg, refineries).[38] There can be inflation caused by high domestic energy prices as well.[39] The resulting inflation risk would harm people's livelihood.[40]

China's energy policymakers have also been aware of the risk of insecure supply sources or transportation channels to oil and gas supplies to China,[41]

[30] X Yin, 'Energy Security: China's Choices against the Complex and Changing Background' [《能源安全:复杂多变形势下的中国政策选择》] (2020) 01 *Energy* 87, 91.

[31] K Wu, 'China's Energy Security: Oil and Gas' (2014) 73 *Energy Policy* 4, 6.

[32] State Council, *China's Energy Policy 2012* (2012).

[33] See, eg, C Zhao and B Chen, 'China's Oil Security from the Supply Chain Perspective: A Review' (2014) 136 *Applied Energy* 269, 271; JB Geng and Q Ji, 'Multi-Perspective Analysis of China's Energy Supply Security' (2014) 64 *Energy* 541.

[34] See, eg, State Development and Planning Commission, *The 10th Energy Development Five-Year-Plan* [《国民经济和社会发展第十个五年计划能源发展重点专项规划》] (2001).

[35] ibid.

[36] National Development and Reform Commission (NDRC), *The 11th Five-Year Plan of Energy Development* [《能源发展"十一五"规划》] (2007); NDRC, *The 12th Energy Five-Year Plan* [《能源发展"十二五"重点专项规划》] (2013); see also NDRC, *The 12th Natural Gas Development Five-Year Plan* [《天然气发展"十二五"重点专项规划》] (2012); J Lee, 'China's Geo-strategic Search for Oil' (2012) 35 *The Washington Quarterly* 75, 77.

[37] L Zhou and J Hang, 'High Reliance on External Oil Supply and China's Energy Security' [《石油对外依存度高企与中国能源安全》] (2014) 68 *Review of Economic Research* 34, 36.

[38] Geng and Ji (n 33) 541; B Kong, *An Anatomy of China's Insecurity and Its Strategies* (Pacific Northwest National Laboratory, December 2005) 19–20.

[39] Lee (n 36) 78.

[40] JX Liao, 'The Chinese Government and the National Oil Companies (NOCs): Who is the Principal?' (2015) 21 *Asia Pacific Business Review* 44, 53.

[41] NDRC, *The 13th Petroleum Development Five-Year Plan* [《石油发展"十三五"规划》] (2016); State Council (n 32).

because developed states have taken up global oil and gas fields and exerted control over transportation routes, according to *China's Energy Policy 2012* and other five-year energy development plans.[42] For example, the two Iraq wars and the Gulf War impeded Middle-Eastern oil flow to the global market.[43] The US encouraged its energy companies to invest in oil and gas fields in the region,[44] thus reducing the possibility that Central Asian states might collaborate with China's energy companies.[45] Additionally, China's leadership has been worried about reliable oil and gas transportation due to the potential military presence of the US in the Malacca Strait.[46] In 2003, the then President Hu coined the phrase 'Malacca dilemma' to describe the threats to crucial sea routes in the Malacca Strait.[47]

The challenges of price shocks and physical interruptions can be largely explained by China's non-advantageous position on foreign oil and gas markets.[48] At the very beginning of seeking foreign resources, *The 10th Petroleum Industrial Development Five-Year Plan* (2001) predicted that against the background of low oil prices, NOCs would face the huge pressure of participating in the competition on the global oil market after the restructuring and merger of big international oil companies (IOCs).[49] The western states are more experienced in the oil and gas business, and their IOCs control most of the quality reserves.[50] The global institutions created to govern the international oil market also favour western IOCs.[51] These IOCs are able to manipulate energy spots as well as futures markets through hedge funds,[52] thus frustrating China's acquisition of oil and gas.[53] It has been

[42] State Council (n 32); NDRC (n 41); NDRC (n 36); NDRC and National Energy Administration (NEA), *Mid- and Long-Term Oil and Gas Pipelines Networks Planning* [《中长期油气管网规划》] (2017); S Handke, 'Securing and Fuelling China's Ascent to Power' *CIEP* (August 2006) 27 at www.clingendaelenergy.com/inc/upload/files/Chinese-Kazakh_Oil_Pipeline.pdf.

[43] D Zha, 'China's Energy Security and its International Relations' (2005) 3 *The China and Eurasia Forum Quarterly* 39, 49.

[44] B Hu, 'Oil and Gas Cooperation between China and Central Asia in An Environment of Political and Resource Competition' (2014) 11 *Petroleum Science* 596, 598.

[45] Q Zhou, Z He and Y Yang, 'Energy Geopolitics in Central Asia: China's Involvement and Responses' (2020) 30 *Journal of Geographical Sciences* 1871, 1878.

[46] Tunsjø (n 17).

[47] Q Akram and M Fareed, 'China's Malacca Dilemma: Power Politics in Indian Ocean' (2019) 5 *Journal of Politics and International Studies* 29, 29.

[48] H Yu, 'System Equilibrium in Geo-Security: Challenges and Responses to China's Energy Security in the New Era' [《地缘安全中的体系均衡：新时期中国能源安全的挑战与应对》] (2019) 4 *West Asia and Africa* 143, 144.

[49] State Development and Planning Commission, *The 10th Petroleum Chemical Industrial Development Five-Year-Plan* [《石油工业"十五"规划》] (2001).

[50] S Chen, 'Motivations behind China's Foreign Oil Quest: A Perspective from the Chinese Government and the Oil Companies' (2008) 13 *Journal of Chinese Political Science* 79, 88.

[51] H Kreft, 'China's Quest for Energy' (Hoover Institution of Stanford University, October 2006) at www.hoover.org/research/chinas-quest-energy.

[52] ibid.

[53] Z Jiang, 'Thinking China's Energy Security' [《对中国能源问题的思考》] (2008) 30 *China Energy* 5, 7; K Ma, *China's Current Energy Situation and the '11th Five-Year Plan' for Energy Development* [《我国当前的能源形势与"十一五"能源发展》] (a Report at the Conference on the Current Situation jointly sponsored by six ministries in the Central Propaganda Department of PRC, 2006) at www.gov.cn/jrzg/2006-07/15/content_336446.htm.

problematic that China has still not adapted well to the volatile international oil market, despite its current massive international oil cooperation, according to *The 13th Petroleum Development Five-Year Plan* (2016).[54]

Domestic non-competitive energy companies may not only impede China's foreign oil and gas supplies, but also prevent the country's adaptation to global renewable energy development.[55] *The 13th Energy Development Five-Year Plan* (2016) expressly confirmed that the current focus of competition in the energy sector has shifted from control over resources and transmission to broader dimensions, such as leading energy transition.[56] *The 13th Power Development Five-Year Plan* (2016) suggested that China's power companies should enhance their competitiveness to join in the establishment of a new global power system.[57] Under *The 14th Five-Year Plan of Renewable Energy Development* (2022), competitive renewable energy companies should export their equipment, technologies and standards, thus helping China to deepen cooperation on the transition to clean energy.[58]

# V. China's External Energy Strategies

## A. Diversification

China's diversification strategy is currently based on a wide-ranging mix of fossil fuels and renewable energy.[59] Five-year plans once stated that natural gas should be a pillar of China's energy mix to alleviate the anxiety surrounding oil.[60] *The 13th Energy Development Five-Year Plan* (2016) set a target of 15 per cent non-fossil fuel use and 10 per cent natural gas use in the energy mix.[61] Stimulating clean energy use is another crucial dimension of China's diversification strategies.[62] More

[54] NDRC (n 41); GCK Leung, 'China's Energy Security: Perception and Reality' (2011) 39 *Energy Policy* 1330, 1335.

[55] See, eg, L Hu and Y Song (eds), *Research on SOEs Reform and Development: Take CNOOC as the Example* [《国有企业改革发展研究：以中海油为例》] (Beijing, Economic & Management Publishing House, 2012) 12–14.

[56] NDRC and NEA, *The 13th Energy Development Five-Year Plan* [《能源发展"十三五"规划》] (2016).

[57] ibid.

[58] NDRC et al, *The 14th Five-Year Plan of Renewable Energy Development* [《"十四五"可再生能源发展规划》] (2022).

[59] State Development and Planning Commission (n 34); C Len, 'China's 21st Century Maritime Silk Road Initiative, Energy Security and SLOC Access' (2015) 11 *Maritime Affairs* 1, 2.

[60] State Development and Planning Commission (n 49); NDRC and NEA (n 42); M Bradshaw and A Waterworth, 'China's Dash for Gas: Local Challenges and Global Consequences' (2020) 61 *Eurasian Geography and Economics* 266, 289.

[61] NDRC and NEA (n 56).

[62] PRC Renewable Energy Law (adopted in 2005); Y Wang and A Gu, 'Recent Development of Energy Supply and Demand in China, and Energy Sector Prospects Through 2030' (2011) 39 *Energy Policy* 6745, 6746.

recently, the *Mid- and Long-Term Hydrogen Industrial Development Plan* (2022) highlighted the importance of hydrogen for developing a safe and climate-neutral energy supply.[63]

Additionally, China's energy policies have stressed that domestic oil production should be complemented by various sources of foreign oil supply.[64] Through diversifying suppliers, Beijing can minimise the possibility that a specific exporting state will enjoy political leverage over China.[65] China has diversified suppliers through investing in foreign energy reserves and cross-border energy infrastructure.[66] To facilitate the realisation of these investments, the five-year plans have suggested that the state should maintain good relationships with various oil and gas suppliers, such as the Middle East, Russia and Central Asia.[67] Identifying these key energy suppliers may explain why there is a list of preferred investment destinations in energy policies (see chapter four). China can transport oil and gas to China by relying on Chinese companies' assets in these key energy suppliers, rather than by buying oil and gas on the open market.[68] The five-year plans have also advised that the diversification of transportation routes requires substantial investment in pipelines and LNG terminals, such as those built or planned to be built in the Land Silk Road, China–Pakistan Economic Corridor and Bangladesh–China–Myanmar Economic Corridor.[69] The China–Kazakhstan oil pipeline is an example of diversification of transportation routes, and will be discussed in the case studies in chapter seven.

## B. Building Strategic Stocks

Similar to other import-dependent states, China has made progress in building strategic reserves of fossil fuels to ensure stable supply.[70] The five-year plans suggested building strategic petroleum reserves to secure the oil supply, and to strengthen the Government's capacity for managing price shocks from the international oil market.[71] China has built up stocks of oil and gas, and its storage level

[63] NDRC, *The Mid- and-Long-Term Hydrogen Industrial Development Plan (2021–2035)* [《氢能产业发展中长期规划（2021–2035 年）》] (2022).

[64] See, eg, NDRC and NEA (n 42).

[65] B Tessman and W Wolfe, 'Great Powers and Strategic Hedging: The Case of Chinese Energy Security Strategy' (2011) 13 *International Studies Review* 214, 224.

[66] E Downs, 'The Chinese Energy Security Debate' (2004) 177 *The China Quarterly* 21, 32–39; Vivoda (n 9) 4621.

[67] See, eg, State Development and Planning Commission (n 49); NDRC, *The 13th Natural Gas Development Five-Year Plan* [《天然气发展"十三五"规划》] (2016).

[68] MJ Bambawale and B Sovacool, 'China's Energy Security: The Perspective of Energy Users' (2011) 88 *Applied Energy* 1949, 1951.

[69] State Development and Planning Commission (n 34); NDRC (n 36).

[70] GCK Leung, R Li and M Low, 'Transitions in China's Oil Economy, 1990–2010' (2011) 52 *Eurasian Geography and Economics* 483, 496.

[71] See, eg, State Development and Planning Commission (n 35); State Development and Planning Commission (n 49); NDRC (n 36); NDRC (n 41); NEA, Notice on Guidance of the National Energy Administration's Working Plan in 2020 [《2020年能源工作指导意见》] (2020).

has reached that of developed states, according to the *Mid- and Long-Term Oil and Gas Pipelines Networks Planning* (2017).[72] Although energy policies do not specify those responsible for undertaking the construction of strategic oil and gas stocks, Chinese NOCs have played a crucial role in building, maintaining and managing storage facilities.[73] For example, CNPC is operating six strategic gas stocks, located in Northeast China, North China, Southwest China, Northwest China, mid-West China and mid-East China respectively.[74] However, the current storage volume of China's strategic reserves is still insufficient to deal with anything other than a short-term interruption of supply.[75]

## C. Increasing Influence on the International Energy Market

China's external energy strategy is not just about controlling energy resources.[76] It should help China to enhance its influence on international energy governance.[77] Nurturing internationally competitive energy SOEs,[78] facilitating industrial upgrading,[79] expanding business into global energy value chains[80] and influencing the standard-setting of clean energy technologies[81] would help China to exert an influence on the international energy market. By optimising the pace of investment and the asset structure, NOCs can improve the profitability and quality of oil investments, according to *The 13th Petroleum Development Five-Year Plan* (2016).[82] Upgrading China's energy industry assists in reducing its supply vulnerabilities as well,[83] because it will prepare China for providing more cost-effective and high-quality energy products to the rest of the world.[84] Furthermore,

[72] NDRC and NEA (n 42).
[73] Tunsjø (n 17) 62; Bahgat (n 8) 72.
[74] CNPC, 'Key Implications of the 14th Five-Year Plan of Modern Energy System for the Oil-and-Gas Industry' [《<"十四五"现代能源体系规划>中的油气行业要点》] (15 April 2022) at news.cnpc.com.cn/system/2022/04/15/030065552.shtml.
[75] Yin (n 30) 91.
[76] J Husar and D Best, *Energy Investments and Technology Transfer Across Emerging Economies: The Case of Brazil and China* (IEA, 2013) 12.
[77] NEA, Notice on Guidance of the National Energy Administration's Working Plan in 2014 [《2014年能源工作指导意见》] (2014); JYS Cheng, 'A Chinese View of China's Energy Security' (2008) 17 *Journal of Contemporary China* 297, 314.
[78] Hu and Song (eds) (n 55).
[79] P Andrews-Speed, M Qiu and C Len, 'Chinese Engagement in Southeast Asian Energy and Mineral Resources: Motivations and Outlook' (2016) 57 *Eurasian Geography and Economics* 316.
[80] Energy Charter Secretariat, *China Investment Report* (2017).
[81] Andrews-Speed, Qiu and Len (n 79).
[82] NDRC (n 41).
[83] H Zhao and H Wu, 'China's Energy Foreign Policy towards the Caspian Region: The Case of Kazakhstan' in M Amineh and Y Guang (eds), *Secure Oil and Alternative Energy* (Leiden, Brill, 2012) 167–95, 173.
[84] See, eg, the State Council, *Energy in China's New Era* [《新时代的中国能源发展》] (2020), which briefly highlights the relevance of China's industrial capacities for the supply of energy products to the world.

as directed by NDRC and NEA, China's energy companies should 'move up to the higher end of the value chain' in both the conventional and renewable energy sectors.[85]

Particularly by integrating into global energy value chains, China can participate in the standard-setting of advanced energy technologies, to internationalise domestic energy technology standards and thus to influence global energy transition, according to the *Energy Production and Consumption Transition Strategy (2016–2030)* (2016).[86] In addition to exporting the standards for oil and gas pipelines,[87] China's energy policymakers have placed a value on influencing the standard-setting of clean energy technologies (eg, solar power, wind power and hydrogen), because such influence is an entry-point for strengthening their foothold in future clean-energy-related value chains. During the 14th five-year period, China aims to continue enhancing the mutual recognition of renewable energy technology with international organisations, including the International Electrotechnical Commission, and to contribute more to global energy standard-setting.[88]

## D. Establishing a Supportive Regulatory Environment for Implementing Strategies

*The 10th Five-Year Plan* (2001) highlighted that the Chinese Government should establish a supportive regulatory environment for implementing external energy strategies, especially overseas energy investments, by 'updating existing investment policies and regulations'.[89] China has designed a policy support system to promote global energy expansion (see chapter four).[90] Simultaneously, China has introduced administrative reform (eg, streamlining investment approval procedures) to impose fewer administrative burdens on energy companies (see chapter five).[91] Furthermore, as these foreign energy projects are mainly

[85] NDRC and NEA, *Vision and Actions on Energy Cooperation in Jointly Building the Silk Road Economic Belt and 21st-Century Maritime Silk Road* [《推动丝绸之路经济带和21世纪海上丝绸之路能源合作愿景与行动》] (2017); T Brink, *China's Capitalism – A Paradoxical Route to Economic Prosperity* (Philadelphia, PA, University of Pennsylvania Press, 2019).

[86] See NDRC and NEA, *Energy Production and Consumption Transition Strategy (2016–2030)* [《能源生产和消费革命战略（2016–2030）》] (2016); NDRC, *The 14th Five-Year Plan of Renewable Energy* [十四五可再生能源规划] (2022); K Lo, 'A Critical Review of China's Rapidly Developing Renewable Energy and Energy Efficiency Policies' (2019) 29 *Renewable and Sustainable Energy Reviews* 508, 509.

[87] NDRC (n 41); NDRC and NEA (n 42).

[88] NDRC (n 86).

[89] State Council, *The 10th Five-Year Plan* [《"十五"计划纲要》] (2001).

[90] See, eg, State Development and Planning Commission (n 49); NDRC (n 36).

[91] NDRC, *The 12th FDI Five-Year Plan* [《"十二五"利用外资和境外投资规划》] (2012); NDRC, *The 13th Coal Development Five-Year Plan* [《煤炭工业发展"十三五" 》] (2016).

carried out by China's energy SOEs,[92] the SOEs' efficiency is a crucial factor in ensuring energy security, as suggested by the World Bank Group. China is corporatising its energy industry to manage external supply risks (see chapter six).[93]

In addition to domestic institutional support, guaranteeing overseas economic interests is equally vital for implementing China's external energy strategy, according to *The 14th Five-Year Plan* (2020).[94] The State Council and ministries subordinated to it have aimed to hold regular dialogues with host states, as well as to sign economic cooperation agreements (eg, China–Kazakhstan Cooperation Framework Agreement) and investment treaties (eg, China–Turkmenistan BIT) to remove barriers to investments.[95] The State Council aimed to build an investment promotion system to facilitate energy companies' access to foreign markets and an investment protection system to protect them from political risks.[96] For instance, to mitigate security threats, China and other Belt and Road Initiative (BRI) states 'will jointly secure international energy production and transmission pathways', according to the *Vision and Actions on Energy Cooperation in Jointly Building Silk Road Economic Belt and 21st-Century Maritime Silk Road* (2017).[97] The promotion and protection of China's overseas energy investments will be discussed in chapters eight and nine respectively.

## VI. The Role of Overseas Investments in Diversification and Building Strategic Stocks

To diversify oil and gas suppliers and build strategic stocks, energy policymakers have provided guidance on investing in foreign oil and gas reserves and building cross-border transmission infrastructure.[98]

[92] V Vivoda and J Manicom, 'Oil Import Diversification in Northeast Asia: A Comparison Between China and Japan' (2011) 11 *Journal of East Asian Studies* 223, 243; Tessman and Wolfe (n 65) 225. However, China's energy policymakers also encourage and facilitate POEs' outbound energy investments, see, eg, State Council, *Several Opinions of the State Council on Encouraging, Supporting and Guiding the Development of Individual and Private Economy and Other Non-Public Sectors of the Economy* [《国务院关于鼓励支持和引导个体私营等非公有制经济发展的若干意见》] (2005).

[93] Zhao and Wu (n 83).

[94] State Council, *The 14th Five-Year Plan* [《国民经济和社会发展第十四个五年规划和二〇三五年远景目标的建议》] (2020).

[95] State Council, *Opinions on Encouraging and Regulating the Cooperation of Enterprises in Foreign Investment* [《国务院关于鼓励和规范企业对外投资合作的意见》] (2007); State Council, *The 12th Five-Year-Plan* [《"十二五"计划纲要全文》] (2011); NDRC, *The 12th FDI Five-Year Plan* (n 91).

[96] State Council (n 95); State Council, *Opinions on Encouraging and Promoting Wholesome Development of Private Investment* [《国务院关于鼓励和引导民间投资健康发展的若干意见》] (2010).

[97] NDRC and NEA (n 85).

[98] NDRC and NEA (n 86); C Zhang, *The Domestic Dynamics of China's Energy Diplomacy* (Singapore, World Scientific, 2015) 15. Zhang described the period from 2006 to present as the 'outward investment' stage.

## A. Building Overseas Oil and Gas Production Bases

The heavy reliance on foreign oil and gas supplies has forced China's energy policymakers to direct domestic capital flows to foreign oil and gas projects.[99] Five-year plans, have suggested that building overseas production bases could help China secure foreign oil and gas supplies by owning the oil and gas produced in these projects.[100] For example, *The 12th FDI Five-Year Plan* (2012) confirmed that 'investments in overseas production and development of energy resources secure economical, stable and safe energy supply for domestic economic development'.[101] The international oil projects should contribute to the security of the oil supply, according to *The 13th Petroleum Development Five-Year Plan* (2016).[102] During the 14th five-year period, China aims to continue guaranteeing the smooth operation of overseas oil and gas production bases.[103]

In addition the direct production of oil and gas, China's overseas upstream investments can also facilitate oil and gas imports from a specific exporting state.[104] For instance, China sought long-term inter-governmental deals with the Middle East, Central Asia and Russia, while China's NOCs invested in these areas.[105] When the investment destination is not subject to embargo but China is the target of an oil embargo, overseas oil and gas production might be brought back to China.[106] However, the contribution of building overseas oil and gas production bases to securing China's external oil-and-gas supply is still questionable,[107] as China still needs to deal with transmission insecurity.

## B. The Construction of Cross-Border Oil and Gas Pipelines

To ensure the uninterrupted transmission of oil and gas back to China, China's energy policymakers have encouraged energy companies to invest in

[99] X Liu, F Zhou and J Li, 'Adjustment and Optimization of Energy Supply Structure in China' in *China National Energy Strategy and Policy 2020* (Energy Research Institute of NDRC, 2004) 617; P Andrews-Speed, X Liao and R Dannreuther, *The Strategic Implication of China's Energy Needs* (London, Routledge, 2009) 25; B Li, 'China's Energy Development and Energy Security' [《中国能源发展与能源安全》] (2004) 10 *Development* 2, 2.
[100] Leung (n 54) 1335; State Council, *The 11th Five-Year Plan* [《中华人民共和国国民经济和社会发展第十一个五年规划纲要》] (2006); State Council (n 95); State Development and Planning Commission (n 34).
[101] NDRC (n 91).
[102] NDRC (n 41); X Shu and G Yan, 'Petroleum: The Core of Chinese Energy Sources Security and the International Strategy' [《中国能源安全的核心与国际战略》] (2004) 20 *Petrochemical Technology and Economics* 12, 18.
[103] NDRC (n 86).
[104] Y Zhao, X Shi and F Song, 'Has Chinese Outward Foreign Direct Investment in Energy Enhanced China's Energy Security?' (2020) 146 *Energy Policy* 1.
[105] Li (n 99).
[106] Leung (n 54) 1335.
[107] ibid.

cross-border oil and gas transmission infrastructure, including pipelines and LNG terminals.[108] The transmission of oil and gas by land provides an alternative to oil imports from, for example, the Middle East and Africa by sea.[109] By the time of issuing *The 12th Energy Development Five-Year Plan* (2011), the north-western, north-eastern, south-western and seaborne channels existed for facilitating oil and gas imports.[110] In addition to expanding the capacities of the existing pipelines and the storage capacities of the existing LNG terminals and crude oil ports, especially those connected with the BRI states,[111] China's energy policymakers also stressed the need for guaranteeing the safe operation of these pipelines, by collaboratively working with the BRI states.[112] By 2025, China is expected to make further achievements in seaborne shipping and pipeline transport.[113]

## C. The Potential for Importing Electricity Through Building Grids

Apart from oil and gas transportation, a certain volume of electricity is transmitted back to China.[114] Therefore, the construction of power transmission infrastructure is important for the stability of China's electricity imports. Energy cooperation in the BRI should help to enhance electricity interconnection and thereby strengthen regional electricity supply capacities, according to the *Energy Production and Consumption Transition Strategy (2016–2030)* (2016) and other policies governing the power sector.[115] More specifically, China should 'advance the construction of cross-border power transmission lines, upgrade and retrofit the regional power grid, [and] negotiate to establish the regional power market', according to the *Vision and Actions on Energy Cooperation in Jointly Building Silk Road Economic Belt and 21st-Century Maritime Silk Road* (2017).

[108] NEA (n 71); X Zhao, J Shen and L Long, 'China's Energy Security and International Energy Cooperation in the BRI' [《"一带一路"战略下中国能源安全与国际合作》] (2017) 37 *Journal of Chifeng University* 76, 78.
[109] Z Zhang, 'An Analysis of China's Energy Demand and Supply Policy Framework' (2013) 2 *WIREs Energy and Environment* 422, 430.
[110] NDRC (n 36).
[111] NEA, Notice on Guidance of the National Energy Administration's Working Plan in 2017 [《2017年能源工作指导意见》] (2017); NDRC and NEA (n 42).
[112] NDRC and NEA (n 56); NDRC (n 41).
[113] NDRC and NEA (n 42).
[114] Andrews-Speed, Qiu and Len (n 79); S Ji, 'China Ramps Up Electricity Imports From North Korea, Russia, Myanmar In Bid To Ease Power Crisis' *SCMP* (22 October 2021) at www.scmp.com/economy/china-economy/article/3153342/china-ramps-electricity-imports-north-korea-russia-myanmar; 'Electricity in China', OEC at oec.world/en/profile/bilateral-product/electricity/reporter/chn?redirect=true. This data centre reported that 'in 2021, China imported $254M in Electricity, becoming the 42nd largest importer of Electricity in the world'.
[115] NDRC and NEA (n 56).

# VII. The Role of Investment in Increasing Influence on the Global Energy Market

China has become a dominant investor in the global energy sector since 2008.[116] Investments made by Chinese energy companies have helped the Chinese Government to upgrade the domestic energy industry, integrate into global energy value chains and internationalise China's energy-related standards.[117]

## A. Improving the Competitiveness of China's Energy Companies

China's oil and gas companies can build their managing capacity during their global expansion.[118] These companies have been encouraged to join together by NDRC to invest abroad, to participate in international market competition and to improve their capacity to deal with market volatility.[119] By acquiring technical and managerial know-how in outbound investments, the NOCs have grown into mature players in energy value chains.[120] For instance, CNPC has grown into a competitive multilateral corporation like Exxon-Mobil.[121] The more shares China's NOCs take in the global market, the stronger their capacity to manage price volatility.[122] Therefore, China is likely to reduce its dependence on western oil companies for energy imports and have a stronger position in the global market.[123]

## B. Upgrading China's Energy Industry Through Technologies Cooperation

The *Energy Production and Consumption Transition Strategy (2016–2030)* (2016) highlighted the importance of investment cooperation on energy technology for developing the domestic energy industry.[124] Such investment cooperation will

[116] K Gallagher et al, 'Fueling Global Energy Finance: The Emergence of China in Global Energy Investment' (2018) 11 *Energies* 2804, 2805.

[117] A Boute, 'China's External Energy Security: Energy Trade and Investment Along the "Belt and Road": An Introduction' (2019) 20 *Journal of World Investment and Trade* 195, 196.

[118] C McPherson, 'National Oil Companies: Ensuring Benefits and Avoiding Systemic Risks' in A Goldthau (ed), *The Handbook of Global Energy Policy* (New York, John Wiley & Sons, 2013) 146–56, 149.

[119] See, eg, NDRC (n 36); State Development and Planning Commission (n 49).

[120] Leung, Li and Low (n 70) 495 and 497.

[121] E Downs, *Energy Security Series: China* (The Brookings Foreign Policy Studies, December 2006) 51.

[122] Chen (n 50) 90.

[123] Andrews-Speed, Liao and Dannreuther (n 99) 52.

[124] NDRC and NEA (n 86); O Gippner and D Torney, 'Shifting Policy Priorities in EU–China Energy Relations: Implications for Chinese Energy Investments in Europe' (2017) 101 *Energy Policy* 649, 652;

bring advanced technology back for use in China,[125] and thus enable the domestic energy system to perform in an effective way, as well as to supply energy in a cost-competitive way.[126] As far back as 2007, *China's Energy Conditions and Policies* (2007) and the *Opinions on Encouraging and Regulating the Cooperation of Enterprises in Foreign Investment* (2007) encouraged energy companies to 'steadily expand cooperation in energy engineering technology'.[127] In the more recent energy cooperation in the BRI, both the *Vision and Actions on Jointly Building Silk Road Economic Belt and 21st-Century Maritime Silk Road* (2015) and the *Vision and Actions on Energy Cooperation in Jointly Building Silk Road Economic Belt and 21st-Century Maritime Silk Road* (2017) promoted cooperation in energy technology (eg, deep-processing technology).[128] For example, Sinopec proposed to learn the technology of deep-sea exploration when investing in Brazil.[129] The *Guidelines on Promoting the Joint Establishment of Green Development of the BRI* (2022) and *The 14th Five-Year Plan of Renewable Energy Development* (2022) further promote the communication of and cooperation in technology innovation regarding cost-effective power generation by renewable energy, smart grid, hydrogen energy, energy storage and carbon capture, usage and storage (CCUS).[130] In practice, China's investments in the European renewable energy industry enable domestic energy companies to develop renewable energy technologies and to become more competitive in this sector.[131]

## C. Expansion in Global Energy Value Chains

China's overseas energy investments can help the Government to influence global energy governance by providing energy products for host states.[132] Dating back

S Liedtke, 'Chinese Energy Investments in Europe: An Analysis of Policy Drivers and Approaches' (2017) 101 *Energy Policy* 659.

[125] A Hove, 'Renewable Energy: Is China's Innovation System Adequate to Enable a Low-Carbon Transition?' (2021) 1 *GREEN* 72, 78; N Gao and J Schaaper, 'Chinese Companies Go Global: The Case of Chinese Investments in France' in R Taylor and J Jaussaud (eds), *China's Global Political Economy: Managerial Perspectives* (London, Routledge, 2018) 125–46; E Vermeer, 'The Global Expansion of Chinese Oil Companies: Political Demands, Profitability and Risks' (2015) 29 *China Information* 3.

[126] See, eg, S Zhang et al, 'Review of China's Wind Power Firms Internationalization: Status Quo, Determinants, Prospects and Policy Implications' (2015) 43 *Renewable and Sustainable Energy Reviews* 1333; X Tan et al, *China's Overseas Investments in the Wind and Solar Industries: Trends and Drivers*, Working Paper Series (World Resources Institute, 2013) 15.

[127] State Council (2007) (n 95).

[128] NDRC, MFA and MOFCOM, *Vision and Actions on Jointly Building Silk Road Economic Belt and 21st-Century Maritime Silk Road* (2015); NDRC and NEA (n 85).

[129] Husar and Best (n 76) 6.

[130] NDRC, *Guidelines on Promoting the Joint Establishment of Green Development of the BRI* [《关于推进共建"一带一路"绿色发展的意见》] (2022); NDRC (n 86).

[131] B Conrad and G Kostka, 'Chinese Investments in Europe's Energy Sector: Risks and Opportunities?' (2017) 101 *Energy Policy* 644, 646; Energy Charter Secretariat (n 80); Gippner and Torney (n 124) 656.

[132] P Andrews-Speed, 'China's International Energy Engagement' in K Zeng (ed), *Handbook on the International Political Economy of China* (Cheltenham, Edward Elgar Publishing, 2019) 132–50, 136; H Wang, 'China's Approach to the Belt and Road Initiative: Scope, Character and Sustainability' (2019) 22 *Journal of International Economic Law* 29, 54–55.

to the 10th five-year period (2001–05), China promoted the export of domestic equipment, technology and labour.[133] The *Energy Production and Consumption Transition Strategy (2016–2030)* (2016) highlighted again that foreign energy projects could export technology, services and equipment, help domestic energy companies to play a crucial role in global energy supply chains for both the conventional and renewable energy, and thus enhance China's influence on global energy market.[134]

In the BRI, broadening investment cooperation in different segments of the energy value chains will help to lay the foundation for 'creating an integrated network of supply and value chains' in the energy sector,[135] thus shaping global energy development. By promoting investments in 'the processing and conversion of energy resources at or near places where they are exploited', and exporting energy equipment, technology and construction services in the investments,[136] China can 'create an integrated energy industrial chain', according to the *Vision and Actions on Jointly Building Silk Road Economic Belt and 21st-Century Maritime Silk Road* (2015).[137] As explained by policymakers, by exporting the equipment for pipelines and providing construction services in the investments in the construction of pipelines, China's NOCs can provide downstream services and expand shares in the oil markets of other states (eg, refining).[138] Indeed, China's NOCs, together with POEs, have established their presence in the petrochemical industry of the Middle East, from exploration, transportation and refining to engineering services and equipment sales.[139] Similarly, when contracting on projects for the infrastructure of power generation and transmission, electricity companies should actively provide services such as upgrading and designing power grids, according to *The 12th Energy Five-Year Plan* (2013).[140]

In particular, NDRC and NEA have highlighted that clean energy sectors along the BRI are important investment destinations for China's capital, and that manufacturing companies in the renewable energy sector should actively carry out overseas projects.[141] Analysts argue that this is because China views renewable energy development as a pillar industry and hopes to become 'a global leader and exporter of green technologies'.[142] By supplying clean-energy products to host

[133] State Development and Planning Commission (n 49); State Council (2007) (n 95).

[134] NDRC and NEA (n 86); NEA, Notice on Guidance of the National Energy Administration's Working Plan in 2016 [《2016年能源工作指导意见》] (2016); NEA (n 111).

[135] F Umbach, 'China's Belt and Road Initiative and Its Energy-Security Dimensions', RSIS Working Paper Series No 320 (January 2019) 3.

[136] NDRC and NEA (n 56).

[137] NDRC, MFA and MOFCOM (n128).

[138] NDRC (n 36); NDRC (n 41).

[139] T Kenderdine and P Lan, 'China's Middle East Investment Policy' (2018) 59 *Eurasian Geography and Economics* 557, 565. Energy POEs have been important players in exporting equipment and products. However, according to an interviewee, energy SOEs have paid increasing attention to the manufacturing of equipment and products in recent years.

[140] NDRC (n 36).

[141] NDRC (n 86); NDRC (n 130).

[142] X Zhao et al, 'China's Wind, Biomass and Solar Power Generation: What the Situation Tells Us?' (2012) 16 *Renewable and Sustainable Energy Reviews* 6173; Z Wang, H Qin and J Lewis, 'China's Wind

states or third states, clean energy investments will play an increasingly important role in assisting China to take up significant shares in the global energy supply chains.[143] The State Council has also explained that the expanded export of clean energy technology would alleviate host states' concerns regarding the impact of China's investments on their environment.[144]

Generally, Chinese electricity companies should facilitate the export of equipment for clean coal power, hydro-electric power, nuclear power, power transmission and transformation and others, according to *The 13th Power Development Five-Year Plan* (2016).[145] More specifically, under *The 13th Wind Power Development Five-Year Plan* (2016), wind-power companies are encouraged to provide services such as consultation, design, engineering, procurement, construction (EPC) and operation to access foreign markets, to form competitive industrial clusters and ultimately to increase the influence of China's wind-power industry on global energy governance.[146] Solar-energy companies should boost cooperation with their counterparts in Europe, South-East Asia, Africa and other continents, to form industrial alliances and to establish a platform for the communication of technology, according to *The 13th Solar Energy Development Five-Year Plan* (2016).[147]

## D. Influencing the Standard-Setting of Clean Energy Technologies

Given the importance of influencing the standard-setting of clean energy technologies (see section V.C.), electricity companies should introduce grid-related technological standards when upgrading and designing power grids of host states, according to *The 12th Energy Five-Year Plan* (2013).[148] For instance, solar-energy companies should participate in the standardisation of solar power, according to *The 13th Solar Energy Development Five-Year Plan* (2016).[149] Under the more recent *Guidelines on Promoting the Joint Establishment of Green Development of the BRI* (2022), China's energy-related industrial associations should actively participate in the setting of 'green' standards (eg, standards for environmentally friendly energy technology).[150]

Power Industry: Policy Support, Technological Achievements, and Emerging Challenges' (2012) 51 *Energy Policy* 80.

[143] Lo (n 86) 509.

[144] State Council, Notice by the State Council of the Action Plan for Carbon Dioxide Peaking Before 2030 [《国务院关于印发2030年前碳达峰行动方案的通知》] (2021).

[145] NDRC and NEA (n 56).

[146] NEA, *The 13th Wind Power Development Five-Year Plan* [《风电发展"十三五"规划》] (2016).

[147] NEA, *The 13th Solar Energy Development Five-Year Plan* [《太阳能发展"十三五"规划] (2016).

[148] NDRC (n 36).

[149] ibid.

[150] NDRC (n 130).

If China can leverage its potentially advantageous position in setting standards for clean energy technologies, it can offset its dependence on oil and gas imports and minimise its supply vulnerabilities.[151] China can deepen its 'strategic collaboration' with resource-rich states by assisting these states to build industrial capacities of clean energy (eg, by talent training) in the transition to low-carbon energy.[152] Ultimately, the Chinese Government may grow into a price maker in the global market, due to its greater presence in the global energy value chains.[153]

## VIII. Conclusion

The external dimension of China's energy security is important, given its dependence on oil and gas imports, the increase in electricity imports and the development of global supply chains for clean energy. Overseas investments in both the conventional and renewable energy sectors are crucial for implementing China's external energy strategy. Outbound oil and gas investments have played a role in diversifying oil and gas suppliers and transportation routes, as well as in building strategic stocks. Against the background of the global transition to low-carbon energy, China is actively seeking opportunities to influence that transition by enhancing technology cooperation, exporting its cost-competitive equipment and participating in the standard-setting of clean energy technology. China's foreign electricity projects can export relevant technologies, equipment and standards for realising the goal of influencing global energy governance.

Given the importance of overseas energy investments for China's external energy strategies, the remaining chapters of this book will look at how the Chinese Government has established a supportive regulatory framework for governing such investments. Do the regulations, laws, investment treaties, memorandums of understanding and inter-governmental agreements relevant for overseas energy investments leave space for state control over these investments to achieve the policy goals discussed above?

[151] Q Xu and Y Miao, 'Belt and Road Initiative and China's International Energy Cooperation' (2019) 29(4) *Modern International Relations* 66, 67; P Cai, *Understanding China's Belt and Road Initiative* (Lowy Institute, March 2017) 7.

[152] X Gong, 'Time for Action: Chinese Companies and "One Belt One Road"', *IPP Review* (10 June 2016); Xu and Miao (n 152) 67.

[153] M Meidan, *China's 13th Five-Year Plan: Implications for Oil Markets* (Oxford Institute for Energy Studies, June 2016) 16.

# 3

# The Conceptualisation of Commercial Investments

## I. Introduction

The energy geopolitics literature throws valuable light on the phenomenon of strategic investments and the security risks they present, but does not establish clear criteria to distinguish a profit-driven (commercial) investment from a government-driven (strategic) project. This limitation prevents us from assessing whether the Chinese Government has instruments for influencing overseas energy investments. Therefore, to offer benchmarks for the legal analysis in chapters four, five and six, this chapter aims to introduce the criteria for commercial investments. More generally, delineating the legal criteria for commercial investments will provide an objective criterion for assessing the potential regulatory control exerted by the Government over state-owned investors. Identifying the legal criteria for commercial investments relies on international soft rules governing commercial activities of SOEs and sovereign wealth funds (SWFs), customary international law and adjudications made by international courts or arbitration tribunals. Such criteria offer guidelines on delimiting the role of the government in managing state-owned investors and their investment-making.

The following three sections discuss the elements of commercial investments, including the commercial basis of investments (section II), disclosure and transparency (section III), and the autonomy of making investment decisions (section IV). Section V sums up and set out the implications for assessing China's investment-related law, regulations and policies.

## II. Commercial Basis of Investments

Under *the Convention Establishing the Multilateral Investment Guarantee Agency* (1985), the commercial basis of investments is important for determining whether state enterprises should be treated the same as private ones.[1] There is a growing

[1] Convention Establishing the Multilateral Investment Guarantee Agency (came into effect in 1988), Art 13(a)(iii), at www.miga.org/sites/default/files/archive/Documents/MIGA%20Convention%20(April%202018).pdf.

expectation that state-owned investment vehicles should aim to maximise financial returns and operate in accordance with the principles of sound asset management. As demonstrated by the *OECD Guidelines on Corporate Governance of SOEs* (2015), 'SOEs' economic activities should be required to earn rates of return that are consistent with those obtained by competing private enterprises.'[2] The *Santiago Principles on Sovereign Wealth Funds* (2008) also provide generally accepted practices for investments made by SWFs.[3] These principles stress that SWFs should invest 'on the basis of economic and financial risks and return-related considerations'.[4] Because the commercial basis is 'a mix of subjective and objective standards',[5] the *United Nations Convention on Jurisdictional Immunities of States and Their Property* (2004)[6] provides a globally recognised approach to examining the commercial basis of investments, namely the consideration of the nature of the investment (the fundamental element) and the purpose of the investment, although this instrument has not yet entered into force.[7]

## A. Commercial Nature

The commercial nature of investments is decisive for distinguishing state-driven investments from commercial investments, even if the SOE implements national policies, according to *CSOB v Slovakia*.[8] In *Certain Iranian Assets (Islamic Republic of Iran v United States of America)*, the International Court of Justice (ICJ) examined whether the bank Markazi, which was wholly owned by the Iranian state, carried out industrial or commercial activities in the US, when deciding whether the bank came within the definition of a company in *the Treaty of Amity, Economic Relations and Consular Rights between Iran and the United States* (1955).[9] This case thus offered an example of how the ICJ distinguished commercial investments

[2] *OECD Guidelines on Corporate Governance of State-Owned Enterprises* (OECD, 2015) 21 at www.oecd.org/corporate/guidelines-corporate-governance-soes.htm.

[3] *Santiago Principles on Sovereign Wealth Funds* (International Forum for Sovereign Wealth Funds, 2008) at www.ifswf.org/santiago-principles-landing/santiago-principles.

[4] ibid.

[5] L Wang, 'State Controlled Entities as Qualified "Investors": Implications for the Pacific Region Investment Treaty Making' (2015) 12 *Transnational Dispute Management* 1, 27; S Hu, 'State Enterprises in International Investment Disputes: Focus on Actor or Action?' (2020) 51 *Georgetown Journal of International Law* 323, 330. Hu characterised the purpose approach as an 'actor-focused method'.

[6] United Nations Convention on Jurisdictional Immunities of States and Their Property (2004), Art 2, at treaties.un.org/doc/source/recenttexts/english_3_13.pdf.

[7] S Hu, 'Clash of Identifications: State Enterprises in International Law' (2019) 19 *UC Davis Business Law Journal* 171, 195.

[8] *Ceskoslovenska Obchodni Banka v Slovakia*, ICSID Case ARB/97/4, Decision on Objections to Jurisdiction, 24 May 1999, paras 16 and 21; R Dolzer and C Schreuer, *Principles of International Investment Law*, 2nd edn (Oxford, Oxford University Press, 2012) 242; L Bouchez, 'The Prospects for International Arbitration: Disputes Between States and Private Enterprises' (1991) 8 *Journal of International Arbitration* 81, 84.

[9] *Certain Iranian Assets (Islamic Republic of Iran v United States of America)*, Judgment of 6 November 2003, para 86.

from strategic ones, based on the commercial nature of the activities in question. Similarly, to determine whether the SOE acted on a commercial basis or as an agent of the state, the tribunal in *Beijing Urban Construction Group (BUCG) v Yemen* considered the nature of BUCG's action, namely the commercial background of the investment (eg, the SOE's participation in the competitive selection of bids for realising the project).[10]

## B. Commercial Purpose

In addition to considering the nature of the activities in question, under *the United Nations Convention on Jurisdictional Immunities of States and Their Property* (2004), the purpose of the transaction should also be considered to distinguish commercial transactions from strategic ones.[11] An OECD policy paper defines political objectives as 'any goal related to the implementation of any aspect of public policy' and commercial objectives as 'the desire to earn money or reduce costs'.[12] Because private entities rarely pursue public interests in their investments,[13] a review of the investment purpose helps when examining the potential state control over SOEs for instrumental use.[14] A strategic purpose of a specific investment may imply the existence of government direction or control.[15] For Petrochilos, SOEs have non-state status as long as they pursue profit maximisation.[16]

Investment-related treaties adopt this approach and consider commercial purposes. In the Annex of Financial Services listed in the General Agreement on Trade in Services (GATS), if an entity aims to realise government goals, this

[10] *Beijing Urban Construction Group Co Ltd (BUCG) v Republic of Yemen*, ICSID Case No ARB/14/30, Decision on Jurisdiction; A Zhang, 'The Standing of Chinese State-Owned Enterprises in Investor–State Arbitration: The First Two Cases' (2018) 17 *Chinese Journal of International Law* 1147, 1150; Hu (n 5) 339.

[11] UN Convention on Jurisdictional Immunities of States and Their Property (n 6) Art 2(2).

[12] *Foreign Government-Controlled Investors and Recipient Country Investment Policies*, A Scoping Paper (OECD, January 2009).

[13] P Blyschak, 'State-Owned Enterprises and International Investment Treaties: When are State-Owned Entities and Their Investments Protected?' (2011) 6 *Journal of International Law and International Relations* 1, 31; Hu (n 5) 332.

[14] C Beus, 'Sovereign Wealth Funds in the ICSID' (2014) 1 *The Indonesian Journal of International & Comparative Law* 543, 559; see also WB Hamida, 'Sovereign FDI and International Investment Agreements: Questions Relating to the Qualification of Sovereign Entities and the Admission of their Investments under Investment Agreements' (2010) 9 *The Law and Practice of International Courts and Tribunals* 17.

[15] J Chen and C Yang, 'SOEs' Standing in International Investment Arbitration: Structure, Trend and Responses' [《国际投资仲裁中的国有企业投资者地位认定:构造、趋势与因应》] (2018) 6 *Modern Economic Research* 119, 123; M Feldman, 'The Standing of State-Owned Entities under Investment Treaties' in K Sauvant (ed), *Yearbook on International Investment Law and Policy 2010–2011* (Oxford, Oxford University Press, 2012) 615–38, 630.

[16] G Petrochilos, 'Attribution: State Organs and Entities Exercising Elements of Governmental Authority' in K Yannaca-Small (ed), *Arbitration under International Investment Agreements: A Guide to the Key Issues*, 2nd edn (Oxford, Oxford University Press, 2018) 328–73, 343.

entity does not act on a commercial basis.[17] Chapters of Investments in some free-trade agreements also require the contracting parties to ensure that SOEs 'act in accordance with commercial considerations' and 'with an orientation towards profit-making'.[18] For instance, the Comprehensive and Progressive Agreement for Trans-Pacific Partnership (CPTPP) and the US–Singapore Free Trade Agreement require that SOEs should aim at profits when engaging in commercial activities.[19]

Host states also consider the purposes of incoming investments in their national security reviews, by assessing whether these investments have been 'based solely on commercial grounds'[20] or 'may be pursuing broader political or strategic objectives'.[21]

## III. Disclosure and Transparency

The *OECD Guidelines for Corporate Governance of State-Owned Enterprises* (2015) allow state-owned entities to pursue public interests as long as these strategic objectives are transparent and can be differentiated from commercial ones.[22] While it is probably naive to expect that an SOE will disclose sensitive strategic objectives,[23] a clear explanation of an SOE's economic and political mandate to host states can help to address national security concerns of host states when the commercial rationale of an investment is unclear.[24]

[17] The General Agreement on Trade in Services (GATS) (signed in 1994), the Annex of Financial Services, at www.wto.org/english/docs_e/legal_e/26-gats_02_e.htm#annfin; Hu (n 7) 183.

[18] See, eg, EU–Vietnam Trade Agreement (signed in June 2019) Arts 11.1 and 11.4, at policy.trade.ec.europa.eu/eu-trade-relationships-country-and-region/countries-and-regions/vietnam/eu-vietnam-agreement_en; see also L Borlini, 'When the Leviathan Goes to the Market' (2020) 33 *Leiden Journal of International Law* 313, 330; M Matsushita and CL Lim, 'Taming Leviathan as Merchant' (2020) 19 *World Trade Review* 402.

[19] Comprehensive and Progressive Agreement for Trans-Pacific Partnership (CPTPP) (signed in 2018) Art 17(1), at www.dfat.gov.au/trade/agreements/in-force/cptpp/comprehensive-and-progressive-agreement-for-trans-pacific-partnership; J Lee, 'Trade Agreements' New Frontier – Regulation of State-Owned Enterprises and Outstanding Systemic Challenges' (2019) 14 *Asian Journal of WTO and International Health Law and Policy* 33, 50; EU–Vietnam Trade Agreement (n 18) Art 11.1; EU–Canada Comprehensive and Economic Trade Agreement (entered into force in 2017) Art 18.5, at policy.trade.ec.europa.eu/eu-trade-relationships-country-and-region/countries-and-regions/canada/eu-canada-agreement_en; US–Singapore Free Trade Agreement (signed in 2003) Art 12.8, at ustr.gov/trade-agreements/free-trade-agreements/singapore-fta; R Bhala, 'Exposing the Forgotten TPP Chapter: Chapter 17 as a Model for Future International Trade Disciplines on SOEs' (2017) 14 *Manchester Journal of International Economic Law* 2, 31.

[20] Guidance Concerning the National Security Review Conducted by the Committee on Foreign Investment in the United States, 73 Fed Reg 74,567, 74,571, 8 December 2008, at www.treasury.gov/resource-center/international/foreign-investment/Documents/CFIUSGuidance.pdf.

[21] Australian Government Foreign Investment Review Board, Guidance Note on 'The National Interest Test' (2019).

[22] OECD (n 2) 20.

[23] R Bismuth, 'The "Santiago Principles" for Sovereign Wealth Funds' (2017) 28 *European Business Law Review* 69, 82.

[24] *Santiago Principles* (n 3).

## IV. Investment – Exercising Autonomy

The commercial basis requires that the SOE's act should be 'within the competency of a private commercial entity'.[25] An important dimension of the competency of a private commercial entity is operational independence.[26] The credibility of SOEs in the eyes of commercially-oriented international investors would be hampered if the SOEs could not exercise autonomy in their daily operation.[27] The *OECD Guidelines* and the *Santiago Principles* make recommendations on guaranteeing the autonomy of these investing entities.[28] For instance, they aim to protect the investing autonomy of SOEs and SWFs by limiting excessive administrative intervention in their daily operation, or by preventing the state shareholders from abusing their shareholder power.[29]

As the ICSID Convention aims to encourage private capital flows, and to protect only those investors that do not have governmental capacities, the assessment of whether the investor in question falls within the scope of the definition of 'investors' in the Convention offers more detailed indications when examining whether the competency of investment-making lies with private or state entities.[30] More specifically, the assessment looks at whether SOEs discharge an essentially government function or act as agents of the Government.[31] *The International Law Commission's (ILC's) Articles on Responsibility of States for Internationally Wrongful Acts* (2001) provide guidance on carrying out this assessment.[32] Articles 4, 5 and 8 respectively describe the institutional, functional and factual links between entities (eg, SOEs) and governments, all of which can damage the

[25] Blyschak (n 13) 29.

[26] Treasury of the Commonwealth of Australia, Foreign Investment Reforms (2020) 12 at treasury.gov.au/sites/default/files/2020-06/p2020-87595_0.pdf.

[27] OECD Secretariat, *Assessing Foreign State-Owned Enterprises: Guidance for Regulators Based on the OECD Guidelines on Corporate Governance of SOEs* (OECD Publishing, 2016) 20. The *OECD Guidelines on Corporate Governance of SOEs* (*OECD Guidelines*) have been used in national security revies of host states to assess the autonomy of state investors, see, eg, P Kowalski and D Rabaioli, 'Bringing Together International Trade and Investment Perspectives on State Enterprises', OECD Trade Policy Papers, No 201 (OECD Publishing, 2017).

[28] See, eg, D Park and G Estrada, 'Developing Asia's Sovereign Wealth Funds: The Santiago Principles and the Case for Self-Regulation' (2011) 1 *Asian Journal of International Law* 383.

[29] ibid 396.

[30] International Centre for Settlement of Investment Disputes, Convention on the Settlement of Investment Disputes between States and Nationals of Other States (opened for signature 18 March 1965, entered into force 14 October 1966) (ICSID Convention) Art 25; A Broches, 'The Convention on the Settlement of Investment Disputes between States and Nationals of Other States' (1972) 136 *Recueil des Cours* 331.

[31] Broches (n 30); *CSOB v Slovakia* (n 8) para 17.

[32] International Law Commission, Responsibility of States for Internationally Wrongful Acts (2001), at legal.un.org/ilc/texts/instruments/english/draft_articles/9_6_2001.pdf; M Ussama, 'Sovereign Wealth Funds and Investor-State Dispute Settlement: Examining Questions of ICSID's Jurisdiction and the Impact of Investment-Treaty Arbitration' (2021) 7(1) *Washington College of Law Journals & Law Reviews* 11, 50; Petrochilos (n 16) 334; Beus (n 14) 563; Hu (n 5) 343; K Hobér, 'State Responsibility and Attribution' in P Muchlinski, F Ortino and C Schreuer (eds), *The Oxford Handbook of International Investment Law* (Oxford, Oxford University Press, 2008) 549–83, 554.

independence of the entities.[33] The existence of an institutional link (Article 4) leads to attribution of the investment in question to the state. Although the SOEs that made investments are independent legal entities, they may exercise government powers in the investments (Article 5). In the absence of an institutional link and a functional link, a factual link (Article 8) may exist.

An SOE will not be independent if it has been created as a state organ to exercise public functions, according to Article 4 of *the ILC Articles on Responsibility of States for Internationally Wrongful Acts*.[34] The nature of the act (eg, making investments) is not relevant here as long as the entity has the status of a state organ.[35] The SOE can be an executive branch of a sovereign power in accordance with the laws of the state.[36] In the energy sector, if energy companies are part of the ministry/department of energy, they are state organs under Article 4.

Article 5 of the ILC Articles is useful in assessing whether SOEs are discharging government functions.[37] If domestic laws empower an entity to exercise government authority that is usually reserved to the government (eg, the pursuit of public interests, management of state assets or the approval of specific projects[38]) or to have privileges that are not enjoyed by private parties (eg, subsidies), its act should be viewed as an act of the state.[39] For instance, if a national oil company has the exclusive power to conclude oil contracts with foreign companies then the conclusion of oil contracts with foreign companies may be viewed as an act of the state.[40] The assessment further requires application of the structural test for the existence of the authority and the functional test.[41] The structural test is more relevant for the discussion of investment-making autonomy, while the functional test essentially addresses whether the investments made by SOEs are of a sovereign or commercial nature (see section II.A).[42] The structural test can examine the way in which political power is granted, the purpose for which the power is granted, the content of the power and the entity's responsibilities to the state organ.[43] This examination depends heavily on the specific context of a state.[44] In sum, if an SOE's decision-making is influenced by its exercising government authority, its investments are likely to be viewed as acts of the state.

[33] C Stefano, *Attribution in International Law and Arbitration* (Oxford, Oxford University Press, 2020) 121, 135.

[34] ILC (n 32) Art 4; Petrochilos (n 16) 341.

[35] Hobér (n 32) 551.

[36] Stefano (n 33) 136.

[37] Feldman (n 15) 28.

[38] Stefano (n 33) 154–56; Petrochilos (n 16) 351.

[39] ILC (n 32) Art 5; J Crawford, *The International Law Commission's Articles on State Responsibility: Introduction, Text and Commentaries* (Cambridge, Cambridge University Press, 2002) 101; Dolzer and Schreuer (n 8) 220; Petrochilos (n 16) 349.

[40] Petrochilos (n 16) 355.

[41] Stefano (n 33) 153; Hobér (n 32) 555.

[42] *Emilio Agustín Maffezini v The Kingdom of Spain*, ICSID Case No ARB/97/7, Award, 13 November 2000, paras 52, 57; Hobér (n 32) 559.

[43] Crawford (n 39) 101; Dolzer and Schreuer (n 8) 220.

[44] Hobér (n 32) 556; Hu (n7) 351.

Article 8 of *the ILC Articles on Responsibility of States for Internationally Wrongful Acts* helps to assess whether an SOE is acting as the agent of the government in the absence of the exercise of state authority.[45] Establishing the agency relationship between a SOE and the government requires the SOE to be 'in fact acting on the instructions of, or under the direction and control of, that State'.[46] It is argued that the link between state instructions and individual operation can be assessed through examining the relationship between the home government and the decision-making body of the SOE.[47] For instance, according to the US–Singapore FTA, a government may interfere with the decision-making of its SOEs by subsidising SOEs and exercising the power of appointment of the management of SOEs.[48] For Petrochilos and others, an SOE's compliance with government instructions implies that the company carries out the state's decisions without considering its own commercial interests.[49]

Given the focus of this book on Chinese companies (especially SOEs), two arbitration cases, in which the standing of Chinese SOEs before investor–state arbitration was challenged by the respondents, give a closer look at how to guarantee the independence of China's SOEs in commercial investments. Host states are usually concerned about how China's investment decisions are influenced by China's policies, investment approval and the Party's political leadership.

In *China Heilongjiang v Mongolia*, the respondent argued that the two SOEs were under direct state control, by alleging that the parent company of Beijing Shougang was supervised by the State Council and its investment decision-making complied with China's policies of investing in mineral resources.[50] However, the tribunal held that there was no evidence that these companies acted under the Chinese Government's 'express instruction to implement China's foreign policies'.[51] This case thus highlights that an explicit government order to implement policies was needed to establish a factual link between an SOE's decision-making body and the Government.

In *Beijing Urban Construction Group v Yemen*, the respondent claimed that the SOE, BUCG, 'is an agent of the Chinese Government and discharges government functions even in its ostensible commercial undertakings', making reference to Article 5 of the ILC's Articles.[52] The respondent argued that the boards of Chinese

[45] Regarding the Broches test of whether the investment in question is of a commercial nature or not, see A Broches, *Selected Essays, World Bank, ICSID, and other Subjects of Public and Private International Law* (Boston, MA, Martinus Nijhoff Publishers, 1995) 202; Crawford (n 39) 112–13; Blyschak (n 13) 35.

[46] ILC (n 32) Art 8; Crawford (n 39) 110; Dolzer and Schreuer (n 8) 219–21.

[47] Blyschak (n 13) 40; Bouchez (n 8) 91–92.

[48] M Kim, 'Regulating the Visible Hands: Development of Rules on State-Owned Enterprises in Trade Agreements' (2017) 58 *Harvard International Law Journal* 225, 247; Petrochilos (n 16) 345; Stefano (n 33) 79.

[49] Petrochilos (n 16) 346; Chen and Yang (n 15) 124.

[50] *China Heilongjiang International Economic & Technical Cooperative Corp, Beijing Shougang Mining Investment Company Ltd, and Qinhuangdaoshi Qinlong International Industrial Co Ltd v Mongolia*, UNCITRAL, PCA, 2017, para 271.

[51] ibid para 418.

[52] *BUCG v Republic of Yemen* (n 10) para 29.

SOEs such as BUCG considered China's national interests in investment-making, and that the embedded status of Party branches also forced these SOEs to carry out national policies.[53] The respondent added that the PRC Foreign Economic and Trading Department (the previous name of MOFCOM) was the final decision-maker regarding BUCG's foreign business, because of the requirement for foreign business approval by that Department.[54]

However, the tribunal found that Yemen's termination of contracts did not relate to China's decisions or policies.[55] In other words, China's policy guidance did not result in BUCG's failure to provide the commercial service.[56] The tribunal also concluded that building the airport in Yemen was not a government function because there was no close causal link between the approval of the Chinese Foreign Economic and Trading Department and the construction of the airport.[57] Therefore, the existence of investment approval procedures in China does not necessarily indicate SOEs' implementation of government functions. Furthermore, the tribunal recognised that it would be an oversimplification of China's corporate structure to conclude, simply on the basis of the Party's control, that foreign investments are presently dictated by the Government.[58]

## V. Conclusion

The regulatory assessments in the following chapters will discuss whether China's investment-related law, regulations and policies enable energy companies to seek profits, to disclose strategic objectives and to obtain investment autonomy, or whether these investment-related laws, regulations and policies are official channels for exerting state influence over energy companies. More specifically, in chapter four, do China's energy policies describe the state's strategic objectives? Is policy guidance a form of government instruction? Is state support a form of government control? In chapter five, is the right to invest abroad exclusively granted to SOEs? If not, do the investment approval procedures grant authority to energy companies, regardless of ownership, to invest abroad for the purpose of exercising government functions? In chapter six, how does China's corporate law deal with the appointment of the board of directors, the decision-making process and management of state-owned assets, all of which can be subject to government control, after China's energy SOEs are no longer part of state organs (eg, the petroleum ministry)? Does the Chinese Government maintain regulatory tools for controlling POEs' corporate governance as well, especially those connecting

[53] ibid para 38.
[54] ibid para 12.
[55] ibid para 40.
[56] Hu (n 5) 354.
[57] *BUCG v Republic of Yemen* (n 10) para 43.
[58] ibid para 39.

with the Government, as claimed by scholars in the current discussion of China's overseas energy investments?

Furthermore, case studies of various foreign energy projects are necessary to assess the specific act in the context of the overall background (eg, the general contexts of different types of energy project), as demonstrated in *Beijing Urban Construction Group v Yemen*. Therefore, this book will comprehend how investment approval procedures and policy guidance are carried out and how the corporate setting works in different types of energy projects operated by Chinese companies in chapter seven.

# 4

# State Guidance and Support

## I. Introduction

China's global energy expansion follows the path of policy guidance and enterprise decision-making, given that energy policies are powerful tools for governing overseas energy investments, as discussed in chapter two.[1] Energy policy literature includes an intensive discussion of the role of policy guidance and support for China's overseas energy investments,[2] and the scholars have argued that the Chinese Government interferes with overseas energy investments by granting support such as public financing to energy companies, especially SOEs.[3] However, China's energy policies regarding overseas energy investments have rarely been discussed in the energy law literature. Building on the current discussion, this chapter aims to discuss whether the implementation of energy policies offers a channel for the Chinese Government to influence overseas energy investments and, if so, how the government influence manifests itself.

This chapter looks at state guidance on overseas energy investments specified in energy policies, long-term economic plans and catalogues of preferred investments, as well as financial support mechanisms. The discussion of financial support mechanisms mainly looks at the policies or official internal governance documents adopted by policy banks, the Asian Infrastructure Investment Bank (AIIB) and the Silk Road Fund (SRF). Policy banks are state-owned banks that implement policy directives,[4] and thus they may be avenues for exerting state influence over investments. Among the international financing institutions dominated by China, this chapter focuses on the AIIB and the SRF, because they are frequently described as instruments of the Chinese Government by which to exert strategic influence over overseas energy projects.[5]

[1] M Du, 'When China's National Champions Go Global: Nothing to Fear but Fear Itself?' (2014) 48 *Journal of World Trade* 1127, 1134.

[2] See, eg, S Liedtke, 'Chinese Energy Investments in Europe: An Analysis of Policy Drivers and Approaches' (2017) 101 *Energy Policy* 659.

[3] X Qian, 'China's Outward Direct Investments and Its Oil Request' in YW Cheung, J Haan and C Fuest (eds), *The Evolving Role of China in the Global Economy* (Cambridge, MIT Press, 2014) 375–417. See, eg, Ø Tunsjø, *Security and Profit in China's Energy Policy: Hedging Against Risk* (New York, Columbia University Press, 2013) 42.

[4] D Dollar, 'Is China's Development Finance a Challenge to the International Order?' (2018) 13 *Asian Economic Policy Review* 283, 285.

[5] See, eg, B Kong and K Gallagher, 'Globalizing Chinese Energy Finance: The Role of Policy Banks' (2017) 26 *Journal of Contemporary China* 834; B Kong, *Modernization Through Globalization: Why*

In light of the criteria for commercial investments and the literature on home states' efforts in promoting outbound investments,[6] the principle of disclosure and transparency has been developed to require home states to disclose their public interests and their strategic assistance to domestic enterprises (eg, the EU's mechanism regarding 'Projects of Common Interest'). This chapter will discuss whether the Chinese Government has disclosed its objectives and whether the criteria for eligibility for financing are transparent. Also, this chapter will examine whether state guidance (namely, translating energy policy objectives into the realisation of different types of foreign energy projects) and support mechanisms enable energy companies, especially SOEs, to discharge government functions.

This chapter points out that policy guidance and support remain channels for exerting government influence on China's overseas energy investments, although the Chinese Government has disclosed its objectives associated with external energy security to justify its potential influence on investments. Policy guidance is not the only factor in proposing foreign energy projects, as some projects were initiated ahead of policy guidance. Moreover, given SOEs' influence on energy policymaking, SOEs can align their corporate development with policy objectives and thus use state support mechanisms to realise their corporate goals. This observation will enrich the existing discussion of how international investment law may regulate home-country measures, especially advantages granted to SOEs.

Section II discusses the governance of home states' practice of promoting outward investments. Section III introduces the literature on the contribution of the implementation of energy policies in foreign projects to realising China's strategic goals. Section IV examines what guidance China's energy policies provide for energy companies, and how these policies are put into practice. Section V discusses how the Chinese Government promotes the implementation of energy policies as part of the global energy expansion via the incentive regime. This section specifically examines the role of public financing in facilitating the realisation of foreign energy projects. Section VI sums up and suggests implications.

## II. Theory on the Requirement for Disclosure and Transparency for ODI Policies

The United Nations Conference on Trade and Development (UNCTAD) defines outward direct investment (ODI) policies as 'all policy measures that are taken

*China Finances Foreign Energy Projects Worldwide* (Singapore, Palgrave Macmillan, 2019); M Chen, *Official Aid or Export Credit: China's Policy Banks and the Reshaping of Development Finance* (Boston, MA, Global Development Policy Center, Boston University, 2018) 14; X Gong, 'China's Belt and Road Initiative Financing in Southeast Asia' (2020) *Southeast Asian Affairs* 77; D Chow, 'Why China Established the Asia Infrastructure Investment Bank' (2016) 49 *Vanderbilt Journal of Transnational Law* 1255, 1298.

[6] K Sauvant et al, 'Trends in FDI, Home Country Measures and Competitive Neutrality' in A Bjorklund (ed), *Yearbook on International Investment Law & Policy 2012–2013* (Oxford, Oxford University Press, 2014) 3–108.

by the home countries of firms that choose to invest abroad and that are designed to encourage ODI flows to other countries'.[7] States can set goals for their SOEs to fulfil 'overall political priorities', including the priorities for promoting ODI.[8] Given that ODI policies are designed to encourage capital flows to other states, they include support mechanisms, such as information services, financial support, insurance and feasibility studies, that help to realise ODI policy goals.[9] As the support granted to SOEs is usually viewed as offering 'specific advantages' to them,[10] Sauvant and others have expressed concern that SOEs 'operate as an instrument of the national government to advance not only economic goals, but also political interests in a manner that potentially threatens the national security of others'.[11] Capobianco and Christiansen have also argued that if SOEs pursued public objectives 'at zero profit, or even at a loss', their activities could not be commercial,[12] because the home government would compensate SOEs for their non-profitable investments.[13] The compensation may take the form of cheap loans from home governments.[14]

To limit state influence on commercial activities, international trade and investment treaties require that the support should be granted to SOEs in a transparent manner.[15] This requirement helps to clarify the state's involvement in commercial affairs. The articles in the General Agreement on Tariffs and Trade (GATT) and GATS require states to disclose policy objectives and support mechanisms, but do not include an enforcement mechanism.[16] The disclosure of support mechanisms enables contracting parties to review other contracting parties' subsidy regime.[17] To reduce the possibility of 'pursuing governmental economic policies' through granting special advantages to SOEs, the EU stated in its proposal for WTO modernisation that there should be 'transparency with regard to the level

[7] *Home Country Measures* (UNCTAD, 2001) 65: unctad.org/system/files/official-document/psiteiitd24.en.pdf.

[8] A Capobianco and H Christiansen, 'Competitive Neutrality and State-Owned Enterprises: Challenges and Policy Options', OECD Corporate Governance Working Paper No 1 (2011).

[9] ibid.

[10] Sauvant et al (n 6) 14.

[11] ibid 25.

[12] Capobianco and Christiansen (n 8) 12.

[13] I Willemyns, 'Disciplines on SOEs in International Economic Law' (2016) 19 *Journal of International Economic Law* 657; P Kowalski and D Rabaioli, 'Bringing Together International Trade and Investment Perspectives on State Enterprises', OECD Trade Policy Papers, No. 201 (OECD Publishing, 2017) 28; R Bhala, 'Exposing the Forgotten TPP Chapter: Chapter 17 as a Model for Future International Trade Disciplines on SOEs' (2017) 14 *Manchester Journal of International Economic Law* 2, 36.

[14] Kowalski and Rabaioli (n 13) 34.

[15] See, eg, Agreement on Subsidies and Countervailing Measures (entered into force in 1995) Art 14.

[16] The General Agreement on Tariffs and Trade (GATT) (signed in 1947), at www.wto.org/english/docs_e/legal_e/gatt47_01_e.htm; The General Agreement on Trade in Services (GATS) (signed in 1994), at www.wto.org/english/docs_e/legal_e/26-gats_02_e.htm#annfin; Willemyns (n 13) 669; M Kim, 'Regulating the Visible Hands: Development of Rules on State-Owned Enterprises in Trade Agreements' (2017) 58 *Harvard International Law Journal* 225, 246.

[17] 'WTO modernization – Introduction to future EU proposals', Concept Paper (European Commission, 28 June 2018) at trade.ec.europa.eu/doclib/docs/2018/september/tradoc_157331.pdf.

and degree of state control in SOEs'.[18] Furthermore, the transparency provisions in the Transatlantic Trade and Investment Partnership (TTIP) require contracting parties to provide information on their strategic assistance to domestic companies.[19] Other contracting parties can review the policy objectives, and the amount and the duration of the non-assistance, and thus are able to determine the effects of the assistance on trade and investments.[20]

International soft rules governing commercial activities of SOEs and SWFs also advocate guaranteeing transparency.[21] The OECD Guidelines recommend that where SOEs pursue both economic and public policy objectives, high standards of transparency and disclosure should be maintained.[22] Similarly, the *Santiago Principles* recommend that if investment decisions are subject to considerations other than economic and financial ones, these should be clearly defined and publicly disclosed.[23] It is expected that transparency and disclosure will ensure that investments are made 'without any intention to fulfil any geopolitical agenda of the government'.[24]

In practice, national security reviews are concerned about transparency as well. Host governments inquire about the source of investment capital when questioning the purposes of foreign investments.[25] Australia suggested that 'foreign owned or controlled investors that operate on a transparent and commercial basis are less likely to raise national interest concerns than proposals from those that do not'.[26] A review by the Committee on Foreign Investment in the United States (CFIUS) also looks at 'the degree of transparency and disclosure of investment objectives, institutional arrangements, and financial information of the investor'.[27] Similar to Australia and the US, the EU requires investors to disclose 'the funding of the investment and its source'.[28]

[18] ibid.

[19] The negotiation of the Transatlantic Trade and Investment Partnership ended in 2016. JS Fleury and JM Marcoux, 'US Shaping of SOE Disciplines in TPP' (2016) 19 *Journal of International Economic Law* 445, 462–63.

[20] ibid 463; T Kawase and M Ambashi, 'Disciplines on State-Owned Enterprises under the Trans-Pacific Partnership Agreement: Overview and Assessment', ERIA Discussion Paper Series (February 2018) 13.

[21] Regarding the aim of the US in TPP negotiation, see Fleury and Marcoux (n 19) 462.

[22] OECD, *OECD Guidelines on Corporate Governance of State-Owned Enterprises* (OECD Publishing, 2015) 20 and 24.

[23] *Santiago Principles on Sovereign Wealth Funds* (International Forum for Sovereign Wealth Funds, 2008) at www.ifswf.org/santiago-principles-landing/santiago-principles.

[24] ibid 12.

[25] OECD Secretariat, *Assessing Foreign State-Owned Enterprises: Guidance for Regulators Based on the OECD Guidelines on Corporate Governance of SOEs* (OECD Publishing, 2016) 33; K Sauvant, L Sachs and W Jongbloed, 'Sovereign Investment: An Introduction' in K Sauvant, L Sachs and W Jongbloed (eds), *Sovereign Investment: Concerns and Policy Reactions* (Oxford, Oxford University Press, 2012) 3–26, 11–12.

[26] See, eg, Treasury of the Commonwealth of Australia, *Australia's Foreign Investment Policy* (2019) 10.

[27] Guidance Concerning the National Security Review Conducted by the Committee on Foreign Investment in the United States, 73 Fed Reg 74,567, 74,571 (8 December 2008) at www.treasury.gov/resource-center/international/foreign-investment/Documents/CFIUSGuidance.pdf.

[28] Regulation (EU) 2019/452 of the European Parliament and of the Council of 19 March 2019 establishing a framework for the screening of foreign direct investments into the Union [2019] OJ L791/1.

## III. Literature on Chinese Government Control of SOEs Through Support Mechanisms

A majority of scholars believe that China's SOEs, including energy ones, are tools for implementing national industrial policies,[29] although Andrews-Speed and Dannreuther argue that SOEs have the ability to influence policy-making.[30] It is reported that China has relied heavily on energy SOEs in carrying out its five-year plans, because it does not trust the market to determine the structure of the energy industry.[31] For Brink and others, support mechanisms play important roles in motivating SOEs to implement energy policies.[32]

The support mechanisms include financial incentives, privileged access to government networks, preferential treatment and monopoly production rights.[33] For Andrews-Speed and others, these mechanisms are institutional-specific advantages that have ensured the success of China's NOCs in the global energy market.[34] In particular, cheap state financing allows SOEs to be free from the need to improve operational efficiency.[35] Cheap state financing thus suggests that the Chinese Government forgoes profits in favour of increasing influence over the global market and realising strategic goals.[36] Sanderson and Forsythe took the China Development Bank (CDB) as an example, summarising how CDB's energy-backed financing posed threats to the development of

[29] P Buckley et al, 'Explaining China's Outward FDI: An Institutional Perspective' in K Sauvant, K Mendoza and I Irmak (eds), *The Rise of Transnational Corporations from Emerging Markets: Threats or Opportunities?* (Cheltenham, Edward Elgar Publishing, 2008) 107–43, 117; A Szamosszegi and C Kyle, 'An Analysis of State-owned Enterprises and State Capitalism in China' (US–China Economic and Security Review Commission, 26 October 2011) 91 at www.uscc.gov/sites/default/files/Research/10_26_11_CapitalTradeSOEStudy.pdf; J Wang, 'The Political Logic of Corporate Governance in China's State-Owned Enterprises' (2014) 47 *Cornell International Law Journal* 634, 662.

[30] P Andrews-Speed and R Dannreuther, *China, Oil and Global Politics* (London, Routledge, 2011) 54.

[31] Szamosszegi and Kyle (n 29); D Chen, 'China's State-Owned Enterprises: How Much Do We Know? From CNOOC to Its Siblings' (2019) 6 *The School of Public Policy Research Papers* 1, 3–5; Wang (n 29) 662; J Lee, 'China's Geostrategic Search for Oil' [2012] *The Washington Quarterly* 75, 79.

[32] T Brink, 'The Challenges of China's Non-Liberal Capitalism for the Liberal Global Economic Order' (2014) 16 *Harvard Asia Quarterly* 36, 39; F He and B Wang, 'Chinese Interests in the Global Investment Regime' (2014) 7 *China Economic Journal* 4, 10; N Salidjanova, *Going Out: An Overview of China's Outward Foreign Direct Investment* (USCC Staff Research Report, 30 March 2011) 3.

[33] D Holtbrügge and SC Berning, 'The National Government's Role in Chinese Outward FDI' in C Julian, Z Ahmed and J Xu (eds), *Research Handbook on the Globalization of Chinese Firms* (Cheltenham, Edward Elgar Publishing, 2014) 94–134.

[34] P Andrews-Speed, *Energy Policy and Regulation in People's Republic of China* (London, Kluwer Law International, 2004) 178; O Odgaard and J Delman, 'China's Energy Security and Its Challenges Towards 2035' (2014) 71 *Energy Policy* 104, 116.

[35] AM Jaffe and R Soligo, 'State-Backed Financing in Oil and Gas Projects' in A Goldthau and JM Witte (eds), *Global Energy Governance: The New Rules of the Game* (Berlin, Global Public Policy Institute, 2010) 107–32, 130.

[36] Salidjanova (n 32) 11; W Norris, *Chinese Economic Statecraft* (Ithaca, NY, Cornell University Press 2016) 99; P Evans and E Downs, 'Untangling China's Quest for Oil through State-Backed Financial Deals' (2006) 154 *Brookings Policy Brief* 1, 90.

the global energy market.[37] They explained that 'CDB's loans lock the countries into supply contracts that make them increasingly dependent on China's purchasing power'.[38]

However, scholars such as Hameiri and Jones have explained that a fragmented and decentralised financing system in China has restricted the ability of the Government to realise geopolitical goals through state financing.[39] Instead, Chinese companies (SOEs in particular) can manipulate state financing in pursuit of commercial opportunities.[40] According to Jones and Zou, the involvement of multiple administrative departments 'allows SOEs considerable space to "interpret" central guidelines according to their own pecuniary interests'.[41] Thus, SOEs can present their profit-seeking schemes as putting top-level policies into practice, and can thereby attain policy and financial concessions.[42] For example, Erie observed that 'Chinese enterprises have labelled many of their earlier deals (including energy ones) as BRI ones'.[43] Furthermore, by relying on the recipient-led financing mode, which is usually defined as the way in which capital-importing states propose energy projects,[44] Chinese energy companies can push foreign governments to apply for Chinese financing.[45] Therefore, in this mode, foreign governments are leading players that enable energy companies to receive state financing.[46]

## IV. Policy Guidance on Overseas Energy Investments

According to the *Measures for Managing Outbound Investment of Enterprises* (2017), 'the NDRC shall develop specific plans and industry policies in the relevant fields as needed for the national economic and social development to provide general guidance for investors to make overseas investments'.[47] To enforce the

[37] H Sanderson and M Forsythe, *China's Superbank: Debt, Oil and Influence* (Hoboken, NJ, Bloomberg Press, 2012) 125.

[38] ibid.

[39] S Hameiri and L Jones, 'China Challenges Global Governance? Chinese International Development Finance and the AIIB' (2018) 94 *International Affairs* 573, 583–85; KE Brødsgaard, 'Politics and Business Group Formation in China: The Party in Control?' (2012) 211 *The China Quarterly* 624, 633.

[40] Hameiri and Jones (n 39) 585.

[41] L Jones and Y Zou, 'Rethinking the Role of State-owned Enterprises in China's Rise' (2017) 22 *New Political Economy* 743, 751.

[42] ibid.

[43] M Erie, 'Chinese Law and Development' (2020) 62 *Harvard International Law Journal* 51.

[44] B Kong and K Gallagher, 'Chinese Development Finance for Solar and Wind Power Abroad', GCI Working Paper 01 (2020) 9.

[45] Hameiri and Jones (n 39) 584.

[46] ibid.

[47] NDRC, *Measures for Managing Outbound Investment of Enterprises* [《企业境外投资管理办法》] (2017) Arts 9 and 10. L Li, 'Viewing the "Going Out" Strategy from the Perspective of the Government' [《从政府角度看"走出去"战略》] (2014) 6 *Commercial Research* 134, 135; J Chen, 'Thoughts about Improving the Overseas Investments Management System' [《完善中国企业"走出去"政策措施体系之思考》] (2013) 10 *International Trade* 25, 25.

'Going Out' strategy,[48] China's five-year plans play a crucial role in guiding and coordinating overseas energy investments.[49] These plans provide 'overall strategic guidance' for domestic companies as to investing in specific industries or states.[50] In other words, international energy expansion should contribute to China's security of supply and its greater influence on the global energy market.[51] With the guidance, energy companies exercise their decision-making rights under the macro control of the Chinese Government.[52]

## A. The Mode of 'Encouraging Investments and Negative Lists'

The Chinese Government has adopted the mode of 'encouraging investments and negative lists' to boost capital flows in areas that are essential to social and economic development.[53] Broad state guidelines set the parameters of making outbound energy investments[54] and channel the information from the central leadership to different administrative departments.[55]

The *Policies on Industry Guidance on Overseas Investments* (2006) generally divided investments into three types: encouraged investments; restricted investments; and forbidden investments.[56] In the energy sector, NDRC is concerned with energy security.[57] This has been translated into policy goals amid an overseas scramble for energy resources.[58] Investments in energy resources or raw materials

[48] State Council, *The 12th Five-Year-Plan* [《"十二五"计划纲要全文》] (2011); D Rosen, 'The CCP and Free-Market Principles' in S Kennedy (ed), *State and Market in Contemporary China: Toward the 13th Five-Year Plan* (Centre for Strategic & International Studies, 2016) 2–5, at 2.

[49] NDRC, *The 10th FDI Five Year Plan* [《"十五"利用外资和境外投资规划》] (2001); NDRC, The *12th Energy Five-Year Plan* [《能源发展 " 十二五 " 重点专项规划》] (2013); Szamosszegi and Kyle (n 29) 61.

[50] NDRC, MOFCOM, People's Bank of China (PBOC) and Ministry of Foreign Affairs (MFA), *Opinions on Guiding and Regulating the Direction of Overseas Investments* [《关于进一步引导和规范境外投资方向的指导意见》] (2017); NDRC and NEA, *13th Energy Development Five-Year Plan* [《能源发展"十三五"规划》] (2016); O Melton, 'China's Five-Year Planning System: Implications for the Reform Agenda', Testimony for the US–China Economic and Security Review Commission (22 April 2015) 2–3.

[51] Chapter 2 discusses objectives of China's external energy strategy.

[52] Y Qiu, H Lai and H Ye, 'Institution, Marketization and Domestic Investment Management System Reform' [《制度、市场化与我国投资体制改革》] (2000) 1 *Economic System Reform* 216, 217.

[53] NDRC, MOFCOM, PBOC and MFA (n 50). W Yin, 'China's Approach Towards Investment Agreements and Its Interests Involved in International Investment Rule Making' in J Nakagawa (ed), *Asian Perspectives on International Investment Law* (London, Routledge, 2019) 10–29, 12.

[54] X Ma and P Andrews-Speed, 'The Overseas Activities of China's National Oil Companies: Rationale and Outlook' (2006) 21 *Minerals & Energy* 17, 27; A Collier, *China Buys the World: Analyzing China's Overseas Investments* (Singapore, Springer, 2018) 55.

[55] L Corkin, 'Redefining Foreign Policy Impulses toward Africa: The Roles of the MFA, the MOFCOM and China Exim Bank' (2011) 40 *Journal of Current Chinese Affairs* 61, 63.

[56] NDRC, MOFCOM, MFA, *Policies on Industry Guidance on Overseas Investments* [《境外投资产业指导政策》] (2006) Art 4.

[57] Y Jiang, 'Red Trojan Horses? A New Look at Chinese SOEs' Outward Investment' (2014) 2 *Journal of China and International Relations* 1.

[58] ibid.

that are in short supply therefore fall into the category of encouraged investments.[59] For example, investments in oil and gas exploration and related services are clearly listed as encouraged investments.[60]

According to the *Opinions on Encouraging and Regulating the Cooperation of Enterprises in Foreign Investment* (2007), the categorisation of restricted investments was determined by the need to implement diplomatic policies and upgrade domestic industries.[61] The central Government restricts investments that cannot contribute to domestic industrial development or that are located in places in political crisis and which may require the Chinese Government to step in.[62] The possible requirement for the involvement of the Chinese Government will prevent it from complying with the diplomatic principles of non-intervention in other states.[63] Therefore, in these restricted investments, administrative departments will remind investors to remain cautious.

As for forbidden investments, investments relevant to core military technology are forbidden due to their threats to national interests or security.[64]

Accordingly, given that energy investments can help to realise energy policy goals and may be located in politically unstable regions, the governance of encouraged investments and restricted investments is relevant for the management of China's overseas energy investments.

## B. Preferred Energy Projects and Destinations for Energy Investments

In addition to encouraging investments that help to develop the domestic energy sector, the policy guidelines provide a choice of projects and investment destinations (Appendix 1 to this book).[65] The catalogues for preferred foreign energy projects and investment destinations represent government prospects for encouraged overseas energy investments without mandatory force.[66] These preferred host states where energy investments can be made and preferred projects in policies acknowledges the importance of these states and projects

[59] NDRC, MOFCOM, MFA (n 50) Art 6.

[60] ibid App 1 to the book.

[61] State Council, *Opinions on Encouraging and Regulating the Cooperation of Enterprises in Foreign Investment* [《国务院关于鼓励和规范企业对外投资合作的意见》] (2007).

[62] ibid; J Yu and Z Chen, 'The Discussion of China's Overseas Investments Approval Procedure' [《中国境外投资核准制度改革自议》] (2013) 2 *The Jurist* 43, 44.

[63] Yu and Chen (n 62).

[64] NDRC, MOFCOM, PBOC and MFA (n 50).

[65] Z Chen, 'The Historical Development and Current Status of the Domestic Investment Approval System' [《我国投资审批制度的沿革和现状浅述》] (2017) 5 *Modern Business* 41, 42; H Qiao, 'The Role of the Government in China's Outbound Investments' [《中国企业海外投资中政府的角色定位》] (2002) 1 *Asia Pacific Economic Review* 57, 59.

[66] D Freeman, 'China's Outward Investment Institutions, Constraints, and Challenges' (2013) 7 *Asia Paper* 2.

for the security of China's supply.[67] The five-year plans specifically require the realisation of certain energy infrastructure projects that are usually highly capital-intensive investments regarding special energy interests.[68] Also, the catalogues for investment destinations comply with the principle of protecting diplomatic interests. Sudan was removed from the list of preferred investment destinations by NDRC and MOFCOM, to fulfil China's commitments to the international community.[69] Therefore, by following these investment guidelines, companies can help the Government to realise its policy goals, such as building overseas oil and gas production bases as highlighted in chapter two, without hampering the Government's diplomatic interests.[70]

## C. The Guidance Specifically Provided for Energy SOEs

China's energy policymakers have stressed that overseas investments made by energy SOEs need to help achieve policy goals.[71] In other words, energy SOEs should translate the policy goals introduced in chapter two into various energy projects. Before the corporatisation of SOEs, '[the Government] shall formulate and adjust industrial policies, and guide the enterprises in working out their development plans', according to the Law of the People's Republic of China on Industrial Enterprises Owned by the Whole People (1988, revised 2009).[72] For example, in the early 1990s, China's NOCs made investment decisions in accordance with the 'broader macro-economic goals' set out by policymakers.[73] After their corporatisation, central energy SOEs still bear the mission of investing in overseas oil and gas exploration, technology innovation and the construction of power grids, the development of hydro power, solar power and nuclear power, the export of services and equipment, and the improvement of coal-efficient use.[74] Under *The*

[67] H Voss, P Buckley and A Cross, 'An Assessment of the Effects of Institutional Change on Chinese Outward Direct Investment Activity' in I Alon et al (eds), *China Rules: Globalization and Political Transformation* (London, Palgrave Macmillan, 2009) 135–65, 153; Corkin (n 55) 63.

[68] Melton (n 50).

[69] E Downs, 'Who's Afraid of China's Oil Companies' in C Pascual and J Elkind (eds), *Energy Security* (Washington, DC, Brookings Institution Press, 2010) 73–102, 78.

[70] Y Luo, Q Xue and B Han, 'How Emerging Market Governments Promote Outward FDI: Experience from China' (2010) 45 *Journal of World Business* 68, 76; K Sauvant and VZ Chen, 'China's Regulatory Framework for Outward Foreign Direct Investment' (2014) 7 *China Economic Journal* 141, 144.

[71] State-Owned Asset Supervision and Administration Commission (SASAC), *The 12th Five-Year Plan of Developing Central SOEs* [《中央企业"十二五"和谐发展战略实施纲要》] (2011); W Wu, *Chinese Oil Enterprises in Latin America* (Singapore, Springer, 2019) 29; H Zhao, 'China's Overseas Energy Investment: Myth and Reality' [2009] *Contemporary International Relations* 89, 109.

[72] Law of the People's Republic of China on Industrial Enterprises Owned by the Whole People [《中华人民共和国全民所有制工业企业法》] (1988, revised in 2009) Art 56.

[73] M Meidan, *The Structure of China's Oil Industry: Past Trends and Future Prospects* (Oxford Institute for Energy Studies, May 2016).

[74] State Council, *Guiding Opinions of the General Office of the State Council on Promoting the Restructuring and Reorganisation of Central State-Owned Enterprises* [《国务院办公厅关于推动中央

*12th Energy Five-Year Plan* (2013), SOEs should play a leading role in developing strategic new energy industries.[75]

As the leading administrative department governing SOEs in China, SASAC has formulated measures for ensuring the compliance of SOEs' investments with energy policies.[76] According to *Management Measures of Development Strategies and Plans of Central SOEs* (2004), SASAC evaluates whether SOEs' investment strategies comply with industrial policies.[77] For energy SOEs, SASAC assesses how their global energy expansion can help the state to secure energy supplies and influence the global energy market.[78] For instance, with *The 13th Petroleum Development Five-Year Plan* (2016), 'the evaluation system of SOEs' management should strengthen the appraisal of the contribution of overseas oil investments to the security of oil supply'.[79] Chapter six will include a more detailed discussion of how SASAC ensures the consistency of SOEs' investment plans with policies.

## D. The Implementation of Policy Guidance

Policy guidance on investing abroad does not necessarily mean that energy companies do not have investment autonomy. The mode of 'encouraged investments and negative lists' reflects that the Chinese Government has 'shifted from a commander who assigns specific tasks towards a planner who offers general guidance only'.[80] As suggested by *The 10th Five-Year Plan* (2001), 'the proposed direction of industrial development and the proposed key industries are suggestions to market entities'.[81] Also, 'China respects the self-willingness of enterprises' according to *The 12th Five-Year Plan*.[82] Therefore, policies shape but do not determine Chinese companies' investment decisions.[83]

企业结构调整与重组的指导意见》] (2016); SASAC, *Interpreting the 11th Five-Year Plan of Developing Central SOEs* [《中央企业十一五规划发展规划纲要解读》] (2006); SASAC, *Interpreting the 13th Five-Year Plan of Developing Central SOEs* [《中央企业十三五规划发展规划纲要解读》] (2017).

[75] NDRC (2013) (n 49).

[76] SASAC, *Measures for the Supervision and Administration of Overseas Investments by Central Enterprises* [《中央企业境外投资监督管理办法》] (2017) Art 11.

[77] SASAC, *Management Measures of Development Strategies and Plans of Central SOEs* [《中央企发展规略和规划管理办法》] (2004) Art 13.

[78] F Robins, 'The Uniqueness of Chinese Outward Foreign Direct Investment' (2013) 12 *Asian Business & Management* 525, 525.

[79] NDRC, *The 13th Petroleum Development Five-year Plan* [《石油发展"十三五"规划》] (2016).

[80] L Che, *China's State-Directed Economy and the International Order* (Singapore, Springer, 2019) 44; Voss, Buckley and Cross (n 67) 154.

[81] State Council, *The 10th Five-Year-Plan* [《"十五"计划纲要全文》] (2001).

[82] State Council (n 48).

[83] CS Liou, 'Bureaucratic Politics and Overseas Investment by Chinese State-Owned Oil Companies: Illusory Champions' (2009) 49 *Asian Survey* 670, 679; H Ai, 'Reforming the Investment Management System and Increase Returns of Investments' [《改革现行投资体制，提高政府投资效益》] (2004) 5 *Guangdong Accountancy* 19, 20; YC Xu, 'China's Giant State-Owned Enterprises as Policy Advocates: The Case of the State Grid Corporation of China' (2017) 79 *The China Journal* 21.

Furthermore, the extent to which five-year plans are enforceable is unclear,[84] as the plans do not charge a specific energy company with the fulfilment of a specific project.[85] The five-year plans are developed by the State Council, subject to the guidance of the Party, and are then adopted by the National People's Congress.[86] Although there is no explicit indication as to whether the five-year plans are binding, Chinese scholars generally agree that the they are obligatory and that their implementation affects the evaluation of local governments.[87] This is because of their standardised drafting process and the involvement of the highest administrative department, the Party and the highest legislative authority.[88] More specifically, these scholars believe that the targets (eg, the carbon emission targets) set out in the plans are binding on local governments, and that local governments are accountable for the achievement of those targets.[89] However, other plan content, including recommendations on investing abroad, are far from enforceable and are drafted in non-binding language. For Andrews-Speed and Dannreuther, 'the five-year energy plans continue to be characterised by specific targets for each component of the energy industry, but by only vague statements relating to measures and mechanisms that would apply across the energy sector'.[90] Therefore, scholars such as Ye have argued that policy guidance on investing abroad was directional and complemented regulatory governance, and that Chinese companies were free to comprehend the strategy and to manage their foreign business.[91] In other words, the general and vague language of some content of these policies leaves room for companies

[84] T Hao, 'Does National Economic and Social Plans Have Legal Forces?' [《我国国民经济和社会发展规划具有法律约束力吗?》] (2007) 2 *Learning and Discovery* 99, 100; X Dong, 'Legal Guarantee for the Implementation of the Development Plan' [《论发展规划法中的实施机制》] (2018) 1 *Economic Law Review* 225.

[85] State Council (n 48) (on the autonomy of energy companies in the making of energy investments).

[86] Constitution of the People's Republic of China [《中华人民共和国宪法》] (1982, as amended in 1993, 1999, 2004 and 2018) Arts 62 and 89(5); see also M Xu, 'Development Plans of Economy and Society and the Legal Development of Plans' [《论经济社会发展规划与规划法制建设》] (2012) 2 *The Jurist* 43, 51.

[87] Xu (n 86) 45–46; AG Hu, 'The Five-Year Plan: A New Tool for Energy Saving and Emissions Reduction in China' (2016) 7 *Advances in Climate Change Research* 222, 223; C Guo, 'Analysis of the Legal Nature of Plans' [《规划纲要的法律性质探析》] (2018) 3 *Academic Journal of Shanghai University of Political Science and Law* 57, 62–64.

[88] Xu (n 86) 45–46; Guo (n 87); Hao (n 84).

[89] See also J Jiang, 'The Research of the Implementation Mechanisms of National Five Year Plans: Implementation Paths, Implementation Difficulties and Solutions' [《国家五年规划的实施机制研究: 实施路径、困境及其破解》] (2017) 3 *North Western Normal University (Social Science)* 1; X Xu, Plans as A Governance Tool: Essence, Reasons and Paths [《作为治理工具的规划: 内涵、缘起与路径》] (2017) 2 *South East Academic* 1.

[90] Andrews-Speed and Dannreuther (n 30) 54–55.

[91] M Ye, *The Belt Road and Beyond – State-Mobilized Globalization in China: 1998–2018* (Cambridge, Cambridge University Press, 2020) 102–03; Jiang (n 89); I Casaburi and CB Broggi, 'The Internationalization of Chinese Companies and Their Presence in Europe' in J Solana and A Saz-Carranza (eds), *The Global Context: How Politics, Investment, and Institutions Impact European Businesses* (ESADEgeo – Center for Global Economy and Geopolitics, 2015) 110–27.

to pursue their commercial interests.[92] However, the PRC Energy Law (2020 Draft), if adopted, will contribute to the achievement of energy five-year plans, as it explicitly requires domestic energy investors to 'comply with the national energy strategy and plans'.[93]

In practice, the profile of China's foreign energy projects indicates gaps in carrying out five-year energy plans. For instance, the construction of Line D of the China–Central Asia gas pipeline was 'indefinitely postponed' in 2017, despite the inclusion of this project in *The 13th Gas Development Five-Year Plan* (2016).[94] The reason why China's energy companies failed to complete projects might be the delays and resistance to approval by, and cooperation with, host states and their national energy companies. At the same time, China's companies and their local partners have started to develop projects before the Chinese Government includes those projects in five-year plans. Examples include the expansion of the China–Kazakhstan oil pipeline[95] and the development of the China–Myanmar oil and gas pipelines.[96] Chapter seven provides case studies of China's foreign energy projects.

## V. Policies in Support of Global Energy Expansion

The state support mechanisms can facilitate the implementation of the policy guidance.[97] The support mechanisms that benefit encouraged overseas energy

[92] L Jakobson, 'Does China Have an "Energy Diplomacy"? Reflections on China's Energy Security and its International Dimensions' in A Marquina (ed), *Energy Security: Visions from Asia and Europe* (London, Palgrave Macmillan 2008) 121–34; M Meidan, *China's 13th Five-Year Plan: Implications for Oil Markets* (Oxford Institute for Energy Studies, June 2016).

[93] National Energy Administration, Public Consultation on the Energy Law of the PRC (Draft)' [国家能源局关于《中华人民共和国能源法(征求意见稿)》公开征求意见的公告] (3 April 2020) Art 87.

[94] C Michel, 'The Central Asia-China Gas Pipeline Network: Line D(ead)' at thediplomat.com/2017/03/the-central-asia-china-gas-pipeline-network-line-dead/.

[95] In 2009, CNPC committed to construct Phase II of the pipeline (CNPC in Kazakhstan at www.cnpc.com.cn/cnpc/Kazakhstan/country_index.shtml), before official endorsement in 2013 (NDRC, n 49); in 2013, CNPC committed to expanding and modernising the pipeline (CNPC in Kazakhstan at www.cnpc.com.cn/cnpc/Kazakhstan/country_index.shtml), before official endorsement in 2016 (NDRC and NEA, n 50).

[96] In 2003, CNPC and the Yunnan government proposed the pipelines to NDRC, which first rejected the projects as unfeasible before endorsing them in 2006. See Jones and Zou (n 41) 751; A Erickson and G Collins, 'China's Oil Security Pipe Dream' (2010) 63 *Naval War College Review* 89, 98.

[97] X Zheng, *China's 40 Years of Economic Reform and Development: How the Miracle Was Created* (Singapore, Springer, 2018) 186; The Research Team of State Planning Commission, 'China's Investment Management Reform: Transforming to the Socialist Market Economy' [《转向市场经济的中国投资体制改革》] (1993) 11 *Economic Discovery* 23, 26; B Wang and K Gao, 'Forty Years Development of China's Outward Foreign Direct Investment' (2019) 27 *China & World Economy* 1, 11; H Li, M Xu and Q Zhang, 'Review of Energy Policies in the 40 Years of Reform and Opening in China: from Structure to Logic' [《改革开放 40 年中国能源政策回顾:从结构到逻辑》] (2019) 29 *China Population, Resources and Environment* 167, 273; J Tian, 'The Retrospects and Prospects of the Reform of the Investment Management System' [《我国投资体制改革回顾与展望》] (2008) 7 *China Technology Investment* 35, 36.

investments include insurance services, financial support, simplified investment approval procedures, and the system for providing information on the investment environment.[98] Information services and insurance services will be discussed in chapters eight and nine respectively.

## A. The Official Call for Simplifying Investment Approval Procedure

Policymakers confirm that pinning down the scope of projects subject to approval has been one objective of reforming the investment system.[99] The *Decision on Reform of Investment System* (2004)[100] stated that strict investment approval procedures restricted investors' autonomy and imposed heavy administrative burden on them.[101] The Government therefore tried to simplify the investment approval procedure and to establish a new investment management system in which investors are able to exercise autonomy in their global energy expansion, according to the *Opinions on Encouraging and Regulating the Cooperation of Enterprises in Foreign Investment* (2007).[102] The *Guiding Opinions on Promotion of International Production Capacity and Equipment Manufacturing Cooperation* (2015) also proposed that 'we should move from pre-event management mode to the mode of in-process and after-event management'.[103] With five-year plans and investment-related policies:

> the government should ensure enterprises' decision-making power in investments, gradually narrow down the scope of investments that are subject to approval, limit governmental intervention with enterprises, strengthen transparency of the procedure and increase the processing efficiency.[104]

[98] NDRC (n 47); NDRC, MOFCOM, PBOC and MFA (n 50) Art 8; Sauvant and Chen (n 70) 142; G Liang, 'China Goes Global: Outward Investment' in H Wang and L Miao (eds), *Handbook on China and Globalization* (Cheltenham, Edward Elgar, 2019) 115–38, 125.

[99] National People's Congress, Decision of the First Session of the Twelfth National People's Congress on the Plan for Restructuring the State Council and Transforming Functions [《国务院机构改革和职能转变方案》] (2013); S Li and Y Gao, 'A Small Discussion on the Main Content of Decision of the State Council on Reforming the Investment System' [《浅谈投资体制改革的主要内容》] (2004) 10 *Finance and Accounting for Foreign Economic Relations and Trade* 9, 9; Sauvant and Chen (n 70) 144.

[100] State Council, Decision of the State Council on Reforming the Investment System [《国务院关于投资体制改革的决定》] (26 July 2004).

[101] W Zhang, 'The Impacts of the Reform of the Investment Management System on Enterprises' [《投资体制改革对企业的影响》] (1995) 7 *Academic Journal of Central University of Finance and Economics* 29, 30. Investors' autonomy includes independently selecting financing methods, freely choosing a specific project and defining their business scope.

[102] State Council, *Opinions on Encouraging and Regulating the Cooperation of Enterprises in Foreign Investment* [《国务院关于鼓励和规范企业对外投资合作的意见》] (2007); J Zhang and X Zhou, 'Thoughts on Policy-Making of China's Overseas Investments against the Background of the "Going Out" Strategy' [《"走出去"战略背景下中国对外直接投资政策体系的思考》] (2007) 4 *International Trade* 27, 28.

[103] State Council, *Guiding Opinions on Promotion of International Production Capacity and Equipment Manufacturing Cooperation* [《国务院关于推进国际产能和装备制造合作的指导意见》] (2015).

[104] NDRC, *The 13th Five Year Plan* [《"十三五"国民经济规划》](2016); NDRC, MOFCOM, PBOC and MFA (n 50).

By relaxing the ex ante approval procedures, China's companies can minimise their transaction costs in launching foreign projects.[105]

In the energy sector, the officials of NDRC stated in a 2015 press conference that the gradual liberalisation of the investment approval procedure should facilitate global energy expansion.[106] Dating back to 2001, *The 10th Petroleum Development Five-Year Plan* (2001) suggested '[removal of] the limit on the amount of outward investments in oil'.[107] Later, with the *China National Energy Strategy and Policy 2020* (2004), it became necessary to simplify the procedure for approving oil companies' overseas investments.[108] *The 12th Energy Five-Year Plan* (2013) further advocated an improved record-keeping regime for limiting government intervention in overseas energy investments.[109] Chapter five provides more detail on the relaxing of state control through reformation of the investment approval procedure.

## B. Financial Support

Policy banks, the AIIB and the SRF have financed China's overseas energy investments in the form of lines of credit to SOEs,[110] because these institutions have a stronger financial capacity for granting loans to capital-intensive energy projects, compared with China's commercial banks.[111] As stressed by *The 10th Energy Five-Year Plan* (2001), policy loans should help NOCs establish overseas oil production bases.[112] China's financial support is 'state-supported but market-based'.[113] State ownership enhances credibility of the financing and reduces the financial risks of domestic energy companies;[114] and meanwhile, these state-financing institutions

[105] Chen (n 47) 25.

[106] NDRC, *Interpretation on Guiding Opinions on Promotion of International Production Capacity and Equipment Manufacturing Cooperation* [《发改委解读推进国际产能和装备制造合作指导意见》] (2015).

[107] State Commission for Economics and Trade, *The 10th Petroleum Development Five-Year Plan* [《石油工业"十五"规划》] (2001).

[108] X Liu, F Zhou and J Li, 'Adjustment and Optimization of Energy Supply Structure in China' in *China National Energy Strategy and Policy 2020: Renewable Energy Development Policy and Strategy* (Energy Research Institute of NDRC, 2004) 17.

[109] NDRC (n 49).

[110] NDRC and NEA, 'Energy Production and Consumption Transition Strategy (2016–2030)' [《能源生产和消费革命战略（2016–2030）》] (December 2016); P Andrews-Speed, 'China's International Energy Engagement' in K Zeng (ed), *Handbook on the International Political Economy of China* (Cheltenham, Edward Elgar Publishing, 2019) 132–50, 142; J Meckling, B Kong and T Madan, 'Oil and State Capitalism: Government-Firm Coopetition in China and India' (2015) 22 *Review of International Political Economy* 1159, 1183; H Wang, 'China's Approach to the Belt and Road Initiative: Scope, Character and Sustainability' (2019) 22 *Journal of International Economic Law* 29, 33.

[111] Kong and Gallagher (n 5); E Downs, *Inside China, Inc: China Development Bank's Cross-Border Energy Deals* (Brookings Institute, March 2011) 26.

[112] NDRC, *The 10th Energy Five-Year Plan* [《国民经济和社会发展第十个五年计划能源发展重点专项规划》] (2001).

[113] Chen (n 5) 2.

[114] D O'Neill, 'Playing Risk: Chinese Foreign Direct Investment in Cambodia' (2014) 36 *Contemporary Southeast Asia* 173, 189.

grant financing to energy companies at market rates and conduct due diligence to protect their financial interests.[115] As stressed by Keming Qian, the previous Vice Minister of MOFCOM, policy banks have their own transparent and high-quality procedures to assess projects.

### *i. China Development Bank and Export-Import Bank*

With the *Measures for the Supervision and Administration of the Export-Import Bank of China* (2017) and the *Measures for the Supervision and Administration of the China Development Bank* (2017), the Export-Import Bank (EXIMB) and CDB shoulder the mission of implementing national strategies such as international energy cooperation.[116] More specifically, the head of CDB publicly stated that 'CDB should finance the construction of infrastructure projects in the BRI'.[117] In practice, both CDB and EXIMB play central roles in China's global energy expansion, especially in the renewable power sector.[118] For example, CDB has financed the development of pipeline infrastructure projects (eg, the Kazakhstan–China oil pipeline and the Central Asia–China gas pipeline).[119] It has also issued loans of US$ 6.4 billion to renewable electricity projects in the BRI.[120] Solar power investments have been financed by EXIMB in Pakistan.[121]

The criteria for eligible overseas energy investments reflect the financial support target for facilitating the implementation of energy policies.[122] According to the *Notice on Giving Credit Support to the Key Overseas Investment Projects Encouraged by the State* (adopted in 2004) and the *Notice on the Relevant Issues of Providing More Financing Support to Key Overseas-Invested Projects* (adopted in 2005), EXIMB and CDB respectively set up a mechanism for financing eligible overseas investments.[123] The investments in question are those that acquire

[115] Chen (n 5) 15 and 22; J Mathews and H Tan, 'China's New Silk Road: Will It Contribute to Export of the Black Fossil-Fuelled Economy?' (2017) 15 *The Asia-Pacific Journal* 1, 8.

[116] China Banking Regulatory Commission, *Measures for the Supervision and Administration of the Export-Import Bank of China* [《中国进出口银行监督管理办法》] (2017) Art 5; China Banking Regulatory Commission, *Measures for the Supervision and Administration of China Development Bank* [《国家开发银行监督管理办法》] (2017) Art 3.

[117] CDB, *The Annual Report 2015 of CDB* [《国开行2015年度报告》] (2015).

[118] X Tan et al, 'China's Overseas Investments in the Wind and Solar Industries: Trends and Drivers', World Resources Institute Working Paper (April 2013) 15 (last accessed 10 May 2019); Kong and Gallagher (n 44) 2.

[119] See, eg, F Aminjono, et al, 'BRI in Central Asia' (2019) 22 *Central Asia Regional Data Review* 1.

[120] 'The Trends of and Suggestions on Renewable Energy Investments in the BRI' [《"一带一路"国家可再生能源投资趋势及建议》] (Chinese Renewable Energy Industries Association, February 2020) at www.greenbr.org.cn/cmsfiles/1/editorfiles/files/c23b773ab3454b9b978c4d70401587d8.pdf.

[121] 'China Funds Mega Yamal LNG Project' *Global Trade Review* (4 May 2016) at www.gtreview.com/news/europe/china-funds-mega-russian-lng-project/; A Bros and T Mitrova, 'Yamal LNG: An Economic Project under Political Pressure', Note de la FRS n°17/2016 at www.frstrategie.org/en/publications/notes/yamal-lng-economic-project-under-political-pressure-2016.

[122] Kong (n 5) 41.

[123] NDRC and EXIMB, *Notice on Giving Credit Support to the Key Overseas Investment Projects Encouraged by the State* [《国家发展和改革委员会、中国进出口银行关于对国家鼓励的境外

energy resources, export energy-related technologies, products, equipment and services, utilise foreign advanced technologies and improve domestic companies' international competitiveness.[124] Therefore, overseas energy investments qualify for financing by CDB and EXIMB if they can strengthen the external energy supply and increase China's influence over the global energy market. For eligible conventional energy investments, oil and gas projects should secure oil and gas supplies.[125] For renewable energy projects, firms need to export China's renewable energy technologies, services and products and, meanwhile, 'shorten the technological learning curve or enhance global competitiveness' in power projects operation.[126] Annual reports and manuals of two policy banks provide examples of investments that contributed to the realisation of energy policy goals. The *Global Business Manual* of CDB recorded that the CDB granted US$ 4.15 billion to a joint venture established by CNPC and Petróleos de Venezuela, SA (PDVSA) for developing the MPE3 oil field in Venezuela.[127] This project ensured an oil supply to China and exported domestic energy equipment.[128] EXIMB also financed the Karot Hydropower Station, which 'is of great significance to developing the China–Pakistan Economic Corridor (CPEC)'.[129]

While assessing whether the projects can help to achieve energy policy goals, China's policy banks closely scrutinise the financial viability of energy projects by carrying out risk assessments.[130] The assessments centre on the financial and technical aspects of foreign energy projects, such as the return rate.[131] Based on these, these two policy banks can refuse to grant financing to energy companies, despite the 'political pressure of implementing "Going Out" policies or the BRI'.[132] For instance, although renewable energy investments help to implement energy policies, policy banks do not actively pursue renewable power projects in practice.[133] Instead, they approve loans when the return rate of the particular project meets the standards that are required in risk assessments.

The State Council and central ministries subordinated to it clearly established that POEs should be treated the same as SOEs in obtaining financing granted by

投资重点项目给予信贷支持政策的通知》] (2004); NDRC and CDB, *Notice on Providing More Financing Support to Key Overseas-invested Projects* [《关于进一步加强对境外投资重点项目融资支持有关问题的通知》] (2005).

[124] NDRC and EXIMB (n 124); NDRC and CDB (n 124); Sauvant and Chen (n 70) 143.

[125] Kong and Gallagher (n 44) 8.

[126] ibid.

[127] CDB, 'Global Business Manual' [《国际业务宣传手册》] 12 at www.cdb.com.cn/ywgl/xdyw/gjhzyw/201512/W020160311572457861502.zip.

[128] ibid.

[129] EXIMB, 'Annual Report 2016' [《2016年度报告》] (2016) 49; EXIMB, 'The abstract of EXIMB's Articles of Association' [《章程（摘要）》] at www.eximbank.gov.cn/tm/second/index_1162.html.

[130] EXIMB, 'Loans for Overseas Investments' at www.eximbank.gov.cn/tm/Fm2/index_1168.html; Kong and Gallagher (n 44) 10.

[131] Kong and Gallagher (n 44) 10.

[132] Hameiri and Jones (n 39) 583.

[133] Kong and Gallagher (n 44) 9.

policy banks.[134] Indeed, CDB financed the projects invested in by a POE – LDK Solar.[135] Nevertheless, in practice, energy SOEs have benefited from more support than their private counterparts.[136] Interviews with lawyers also indicated that it is more probable that SOEs will receive financing. The empirical research conducted by Gallagher and Irwin illustrated that energy SOEs and private ones with close ties to the Government are major recipients.[137] The *Annual Report 2017 of CDB* recorded that CDB provided US$ 13.4 billion for large group clients – central SOEs in their overseas investments.[138]

## *ii. AIIB and SRF*

In addition to policy banks, the AIIB and SRF fill the gap between financing and the needs of energy infrastructure investments.[139] The Articles of Agreement adopted by the AIIB provide that this bank aims to 'strengthen infrastructure connectivity in Asia by investing in infrastructure projects'.[140] *The Energy Sector Strategy: Sustainable Energy for Asia* specifies that financing will be provided for investments that increase access to energy and investments in cross-border energy transportation networks.[141] Indeed, the AIIB has financed a wide range of energy projects, from power-generation plants to pipelines.[142] The Articles of Association (Abstract) adopted by the SRF also require the fund to push cooperation in the BRI and to fill the funding gap in infrastructure projects and the development of energy resources.[143] Development of energy resources includes projects involving

[134] State Council, *Opinions on Encouraging and Guiding Investments of Private Owned Enterprises* [《国务院关于鼓励和引导民间投资健康发展的若干意见》] (2010); NDRC et al, *Instruction of Encouraging and Guiding Overseas Investment of Private Owned Enterprises* [《关于鼓励和引导民营企业积极开展外投资的实施意见》] (2012); State Council, *Opinions on Encouraging the Development of the Private Economy* [《国务院关于鼓励支持和引导个体私营等非公有制经济发展的若干意见》] (2005); YC Xu, 'Chinese State-owned Enterprises in Africa: Ambassadors or Freebooters' (2014) 23 *Journal of Contemporary China* 822, 830.

[135] Kong (n 5) 39.

[136] Downs (n 111); J Jiang and J Sinton, *Overseas Investments by Chinese National Oil Companies* (IEA, 2011); K Sauvant and M Nolan, 'China's Outward Foreign Direct Investment and International Investment Law' (2015) 18 *Journal of International Economic Law* 893, fn 27.

[137] K Gallagher and A Irwin, 'China's Economic Statecraft in Latin America' (2015) 88 *Pacific Affairs* 1, 15–17.

[138] CDB, *The Annual Report 2017 of CDB* [《国开行2017年度报告》] (2017) 48.

[139] C Cai, *The Rise of China and International Law* (Oxford, Oxford University Press, 2019) 192.

[140] AIIB, Articles of Agreement, Art 1 at www.aiib.org/en/about-aiib/basic-documents/_download/articles-of-agreement/basic_document_english-bank_articles_of_agreement.pdf.

[141] AIIB, 'Energy Sector Strategy: Sustainable Energy for Asia' (11 April 2018) 11 at www.aiib.org/en/policies-strategies/strategies/sustainable-energy-asia/.content/index/_download/energy-sector-strategy.pdf; AIIB, 'Thematic Priorities' at www.aiib.org/en/policies-strategies/strategies/index.html#strategies.

[142] P Galkin, D Chen and J Ke, *China's Energy Investment Through the Lens of the Belt and Road Initiative* (King Abdullah Petroleum Studies and Research Centre, 2019) 20.

[143] Silk Road Fund, Articles of Association (Abstract) at www.silkroadfund.com.cn/cnweb/19882/19886/index.html; 'Interview with CEO of the Silk Road Fund' *Closer to China* (2 September 2018), broadcast on CGTN.

conventional and renewable energy.[144] For instance, the SRF financed the Yamal LNG project.[145]

By making use of financing granted by AIIB, China is able to accomplish its policy goal of securing an uninterrupted energy supply through prioritised infrastructure investments.[146] China has also exported its energy-related services, technology and equipment in energy projects financed by the AIIB.[147]

Although the AIIB has facilitated the implementation of China's energy policies, such as diversifying transportation routes in the BRI, the Bank's Vice President announced that 'the AIIB is not a financial subsidiary for the BRI but an independent actor that consider members' ideas'.[148] With the *Operation Policy of Financing*, a main criterion is whether the project helps the Bank to realise development goals (eg, energy inter-connectivity).[149] Additionally, the delicate decision-making process for approving loans provides all stakeholders with opportunities to express infrastructural needs, and therefore restricts China's influence on the direction of funding flows.[150] The *Operation Policy of Financing* establishes that the board of directors makes decisions on financing infrastructure projects.[151] The Articles of Agreement further provides that the approved financing should be permitted by no less than three-quarters of the total voting power of the members.[152] China's absolute power of veto (26.06 per cent voting rights) cannot be used in this decision-making process, because this power mainly affects the general management of the Bank, such as membership, the volume of capital stock and the appointment of directors.[153] Moreover, in the long run, China will welcome more members, which will dilute its share of the vote, and therefore may lose the de facto power of veto.[154]

[144] Silk Road Fund, 'Scope of Investments' at www.silkroadfund.com.cn/enweb/23798/23805/index.html.

[145] 'Yamal LNG: A Titanic Gas Project in Arctic Siberia' *Alten around the World* (4 December 2019) at www.alten.com/yamal-lng-project-gas-arctic-anotech-energy/; 'Yamal LNG', CNPC at www.cnpc.com.cn/en/xhtml/pdf/2018YamalLNG.pdf.

[146] M Dian and S Menegazzi, *New Regional Initiatives in China's Foreign Policy* (Cham, Springer International Publishing, 2018) 62. 'Interview with Danny Alexander' *Closer to China* (26 August 2018), broadcast on CGTN.

[147] M Kon, SM Hsu and LS Kung, 'Why did China Take the One Belt and One Road (OBOR) Strategy and Initiate the Asian Infrastructure Investment Bank (AIIB)?' (2016) 6 *International Journal of Economics, Commerce and Research* 39, 44.

[148] 'Interview with Danny Alexander' (n 146).

[149] AIIB, *Operation Policy of Financing* (January 2016, updated 21 March 2017) 5 at www.aiib.org/en/policies-strategies/_download/operation-policy/policy_operational_financing_new.pdf.

[150] B Gu, 'Chinese Multilateralism in the AIIB' (2017) 20 *Journal of International Economic Law* 137, 146; M Callaghan and P Hubbard, 'The Asian Infrastructure Investment Bank: Multilateralism on the Silk Road', EABER Working Paper Series Paper No 116 (East Asian Bureau of Economic Research, 2016) 16.

[151] AIIB (n 149) 7.

[152] AIIB (n 140) Art 26.

[153] ibid Arts 23 and 28; Kon, Hsu and Kung (n 147) 43.

[154] Gu (n 150) 150; Cai (n 139) 193.

The SRF was jointly financed by the State Administration of Foreign Exchange (the biggest shareholder with 65 per cent of the shares), the China Investment Corporation, CDB and EXIMB.[155] The SRF prioritises renewable energy investments that respond to the policy needs of exporting energy-related services, equipment and technology.[156] Despite the requirement to fulfil energy policy mandates, the SRF determines whether the Fund will approve the financing based on the profitability of projects, to maintain the financial viability of the SRF over the medium and long term.[157]

## C. Companies' Continuing Pursuit of Corporate Interests?

By leveraging state support, China's companies can overcome difficulties such as insufficient information on the investment environment of host states and insufficient financing capacity.[158] State support supplies a distinct competitive advantage.[159] Accordingly, state support should in principle incentivise energy companies to help the Chinese Government in implementing its external energy strategy.[160]

However, benefiting from state support does not necessarily imply that NOCs sacrifice business interests for policy interests.[161] The *Opinions on Guiding and Regulating the Direction of Overseas Investments* (2017) stressed that enterprises make investments in accordance with commercial principles.[162] Norris has explained that the Government has achieved its policy goals in alignment with energy companies' pursuit of foreign business development.[163] Moreover, policy financing is conditioned on the profitability of energy investments, as discussed above.

The following projects demonstrate the coexistence of business interests and energy policy interests in the course of global energy expansion (for more details,

[155] Silk Road Fund, 'About Us' at www.silkroadfund.com.cn/enweb/23775/23767/index.html.

[156] Silk Road Fund (n 144).

[157] Silk Road Fund, 'FAQs' at www.silkroadfund.com.cn/cnweb/19954/20355/index.html; R Pantucci, 'China's Development Lenders Embrace Multilateral Co-Operation' *Financial Times* (1 November 2016) at www.ft.com/content/a3192fa0-c59a-30cc-968a-6651ca9310b9; G Wei, 'New Landscapes for Investments and Financing in the BRI – Interviews with Qi Jin' [《开创"一带一路"投融资合作新格局--访丝路基金董事长金琦》] (2017) 9 *China Finance* 20, 21.

[158] C Wang et al, 'What Drives Outward FDI of Chinese Firms? Testing the Explanatory Power of Three Theoretical Frameworks' (2012) 21 *International Business Review* 425.

[159] Voss, Buckley and Cross (n 67) 154.

[160] A Kärkkäinen, 'Does China Have a Geoeconomic Strategy Towards Zimbabwe? The Case of the Zimbabwean Natural Resource Sector' (2016) 14 *Asia Europe Journal* 185, 190; L Corkin, *Uncovering African Agency: Angola's Management of China's Credit Lines* (London, Routledge, 2013) 96.

[161] X Gong, 'The Role of Chinese Corporate Players in China's South China Sea Policy' (2018) 40 *Contemporary Southeast Asia: A Journal of International and Strategic Affairs* 301, 303; Chen (n 31) 13; J Li, *The Clash of Capitalisms? Chinese Companies in the United States* (Cambridge, Cambridge University Press, 2018) 219.

[162] NDRC, MOFCOM, PBOC and MFA (n 50).

[163] Norris (n 36) 31–32.

see chapter seven). The construction of the China–Myanmar pipelines not only contributed to the diversification of China's oil and gas import routes, but also helped CNPC to penetrate domestic south-western downstream markets.[164] The 30-year Gas Sale–Purchase Agreement by CNPC with Gazprom, in the context of the construction of the Power of Siberia pipeline, has diversified China's gas import routes and sources on 'very good commercial terms for the gas'.[165] Similarly, CNPC's investment in the Yamal LNG project not only helped to develop the 'Polar Silk Road',[166] but also enabled CNPC to access Russian upstream assets, acquire advanced technology and gain operational expertise on the Arctic frontier.[167] The China National Offshore Oil Corporation (CNOOC) advanced its investments in oil and gas exploration in the South China Sea to realise the goals of safeguarding China's 'maritime sovereignty' and safeguarding the company's business interests.[168] By investing in the projects involving electricity generation and transmission abroad, State Grid (eg, in Brazil) and the China Three Gorges Corporation (eg, in Pakistan) helped the Chinese Government to export Chinese electricity-related standards and secure influence in these host states.[169] Meanwhile, these investments have provided more profitable opportunities, compared with projects in the more strictly regulated domestic market.[170]

In the long run, energy SOEs may seek to marginalise the contribution made by their investments to the carrying out of energy policies if they find that they are able to rely less on state financing.[171] Secure access to foreign capital is another source of autonomy for energy companies,[172] because less dependence on state financing enable SOEs to view the realisation of policy goals as a minor consideration.[173] For example, State Grid, an electricity SOE, raised funds on the international financial market to accomplish its corporate strategy of utilising international financial resources.[174]

[164] Tunsjø (n 3) 173; D Liu, K Yamaguchib and H Yoshikawa, 'Understanding the Motivations Behind the Myanmar-China Energy Pipeline' (2017) 107 *Energy Policy* 403, 408.

[165] J Henderson and A Moe, *The Globalization of Russian Gas* (Cheltenham, Edward Elgar 2019) 108.

[166] ibid 120.

[167] Q Liu, 'Investing in the Yamal LNG Project' [《入股亚马尔:中石油夙愿已偿》] (2013) 19 *China Petroleum and Chemical Products* 45; L You, 'China-Russia Energy Cooperation' [《中俄能源产业合作动因、风险及路径选择—以亚马尔 LNG 项目为例》] (2018) *4 International Economic Cooperation* 15.

[168] Gong (n 161).

[169] YC Xu, *Sinews of Power* (Oxford, Oxford University Press, 2016) 278–81; F Leverett and B Wu, 'The New Silk Road and China's Evolving Grand Strategy' (2016) 77 *The China Journal* 110; SA Khan and Z Marwat, 'CPEC: Role in Regional Integration and Peace' (2016) 31 *South Asian Studies* 499.

[170] Andrews-Speed (n 110) 140; Jones and Zou (n 41) 744; P Andrews-Speed, M Qiu and C Len, 'Chinese Engagement in Southeast Asian Energy and Mineral Resources' (2016) 57 *Eurasian Geography and Economics* 316.

[171] Xu (n 169) 287.

[172] Meidan (n 73) 40.

[173] On impacts of the dependence on the government on autonomy of making outbound investments, see, eg, T Bai, S Chen and Y Xu, 'Formal and Informal Influences of the State on OFDI of Hybrid State-Owned Enterprises in China' (2021) *International Business Review* 1, 9.

[174] Xu (n 169) 287.

# VI. Conclusion

A substantial body of literature claims that the Chinese Government advances its strategic interests through supporting its preferred outward investments. Due at least to the coexistence of policy interests and business interests, China's policy guidance and support mechanism remains a potential channel for exerting state influence over foreign energy projects. However, this approach does not necessarily conflict with the international practice of commercial activities conducted by state-owned entities, or the governance of investments made by state-owned entities in trade or investment agreements. China's support mechanism for energy investments is implemented in a relatively transparent way, at least with regard to the disclosed criteria for receiving state support, namely, achieving energy policy objectives. Five-year plans outline which projects are encouraged and why. In this respect, China's approach to stimulating global energy expansion is consistent with the recommended practice of disclosure and transparency. This nuanced view from the regulatory perspective is important for assessing Chinese investments in national security reviews that investigate state support (eg, financial support) for the investment in question.

# 5

# Administrative Law Requirements for Outbound Energy Investments

## I. Introduction

Host states have frequently perceived that, similar to policy guidance, China's administrative law on approving investments helps to realise the strategic purpose of the Chinese Government.[1] The discussion of China's investment approval procedure as a tool for influencing global energy expansion has so far been dominated by the analysis in the field of international relations.[2] Regarding the existing discussion of China's legal framework for outbound investments, legal scholars have failed to examine how these regulations govern global energy expansion.[3] Building on the current discussion, this chapter aims to assess whether China's administrative regulatory system of governing outbound investments remains a channel for the Government to influence outbound energy investments.

The analysis of government control over energy companies through administrative law requirements relies on the international expectations as to guaranteeing the operational independence of SOEs and SWFs, and literature on guaranteeing SOEs' operational independence. It is crucial to isolate SOEs from administrative intervention (eg, government approval of participation in international commercial activities). The National Development and Reform Commission (NDRC), the Ministry of Commerce (MOFCOM) and the State Administration of Foreign Exchange (SAFE) are key players in regulating outbound investments. The examination of domestic administrative regulations adopted by NDRC, MOFCOM and

[1] See, eg, Ø Tunsjø, *Security and Profit in China's Energy Policy: Hedging Against Risk* (New York, Columbia University Press, 2013); T Hanemann and D Rosen, *Chinese Invests in Europe: Patterns, Impacts and Policy Implications* (New York, Rhodium Group 2012) 54–61; J Garlick, 'China's Principal–Agent Problem in the Czech Republic' (2019) 17 *Asia Europe Journal* 437.

[2] See, eg, D Brautigam, *The Dragon's Gift: The Real Story of China in Africa* (Oxford, Oxford University Press, 2009) 299–306; M Forstater et al, 'Corporate Responsibility in African Development: Insights from an Emerging Dialogue', Corporate Social Responsibility Initiative Working Paper No 60 (2010); P Yeophantong, 'China's Hydropower Expansion and Influence over Environmental Governance in Mainland Southeast Asia' in E Goh (ed), *Rising China's Influence in Developing Asia* (Oxford, Oxford University Press, 2016) 174–92.

[3] See, eg, K Sauvant and VZ Chen, 'China's Regulatory Framework for Outward Foreign Direct Investment' (2014) 7 *China Economic Journal* 141; K Sauvant and M Nolan, 'China's Outward Foreign Direct Investment and International Investment Law' (2015) 18 *Journal of International Economic Law* 893.

SAFE on approving and managing overseas investments focuses on whether these regulations guarantee the operational independence of energy companies.

This chapter argues that with the relaxed control by the investment approval procedure over domestic companies, regardless of ownership, these companies have increasing autonomy to pursue commercial interests in their foreign energy projects. Meanwhile, this procedure also enables the Government to protect its diplomatic interests and to promote domestic industrial development, by imposing stricter regulatory requirements on proposed investments that will be located in unstable regions or that are made in a specific industry. This conclusion may not only reflect the implementation of the principle of isolating SOEs from administrative intervention, but also broaden the current legal discussion around guaranteeing the commercial integrity of outbound investments. China's POEs can invest abroad; the potential state influence on POEs therefore deserves attention.

Section II looks at the general practice of isolating SOEs' decision-making from administrative interference. Section III is an introduction to how the international relations literature perceives China's investment approval procedure. Section IV examines how NDRC and MOFCOM have come to regulate outbound investments made by companies, regardless of ownership, from a historical perspective. Section V discusses how these two departments have supervised the management of existing energy investments. Section VI concludes and suggests implications.

## II. Theory on Operational Independence of State-Owned Investors

Independent investment-making is an important dimension when assessing whether the investments have been made to realise the strategic goals of home states.[4] Investments may not be commercial if the investor is authorised by the state to exercise government functions, as discussed in chapter three. Under the *OECD Guidelines* and the *Santiago Principles*, limiting excessive administrative intervention in the daily operation of SOEs and SWFs is crucial for safeguarding their investing autonomy.[5] Therefore, it is necessary to look at how the administrative law and regulations of home states govern outbound investments.

[4] See, eg, Guidance Concerning the National Security Review Conducted by the Committee on Foreign Investment in the United States, 73 Fed Reg 74,567, 74,571, 8 December 2008, at www.treasury.gov/resource-center/international/foreign-investment/Documents/CFIUSGuidance.pdf; Australian Government Foreign Investment Review Board, Guidance Note on 'The National Interest Test' (2019) at firb.gov.au/guidance-resources/guidance-notes/gn23; 'Foreign Investment Policy and National Interest Guidance', Guidance Note (May 2020) New Zealand Government at www.treasury.govt.nz/sites/default/files/2020-05/for-invest-policy-nat-interest-guidance-may20-v2.pdf; Regulation (EU) 2019/452 of the European Parliament and of the Council of 19 March 2019 Establishing a Framework for the Screening of Foreign Direct Investments into the Union (2019), Art 4.

[5] *OECD Guidelines on Corporate Governance of State-Owned Enterprises* (OECD, 2015) at www.oecd.org/corporate/guidelines-corporate-governance-soes.htm; *Santiago Principles on Sovereign Wealth Funds*

More specifically, Bouchez has stressed the potential harm caused by domestic investment approval/authorisation procedures to the investing autonomy of state-owned investors. State-owned enterprises may be classed as: (i) enterprises with sole responsibilities and independent decision-making power regarding their business activities; and (ii) enterprises requiring the formal approval or authorisation of state organs to take part in international business transactions.[6] The second type of SOEs cannot make commercial investments because their overseas investments must be approved/authorised by the relevant government departments. Therefore, domestic investment approval/authorisation procedures can be a state tool, damaging the operational independence of state-owned investors and preventing those investors from pursuing commercial interests.

## III. Current Discussion of China's Administrative Management of Overseas Investments

In contrast to the investment law of other capital-exporting states, China's investment regulations govern both the making of investments by foreign companies in China and the making of investments by Chinese companies abroad. Domestic regulations on China's outbound investments have led many scholars, such as Norris, to conclude that the Government can instruct companies to invest abroad for geopolitical purposes.[7] Outbound energy investments are no exception. Andrews-Speed and Dannreuther believe that China's investment approval procedure is designed as a mechanism for controlling NOCs.[8] For Zhang and Tunsjø, by deciding whether the proposed energy project can go forward, the State Council and NDRC subordinated to it can control NOCs.[9] Given the existence of an investment approval procedure, Chinese energy companies cannot be independent investors, according to Moran.[10]

(International Forum for Sovereign Wealth Funds, 2008) at www.ifswf.org/santiago-principles-landing/santiago-principles; D Park and G Estrada, 'Developing Asia's Sovereign Wealth Funds: The Santiago Principles and the Case for Self-Regulation' (2011) 1 *Asian Journal of International Law* 383, 396.

[6] L Bouchez, 'The Prospects for International Arbitration: Disputes Between States and Private Enterprises' (1991) 8 *Journal of International Arbitration* 81, 91–92.

[7] See, eg, J Lee, 'China's Geostrategic Search for Oil' [2012] *The Washington Quarterly* 75; S Chen, 'Motivations behind China's Foreign Oil Quest: A Perspective from the Chinese Government and the Oil Companies' (2008) 13 *Journal of Chinese Political Science* 79, 93; P Buckley et al, 'Explaining China's Outward FDI: An Institutional Perspective' in K Sauvant, K Mendoza and I Irmak (eds), *The Rise of Transnational Corporations from Emerging Markets: Threats or Opportunities?* (Cheltenham, Edward Elgar Publishing, 2008) 107–57, 117; W Norris, *Chinese Economic Statecraft* (Ithaca, NY, Cornell University Press, 2016) 80–83.

[8] P Andrews-Speed and R Dannreuther, *China, Oil and Global Politics* (London, Routledge, 2011) 84.

[9] Tunsjø (n 1) 42; C Zhang, *The Domestic Dynamics of China's Energy Diplomacy* (Singapore, World Scientific, 2015) 264.

[10] T Moran, *China's Strategy to Secure Natural Resources: Risks, Dangers and Opportunities* (New York, Columbia University Press, 2010) 47.

Nevertheless, some scholars have observed that energy companies have the capacity to pursue business interests. For instance, Li and Hendrischke believe that Chinese companies, including energy firms, have been increasingly independent from the Government and have sought commercial interests in the global expansion.[11] Commercial dimensions are at play in China's global energy expansion, including the search for market shares due to domestic overcapacity, and the desire to foster new capabilities and technical expertise.[12] Dannreuther has observed that energy investors have pursued profits without taking into account government orders.[13]

## IV. The Gradual Deregulation of Outbound Investments

By following the policy guidance on simplifying the administrative approval of outbound investments (see chapter four), starting in 2001 and more specifically after 2013, the Government has made various reforms of the approval procedure.[14] Since 2017, the simpler record-keeping procedure has become 'a priority in the overseas investments management system', according to NDRC, MOFCOM, PBOC and MFA.[15] To ensure compliance with record-keeping/approval proceedings, SAFE requires a record-keeping/approval certificate before foreign currency transfers will be permitted. This agenda has been simplified as well, as confirmed by interviewees. As a result of these reforms, can the Government still use these procedures to give Chinese companies 'express instructions to invest abroad'?[16]

### A. Reform and Opening Up (1979–2000)

The Chinese Government's 1979 economic reforms allowed Chinese companies to invest abroad.[17] The Government recognised the right of legal entities to establish enterprises abroad and engage in foreign investment activities, but aimed

[11] W Li and H Hendrischke, 'Chinese Outbound Investment in Australia: From State Control to Entrepreneurship' [2019] *The China Quarterly* 1.

[12] International Energy Agency, *World Energy Outlook 2017* (OECD Publishing, 2017) 486–87.

[13] R Dannreuther, 'China and Global Oil: Vulnerability and Opportunity' (2011) 87 *International Affairs* 1345, 1349.

[14] X Zhang and B Corrie, *Investing in China and Chinese Investment Abroad* (Singapore, Springer, 2018); X Tan, 'China's Overseas Investment in the Energy/Resources Sector' (2013) 36 *Energy Economics* 750, 753.

[15] NDRC, MOFCOM, PBOC and MFA, Opinions on Guiding and Regulating the Direction of Overseas Investments [《关于进一步引导和规范境外投资方向的指导意见》] (August 2017).

[16] *China Heilongjiang International Economic & Technical Cooperative Corp, Beijing Shougang Mining Investment Company Ltd, and Qinhuangdaoshi Qinlong International Industrial Co Ltd v Mongolia*, UNCITRAL, PCA, 2017, para 418.

[17] G Lv, *Historical Development of the Overseas Investment Approval Procedure* [《我国境外投资行政审批制度的历史沿革》] (Development Research Center of the State Council, 2002); Y Dong,

to closely control foreign investment decisions.[18] There were several reasons for limiting domestic investors' freedom at this early stage. First, the planned economy, in which the state exercises micro-control over the national economy, led to the leading role of the Government in investment-making.[19] Second, the Chinese Government promoted 'an inward-looking development strategy', and thus developed conservative policy-making regarding outbound investments.[20] Third, the central Government tried to manage excessive and poorly-operated outward investments.[21] 'China has not been competent enough to invest abroad on a large scale', according to the *Opinions on Strengthening the Management of Overseas Investment Projects* (1991).[22] Because of their lack of familiarity with international commercial practice, Chinese investors suffered substantial economic losses from foreign investments.[23]

## i. *The State's Tight Control Over Outbound Investments*

The State Council determined investment destinations and specified priorities for investment projects, and had the right of approval of any proposed project where the value of the investment was US$30 million or more.[24] At a lower administrative level, all overseas investments were, in principle, subject to the approval of NDRC (formerly the State Planning Commission) and MOFCOM (formerly the Ministry of Foreign Trade and Economic Cooperation),[25] NDRC's being responsible for appraising investment proposals while MOFCOM reviewed contracts and articles of association.[26] Both departments centred their evaluation primarily on the economic viability of projects, but also, to a lesser extent, on their diplomatic implications.[27] MOFCOM explained that the projects needed to

'The Analysis on Evolvement of Institutions of China's Overseas Investment Promotion: 1979–2009' [《我国境外投资促进体系的制度演进分析: 1979–2009》] (2012) 3 *Research on Theoretical Economy* 34, 34.

[18] State Council, Decision on Further Deepening the Reform of the Foreign Trade System [《关于进一步深化对外贸易体制改革的决定》] (1994); State Planning Commission, *Opinions on Strengthening the Management of Overseas Investments* [《关于加强海外投资项目管理的意见》] (1991).

[19] Dong (n 17) 34.

[20] H Voss, P Buckley and A Cross, 'An Assessment of the Effects of Institutional Change on Chinese Outward Direct Investment Activity' in I Alon et al, (eds), *China Rules: Globalization and Political Transformation* (London, Palgrave Macmillan, 2009) 135–65, 146–47.

[21] ibid 151.

[22] State Planning Commission (n 18).

[23] D Freeman, 'China's Outward Investment Institutions, Constraints, and Challenges' (2013) 7 *Asia Paper* 2, 6.

[24] ibid.

[25] ibid.

[26] Ministry of Foreign Trade and Economic Relations, Interim Regulations on Establishing Joint Ventures Abroad [《在国外开设合营企业的暂行规定》] (1981).

[27] State Planning Commission (n 18); J Zhang and X Zhou, 'Thoughts on Policy-Making of China's Overseas Investments against the Background of the "Going Out" Strategy' [《"走出去"战略背景下中国对外直接投资政策体系的思考》] (2007) 4 *International Trade* 27, 27; Freeman (n 23) 5–6.

have 'market potential',[28] thus reducing the risk of wasting state assets and scarce foreign currency on overseas ventures.[29] Proposals that did not generate sufficient returns, or which seemed to face financial or technical challenges or did not accord with the economic interests of the Party, were sent back for revision or were simply rejected by MOFCOM.[30] The proposed foreign establishment also had to act in accordance with national economic policies, such as technology cooperation and the export of equipment.[31] Although NDRC and MOFCOM paid more attention to the economic implications of outbound investments, MFA would participate in the examination process when the host state did not develop diplomatic relations with China.[32]

SAFE played an equally important role in approving outward investments.[33] First, domestic firms had to report their capital sources and the foreign exchange management of the host state to SAFE before submitting application materials to NDRC and MOFCOM.[34] Second, SAFE helped to enforce regulations issued by NDRC and MOFCOM, because approval documents granted by NDRC and MOFCOM were prerequisites for the outbound transmission of capital.[35]

Accordingly, to prevent the loss of state assets,[36] the central Government took part in structuring investments in a parental manner as it assessed commercial values and technology feasibility, both of which should be achieved by consultation with professional institutions.[37] By questioning the commercial and technological practicality of investments when examining feasibility reports, the state could reject projects, change investment destinations or modify the amount of the invested capital.[38]

[28] Ministry of Foreign Trade and Economic Relations, Provisions on Examining, Approving and Managing Overseas Branches of International Companies [《关于国际公司国外机构审批和管理的有关规定》] (1992).

[29] Voss, Buckley and Cross (n 20) 149.

[30] MOFCOM, *1992–2001: Adjustment and Development of Foreign Direct Investments* [《1992–2001：对外直接投资调整发展》] (MOFCOM, 2002); State Planning Commission, Regulation on Approving Project Proposals of Outbound Investments [《关于编制、审批境外投资项目的项目建议书和可行性研究报告的规定》] (1991) Arts 4–6; Voss, Buckley and Cross (n 20) 148.

[31] Ministry of Foreign Trade and Economic Relations, Approval and Management Regulations on Establishing Enterprises Abroad (Trial) [《关于在境外举办非贸易性企业的审批和管理规定[试行稿]》] (1992).

[32] State Planning Commission (n 30) Arts 4–6.

[33] SAFE, Measure of Managing Foreign Exchange for Outbound investments [《境外投资外汇管理办法》] (1989); SAFE, Regulations on the Examination and Approval of the Verification of Outward Investment Foreign Exchange Risk and Sources of Foreign Exchange Funds [《境外投资外汇风险及外汇资金来源审查的审批规范》] (1993).

[34] SAFE, Measure of Managing (n 33) Art 3.

[35] ibid Art 4.

[36] Y Luo, Q Xue and B Han, 'How Emerging Market Governments Promote Outward FDI: Experience from China' (2010) 45 *Journal of World Business* 68, 75.

[37] M Du, 'When China's National Champions Go Global: Nothing to Fear But Fear Itself?' (2014) 48 *Journal of World Trade* 1127, 1132; J Wu, 'The Discovery of the Reform of the Investment Management System' [《投资体制改革探索》] (2005) 8 *Inquiry into Economic Issues* 37, 39.

[38] Zhang and Zhou (n 27) 27.

### *ii. Application in Energy Investments*

From an energy perspective, foreign investments had not yet become a policy priority, as China only became a net importer of crude oil in 1996 and of natural gas in 2007. Therefore, the state was under no pressure to seek external oil and gas supplies to fuel national economic growth. However, the profile of China's foreign energy investments illustrates that Chinese companies embarked on ambitious overseas activities before the Chinese Government endorsed external energy supply as a policy priority, and sometimes even before obtaining government approval for their investments. A possible reason is that the burdensome approval procedure put NOCs in a disadvantageous position when they competed for bids.[39] For example, CNPC began conducting geological surveys in Sudan in 1994, but official approval of its investment was only granted in 1997.[40]

## B. Going Out (2001–2013)

The Chinese Government began actively encouraging companies to invest abroad for the purpose of carrying out the 'Going Out' strategy introduced in 2001.[41] Energy companies were in favour of the implementation of this strategy, as it enabled them to partly address the negative impact of domestic price controls on their financial operation, and to benefit from government support for their internationalisation.[42] In line with the principle that 'whoever makes the investment shall make the decision, whoever earns profits shall assume the risks', the Government officially recognised companies as dominant entities in foreign investments.[43] MOFCOM stated that 'a domestic enterprise itself shall be responsible for whether it is economically or technically feasible to invest in a foreign enterprise'.[44] In other words, at this stage, the approval process paid less attention to the commercial and technological feasibility of projects, which largely rests with the internal management of companies, and became less cumbersome.[45]

[39] B Kong, *China's International Petroleum Policy* (Santa Barbara, CA, ABC-CLIO, 2009) 97.

[40] L Patey, 'Learning in Africa: China's Overseas Oil Investments in Sudan and South Sudan' (2017) 26 *Journal of Contemporary China* 756; L Jiang and J Xiao, 'China's Oil Diplomacy towards Sudan' [《中国对苏丹的石油外交》] (2011) 5 *Arab World Studies* 40.

[41] Luo, Xue and Han (n 36) 75.

[42] Kong (n 39) 37–47; X Zhang, 'Chinese Capitalism and the Maritime Silk Road' (2017) 22 *Geopolitics* 310, 319.

[43] State Council, Decision on Reforming the Investment System [《国务院关于投资体制改革的决定》] (2004); NPC and CPC, Plan for Restructuring the State Council [《国务院机构改革和职能转变方案》] (2013).

[44] MOFCOM, Provisions on the Examination and Approval of Foreign Investments [《关于境外投资开办企业核准事项的规定》] (2004) Art 5.

[45] Sauvant and Chen (n 3) 142.

## *i. Starting to Simplify the Approval Procedure*

To facilitate the global expansion of Chinese companies, the Government gradually reformed the investment approval procedure.[46] The approval procedure was governed by more explicit standards.[47] This could prevent administrative departments from making expansive interpretation of the standards and from putting obstacles in the way of investors.[48] Small-scale projects in which the investment amount was below US$30 million were subject to the record-keeping procedure rather than to approval by NDRC. In the record-keeping procedure, NDRC only examined whether the application of investments obeyed domestic laws and whether these investments were forbidden by policies.[49] Larger projects in which the investment amount was above US$30 million were subject to approval.[50] The formulation of the standards for investments being subject to approval also took into account China's foreign relations.[51] Investments in the regions that had not yet established diplomatic relations with China, regardless of the amount of the investment, had to obtain NDRC approval.[52] In contrast to NDRC's approval procedure, all outward investments had to be approved by MOFCOM.[53] Simultaneously, NDRC and MOFCOM stressed the importance of the managerial capacities of these companies,[54] as they no longer asked investors about commercial and technological practicalities.[55] Apart from NDRC and MOFCOM, the state-owned Assets Supervision and Administration Commission (SASAC), which was established in 2003, was also charged with reviewing outbound investments, in its capability as a shareholder and a regulator of state-owned assets (see chapter six).

[46] State Council, *Opinions on Encouraging and Regulating the Cooperation of Enterprises in Foreign Investment* [《国务院关于鼓励和规范企业对外投资合作的意见》] (2007); Sauvant and Chen (n 3) 145.

[47] NDRC, Interim Measures on Examination and Approval of Overseas Investments [《境外投资项目核准暂行管理办法》] (2004) Art 18; MOFCOM (n 44) Art 5.

[48] Zhang and Corrie (n 14) 141.

[49] L Kong, 'Interpreting *Decision on Reform of Investment System* (2004): The New Trend of the Reform of the Investment Management System' [《投资体制改革新动向—对<国务院关于投资体制改革的决定>》] (2005) 1 *Macro-Economic Management (under NDRC)* 19, 21; Z Hu, 'Recent Changes in China's Outbound Investment Policies and Their Implications' in X Ding and C Meng (eds), *From World Factory to Global Investor: A Multi-perspective Analysis on China's Outward Direct Investment* (London, Routledge, 2018) 70–98, 75.

[50] NDRC (n 47) Art 18; MOFCOM (n 44) Art 5.

[51] State Council, Catalogue of Investment Projects Subject to Approval of the Government [《国务院关于发布政府核准的投资项目目录 2004》] (2004); State Council, Catalogue of Investment Projects Subject to Approval of the Government [《国务院关于发布政府核准的投资项目目录 2013》] (2013); Zhang and Zhou (n 27) 28.

[52] NDRC (n 47); K Ma, 'Deepening the Reform of the Investment Management System' [《深化投资体制改革》] (2003) 12 *Macro-Economic Management* 9, 10.

[53] MOFCOM (n 44) Art 4; MOFCOM, Measures for Overseas Investment Management [《境外投资管理办法》] (2009) Art 5.

[54] Voss, Buckley and Cross (n 20) 152.

[55] NDRC (n 47) Art 16; MOFCOM, Measures for Overseas Investment Management (n 53) Art 9; MOFCOM (n 44) Arts 5 and 8; J Chen, *Chinese Law: Context and Transformation* (Leiden, Brill, 2015) 877.

To facilitate the implementation of the 'Going Out' policy, SAFE had since 2003 decided to cancel the procedure of assessing foreign exchange risks and simplify the procedure of verifying sources of foreign exchange funds for overseas investments.[56] Therefore, companies could save time when preparing materials in the course of applying for SAFE's approval.[57] Later, according to the *Notice of the State Administration of Foreign Exchange on Issuing the Provisions on the Foreign Exchange Administration of the Overseas Direct Investment of Domestic Institutions* (2009), companies no longer needed to obtain approval to buy foreign exchange before going to NDRC and MOFCOM.[58] However, SAFE still held the 'Ultimate Trump Card', because overseas investments could not occur without foreign exchange registration.[59] SAFE directly verified the funds' source when companies registered foreign exchange and then issued certificates to companies,[60] to ensure the proper use of foreign exchange assets and compliance of foreign exchange use with domestic industry policies.[61]

### ii. *The Requirement to Submit Information Reports*

Although NDRC and MOFCOM began to simplify their approval procedures, starting in 2004, companies nevertheless had to submit information reports on their intended overseas bids or acquisitions before tendering for or signing any binding agreements.[62] If this was not done, companies could not sign binding agreements or make formal commitments.[63] This regulatory requirement aimed at minimising vicious competition among firms,[64] as officials believed that such competition would jeopardise the implementation of the 'Going Out' policy.[65]

[56] SAFE, Circular on Problems Related to the Simplification of the Verification of the Source of Foreign Exchange Funds for Outward Investment [《国家外汇管理局关于简化境外投资外汇资金来源审查有关问题的通知》] (2003); SAFE, Circular on Problems Concerning Further Deepening of Reform of Outward Investment Foreign Exchange Administration [《国家外汇管理局关于进一步深化境外投资外汇管理改革有关问题的通知》] (2003).

[57] MOFCOM required the investor to submit an assessment report on sources of funds, see MOFCOM (n 44) Art 8.

[58] SAFE, Notice of the State Administration of Foreign Exchange on Issuing the Provisions on the Foreign Exchange Administration of the Overseas Direct Investment of Domestic Institutions [《国家外汇管理局发布<境内机构境外直接投资外汇管理规定>的通知》] (2009) Art 7.

[59] ibid Art 3.

[60] ibid Art 7.

[61] C Pei and W Zheng, *China's Outbound Foreign Direct Investment Promotion System* (Singapore, Springer, 2015) 87–88.

[62] NDRC (n 47) Art 13; MOFCOM and SAFE, Notice of the Ministry of Commerce and the State Administration of Foreign Exchange about Issuing the Prophase Reporting System for the Overseas Merger and Acquisition Related Matters of Enterprises [《商务部、国家外汇管理局关于印发<企业境外并购事项前期报告制度>的通知》] (2005).

[63] P Huang, 'The Research on Legal Problems of the "Information Reports" Mechanism' [《境外投资"路条"的法律问题研究》] (2015) 9 *Law and Society* 92, 93.

[64] ibid.

[65] YC Xu, 'Chinese State-owned Enterprises in Africa: Ambassadors or Freebooters' (2014) 23 *Journal of Contemporary China* 822, 838.

The Chinese Government established the 'joint conference system' to review information reports.[66] Most of the Chinese legal practitioners believed that only one investor would receive an approval letter.[67] Indeed, NDRC would select one company and issue a confirmation letter that the company was required to submit as part of the future approval procedure.[68] This requirement meant that the Government, rather than market signals, decided the winner in the competitive process.[69] Therefore, whether investors would invest in a specific project was affected by government orders.

### *iii. Application in Energy Investments*

In the energy sector, overseas investments became an imperative as domestic oil and gas fields began to deplete.[70] To ensure energy security, the Government encouraged companies to invest in foreign energy reserves by relaxing regulatory control in the approval procedures, at least in principle.[71] Proposed investments by central SOEs with a value of less than US$30 million were no longer subject to the approval of NDRC.[72] In practice, however, this deregulation measure had little effect, because most energy investments exceeded the threshold of US$30 million.[73] The requirement to submit information reports had implications for overseas energy investments too, as domestic energy companies had been aggressive in acquiring overseas energy assets or shares in foreign energy companies.[74] The central Government urged energy companies to invest in different parts of the world or to make joint bids.[75]

[66] T Wei, J Clegg and L Ma, 'The Conscious and Unconscious Facilitating Role of the Chinese Government in Shaping the Internationalization of Chinese MNCs' (2015) 24 *International Business Review* 331.

[67] J Xiong et al, 'Major Revision of the Procedure for the Information Report' (King Wood Mallesons, 15 April 2014) at www.kwm.com/zh/cn/knowledge/insights/changes-in-regulation-of-cross-border-investment-20160415.

[68] NDRC, Circular on Improving the Administrative Measures of Overseas Investment Projects [《关于完善境外投资项目管理有关问题的通知》] (2009).

[69] Pei and Zheng (n 61) 80.

[70] B Kong, 'Governing China's Energy in the Context of Global Governance' (2011) 2 *Global Policy* 51, 52.

[71] State Commission for Economics and Trade, *The 10th Petroleum Development Five-Year Plan* [《石油工业"十五"规划》] (2001); J Meckling, B Kong and T Madan, 'Oil and State Capitalism: Government-Firm Competition in China and India' (2015) 22 *Review of International Political Economy* 1159, 1177; X Xu, *Chinese NOC's Overseas Strategies: Background, Comparison and Remarks* (James A Baker III Institute for Public Policy, 2007) 4.

[72] NDRC (n 47) Art 6.

[73] H Chen et al, 'Analysis of Chinese Overseas Oil and Gas Investments' [《中国海外油气投资现状分析与对策》] (2015) 37 *China Energy* 38, 40.

[74] Y Liu, 'An Analysis of the 'Going Out' Strategy of China's Energy Development' [《中国能源发展"走出去"战略探析》] (2010) 1 *Journal of University of International Relations* 69, 71 and 73.

[75] S Chen, 'Has China's Foreign Energy Quest Enhanced Its Energy Security?' (2011) 207 *The China Quarterly* 600, 624.

The NEA is responsible for the coordination of overseas investments but does not have the power to block or impose conditions on outbound investments.[76] The former head of NEA, Guobao Zhang, added that the NEA put more energy into drafting and revising energy laws, regulations and policies than approving projects.[77] In practice, NDRC seeks NEA's opinion when reviewing proposed outbound energy investments, according to those interviewed.

According to the interviewees, the Government's uninterrupted control over foreign investments can, at least partly, be explained by its concerns about loss of foreign currency and money laundering. By requiring investors to obtain approval before bidding for or acquiring overseas assets, the Government aimed to reduce the loss of state assets resulting from competition between Chinese SOEs for the same foreign assets.[78] However, in practice the Government's administrative law requirements have sometimes been disobeyed (for more detail, see chapter seven).[79] For instance, in 2003, the subsidiary of CNPC and the subsidiary of Sinopec rejected state coordination and competed with each other for oil-production rights in Sudan to prioritise their financial interests.[80] Similarly, China's energy SOEs bid against each other in Libya and Brazil, although the Chinese Government attempted to coordinate their transactions.[81]

## C. Global Expansion Along the Belt and Road (Since 2014)

The Chinese Government pushed forward further administrative reforms and reduced the administrative burden on energy companies, to put the BRI strategy announced in 2013 into practice.[82] With the adoption of *Measures for the Administration of Approval and Record-Keeping of Overseas Investment Projects* (2014),[83] replaced by the *Measures for Managing Outbound Investment of Enterprises* (2017) by NDRC,[84] as well as the adoption of the *Measures for the*

[76] State Council, Main Responsibilities of the National Energy Administration [《国家能源局主要职责、内设机构和人员编制规定》] (2013); YC Xu, *Sinews of Power: Politics of the State Grid Corporation of China* (Oxford, Oxford University Press, 2017) 121.

[77] M Taylor, *The Chinese State, Oil and Energy Security* (London, Palgrave Macmillan, 2014) 138.

[78] Huang (n 63) 93.

[79] Chen (n 75) 623–24.

[80] CS Liou, 'Bureaucratic Politics and Overseas Investment by Chinese State-Owned Oil Companies: Illusory Champions' (2009) 49 *Asian Survey* 670; Meckling, Kong and Madan (n 71) 1170.

[81] Chen (n 75).

[82] See, eg, MOFCOM, Interpretation on the Administration of Overseas Investments [商务部解读<境外投资管理办法>] (2014) at www.mofcom.gov.cn/article/zcjd/jdtzhz/200903/20090306111066.shtml; D Liu and H Yang, 'Deeply Reforming the Investment Management System, Interpreting the New Approval and Management Rules' [《深化投资体制改革，解读新修核准管理制度》] (2014) 8 *Consultation of China's Projects* 29, 31.

[83] NDRC, *Measures for the Administration of Approval and Record-Keeping of Overseas Investment Projects* [《境外投资项目核准和备案管理办法》] (2014).

[84] NDRC, *Measures for Managing Outbound Investments* [《企业境外投资管理办法》] (2017).

*Administration of Overseas Investment* (2014, still in effect)[85] and the *Interim Measures for Record-Keeping or Approval of Overseas Investments* (2018) by MOFCOM,[86] the 'record-keeping-based and approval-supplemented' regime has represented a significant relaxation of state control over outbound investments.[87] The narrower scope of investments subject to approval and the broader application of the simpler record-keeping procedure, compared with earlier stages, have decreased the possibility of administrative intervention by the Chinese Government.[88] Furthermore, the *Opinions on Guiding and Regulating the Direction of Overseas Investments* (2017) stressed that enterprises should 'take responsibility for profits and losses'.[89] The *Interim Measures for Record-Keeping or Approval of Overseas Investments* (2018) emphasised again that 'domestic companies are decision-makers of outbound investments'.[90] Companies are thus more flexible in their business negotiations.[91] Accordingly, the Chinese Government has changed its role, from an instructor that focused on the economic and technological quality for making outbound investments, to an enabler that directs investments through policies and regulations.[92]

### i. *Greater Relaxation of Control Over Outbound Investments*

The value of investments was still an approval criterion provided for in the regulation issued by NDRC in 2014, although the threshold was lifted to US$1 billion.[93] Nevertheless, in the regulation issued by MOFCOM in 2014 and the one issued by NDRC in 2017, based on the 'negative list' approach, only investments in sensitive destinations and sensitive industries remain subject to approval.[94] All other

[85] MOFCOM, *Measures for the Administration of Overseas Investment* [《境外投资管理办法》] (2014) Art 6.

[86] MOFCOM et.al., *Interim Measures for Record-Keeping or Approval of Overseas Investments* [《对外投资备案（核准）报告暂行管理办法》] (2018).

[87] Li and Hendrischke (n 11) 9; B Wang and K Gao, 'Forty Years Development of China's Outward Foreign Direct Investment' (2019) 27 *China & World Economy* 1, 6.

[88] W Zhang, 'The Impacts of the Reform of the Investment Management System on Enterprises' [《投资体制改革对企业的影响》] (1995) 7 *Academic Journal of Central University of Finance and Economics* 29, 30.

[89] NDRC, MOFCOM, PBOC and MFA, *Opinions on Guiding and Regulating the Direction of Overseas Investments* [《关于进一步引导和规范境外投资方向的指导意见》] (August 2017).

[90] MOFCOM et al, (n 86) Art 5.

[91] H Rao, 'The Transformation of the Regulatory Role after the Issuance of the New Regulation on Central SOEs' investments' [《新版央企投资监管办法背后的监管职能转变》] [2017] *State-Owned Assets Report* 29, 30; Y Wang, 'Implementing Overseas Investments Record-Keeping: Worries of Enterprises about the Nature of Record-Keeping' [《境外投资备案制落地企业忧心"变相审批"》] *Chinese Enterprises News* (22 April 2014) at www.tisino.com/cn/trade/20140422/MTM5ODEZNTU3MTM.html.

[92] Pei and Zheng (n 62) 16; J Yu and Z Chen, 'The Discussion of China's Overseas Investments Approval Procedure' [《中国境外投资核准制度改革自议》] (2013) 2 *The Jurist* 43, 50; Luo, Xue and Han (n 36) 75.

[93] NDRC (n 83) Art 7.

[94] NDRC (n 84) Arts 13–14; MOFCOM (n 85) Art 6.

investments are only subject to record-keeping.[95] Moreover, the regulation issued by NDRC in 2017 allows companies to sign binding agreements even if they have not yet obtained a certificate of approval or record-keeping.[96] An interviewee added that the provincial branches of NDRC and MOFCOM comply strictly with the regulations without imposing additional obligations on investors. Since the investing value is no longer a criterion for approval, investors are free to invest in capital-intensive projects.[97] However, several interviewees cautioned that large companies often inform the Government before filing their overseas investments, thus giving the Government a greater influence over projects than the regulations intend in principle.

The scope of sensitive investments (namely, investments in places that have not yet established diplomatic relations with China, investments located in unstable regions or investments in the development of water resources) overlaps with the scope of restricted investments (discussed in chapter four).[98] The need for approval of 'sensitive investments' reflects the realization of the government objectives of: (i) preventing energy investments from hampering China's diplomatic image; or (ii) forbidding energy investments from adversely impacting economic development.[99] The local embassy is usually consulted by NDRC with regard to the potential diplomatic implications of investment destinations when reviewing the proposed project.[100] MOFCOM reminds investors that the websites of the MFA list states that have not established foreign relations with China and they record states that are sanctioned by the UN.[101] At the same time, MOFCOM considers whether contracts for building infrastructure frustrate the implementation of national economic policies, for example the energy five-year plans.[102] It defines sensitive industries as 'industries involving the export of products and technologies restricted by the People's Republic of China from export or involving the interests of at least one country (or region)'.[103] Therefore, energy infrastructure projects cannot export restricted products or technologies.

[95] NDRC (n 84) Art 29; MOFCOM (n 85) Art 6.
[96] NDRC (n 84) Art 32; MOFCOM (n 85).
[97] Zhang and Zhou (n 27) 27; H Ai, 'Reforming the Investment Management System and Increase Returns of Investments' [《改革现行投资体制，提高政府投资效益》] (2004) 5 *Guangdong Accountancy* 19, 20.
[98] Yu and Chen (n 92) 44; Sauvant and Chen (n 3).
[99] NDRC (n 84) Art 26 and 41; AW Chalmers and ST Mocker, 'The End of Exceptionalism? Explaining Chinese National Oil Companies' Overseas Investments' (2017) 24 *Review of International Political Economy* 119, 123; J Zhang, 'State Structures, Business–State Relations, and Multinational Corporate Behaviours' in X Zhang and T Zhu (eds), *Business, Government and Economic Institutions in China* (Singapore, Springer, 2018) 281–311, 299.
[100] NDRC (n 84) Art 22; Liou (n 80); Zhang (n 9) 282–83.
[101] 'The Format of the Application Form and Record-Keeping Form' (MOFCOM, 6 September 2014) at www.mofcom.gov.cn/article/b/c/201409/20140900723361.shtml.
[102] Y Jiang, 'Red Trojan Horses? A New Look at Chinese SOEs' Outward Investment' (2014) 2 *Journal of China and International Relations* 1.
[103] MOFCOM (n 85) Art 7.

In the case of overseas bidding, under the regulation adopted by NDRC in 2014, investors were required to submit information reports to NDRC when the investment value was more than US$300 million.[104] The requirement to submit information reports was removed by the regulation issued by NDRC in 2017.[105] The NDRC explained that, 'the procedure for submitting information reports has been cancelled to minimise investors' administrative burden in *ex ante* management and to decrease their institutional costs'.[106]

Furthermore, since June 2015, SAFE has delegated the power to review companies' applications for foreign exchange to banks, according to the *Notice on Further Simplifying and Improving Policies for the Foreign Exchange Administration of Direct Investment* (2015).[107] Therefore, companies do not have to go through the administrative procedure but are able to register for foreign exchange at banks. Investors are also able to reinvest directly abroad through an overseas investee, without the need to submit applications to local foreign exchange authorities.[108]

## *ii. The Record-Keeping Procedure*

The Chinese Government claimed the broader application of record-keeping as a way of relaxing government intervention in outbound investments, including energy investments.[109] However, the discussion of whether record-keeping is a form of administrative licence has raised doubts about such a claim.[110] The Government itself remains uncertain about whether record-keeping means the establishment of an administrative licence. In 2016, the guideline on *Measures for the Administration of Overseas Investment (2014)*, issued by MOFCOM, confirmed that record-keeping was categorised as the establishment and implementation of an administrative licence.[111] However, in 2019, the State Council initiated an

[104] NDRC (n 83) Art 10.

[105] NDRC (n 84) Art 32.

[106] NDRC, The Foreign Investment Department of NDRC, *The Explanation on Measures of Managing Outbound Investment of Enterprises (The Exposure Draft)* [《关于<企业境外投资管理办法（征求意见稿>的说明》] (2017).

[107] SAFE, Notice on Further Simplifying and Improving Policies for the Foreign Exchange Administration of Direct Investment [《国家外汇管理局关于进一步简化和改进直接投资外汇管理政策的通知》] (2015).

[108] ibid.

[109] NDRC, *Interpretation of Measures of Managing Outbound Investments (Draft)* [《关于企业境外投资管理办法（征求意见稿）的说明》] (2017); MOFCOM, *Interpretation of Interim Measures of the Record-Keeping of Outbound Investments* [《商务部合作司负责人解读对外投资备案（核准）报告暂行办法》] (2018).

[110] See, eg, X Zhang, 'The Justification of the Mandatory Nature of Administrative Record – Also on the Distinction between Administrative Record and Administrative License' [《行政备案具有强制性之证成—兼论行政备案与行政许可的区分》] (2018) 4 *Graduate Law Review* 62, 62.

[111] State Council, 'The Record-Keeping and Approval System of Overseas Investments' [《境外投资备案和核准》] (28 November 2016) at www.gov.cn/fuwu/2016-11/28/content_5138945.htm; MOFCOM, 'Domestic Enterprises Establish Enterprises Abroad' [《国内企业在境外开办企业（金融企业除外）核准》) (August 2021) at egov.mofcom.gov.cn/xzxksx/18006/.

administrative reform and decided that issues could be subject to the application for an administrative licence or to the system of record-keeping.[112] The categorisation means that the record-keeping system does not require the receipt of an administrative licence.

According to the PRC Administrative Licence Law, an administrative licence covers 'the acts that the administrative organs permit, upon examination according to law, citizens, legal persons or other organisations to engage in as special activities in accordance with their applications'.[113] When confirming applicants' eligibility to engage in an activity, government agencies assess not only the authenticity and legality of the content of the application, but also the content itself.[114] The applicant is able to bring a request for administrative reconsideration or an administrative suit regarding the decision on the administrative licence.[115]

Record-keeping meets the definition of an administrative licence, except that the record-keeping procedure does not include a substantive review of application materials. Government agencies only examine whether formats and the content are structured in accordance with regulatory requirements.[116] By design, it is hard for NDRC to engage in a thorough review of project documents, as a decision has to be made within seven working days. However, the record-keeping procedure is still compulsory. If energy companies fail to apply for a valid record-keeping notice, they will be asked by NDRC to suspend, or even to cease, the implementation of the projects or be found criminally liable.[117] Furthermore, some local governments have stated in record-keeping certificates that the company in question has the right to request administrative reconsideration or an administrative suit.[118] As noted above, this right to remedies applies to administrative licences. The compulsion of this procedure and the available remedies imply that the record-keeping procedure may be perceived as a process of issuing administrative licences, despite

[112] State Council, Decision of the State Council to Cancel or Delegate to Lower-level Authorities a Group of Administrative Licensing Items [《国务院关于取消和下放一批行政许可事项的决定》] (2019).

[113] Administrative Licence Law of the People's Republic of China (issued in 2003, amended in 2019) [《中华人民共和国行政许可法》] Art 2.

[114] X Chen, 'On the Record-Keeping System and Its Legal Nature' [《论备案制度及其法律性质》] (2005) 2 *Journal of Wuyi University* 72; B Zhang, 'The Record-Keeping System in The Governance by Legal Rules: Features, Origins and Drawbacks' [《法治政府视野下的行政许可式备案:特征、成因与弊端》] (2017) 4 *The South China Sea Law Journal* 33.

[115] Administrative Licence Law (n 113) Art 38.

[116] L Wang, 'Comparing the Approval System and the Record-Keeping System' [《浅论行政审批与备案之比较》] (2009) 6 *South-North Bridge* 16.

[117] NDRC (n 84) Art 53.

[118] The notices on granting record-keeping certificates to various companies have been published on official websites, including those of the provincial government of Inner Mongolia at fgw.nmg.gov.cn/zfxxgk/fdzdgknr/bmwj/202108/t20210805_1796757.html; the provincial government of Zhejiang at www.zjzwfw.gov.cn/zjservice/item/detail/index.do?localInnerCode=ca1a353e-e038-490e-b744-93a0a963b4e8; and the provincial government of Guangxi at webcache.googleusercontent.com/search?q=cache:YInnrOcA6EoJ:fgw.gxzf.gov.cn/fzgggz/lywz/wjgg_57314/t2211243.shtml+&cd=10&hl=zh-CN&ct=clnk&gl=hk.

a general review of proposed investments. In practice, the interviewees revealed that NDRC and MOFCOM were reluctant to confirm this legal interpretation,[119] as it conflicts with China's deregulation efforts and the official attitude that companies, not government departments, are responsible for their investments.

### *iii. Application in Energy Investments*

Foreign energy investments help the Government to influence global energy supply chains[120] and are central to energy cooperation in the BRI.[121] The energy investors have certainly benefited from the deregulation process.[122] First, since NOCs do not need to submit information reports before making a formal offer in the bidding process,[123] they are able to become more flexible in order to win deals and can compete with one another.[124] Second, power-grid investments that significantly contribute to energy cooperation in the BRI are no longer classed as sensitive investments and are no longer subject to approval.[125] The interviewees added that, in practice, overseas energy investments are usually categorised as projects subject to record-keeping. Accordingly, energy companies can undertake a cheaper and simpler administrative process, reducing their transaction costs, and are thus more confident in investing abroad.

Although power grids are no longer sensitive investments, the review of sensitivity still applies to energy investments. The strict approval procedure applies to investments in politically unstable areas, because these investments may force the Government to deviate from its diplomatic principle of non-intervention to protect energy projects, where the realisation of these investments could influence China's strategic relationships with big powers.[126] Additionally, cross-border hydropower

[119] State Council, Decision of the State Council on Establishing Administrative Licence for the Administrative Examination and Approval of Matters Considered to be Essential [《国务院对确需保留的行政审批项目设定行政许可的决定》] (2004, amended in 2016) only includes overseas investment approval in the category of administrative licence.

[120] B Conrad and G Kostka, 'Chinese Investments in Europe's Energy Sector: Risks and Opportunities?' (2017) 101 *Energy Policy* 644, 646.

[121] NDRC and NEA, Vision and Actions on Energy Cooperation in Jointly Building Silk Road Economic Belt and 21st-Century Maritime Silk Road [《推动丝绸之路经济带和21世纪海上丝绸之路能源合作愿景与行动》] (2017).

[122] M Ye, 'China Invests Overseas: Regulation and Representation' (2014) 21 *Modern China Studies* 173, 182.

[123] NDRC (n 84) Art 14; MOFCOM, Notice on Effectively Conducting the Record-keeping of Foreign Contracted Projects [《商务部办公厅关于做好对外承包工程项目备案管理的通知》] (2017).

[124] Y Wu, 'Encouraging the National Oil Companies to Go Out' [《鼓励国家石油企业走出去》] (2000) 11 *China Investment* 35, 36.

[125] NDRC (n 84) Art 14; L Zhang, 'Interpreting Measures for the Administration of Overseas Investment of Enterprises' [《<企业境外投资管理办法>解读》] (Deheng Law Office, 28 December 2017) at www.dehenglaw.com/CN/tansuocontent/0008/007813/7.aspx?MID=0902&AID=.

[126] Z Zhang, 'The Overseas Acquisitions and Equity Oil Shares of Chinese National Oil Companies: A Threat to the West but a Boost to China's Energy Security?' (2012) 48 *Energy Policy* 698, 700; Yu and Chen (n 92) 44.

investments, owing to their sensitivity,[127] remain subject to approval.[128] The environmental and social controversy surrounding the construction of the Myitsone hydropower plant in Myanmar probably explains why the Chinese Government felt it necessary to retain control of hydropower investments.[129] The China Power Investment Corporation, an important central energy SOE, 'clearly defied and subverted central regulations' when pursuing its financial interests, thus damaging China's bilateral relations with Myanmar.[130]

## D. Applying the Deregulated Procedure on Private Energy Investments

In contrast to onshore domestic oil and gas production, the making of foreign oil and gas investments by Chinese companies has never been subject to a legal monopoly. The deregulation process contributes to the increasing global expansion of POEs.[131] The empirical research based on China's Overseas Direct Investment (ODI) data demonstrates that the investment approval reforms of 2003 and 2008 significantly accelerated rapid overseas expansion by POEs.[132] Other empirical research also illustrates that a supporting regulatory environment had a positive influence on POEs' investments abroad from 2012 to 2016.[133] For instance, cancelling the mechanism for submitting information reports has facilitated POEs' global expansion because SOEs' non-transparent meetings with government officials could place SOEs in a favourable position.[134] In principle, foreign investments by POEs and SOEs are subject to basically the same approval and record-keeping procedures,[135] except that private investments are not vetted by SASAC. However, it appeared from the interviews that, in practice, POEs can find it more difficult to obtain certificates of approval/record-keeping, as SOEs have better contacts within the Administration and more experience of meeting

[127] P Högselius, *Energy and Geopolitics* (London, Routledge, 2019) 141.
[128] NDRC (n 84) Art 14.
[129] See, eg, L Jones and Y Zou, 'Rethinking the Role of State-owned Enterprises in China's Rise' (2017) 22 *New Political Economy* 743; P Andrews-Speed, M Qiu and C Len, 'Chinese Engagement in Southeast Asian Energy and Mineral Resources: Motivations and Outlook' (2016) 57 *Eurasian Geography and Economics* 316, 334.
[130] Jones and Zou (n 129).
[131] Voss, Buckley and Cross (n 20) 158; Q Wei and H Li, *Entities and Structures in the Embedding Process: A Sociological Analysis of Changes in the Government-enterprise Relations* (Singapore, Springer, 2019) 180.
[132] A Amighini, R Rabellotti and M Sanfilippo, 'Do Chinese State-Owned and Private Enterprises Differ in Their Internationalization Strategies?' (2013) 27 *China Economic Review* 312.
[133] J Guo and X Chen, 'Political Linkages, Government Subsidies and Overseas Direct Investment of Private Enterprises' [《民营企业政治关联、政府补助与境外直接投资》] (2019) 21 *Communication of Finance and Accounting* 61, 65.
[134] Huang (n 63) 93.
[135] State Council, *Opinions on Encouraging the Development of the Private Economy* [《国务院关于鼓励支持和引导个体私营等非公有制经济发展的若干意见》] (2005).

administrative law requirements on outbound investments. Another reason is that NDRC and MOFCOM have transparency concerns about the shareholder structure and the ultimate beneficiaries of investments made by POEs.

## E. Approval: A Form of Strategic Control?

To summarise, the approval of outbound investments in the early phases of China's economic reforms was characterised by a high degree of government control and failed to meet the expectation of the principles of international economic governance regarding investing autonomy (see section II). Although in theory the Government could use its approval powers to pursue strategic objectives, it concentrated mainly on the commercial viability of outbound investments, due to China's weak economic position at the time. The Government has since pursued a policy of deregulating outbound investments. In line with the principle of operational independence, China's deregulation policy aims to enable companies to expand their shares of global markets and take financial responsibility for their investment decisions. With the requirements for approval and record-keeping, the Government maintains a certain degree of control over foreign investments, mainly in sensitive destinations and industries. However, in practice, tight deadlines for the review of projects and the readiness of some companies to defy regulations have limited government interference with investment decisions through the approval/record-keeping procedures.[136]

# V. The Supervision of Overseas Energy Investments

While the Chinese Government has relaxed control over the making of overseas energy investments, it has enhanced supervision of the conduct of investors in the course of their applications for approval/record-keeping certificates and in their investment operations.

## A. At the Ex Ante Stage

While liberalising the approval procedure governing outbound investments, NDRC and MOFCOM aim to close regulatory loopholes and ensure that investors comply with regulatory requirements.[137] First, NDRC requires the company

[136] See more generally X Gong, 'Economic Statecraft' (2017) 22 [国際公共政策研究]1, 9 (emphasising 'a loose control' over SOEs' foreign activities).
[137] E Cunningham, 'The State and the Firm: China's Energy Governance in Context', Global Economic Governance Initiative Working Paper (2015) 5 (last accessed 16 January 2023).

to submit a statement of authenticity of the project to support the application.[138] If a company 'maliciously splits the project, conceals related information or provides false materials', NDRC will reject the application and issue a warning to the company.[139]

Second, NDRC and MOFCOM have taken measures for addressing the establishment of overseas special purpose vehicles (SPVs) that may help investors to evade domestic regulatory requirements.[140] To strengthen supervision of the re-investments through the overseas SPVs, MOFCOM, together with other central ministries, requires companies to disclose the final destination of proposed business operations, and thus obtains knowledge of the direction of domestic capital flows.[141] It is possible for MOFCOM to reject proposed investments if companies fail to disclose information on the business structure and the overseas investee.[142] Meanwhile, NDRC requires companies to submit reports if the amount of the non-sensitive re-investment is US$300 million or more.[143]

## B. At the Ex Post Stage

After investments are made, the Chinese Government endeavours to ensure that companies operate those investments in an honest manner.[144] From 2017 onwards, NDRC, MOFCOM and other central ministries have made lists of companies guilty of misconduct on the National Credit Information Sharing Platform.[145] Leading central ministries such as NDRC, MOFCOM and SAFE should also reject applications from companies that have histories of dishonest behaviour.[146] More specifically, MOFCOM does not allow companies that fail to ensure the integrity

[138] NDRC (n 84) Art 19.

[139] ibid Art 51.

[140] Y Li and W Huang, 'Overseas Investments – Approval or Record-Keeping: Interpreting Measures for the Administration of Overseas Investment of Enterprises' [《境外投资≠核准或备案：解读<企业境外投资管理办法>》] (Zhonglun Law Firm, 27 December 2017) at www.zhonglun.com/Content/2017/12-27/1756065112.html; J Qiu and Y Tao, 'Trial Implementation of New Rules on Overseas Investments: MOFCOM' [《境外投资新规落地"试水"（商委篇）》] (Zhonglun Law Firm, 2018) at www.zhonglun.com/Content/2018/09-19/1044532693.html.

[141] MOFCOM et al (n 90) Art 2; 'Interpreting *Interim Measures for the Record-keeping (or Confirmation) and Reporting of Outbound Investment*' *EY* (12 February 2018), www.ey.com/Publication/vwLUAssets/ey-china-regulations-express-12-feb-2018/$FILE/ey-china-regulations-express-12-feb-2018.pdf.

[142] 'The Interpretation of *Interim Measures for the Record-keeping (or Confirmation) and Reporting of Outbound Investment*' [《解读<对外投资备案（核准）报告暂行办法>》] (Llinks Law Firm, January 2018) at www.llinkslaw.com/uploadfile/publication/87_1517468429.pdf.

[143] NDRC (n 84) Art 42.

[144] Pei and Zheng (n 61) 22; Hu (n 49) 76.

[145] NDRC, *Guiding Opinions on Strengthening the Development of a Credit System in the Foreign Economic Cooperation Field* [《关于加强对外经济合作领域信用体系建设的指导意见》] (2017).

[146] NDRC, MOFCOM, PBOC and other departments, Notice on Joint Punishment of Seriously Dishonest Entities in the Foreign Economic Cooperation Field [《关于对外经济合作领域严重失信主体开展联合惩戒的合作备忘录》] (2017) 4.

of projects to contract for any new overseas projects within a given period.[147] Moreover, if the operation of projects adversely affects the national interest, NDRC will issue a warning to the company, order the suspension of the project and require the company to correct its behaviour within a specified time.[148]

Failure to protect the environment of host states has also been a common problem in China's foreign energy projects, and has damaged the international reputation of Chinese energy companies.[149] For instance, CNPC was criticised by the Government of Chad for an oil spill in 2013.[150] The Ministry of Environment Protection (the former name of the Ministry of Ecology and Environment of PRC) has played an increasingly important role in considering the environmental controversies of outbound energy investments.[151] In 2013, MOFCOM and MEP issued the *Guidance on Environmental Protection in Overseas Investments and Cooperation* (2013).[152] This voluntary guidance suggests that energy companies should comply with environmental-protection-related law and the regulations of host states when operating energy projects.[153]

## C. Guaranteeing the Integrity of Private Energy Investments

Few POEs demonstrate sophisticated investment practices.[154] Some POEs failed to comply with regulatory requirements when applying for approval/record-keeping certificates, made investment decisions without sufficient thought, entered an excessive bid or neglected safe production.[155] For example, they did not conduct careful due diligence before making investments.[156] Also, their unregulated

[147] MOFCOM, The Regulation on Managing the Contracting of Overseas Projects [《对外承包工程管理条例》] (2008) Art 5; NDRC, MOFCOM, PBOC and other departments (n 146).

[148] NDRC (n 84) Arts 51–56.

[149] X Ma and P Andrews-Speed, 'The Overseas Activities of China's National Oil Companies: Rationale and Outlook' (2006) 21 *Minerals & Energy* 17, 28; S Eaton and G Kostka, 'Central Protectionism in China: The Central SOE Problem in Environmental Governance' (2017) 231 *The China Quarterly* 685, 686.

[150] L Fang, 'CNPC Explained the Accident of Oil Spill in Chad' *Xin Hua News* (15 August 2013) at finance.sina.com.cn/chanjing/gsnews/20130815/165516460825.shtml.

[151] P Yeophantong and C Maurin, 'China and the Regulation of Outbound Investment: Toward A "Responsible Investment" Policy Framework' in A Bjorklund (ed), *Yearbook on International Investment Law and Policy 2014–2015* (Oxford, Oxford University Press, 2016) 349–73, 358.

[152] MOFCOM and MEP, Guidance on Environmental Protection in Overseas Investments and Cooperation [《商务部、环境保护部关于印发<对外投资合作环境保护指南>的通知》] (2013) Arts 5, 11 and 12.

[153] ibid Art 5; Yeophantong and Maurin (n 151) 359.

[154] M Erie, 'Chinese Law and Development' (2020) 62 *Harvard International Law Journal* 1.

[155] NDRC answered questions relevant to *The Code of Conduct for the Operation of Overseas Investments by Private Enterprises* in a press conference [国家发展改革委有关负责人就《民营企业境外投资经营行为规范》答记者问] (State Council Information Office, 18 December 2017) at www.scio.gov.cn/xwfbh/gbwxwfbh/xwfbh/fzggw/Document/1613803/1613803.htm.

[156] 'Experts' Opinions on *The Code of Conduct for the Operation of Overseas Investments by Private Enterprises*' [专家解读《民营企业境外投资经营行为规范》] *China Talk* (28 December 2017) at www.china.com.cn/fangtan/2017-12/28/content_50172696.htm.

competition and projects management 'work against the very principles of Chinese foreign policy'.[157] The controversy surrounding the acquisition of a stake in Rosneft by a POE (CEFC), before its chairman was investigated over suspected economic crimes, demonstrated that ex ante procedures did not guarantee the integrity of an investment or investor.[158]

In addition to the general regulatory measures for improving the integrity of outbound investments, POEs are governed by the measures specifically targeted at POEs' overseas investments. The *Code of Conduct for the Operation of Overseas Investments by Private Enterprises* (2017) was issued by NDRC and other administrative departments at ministry level.[159] The central Government attempted to improve the integrity of investments by POEs and to advance their international competitiveness through the following measures.[160] First, corruption is forbidden in the operation of projects. Second, POEs are responsible for protecting the environment and performing social obligations. However, practising lawyers in China pointed out that this document is soft in nature, as it does not provide any punitive measures to enforce the guidance.[161]

## D. Supervision: Improving the Integrity of Overseas Energy Investments

The Chinese Government has thus strengthened the requirement for compliance, while viewing energy companies as independent investors. The aim of the supervision measures is to correct conduct using overseas investments as an excuse for other unlawful business and to fulfil companies' social responsibilities in host states. In this way, the Chinese Government can restore the reputation of China's energy companies. These measures have implications for the international practice of drafting domestic law and regulations governing outbound investments as well. Home states can help to discipline their investors and thus contribute to a more friendly investment environment.

[157] Xu (n 65) 840.

[158] T Paraskova, 'China CEFC Unit Defaults After Failed Rosneft Stake Acquisition' *Oil Price* (22 May 2018) at oilprice.com/Latest-Energy-News/World-News/China-CEFC-Unit-Defaults-After-Failed-Rosneft-Stake-Acquisition.html; D Zhdannikov, 'China's CEFC Investigation Hits $9 Billion Russian Oil Deal' *Reuters* (22 March 2018) at www.reuters.com/article/us-rosneft-cefc/chinas-cefc-investigation-hits-9-billion-russian-oil-deal-idUSKBN1GY1VO.

[159] NDRC et al, Notice on Issuing the Code of Conduct for the Operation of Overseas Investments by Private Enterprises [《国家发展改革委、商务部、人民银行等关于发布<民营企业境外投资经营行为规范>的通知》] (2017).

[160] ibid.

[161] Jincheng Tongda & Neal, 'A Brief Analysis of the Code of Conduct for the Operation of Overseas Investments by Private Enterprises' [《民营企业境外投资经营行为规范》简析] (18 December 2017) at www.jtnfa.com/jp/booksdetail.aspx?type=06001&keyid=0000000000000003295&PageUrl=majorbook&Lan=CN.

## VI. Conclusion

Most of the international relations literature has identified China's investment approval procedure as a channel for exerting state control in order to realise strategic goals, although other scholars have observed that Chinese energy companies have contravened government orders. This analysis of administrative regulations managing China's outward investments provides a more nuanced and detailed answer, which helps us to re-assess the role of the state in China's global energy expansion.

By reviewing the historical development of China's investment approval procedures, this chapter finds that the administrative management of outbound investments has been consistent with the principle of guaranteeing operational independence. The Government has gradually pursued a policy of deregulating outbound investments to remove institutional barriers that hamper the function of market forces in structuring energy investments. In particular, the 'negative list' approach prevents administrative departments from interfering with investments that are not included on the list. The deregulation of governance of outbound investments applies not only to energy SOEs but also to POEs: energy POEs are not forbidden to invest abroad. In other words, domestic law and regulations do not explicitly grant SOEs the privilege of making overseas energy investments. This is a claim rebutting the argument that energy SOEs are instruments of the Chinese Government because of their administrative privilege.

At the same time, the Chinese Government needs to maintain a good diplomatic image and promote national economic development, which is similar to the objectives of other home states regarding the promotion of outbound investments. It still exerts a certain degree of control over foreign investments, in particular those in sensitive destinations and industrial areas. Also, by strengthening supervision of the investing behaviour of energy companies, the Chinese Government helped to enhance the integrity of foreign energy projects and to further promote global energy expansion.

# 6

# Corporate Governance and Investment-Making

## I. Introduction

Corporate governance generally describes the influence of corporate institutional settings on business operations.[1] Host states are concerned that the shareholder rights of the State-Owned Asset Supervision Commission (SASAC) (in SOEs only) and the integration of the Party leadership (in both SOEs and POEs) enable the Chinese Government to pursue strategic interests.[2] The US Government once claimed that the corporate governance of China's companies is an instrument for 'advancing the government's strategic goals rather than profit-maximizing goals'.[3] Building on the existing discussion of how the Chinese Government influences the corporate governance of energy SOEs and POEs,[4] this chapter aims to look at whether the PRC Company Law and policies and rules governing the role of the Chinese Communist Party (CCP) in companies can be channels that facilitate government influence on the decision-making of energy companies.

As highlighted in chapter three, determining the state's influence on the corporate governance of energy companies requires reference to the international soft rules governing the commercial activities of SOEs and SWFs. These generally agreed practices recommend that SOEs' corporate governance should be free from political influence and guarantee the enterprises' autonomy of decision-making.[5] The *OECD Guidelines on the Corporate Governance of SOEs* (2015) attempt to

[1] S Turnbull, 'Corporate Governance: Its Scope, Concerns and Theories' (1997) 5 *Corporate Governance: An International Review* 180.

[2] A Svetlicinii, 'The Interactions of Competition Law and Investment Law: The Case of Chinese State-Owned Enterprises and EU Merger Control Regime' in J Chaisse et al (eds), *Handbook of International Investment Law and Policy* (Singapore, Springer, 2019) 1–21.

[3] White House Office of Trade and Manufacturing Policy, *How China's Economic Aggression Threatens the Technologies and Intellectual Property of the United States and the World* (White House Office of Trade and Manufacturing Policy, June 2018) 11.

[4] See, eg, M Taylor, 'Fuelling China's Rise: Building Oil State Capacity' (2018) 16 *China: An International Journal* 107; W Leutert, 'State-Owned Enterprises in Contemporary China' in L Bernier, M Florio and P Bance (eds), *The Routledge Handbook of State-Owned Enterprises* (London, Routledge, 2020) 201–12.

[5] See, eg, J Norton, 'The "Santiago Principles" for Sovereign Wealth Funds' (2010) 13 *Journal of International Economic Law* 645.

'ensure that SOEs operate efficiently and transparently as well as in an accountable manner'.[6] The *Santiago Principles* also stress the need to guarantee the independence of the decision-making processes of SWFs to ensure the commercial nature of their investments.[7]

To examine whether the PRC Company Law and policies and rules for governing the role of the CCP in companies can indeed be channels that facilitate government influence over the decision-making of energy companies, this chapter questions whether the roles of SASAC, as shareholder, and the Party, as political leader, in corporate governance are compatible with the OECD's recommendation that companies should enjoy 'full operational autonomy' in investment decision-making. More specifically, do the PRC Company Law and regulations adopted by SASAC guarantee the board's decision-making autonomy? What do the rules covering the Party's involvement in corporate governance tell us about the Party's ways of influencing the decision-making of energy companies?

This chapter finds that through SASAC and the Party branches, the Chinese Government continues to participate in the approval of investment programmes and the appointment of top managers, as well as the latter's future career progression. The findings contribute to the energy law literature by discussing, as regards China's global energy expansion, how corporate rules can impact on the investment-making of energy companies. This conclusion also contributes to the discussion of the international soft rules governing SOEs. By referring to the influence by the Party branches on the decision-making of energy companies, future rules may consider limiting the influence of the political leadership in corporate governance of SOEs and even POEs.[8]

Section II introduces the internationally recommended practice of SOEs' corporate governance. Section III introduces the discussion of how the Chinese Government influences the decision-making of both SOEs and POEs. Section IV looks at how the SOE reforms grant SOEs more freedom when making investment decisions. Despite the progress of these reforms, sections V and VI examine how SASAC and the Party branches respectively restrict the independent corporate governance of energy companies. Section VII discusses how the strategic nature of energy requires a certain degree of state control over energy activities. Section VIII summarises and notes the implications.

[6] *OECD Guidelines on Corporate Governance of State-Owned Enterprises* (OECD Publishing, 2015).

[7] *Santiago Principles on Sovereign Wealth Funds* (International Forum for Sovereign Wealth Funds, 2008) at www.ifswf.org/santiago-principles-landing/santiago-principles; R Bismuth, 'The "Santiago Principles" for Sovereign Wealth Funds: The Shortcomings and the Futility of Self-Regulation' (2017) 28 *European Business Law Review* 69.

[8] L Borlini, 'When the Leviathan Goes to the Market: A Critical Evaluation of the Rules Governing State-Owned Enterprises in Trade Agreements' (2020) 33 *Leiden Journal of International Law* 313, 334. Borlini argued that states might view the role of the state in the national economy differently in light of the political economy in that state.

## II. International Soft Rules on Corporate Governance of SOEs

As SOEs and SWFs are playing an increasingly important role in the international economic system, such as in the energy industry,[9] it is crucial to guarantee an arm's-length distance between these state-owned/controlled investors and their home governments, so as to prevent home states from achieving strategic goals through their investments.[10] More specifically, the state ownership function should be centralised in a separate administrative entity that is not allowed to abuse its power as a controlling shareholder.[11] According to the *OECD Guidelines on Corporate Governance of SOEs* (2015), domestic laws should clearly define the government's ownership rights, and should ensure that the state ownership function is separated from other state functions such as the regulatory power.[12] Similarly, with the non-binding *Santiago Principles*, a governance framework characterised by 'the effective division of roles and responsibilities' of the state owner, the governing body and management should ensure companies' operational independence and protect them from political influence.[13]

State shareholders should also respect the autonomy of the board of directors in its daily operation, even when state-owned/controlled entities are implementing national policies.[14] The OECD Secretariat explained that the board's autonomy of decision-making could be constrained by 'the number of independent board members sitting on the board; the extent to which members of the board may take instructions from the government'.[15] In other words, state shareholders' power to appoint board members may facilitate state control.[16] Therefore, the *Santiago Principles* require that the governing body and management of a company should be independent enough to exercise authority and act as a private entity.[17]

[9] ibid 314.

[10] M Rajavuori, 'Governing the Good State Shareholder: The Case of the OECD Guidelines on Corporate Governance of State-Owned Enterprises' (2018) 29 *European Business Law Review* 103, 103.

[11] OECD (n 6) 18–19 and 52.

[12] ibid 26. P Kowalski and D Rabaioli, 'Bringing Together International Trade and Investment Perspectives on State Enterprises', OECD Trade Policy Papers No 201 (OECD Publishing, 2017); see also Q Kong, 'Emerging Rules in International Investment Instruments and China's Reform of State-owned Enterprises' (2017) 3 *The Chinese Journal of Global Governance* 57.

[13] International Forum for Sovereign Wealth Funds (n 7); Bismuth (n 7); SY Chen, 'Positioning SWFs as Claimants in Investment Arbitration' (2013) 6 *Contemporary Asia Arbitration Journal* 299, 307.

[14] OECD (n 6) 18–19 and 52.

[15] OECD Secretariat, *Assessing Foreign State-Owned Enterprises: Guidance for Regulators Based on the OECD Guidelines on Corporate Governance of SOEs* (OECD Publishing, 2016) 9.

[16] ibid 22.

[17] International Forum for Sovereign Wealth Funds (n 7) Principle 9.

## III. The Discussion of State Control Over the Corporate Governance of SOEs and POEs

It is reported that although SOEs have gained increasing autonomy after the SOE reforms, Chinese SOEs are still claimed by various scholars to be instruments of the Chinese Government in the search to fulfil its political and economic interests.[18] Energy SOEs are charged with the mission of investing abroad to secure external energy supplies.[19] For example, Chen argued that CNOOC responded to the policy call for global energy expansion.[20]

SASAC, which is responsible for maximising national interests, dominates the decision-making of SOEs.[21] For Kurlantzick, even if some Chinese SOEs have introduced private capital, the state retains control of decision-making through ownership of 'either a majority of the total shares or a majority of the voting class shares'.[22] Moreover, the mixed ownership reform may aggravate the dilemma of 'state advances and private retreats', because while introducing private capital may improve SOEs' efficiency, private investors are not able to influence their management.[23] Therefore, China's SOE reforms have left room for state influence.[24]

[18] R Hsueh, *China's Regulatory State: A New Strategy for Globalization* (Ithaca, NY, Cornell University Press, 2011) 10–11; T Brink, 'The Challenges of China's Non-Liberal Capitalism for the Liberal Global Economic Order' (2014) 16 *Harvard Quarterly* 36; C Li, 'Holding "China Inc" Together: The CCP and The Rise of China's Yang Qi' (2016) 228 *The China Quarterly* 927, 946; H Yu, 'Reform of State-owned Enterprises in China: The Chinese Communist Party Strikes Back' (2019) 43 *Asian Studies Review* 332, 338; C McNally, 'Sino Capitalism: China's Re-emergence and the International Political Economy' (2012) 64 *World Politics* 741; BB Kar and T Eğri, 'The China Model in the Global Economy' in BB Kar and T Eğri (eds), *The Belt and Road Strategy in International Business and Administration* (IGI Global, 2020) 1–27; C Milhaupt and M Pargendler, 'Governance Challenges of Listed State-Owned Enterprises Around the World: National Experiences and a Framework for Reform' (2017) 50 *Cornell International Law Journal* 473, 526. See, eg, S Eaton, *The Advance of the State in Contemporary China* (Cambridge, Cambridge University Press 2015); B Naughton, 'The Transformation of the State Sector: SASAC, the Market Economy, and the New National Champions' in KS Tsai and B Naughton (eds), *State Capitalism, Institutional Adaptation, and the Chinese Miracle* (Cambridge, Cambridge University Press 2015) 46–72, 63.

[19] Taylor (n 4) 115.

[20] D Chen, 'China's State-Owned Enterprises: How Much Do We Know? From CNOOC to Its Siblings' (2013) 6 *The School of Public Policy Research Papers* 1, 12.

[21] Milhaupt and Pargendler (n 18) 526; K Tsai and B Naughton, 'Introduction: State Capitalism and the Chinese Economic Miracle' in Tsai and Naughton (eds) (n18) 1–24; McNally (n 18); Y Yeo, 'Contextualizing Corporate Governance: The Case of China's Central State Enterprise Groups' (2013) 22 *Journal of Contemporary China* 460, 467–68.

[22] J Kurlantzick, *State Capitalism: How the Return of Statism Is Transforming the World* (Oxford, Oxford University Press, 2016).

[23] W Yin, 'A Comparison of the US and EU Regulatory Responses to China's State Capitalism: Implication, Issue and Direction' (2021) 19 *Asia Europe Journal* 1, 18.

[24] S Tong, 'China's New Push to Reform the State Sector: Progress and Drawbacks' (2018) 16 *China: An International Journal* 35, 36; see also J Wang, 'The Political Logic of Corporate Governance' (2014) 47 *Cornell International Law Journal* 631; LW Lin, 'A Network Anatomy of Chinese State-Owned Enterprises' (2017) 16 *World Trade Review* 583; J Zhang, 'State Structures, Business–State Relations,

Furthermore, it is the Party-building movement that enables the Chinese Government to put national strategies into practice, according to Milhaupt and others.[25] The influence of Party branches may be exercised in all enterprises, regardless of ownership.[26] For Wang, in SOEs, the Party branches' participation in decision-making, together with their power to appoint top management, makes SOEs 'economic entities totally controlled by the CPC'.[27] Thus SOEs will help the Party branches to achieve the strategic objective of 'securing foreign supplies of oil and refining oil products for domestic use'.[28]

For POEs, Andrews-Speed observed that the Party branches exerted state influence over them as well.[29] Moreover, Milhaupt and Zheng have concluded that large POEs, similar to SOEs, are prioritised when they access market and state financing, because of their close connection to political power.[30] By making use of connections within the centres of state power, POEs can minimise discrimination against them in a weak property-right environment and pursue corporate development.[31] This in turn facilitates the state's control over the investment-making of POEs.[32] The connections with state power usually exist in POEs that previously were state-owned, or in POEs whose executives have personal contacts within the Government.[33] The top management of these POEs approach crucial actors, including large SOEs, banks and governors, to seek government support and to ward off new players in their business expansion.[34]

and Multinational Corporate Behaviours: A Case Study of Chinese Multinational Oil Companies' in X Zhang and T Zhu (eds), *Business, Government and Economic Institutions in China* (Cham, Palgrave Macmillan 2018) 281–311, 283.

[25] C Milhaupt, 'Chinese Corporate Capitalism in Comparative Context' in W Chen (ed), *The Beijing Consensus? How China Has Changed Western Ideas of Law and Economic Development* (Cambridge, Cambridge University Press, 2017) 275–99; C Milhaupt, 'The State as Owner – China's Experience' (2020) 36 *Oxford Review of Economic Policy* 1; See also LYH Lin and C Milhaupt, 'Party Building or Noisy Signalling? The Contours of Political Conformity in Chinese Corporate Governance' (2021) 50 *Journal of Legal Studies* 1.

[26] Taylor (n 4) 120.

[27] Wang (n 24).

[28] J Lee, 'China's Geostrategic Search for Oil' [2012] *The Washington Quarterly* 75, 75.

[29] P Andrews-Speed, 'China's Energy Needs and Energy Security' in D Zweig and Y Hao (eds), *Sino-US Energy Triangles: Resource Diplomacy under Hegemony* (London, Routledge, 2016) 38–54, 47.

[30] C Milhaupt and W Zheng, 'Beyond Ownership: State Capitalism and the Chinese Firm' (2015) 103 *The Georgetown Law Journal* 665, 668.

[31] M Peng and Y Luo, 'Managerial Ties and Firm Performance in A Transition Economy: The Nature of a Micro-Macro Link' (2000) 43 *The Academy of Management Journal* 486; JK Kung and C Ma, 'Friends with Benefits: How Political Connections Help to Sustain Private Enterprise Growth in China' (2018) 85 *Economica* 41; Y Wang, 'Beyond Local Protectionism: China's State–Business Relations in the Last Two Decades' (2016) 226 *The China Quarterly* 319.

[32] D Jiang, 'Politics/Party and Enterprises – Civilized Structure of Participation of Political Power in Resources Allocation' [《政治/政党与企业:政治权力参与资源分配的文明结构》] (2018) 1 *Contemporary Law Review* 11.

[33] A García-Herrero and J Xu, 'How to Handle State-Owned Enterprises in EU-China Investment Talks' (2017) 18 *Policy Contribution* 1, 6–11.

[34] C Milhaupt and W Zheng, *Why Mixed-Ownership Reforms Cannot Fix China's State Sector* (Paulson Policy Memorandum, January 2016).

# IV. Contribution of the SOE Reforms to Enhancing SOEs' Autonomy

Although China is conservative as regards provisions on SOEs in investment treaties,[35] the SOE reforms represent the state's proactive response to internationally recommended practices governing SOEs.[36] According to NDRC, China's NOCs should improve their corporate governance to enhance their capacity for managing investments.[37] The SOE reforms includes governance reform and mixed ownership reform.[38] Governance reform essentially aims to reduce excessive state influence on the decision-making of SOEs.[39] In mixed-ownership reform, non-state shareholders are introduced to original SOEs to improve their performance.[40]

## A. Governance Reform

Driven by economic efficiency[41] and higher corporate governance standards in the global expansion,[42] the Chinese Government has worked on SOE reform for almost three decades by acting in accordance with OECD guidelines.[43] On this basis, in the energy sector, the Chinese Government aims to separate state ownership from

[35] H Wang, 'The RCEP and Its Investment Rules: Learning from Past Chinese FTAs' (2017) 3 *The Chinese Journal of Global Governance* 160; M Dian and S Menegazzi, *New Regional Initiatives in China's Foreign Policy* (Cham, Springer International Publishing 2018) 95–117.

[36] W Yin, 'Challenges, Issues in China–EU Investment Agreement and the Implication on China's Domestic Reform' (2018) 26 *Asia Pacific Law Review* 170; X Zhang, 'Integration of CCP Leadership with Corporate Governance' (2019) 1 *China Perspectives* 55; D Ho and A Young, 'China's Experience in Reforming Its State-Owned Enterprises: Something New, Something Old and Something Chinese?' (2013) 2 *International Journal of Economy, Management and Social Sciences* 84, 85.

[37] NDRC, *The 13th Petroleum Development Five-year Plan* [《石油发展"十三五"规划》] (2016); NDRC, *The 13th Natural Gas Development Five-year Plan* [《天然气发展"十三五"规划》] (2016).

[38] R Li and KC Cheong, *China's State Enterprises: Changing Role in a Rapidly Transforming Economy* (Singapore, Palgrave Macmillan, 2018) 49; see also S Wang, L Feng and Y Xu, 'State-owned Equity, Party Organization and Corporate Governance on the Perspective of Mixed Ownership Reform' [《混合所有制改革视野的国有股权、党组织与公司治理》] (2019) 7 *Reform* 27.

[39] M Zhang, 'Research on SOEs' Corporate Governance: Improving State-Owned Assets Regulation and Management System and SOEs' Corporate Governance' [《国有企业公司治理之研究:完善国有资产监管机制和优化国有企业公司治理结构》] (2013) 6 *Reform of Economic System* 88, 88; Ho and Young (n 36) 85.

[40] CPC and State Council, *Opinions on Deepening the Oil and Gas System Reform* [《关于深化石油天然气体制改革的若干意见》] (2017); see also J Wang and C Tan, 'Mixed Ownership Reform and Corporate Governance in China's State-Owned Enterprises' (2020) 53 *Vanderbilt Journal of Transnational Law* 1055; NDRC (n 37 both plans).

[41] See, eg, C Xi, 'Transforming Chinese Enterprises: Ideology, Efficiency and Instrumentalism in the Process of Reform' in J Gillespie and P Nicholson (eds), *Asian Socialism and Legal Change: The Dynamics of Vietnamese and Chinese Reform* (Canberra, ANU Press, 2005) 91–119, 92.

[42] The China Institute of University of Alberta, *State-Owned Enterprises in the Chinese Economy Today: Role, Reform, and Evolution* (2018) 17 at cloudfront.ualberta.ca/-/media/china/media-gallery/research/policy-papers/soepaper1-2018.pdf.

[43] A Keay and J Zhao, 'Transforming Corporate Governance in Chinese Corporations: A Journey, Not a Destination' (2018) 38 *Northwestern Journal of International Law & Business* 187, 190–91; CPC and State Council, Guiding Opinions on Deepening SOEs' Reform [《中共中央、国务院关于深化国有企业改革的指导意见》] (2015).

the management of energy SOEs.[44] The governance reform has helped energy SOEs to gradually distinguish administrative functions from economic functions in the modern enterprise system.[45] These energy SOEs should make investment decisions independently, maximise commercial interests and participate in international market competition.[46]

### i. *Contract Responsibility System*

The Chinese Government principally introduced the contract responsibility system to increase SOEs' autonomy in the first stage of the reforms (1978–83).[47] Expired *Interim Regulations on State-Owned Industrial Enterprises* (1983) provided that SOEs were to enjoy autonomy in production and operation.[48] These Regulations marked the start of delegating rights to energy SOEs.[49] However, SOEs' development plans had to be approved by local governments.[50] This implied that energy SOEs' proposed foreign projects had to be approved by those local governments even before the SOEs underwent NDRC and MOFCOM approval procedures.

### ii. *Asset Operations System*

The SOEs were relieved of their administrative missions to focus on their business operations in the second stage of the reforms (1984–92).[51] The SOEs were able

[44] CPC, Decision on Economic Reform [《中共中央关于经济体制改革的决定》] (1984); W Zhou, H Gao and X Bai, 'Building A Market Economy through WTO-Inspired Reform of State-Owned Enterprises in China' (2019) 68 *International and Comparative Law Quarterly* 977, 980–82; YC Xu, *Powering China: Reforming the Electric Power Industry in China* (Hants and Burlington, Ashgate Publishing, 2002) 109; D Clarke, 'How China's Efforts to Bring Private-Sector Standards into the Public Sector Backfired' in B Liebman and C Milhaupt (eds), *Regulating the Visible Hand?* (Oxford, Oxford University Press, 2016) 29–47; Z Li, 'SOEs Reform: Energy SOEs at the Head' [《国企改革，能源企业站潮头》] (2015) *China Petroleum* 61, 63.

[45] CS Liou and CM Tsai, 'The Governing Paradox in a Transition Economy: Repeated Institutional Reforms and Increasing Regulatory Capture in China's Energy Sector' [2019] *Problems of Post-Communism* 4.

[46] L Brefort, S Valtchev Tenev and C Zhang, *Corporate Governance and Enterprise Reform in China* (The World Bank, 2002); B Jiang, 'China National Petroleum Corporation (CNPC): A Balancing Act between Enterprises and Government' in D Victor, D Hults and M Thurber (eds), *Oil and Governance: State-Owned Enterprises and the World Energy Supply* (Cambridge, Cambridge University Press, 2012) 379–417, 389.

[47] See, eg, L Song, 'State-Owned Enterprise Reform in China: Past, Present and Prospects' in R Garnaut, L Song and C Fang (eds), *China's 40 Years of Reform and Development: 1978–2018* (Canberra, ANU Press, 2018) 345–74.

[48] State Council, Interim Regulations on State-Owned Industrial Enterprises [《国营工业企业暂行条例》] (1983) Art 8.

[49] P Andrews-Speed, 'China's Oil and Gas Industry: Stranded Between the Plan and the Market' in A Belyi and K Talus (eds), *States and Markets in Hydrocarbon Sectors* (Singapore, Palgrave Macmillan, 2015) 214–39, 222. For a criticism of SOE reforms at this stage, see J Wu et al, 'The Failure of State-Owned Enterprise Reforms Under Market Socialism' in J Wu and G Ma (eds), *Whither China?: Restarting the Reform Agenda* (Oxford, Oxford University Press 2016) 59–73.

[50] State Council (n 48) Arts 23 and 24.

[51] C Pei, C Yang and X Yang, *The Basic Economic System of China* (Singapore, Springer, 2019) 193; X Li and KE Brødsgaard, 'SOE Reform in China: Past, Present and Future' (2013) 31 *Copenhagen Journal of Asian Studies* 54, 56.

to possess, utilise and dispose of state-owned assets, in accordance with the *Law on Industrial Enterprises Owned by the Whole People* (1988).[52] As a result, SOEs should become relatively independent economic entities that were responsible for losses and make profits themselves.[53]

However, SOEs were not entirely independent from the Government, because their corporate structures were still embedded in the administrative system.[54] Enterprises 'owned by the whole people' adopted the 'managerial responsibility system'.[55] The factory director or general manager, who also worked as the chief of an administrative department,[56] had the final say on investment plans with the assistance of the management committee.[57] For instance, in compliance with the *Law on Industrial Enterprises Owned by the Whole People* (1988), State Grid issued *Working Rules of the State Grid* (2003) to govern the company with the managerial responsibility system.[58] The general-manager working meeting made investment decisions.[59] The general manager, who was also the chief of an administrative department, hosted this meeting, and invited vice-managers and heads of other corporate departments to attend.[60]

Therefore, the Chinese Government failed to obey the internationally agreed practices of corporate governance at this stage and did not differentiate its shareholder power from administrative functions.[61] Although SOEs in principle no longer shouldered their administrative missions, it was still hard for energy SOEs to make independent investment decisions at this stage.[62]

### iii. Corporatisation of SOEs Since 1993

Corporatisation is important for the commercial basis of China's global energy expansion.[63] The *Decision on Matters Concerning the Creation of a Socialist Market*

[52] Law of the People's Republic of China on Industrial Enterprises Owned by the Whole People [《中华人民共和国全民所有制工业企业法》] (1988) Art 2.

[53] ibid.

[54] G Hu, 'Analysis and Reconstruction of the Delegated Management of State-Owned Property' [《"国有资产授权经营"制度的剖析及其重构》] (2009) 2 *West Law Review* 84, 85; D Liu and D Xu, 'The Approaches and Implementation Mechanism of The Party's Participation in Administering the State-Owned Enterprises Under the Circumstances of Classification Reform' [《党组织参与国企公司治理的路径与法律保障研究——以国企分类改革为视角》] (2017) 23 *Journal of Zhongnan University (Social Science)* 31, 31.

[55] Law of the People's Republic of China on Industrial Enterprises Owned by the Whole People (n 52) Art 7. The revision in 2009 also recognised this system.

[56] ibid Art 7.

[57] ibid Art 47.

[58] State Grid, *Working Rules of the State Grid (Trial Implementation)* [《国家电网工作细则（试行）》] (2003) Art 3.

[59] ibid Arts 4 and 12.

[60] ibid Art 11.

[61] ibid.

[62] M Meidan, *The Structure of China's Oil Industry: Past Trends and Future Prospects* (Oxford Institute for Energy Studies, May 2016).

[63] CS Liou, 'Rent-Seeking at Home, Capturing Market Share Abroad: The Domestic Determinants of the Transnationalization of China State Construction Engineering Corporation' (2014) 54

*Economic System* (1993) gave rise to the concept of a 'modern enterprise system'.[64] This system aims to corporatise SOEs, that is, reorganising SOEs into legal entities with the 'corporate structure found in publicly traded companies'.[65] Gradually corporatising energy SOEs has contributed to increasing their autonomy.[66] This increased autonomy implies that they should be responsible for profits and losses.[67] China's NOCs have indeed become 'more autonomous and influential' in their global expansion,[68] and aim to 'maximise returns for their shareholders'.[69] In 2012–13, CNPC, Sinopec and CNOOC were incorporated under the Company Law of China.[70] In 2002, the State Grid Corporation of China (SGCC) was incorporated under the PRC Company Law and has been an active player in the global energy expansion.[71] These energy SOEs have expanded their shares of foreign markets and enhanced their international competitiveness.[72]

The PRC Company Law has enabled the Chinese Government to 'put ownership in the hands of shareholders and management powers in the hands of directors and senior management'.[73] The shareholders' meeting and the board of directors are two major levels of control mechanisms.[74] The shareholders' meeting

*World Development* 220, 226; Meidan (n 62) 19; M Lelyveld, 'China Revives Oil and Gas Reform Plan' *Radio Free Asia* (11 March 2019) at www.rfa.org/english/commentaries/energy_watch/china-revives-oil-and-gas-reform-plan-03112019105451.html.

[64] CPC, Decision on Matters Concerning the Creation of a Socialist Market Economic System – the concept of modern enterprise system [《中共中央关于建立社会主义市场经济体制若干问题的决定》] (1993).

[65] Xi (n 41) 96; Xu (n 44); W Li and Y Li, 'Corporate Governance Reform of SOEs: from Enterprises Governance and Corporate Governance' [《国企治理改革: 从企业治理到公司治理治理》] *CPC News* (December 2018) at theory.people.com.cn/n1/2018/1210/c40531-30453021.html.

[66] P Andrews-Speed and S Zhang, 'China's Evolving Energy Policy: The Case of Electricity' in J Considine and KW Paik (eds), *Handbook of Energy Politics* (Cheltenham, Edward Elgar, 2018) 179–212, 184; J Alano et al, *Foreign Case Study Report: China Petroleum & Chemical Corporation (Sinopec Corp)* (University of the Philippines Diliman, 2019) 13; X Zheng, *China's 40 Years of Economic Reform and Development: How the Miracle Was Created* (Singapore, Springer, 2018) 95.

[67] H Lai, S O'Hara and K Wyscozanska, 'Rationale of Internationalization of China's National Oil Companies: Seeking Natural Resources, Strategic Assets or Sectoral Specialization?' in H Lai and M Warner (eds), *Managing China's Energy Sector: Between the Market and the State* (London, Routledge, 2016) 77–98, 93.

[68] E Downs, 'Business Interest Groups in Chinese Politics: The Case of the Oil Companies' in L Cheng (ed), *China's Changing Political Landscape* (Brookings Institution, 2008) 121–41, 121; J Meckling, B Kong and T Madan, 'Oil and State Capitalism: Government-Firm Coopetition in China and India' (2015) 22 *Review of International Political Economy* 1159.

[69] SASAC, Guiding Opinions on Building Work of Boards of Directors (Trial Implementation) [《关于国有独资公司董事会建设的指导意见（试行）》] (2004); CNPC, 'Our Goal' at www.cnpc.com.cn/en/ourgoal/about_common.shtml; PetroChina, Rules and Procedures for Shareholders' General Meetings of PetroChina Limited [《中国石油天然气股份有限公司董事会议事规则》] (2017).

[70] SASAC, *SASAC Yearbook* [《中国国有资产监督管理年鉴》] (2012–13).

[71] State Grid, 'Corporate File' at www.sgcc.com.cn/html/sgcc_main_en/col2017112300/column_2017112300_1.shtml.

[72] E Downs, 'Who's Afraid of China's Oil Companies?' in C Pascual and J Elkind (eds), *Energy Security: Economics, Politics, Strategy, and Implications* (Washington, DC, Brooking Institution Press, 2010) 73–102, 75–77; Meidan (n 62).

[73] Clarke (n 44) 33; E Cunningham, 'The State and the Firm: China's Energy Governance in Context', GEGI Working Paper (March 2015) (last accessed 6 June 2018).

[74] J Wang, *Company Law in China: Regulation of Business Organizations in A Social Market Economy* (Cheltenham, Edward Elgar Publishing, 2014); C Lin, 'Corporatisation and Corporate Governance in China's Economic Transition' (2001) 34 *Economics of Planning* 5, 11.

is authorised by the PRC Company Law 'to decide upon investment plans of the company, plus examine and approve the reports by the board of directors'.[75] The boards of directors of SOEs take the lead in making decisions on foreign investments.[76] However, the PRC Company Law does not specify the line between the power of the board of directors and the power of the shareholders' meeting regarding the decisions on making investments.

Central SOEs are wholly state-owned companies. According to the PRC Company Law, a wholly state-owned company is

> a limited liability company funded wholly by the state, and for which the State Council or the State-owned assets supervision and administration authority, authorized by the local people's government at the same level, performs the duties of the capital contributing party.[77]

Therefore, SASAC, representing the state, is authorised to exercise shareholder rights in central SOEs at the first level. *Guiding Opinions on Further Improving SOEs' Corporate Governance Structure* (2017) explained that SASAC was not allowed to intervene with the decision-making process, except when authorised by the law or the Articles of Association.[78] At the same time, under the PRC Company Law and policies covering the reform of SOEs,[79] in wholly state-owned companies, the board of directors is in principle independent when drafting investment plans.[80] Therefore, the board of directors is not an executive committee of the shareholders' meeting but is more competent to make investment decisions.[81]

PetroChina, Sinopec Corp and China Power International Development Ltd have been corporatised under the PRC Company Law. These companies drafted Articles of Associations in accordance with the PRC Company Law to govern the decision-making process (eg, clarifying the authority for approving proposed investments). In PetroChina, both the shareholders' meeting and the board of directors have the right to determine investment plans.[82] If the acquired assets exceed 30 per cent of the latest audited total assets of the company then such an acquisition must be approved by the shareholders' meeting.[83] Compared with the

[75] PRC Company Law [《中华人民共和国公司法》] (1993) Art 38.

[76] ibid Arts 46 and 67.

[77] ibid Art 64.

[78] State Council, *Guiding Opinions on Further Improving SOEs' Corporate Governance Structure* [《国务院办公厅关于进一步完善国有企业法人治理结构的意见》] (2017).

[79] Law on the State-Owned Assets of Enterprises [《中华人民共和国企业国有资产法》] (2008) Art 14; H Zhang, 'Where Is the future: China's SOEs Reform' (2006) 1 *Journal of the Washington Institute of China Studies* 105, 106.

[80] CPC and State Council, Guiding Opinions of the CPC Central Committee and the State Council on Deepening the Reform of State-owned Enterprises [《中共中央、国务院关于深化国有企业改革的指导意见》] (2015); PRC Company Law (1993) (n 75) Art 66.

[81] P Luo, 'The Power Structure of Shareholders' Meeting and the Board of Directors' [《股东会与董事会权力构造论：以合同为进路的分析》] (2016) 2 *Political Science and Law* 122, 131–32.

[82] PetroChina, Articles of Association of PetroChina Limited, Arts 60 and 104 at www.petrochina.com.cn/ptr/gsgg/202006/129f0c18a231464198621cff89d9109a/files/1e74805ea9c14f168ef1bc5fe140ca54.pdf.

[83] ibid Art 60.

Articles of Association of PetroChina, those of Sinopec Corp provide more detail regarding the authority to approve investment plans.[84] The shareholders' meeting will be authorised to approve investment plans and individual investments if the amount to be invested is more than five per cent of the latest audited net asset value of the company.[85] Other small-scale investment plans or individual projects are approved by the board of directors or the chairman of the board.[86] According to the internal manual of China Power International Development Ltd, proposed overseas investments will be reviewed by the chief financial officer and vice-executive president, examined by the risk-control committee under the board and finally approved by the board, if the investment value is more than five million RMB.[87]

## B. Ownership Reform

In China, state-controlled companies and companies with minority state shares have emerged since the Government launched mixed-ownership reform of SOEs. The state-controlled companies and companies with minority state shares are crucial players when investing abroad.[88] By introducing private capital, the mixed-ownership reform has been launched to improve corporate governance of original SOEs, and thus to increase economic returns.[89] This subsection looks at how the involvement of private capital can restrict state influence on the decision-making of the state-controlled companies and companies with minority state shares.

### *i. Diversifying the Composition of Shareholders to Limit State Influence*

The shareholder structure defines the composition of shareholders and the percentage of their capital contribution.[90] This structure determines the extent to which capital contributors can have a say in decision-making.[91] In principle,

[84] Sinopec Corp, Articles of Association of Sinopec Corp [《中石化股份公司章程》] at www.sinopec.com/listco/Resource/Pdf/2019050901.pdf.

[85] ibid Art 12.

[86] ibid Art 6.

[87] China Power International Development Ltd, *Internal Manual of China Power International Development Ltd.* [《中国电力国际发展有限公司内部控制手册》] (Beijing, China Power Press, 2007).

[88] AH Zhang, 'The Antitrust Paradox of China, Inc' (2017) 50 *New York University Journal of International Law and Politics* 159, 206 and 210.

[89] Deloitte, 'The Focus on Ownership Reform' (聚焦混合所有制改革) (2015) 4, at www2.deloitte.com/cn/zh/pages/operations/articles/soe-transformation-whitepaper-issue2.html.

[90] J Jiang, 'State-owned Corporation's Ownership Structure and Its Legal Reform: A View from Corporation Governance Efficiency' [《我国国有公司股权结构及其法律改革——以公司治理效率为主要视角》] (2012) 6 *Journal of Northwest University of Political Science and Law* 131.

[91] ibid.

ownership reform can reduce state control and enable state-controlled companies and companies with minority state shares to direct more attention to business development.[92]

First, decreasing state shares means that the state has less weight for influencing corporate decisions.[93] However, the state's role as regulator gives the impression that the Government de facto has a significant influence on companies' decision-making, even if it is a minority shareholder in mixed-ownership companies.[94] To resolve this problem, the *Opinions of the State Council on the Development of Mixed Ownership Economy by State-Owned Enterprises* (2015) provided that the representatives delegated by the Government cannot take advantage of the shareholder status to intervene with SOEs' daily operation.[95] Also, 'private shareholders should be able to dispatch directors or supervisors for their effective participation in corporate governance', according to the *Operating Guidelines for the Mixed Ownership Reform of Central Enterprises* (2019).[96] Therefore, in mixed-ownership companies, it is hard for the representatives of SASAC to prioritise policy interests in investment decision-making because the representatives need to communicate with other private shareholders to obtain their support in the shareholders' meeting.[97]

Second, central SOEs' subsidiaries with private shares are subject to transparency rules and outside constraints introduced by international markets in Hong Kong, New York and London, if they went public.[98] For instance, listed subsidiaries of three NOCs are governed by the rules of foreign stock exchanges.[99] By complying with the transparency rules and other constraints, these subsidiaries should in principle isolate themselves from state control, take responsibility for their shareholders and disclose information about their foreign projects. Otherwise, these listed subsidiaries may fail to attract private capital.[100] For example, regarding the rule about integration of Party branches into the governance of listed companies

[92] Wang and Tan (n 40).

[93] SASAC, Notice on Issuing the Operating Guidelines for the Mixed Ownership Reform of Central Enterprises [《国资委关于印发<中央企业混合所有制改革操作指引>的通知》] (2019); C Zhu, 'The Shareholder Status of the State Contributor and the Party Leadership from the Perspective of PRC Company Law' [《公司法视角下国有出资人的股东职责与党的领导》] (2017) 2 *Economic Law Review* 47.

[94] Zhang (n 88) 211.

[95] State Council, *Opinions of the State Council on the Development of Mixed Ownership Economy by State-Owned Enterprises* [《国务院关于国有企业发展混合所有制经济的意见》] (2015).

[96] SASAC (n 93).

[97] Zhu (n 93).

[98] P Hubbard, 'Fragmented authoritarianism' and state ownership' *East Asia Forum* (23 January 2017) at www.eastasiaforum.org/2017/01/23/fragmented-authoritarianism-and-state-ownership/.

[99] E Steinfeld, *Playing Our Game: Why China's Economic Rise Doesn't Threaten the West* (Oxford, Oxford University Press, 2010) 216–17.

[100] YH Lin and YC Chang, 'Do State-Owned Enterprises Have Worse Corporate Governance? An Empirical Study of Corporate Practices in China', NYU Center for Law, Economics and Organization, Law & Economic Research Paper Series, Working Paper No 19–28 (December 2019) (last accessed 4 January 2020).

(as discussed in section VI), cross-listed SOEs are more reticent about complying with this rule than those listed only in China, because the cross-listed SOEs are bound by a tighter overseas regulatory environment.[101]

In the energy sector, the *Opinions on Deepening the Oil and Gas System Reform* (2017) suggested that the mixed-ownership reform helped China's NOCs to enlarge the composition of shareholders and develop into independent players on the market.[102] For example, in the mixed-ownership petroleum sales company Sinopec Corp, three directors were nominated by social investors.[103] Also, privatising China's largest electricity company since 2003 has enabled the company to make full use of its competitive advantage, operate independently from state orders and make profits.[104]

## ii. Protecting Non-State Shareholders

As private shareholders aim for commercial interests in investment operations, protecting them is crucial for limiting state influence on investment-making for strategic objectives. The 2005 PRC Company Law is useful in protecting private shareholders of state-controlled companies.[105] Minority shareholders have the right to review internal documents, such as meeting minutes, resolutions and financial reports, for corporate information.[106] Based on the information, minority shareholders have the right to challenge majority shareholders' decisions on transactions and the election of directors.[107] Moreover, shareholders who 'are separately or aggregately holding 1% or more of the company's total shares for 180 consecutive days or more' are able to bring a case against the supervisory board or the board of directors before the court, when directors, supervisors or top management fail to perform their obligations and cause substantial losses.[108] This right is particularly important for passive and dispersed private stockholders, because they cannot directly replace the management like controlling shareholders, nor seek protection via the relevant contracts as other minority shareholders with substantial influence do.[109]

[101] JZ Liu and AH Zhang, 'Ownership and Political Control: Evidence from Charter Amendments' (2019) 60 *International Review of Law and Economics* 1, 2.

[102] CPC and State Council, *Opinions on Deepening the Oil and Gas System Reform* [《关于深化石油天然气体制改革的若干意见》] (2017).

[103] Asian Corporate Governance Association, *The Development History of Chinese Corporate Governance* [《中国公司治理进化史》] (2018) 165–75.

[104] M Tan-Mullins, F Urban and G Mang, 'The Political Ecology of Rising China: Case Study of Chinese Hydropower Dams in Africa and Asia' in G Siciliano and F Urban (eds), *Chinese Hydropower Development in Africa and Asia* (London, Routledge, 2018) 80–99.

[105] OECD, *Corporate Governance of Listed Companies in China* (OECD Publishing, 2011).

[106] PRC Company Law [《中华人民共和国公司法》] (1993, amended in 2005) Art 34.

[107] J Feinerman, 'New Hope for Corporate Governance in China?' in P Keller (ed), *Law and the Market Economy in China* (Burlington, Ashgate, 2011) 97–119.

[108] PRC Company Law (2005) (n 106) Art 152.

[109] Clarke (n 44) 39.

Cumulative voting regarding the election of directors or supervisors can also enhance the power of minority private shareholders in listed state-controlled subsidiaries.[110] According to the PRC Company Law, 'shareholders can multiply their voting rights by the number of candidates and use them all for one candidate for director or supervisor'.[111] It means that minority shareholders have the right to elect their representatives on the board of directors and the supervisory board,[112] and thus to influence corporate decision-making.[113]

In principle, the protection for minority private shareholders can help to implement the mixed-ownership reform of SOEs by preventing the state shareholder from abusing its shareholder power and harming minority private shareholders' rights.[114] Otherwise, the shareholders' meeting is likely to make decisions that sacrifice companies' business interests for policy interests.[115] However, in practice, Chinese courts may be reluctant to support the enforcement of the rights of minority private shareholders.[116]

## V. Remaining State Influence Exerted by SASAC on SOEs' Governance

Before establishing SASAC, the central Government directly imposed political or social mandates on SOEs.[117] The Chinese Government set up SASAC in 2003 to consolidate previously dispersed controlling rights over SOEs in one single decision-maker.[118] SASAC was thus able to influence the investment-making of central energy SOEs.[119] Although SASAC was set up to prevent the state from directly

[110] C Xi, 'Shareholder Voting and Corporate Sustainability in China' in B Sjåfjell and C Bruner (eds), *The Cambridge Handbook of Corporate Law, Corporate Governance and Sustainability* (Cambridge, Cambridge University Press, 2019) 431–45.

[111] PRC Company Law (2005) (n 106) Art 106.

[112] C Xi, 'The Political Economy of Cumulative Voting: The Case of China' (2014) 14 *Asian Business Law* 61.

[113] Feinerman (n 107).

[114] C Zhu, 'The Chinese Corporate Law in Domestic and International Fusion' [《论中国公司法本土化与国际化的融合——改革开放以来的历史沿革、最新发展与未来走向》] (2020) 2 *Oriental Law* 91; X Liang, 'The Reform of the Corporate Governance Structure of the Mixed Ownership and Improvement of Law' [《混合所有制公司治理结构的改革与法律完善》] (2015) 35 *Hebei Academic Journal* 171.

[115] NC Howson, 'Protecting the State from Itself?' in Liebman and Milhaupt (eds) (n 44) 49–67; Z Tang, 'Corporate Governance of China' [《论我国公司法人治理结构》] (2002) 17 *Journal of Tsing Hua University* 58, 60; Q Li and D Wang, 'The Analysis of the Position and Corporate Governance Mechanism of SOEs' [《浅析国有企业定位与治理机制》] (2011) *Corporate Management* 17, 17.

[116] Clarke (n 44) 33.

[117] Naughton (n 18) 62.

[118] LW Lin and C Milhaupt, 'We Are the (National) Champions: Understanding the Mechanisms of State Capitalism in China' (2013) 65 *Stanford Law Review* 697, 735; Hubbard (n 98).

[119] SASAC, The List of Central Enterprises, at www.sasac.gov.cn/n2588035/n2641579/n2641645/index.html. The following national energy companies are listed as central enterprises: the CNPC, Sinopec, CNOOC, State Grid Corporation of China, China Southern Power Grid, China Hua

operating state-owned assets,[120] it maintains important channels for exerting government influence over SOEs.[121] Not only can SASAC's administrative power restrict SOEs' investment autonomy,[122] but its shareholder right also enables this administrative agency to participate in market competition.[123] In practice, SASAC is more used to utilising administrative power to manage central SOEs.[124]

## A. SASAC as a Regulator

SASAC is a 'specialised agency directly under the State Council'.[125] On behalf of the State Council, it 'is responsible for the supervision and administration of the state-owned assets in enterprises', according to the *Interim Regulation on the Supervision and Administration of State-owned Assets of Enterprises* (2011).[126] This Regulation also authorises SASAC to administer the operation of state assets abroad and to draft regulations for governing SOEs' overseas investments, to prevent the loss of state-owned assets.[127] More specifically, SASAC focuses on controlling risks and ensuring economic returns in overseas investments made by central SOEs.[128] The interviewees confirmed that SASAC implemented its tasks as an intermediary between the Government and the SOEs.

Dian Corporation, China Hua Neng Group, China Power Investment Corporation, China Datang Corporation, SHEN HUA GROUP, China National Nuclear Corporation, China General Nuclear Power Corporation and China Coal Energy Group Co Ltd.

[120] J Gordon and C Milhaupt, 'China as A National Strategic Buyer' (2019) 1 *Columbia Law Review* 192, 215–16.

[121] C Zhang, *The World Bank in China's State-Owned Enterprise Reform Since the 1980s* (The World Bank, 2019) 5–6 at https://documents.worldbank.org/en/publication/documents-reports/documentdetail/446121550586445220/the-world-bank-in-chinas-state-owned-enterprise-reform-since-the-1980s; X Chen, 'Legal Regulation and Political Regulation of SOEs: From Competition to Convergence' [《国有企业法律规制与政治规制:从竞争到融合》] (2019) 6 *Law Review* 111, 118–19.

[122] The China Institute of University of Alberta (n 42) 8.

[123] L Che, *China's State-Directed Economy and the International Order* (Singapore, Springer, 2019) 48–50.

[124] D Feng, 'Indigenous Evolution of SOE Regulation' in Liebman and Milhaupt (eds) (n 44) 3–28; Sunshine Law Firm, 'Mixed Ownership Reform | Operation by State Capital Authorization: from Enterprises Management and Capital Management' [《国企混改 | 国资授权经营来了：从管企业到管资本，你准备好了吗？》] (6 May 2019) at www.sunshinelawfirm.com/newsinfo.aspx?id=1883.

[125] The Composition of State Council at www.gov.cn/guowuyuan/zuzhi.htm.

[126] State Council, Interim Regulation on the Supervision and Administration of State-owned Assets of Enterprises [《企业国有资产监督管理暂行条例》] (2011) Art 12.

[127] SASAC, Interim Measures for the Supervision and Administration of Overseas State-owned Assets of Central Enterprises [《中央企业境外国有资产监督管理暂行办法》] (2011) Art 1; C Holz, 'The Unfinished Business of State-owned Enterprise Reform in the People's Republic of China', CESifo Working Paper No 7688 (CESifo, 2019) (last accessed 22 February 2021); Wang and Tan (n 40).

[128] SASAC, *Measures for the Supervision and Administration of Overseas Investments by Central Enterprises* [《中央企业境外投资监督管理办法》] (2017) Art 3; YC Xu, 'Chinese State-owned Enterprises in Africa: Ambassadors or Freebooters' (2014) 23 *Journal of Contemporary China* 822, 829; W Li and H Hendrischke, 'Chinese Outbound Investment in Australia: From State Control to Entrepreneurship' [2019] *The China Quarterly* 1, 10; H Zhao, *The Economics and Politics of China's Energy Security Transition* (San Diego, CA, Elsevier Science & Technology, 2018) 193–94.

SASAC's administration of overseas investments has limited the investment autonomy of the boards of SOEs.[129] According to *Measures for the Supervision and Administration of Overseas Investments by Central Enterprises* (2017), SASAC approves 'investments subject to supervision' of which the investment amount is US$2 billion or more.[130] SASAC also forbids central SOEs from investing in projects that have a low investment return, or that face growing debts.[131] Additionally, SOEs need to communicate with SASAC about their investment plans.[132] As discussed in chapter four, SASAC is involved in developing company-specific five-year plans and outlining how SOEs' plans will implement the national five-year plans.[133] SASAC forbids central SOEs from investing in projects that fall outside the scope provided for in the investment strategies submitted by the SOEs.[134] The interviewees further explained that important investment decisions were normally made by the management of an SOE with the involvement of SASAC, including investments already included in the company's investment plan that complied with national five-year plans.[135]

Furthermore, SASAC annually appraises SOEs that engage in strategic business (eg, the energy sector) on the basis of their contribution to national security (including energy security), the realisation of the BRI and, more generally, compliance with China's economic and social policies.[136] This evaluation system implies that energy SOEs do indeed need to discharge domestic energy policies, but these companies cannot sacrifice financial gains.[137]

Therefore, SASAC can exercise influence over the corporate governance of SOEs through its regulatory power.[138] To limit SASAC's regulatory power over outbound investments,[139] the Government has reduced the number of items that are subject to SASAC's approval or record-keeping, according to the *Opinions*

[129] R Tomasic, 'Company Law Implementation in the PRC' (2015) 15 *Journal of Corporate Law Studies* 285, 307.

[130] SASAC (n 128) Arts 5 and 9; SASAC, The Negative List of Overseas Investments by Central Enterprises [《中央企业境外投资负面清单》] (2017).

[131] The Negative List (n 130).

[132] H Rao, 'The Transformation of the Regulatory Role after the Issuance of the New Regulation on Central SOEs' investments' [《新版央企投资监管办法背后的监管职能转变》] [2017] *State-Owned Assets Report* 29, 31.

[133] SASAC, Management Measures for Development Strategies and Plans of Central SOEs [《中央企业发展规略和规划管理办法》] (2004) Art 13; SASAC, *The 13th Five-Year Plan of Developing Central SOEs* [《中央企业十三五规划发展规划纲要》] (2016); F Robins, 'The Uniqueness of Chinese Outward Foreign Direct Investment' (2013) 12 *Asian Business & Management* 525, 525.

[134] SASAC (n 130).

[135] See State Council (n 126) Art 22.

[136] SASAC, Measures on Assessing Central SOEs' Leadership [《中央企业负责人经营业绩考核办法》] (2018) Art 13; Xu (n 128) 829; X Zhu, 'Performance Evaluation of State-Owned Enterprise in China: A Case of Petroleum Industry' in R Dou (ed), *Proceedings of 2012 3rd International Asia Conference on Industrial Engineering and Management Innovation* (Singapore, Springer, 2013) 843–50, 846.

[137] Xu (n 128) 836; Li and Brødsgaard (n 51) 57.

[138] On influence through the 'nomenklatura system', see Andrews-Speed (n 49) 214; YC Xu, *Sinews of Power: Politics of the State Grid Corporation of China* (Oxford, Oxford University Press, 2017) 103–06.

[139] J Li, 'Managing Capital Still Requires SASAC's Regulation and Supervision' [《"管资本为主"不是不管企业》] (2017) 10 *State Capital Report* 71, 72.

*on Reforming and Improving the Administrative System of State Assets* (2015).[140] *The Notice on Transforming the Function of SASAC: Managing Capital* (2017) also stated that central SOEs are the leading entities that make investment decisions and manage overseas assets.[141] By reducing the regulatory interference by SASAC, SOEs should be more independent.[142] However, it remains to be seen whether SOEs will continue communication with SASAC about investing abroad, which can influence the decision-making of SOEs.

## B. SASAC as a Shareholder

In parallel with SOEs' corporatisation, SASAC can influence the formulation of investment plans as a shareholder in SOEs.[143] There is no shareholders' meeting in wholly state-owned companies.[144] SASAC delegates its right of drafting and approving corporate investment plans to the board of directors.[145] In state-controlled companies, the branches of SASAC can directly propose investments in accordance with the number of their shares,[146] and may also do so indirectly by dispatching shareholder representatives to take part in shareholders' meetings.[147] Therefore, SASAC and its subordinate departments can review investment plans, as the state shareholder, to ensure the compliance of investment plans with national energy policies (in the case of energy SOEs). In practice, SASAC and its subordinate departments also have talks with managers of SOEs about how to achieve policy objectives at the beginning of each year.[148]

Apart from reviewing the investment plans of SOEs, shareholders have the right to 'elect and replace directors' and 'choose managers in proportion to the share of the investment they make in the company', according to the PRC Company Law.[149] For instance, SASAC delegated outside directors and supervisors in Sinopec.[150] The state shareholder dispatches directors to take part in the board meeting when that meeting approves investment plans within its power, to ensure that the management is committed to protecting state-owned assets.[151]

[140] State Council, *Opinions on Reforming and Improving the Administrative System of State Assets* [《关于改革和完善国有资产管理体制的若干意见》] (2015).

[141] State Council, Notice on Transforming the Function of SASAC: Managing Capital [《国务院办公厅关于转发国务院国资委以管资本为主推进职能转变方案的通知》] (2017).

[142] G Gu, 'The Discussion of Policy Targets and Legal Direction of the Reform of State Capital and SOEs' [《论国资国企深化改革的政策目标和法治走向》] (2014) 11 *Politics and Law* 80, 82.

[143] W Zhu, 'Research on Separating SOEs from Government in Mechanism of State-Owned Assets Management' [《国有资产管理体制中的政企分开探析》] (2005) 16 *Journal of Zhongyuan Institute of Technology* 54, 55.

[144] PRC Company Law (1993) (n 75) Art 66.

[145] ibid.

[146] State Council (n 78).

[147] State Council (n 126) Art 22.

[148] Z Wang, 'Corporate Governance under State Control: The Chinese Experience' (2012) 13 *Theoretical Inquiries in Law* 487, 499.

[149] PRC Company Law (1993) (n 75) Arts 4 and 38.

[150] Asian Corporate Governance Association (n 103) 165–75.

[151] PRC Company Law (1993) (n 75) Art 68; Zhu (n 93); Lin (n 24).

Given the dual identity of SASAC, namely as a shareholder in SOEs and as a regulator, the Chinese Government aimed to reform the way in which SASAC exercises shareholder rights. The reform focuses on establishing State Capital Investment and Operation Companies (SIOCs) and enabling them to gradually take over the role of state shareholders.[152] SASAC's shareholder right to propose investments will be partly transferred to SIOCs in order to widen, at least in theory, the separation between state ownership and operational management, according to the *Implementation Opinions of the State Council on Advancing the Pilot Programme of the Reform of State Capital Investment and Operation Companies (SIOCs)* (2018).[153] The SIOCs are responsible for preserving the value of state-owned assets and gaining more revenues from their investments.[154] SASAC has selected pilot SOEs that, in a certain industry, will be restructured or newly established as SIOCs through assets transfers.[155] For example, the State Power Investment Corporation Ltd will be managed on this basis.

This latest reform represents another nod towards China's declared commitment to the operational autonomy of SOEs, as it further separates administrative oversight from its shareholder power.[156] SASAC hold the power over major business management and strategic planning.[157] But in future, SIOCs with industrial expertise will invest in or take controlling shares in other central SOEs.[158] In other words, SIOCs will cut the direct link between the Government and SOEs, and will only be economically connected with their funded SOEs.[159] Therefore, the reform is aimed at reducing 'bureaucratic meddling' in China's SOEs.[160] The SOEs invested in by SIOCs will face fewer administrative hurdles when investing abroad.

However, it remains to be seen what practical impacts these measures will have on minimising government control over outbound energy investments.[161]

[152] CPC and State Council (n 800); J Fu, 'State Capitalism and Corporate Law: The Governance of State-Owned Enterprises in China' in R Tomasic (ed), *Routledge Handbook of Corporate Law* (London, Routledge, 2017) 145–62.

[153] State Council, *Implementation Opinions on Advancing the Pilot Program of the Reform of State Capital Investment and Operation Companies* [《国务院关于推进国有资本投资、运营公司改革试点的实施意见》] (2018); Wang and Tan (n 40) 1091.

[154] State Council (n 153); Holz (n 127).

[155] State Council (n 153).

[156] Gu (n 142) 85.

[157] Sunshine Law Firm (n 124).

[158] X Cao and J Wang, 'The Development of State Investment and Operation Companies' (《国有资本投资、运营公司进阶之路》) (Zhong Lun Law Firm, 28 August 2018) at www.zhonglun.com/Content/2018/08-28/1023432080.html.

[159] Z Wen and S Song, 'Reform Logic in Divestiture of Operational Function of State-owned Capital from SOEs and Reconstruction of Performance Appraisal System' [《国有资本运营职能从国有企业剥离的改革逻辑及绩效评价体系》] (2018) 33 *Journal of Beijing Technology and Business University* 10, 13.

[160] Tong (n 24) 36.

[161] For criticism, see eg, Zhou, Gao and Bai (n 44) 993.

The major concerns are that SASAC still has shareholder rights in these SIOCs due to its status as the representative of the State Council to manage state-owned assets, and that SASAC will directly evaluate whether SIOCs properly operate state assets.[162] For scholars such as Zheng and Huang, because of the supervision and administration of SASAC, the newly established state investment vehicles are expected to protect state assets, to create national champions and to support the development of energy and other strategic industries.[163] SIOCs can meet these expectations by participating in the formulation of investment plans of the SOEs funded by them. Naughton also explained that SASAC's selection of SOEs as SIOCs was based on whether these SOEs were closely connected with SASAC itself and whether SASAC could easily control these SOEs.[164]

## VI. Remaining State Influence Through the Party Leadership in SOEs and POEs

All attempts to reform corporate governance of SOEs in China during the past three decades have upheld the fundamental principle of political leadership by the CCP.[165] According to China Securities Regulatory Commission (CSRC), listed companies must set up Party branches, regardless of ownership.[166] The participation of Party branches in corporate governance is subject to the Party rules adopted by the CCP Central Committee, rather than corporate law and regulations.[167] This section assess how the Party branches impact the decision-making process of companies to ensure the consistency of companies' investment plans with policies, such as the five-year plans, and the appreciation of the value of state-owned assets (in the case of SOEs).[168]

[162] State Council (n 153).

[163] Y Zheng and Y Huang, *Market in State: The Political Economy of Domination in China* (Cambridge, Cambridge University Press, 2018) 378–80.

[164] B Naughton, 'The Current Wave of State Enterprise Reform in China: A Preliminary Appraisal' (2017) 12 *Asian Economic Policy Review* 282.

[165] CPC and State Council (n 80); CPC, Decisions on Major Issues Concerning Comprehensively Deepening Reforms [《中共中央关于全面深化改革若干重大问题的决定》] (2013); Wang and Tan (n 40); Gordon and Milhaupt (n 120) 215–16; Zheng and Huang (n 163) 348.

[166] China Securities Regulatory Commission (CSRC), Listed Companies' Corporate Governance Rules [《上 市 公 司 治 理 准 则》] (2012, amended 2018) Art 5; C Cai, *The Rise of China and International Law* (Oxford, Oxford University Press, 2019) 220; Milhaupt, 'Chinese Corporate Capitalism' (n 25); J Wang, 'CEFC in the BRI for New Production of Oil and Gas' [《中国华信:深耕"一带一路"布局"油气新生"》] (2018) 1 *China Report* 60; J Garlick, 'China's Principal–Agent Problem in the Czech Republic' (2019) 17 *Asia Europe Journal* 437.

[167] Lin and Milhaupt (n 25); Brefort, Tenev and Zhang (n 46); B Tricker and G Li, *Understanding Corporate Governance in China* (Hong Kong, HKU Press, 2019) 205; Chen (n 121).

[168] CPC and SASAC, *Opinions on Implementing the Political Core Role of Party Branches of Central Enterprises* [《中央组织部、国务院国资委党委关于中央企业党委在现代企业制度下充分发挥政治核心作用的意见》] (2013); Wang (n 24); Wang and Tan (n 40); Keay and Zhao (n 43) 212–13.

## A. Political Leadership of the Party Over SOEs

Corporate law and regulations as well as Party rules require SOEs to specify the political leadership by Party branches in their Articles of Association.[169] The *Three-Year Action Plans of SOEs Reform (2020–2022)* (2020) highlighted again that the reform of SOEs would not abandon the political leadership by Party branches.[170] More specifically, the Party branches in SOEs guide the making of large-scale investments, according to the *Opinions on Fully Implementing the Political Core Role of Party Branches of Central Enterprises in Modern Enterprise System* (2013).[171] In energy investments, Party branches ensure that foreign energy investments satisfy energy policy interests.[172]

### i. *Influence on Investment Decision-Making*

Between 1978 and 1984, after companies were allowed to invest abroad, Party branches instructed directors or general managers of factories to make decisions.[173] Later, from 1984 to 1992, there was discussion at the central level regarding marginalising the function of the Party branches in business management.[174]

More recently, the CCP has maintained its political control over SOEs through the involvement of its representatives in making major decisions on the basis of the principle of 'collective decision-making'.[175] Since 2010, decisions on large investments (eg, capital-intensive energy projects) must be made in consultation with the Party representatives.[176] In other words, the board of directors must consult with the Party's representatives before approving the company's investment plans and making major investment decisions.[177] The review by Party branches focuses on the objective of the proposed project, the potential problems in operating the

[169] CPC, *Opinions on Improving the Party Building Work in Non State-Owned Enterprises (Trial Implementation)* [《关于加强和改进非公有制企业党的建设工作的意见(试行)》] (2012); CPC and SASAC, Notice on Promoting Integration of Party Building Work in SOEs' Articles of Association [《关于扎实推动国有企业党建工作要求写入公司章程的通知》] (2017); CSRC (n 166) Art 5; PRC Company Law (1993) (n 75) Art 19; CPC and State Council (n 80).

[170] CPC, *The Three-Year Implementation Plan for SOEs Reform* [《国企改革三年行动方案（2020–2022年）》] (2020).

[171] CPC and SASAC (n 168); Zhou, Gao and Bai (n 44).

[172] LW Lin, 'Balancing Closure and Openness: The Challenge of Leadership Reform in China's State-Owned Enterprises' in Liebman and Milhaupt (eds) (n 44) 133–54; Jiang (n 46) 396.

[173] Xi (n 41) 91–114; Brefort, Tenev and Zhang (n 46).

[174] Xi (n 41) 91–114.

[175] Zhang (n 36); H Yu, 'Reform of State-owned Enterprises in China' (2019) 43 *Asian Studies Review* 332, 347; Wang and Tan (n 40).

[176] CPC and State Council, Implementation of the Decision-Making Mechanism 'Three Majors, One Large' in SOEs [《推进国企贯彻落实"三重一大"决策制度的意见》] (2010); CPC and SASAC (n 168); Leutert (n 4).

[177] SASAC, Notice on Accelerating Integration of Party Branches Work in Corporate Governance [《关于加快推进中央企业党建工作总体要求纳入公司章程有关事项的通知》] (2017); CPC, Regulation on the Work of the Party Organisation of CPC (Trial Implementation) [《中国共产党党组工作条例（试行）》] (2015) Art 15; The China Institute of University of Alberta (n 42).

project and the responsibility of different parties.[178] Therefore, Party branches are able to ensure that overseas energy investments help to implement external energy security strategies and do not jeopardise China's national security and diplomatic interests.[179] For instance, in PetroChina and Sinopec Corp, the Party branches are authorised by the their Articles of Association to participate in the decision-making process of the board of directors.[180] Similarly, the Party secretary of State Grid has a say in the drafting of investment strategies.[181] The Articles of Association of Datang International Power authorise the Party branch to participate in the decision-making on investments.[182]

In principle, the decision-making process is supposed to be 'well-coordinated and balanced'.[183] In practice, conflicts are not unusual.[184] Central SOEs are sometimes reluctant to amend their Articles of Association, as they try to resist the Party's influence on corporate decision-making.[185] Furthermore, the Party branches have the ability to sideline the boards of directors to pursue policy interests through the prior-consultation procedure.[186] In these cases, the PRC Company Law does not provide remedies for shareholders or the company to allow them to initiate legal proceedings if Party branches implement national policies at the cost of profits.[187] Nevertheless, Chinese lawyers are of the opinion that the Party branches are not allowed to inappropriately intervene with investment-making in daily operations.[188]

The involvement of the Party branches in SOEs' decision-making may be partly justified by the state's objective of resolving the insider control problem and protecting state assets.[189] It is a long-existing problem in Chinese SOEs that top executives pursue their own economic interests rather than maximising corporate profits.[190] The Party branches in practice focus more on potential corruption and

[178] CPC and SASAC, *Strengthen and Improve Party Work of Central SOEs* [《中央组织部、国务院国资委党委关于加强和改进中央企业党建工作的意见》] (2004).

[179] Ø Tunsjø, *Security and Profit in China's Energy Policy: Hedging Against Risk* (New York, Columbia University Press, 2013) 48–49.

[180] PetroChina (n 82) Arts 8 and 105.

[181] Xu (n 138) 139.

[182] Zhou, Gao and Bai (n 44); Gordon and Milhaupt (n 120).

[183] State Council (n 78); CPC and State Council (n 176).

[184] J Hughes, 'China's Communist Party Writes Itself into Company Law' *Financial Times* (14 August 2017) at www.ft.com/content/a4b28218-80db-11e7-94e2-c5b903247afd.

[185] Milhaupt, 'The State as Owner' (n 25) 376; Wang and Tan (n 40); LYH Lin, 'Institutionalizing Political Influence in Business: Party-Building and Insider Control in Chinese State-Owned Enterprises' (2021) 45 *Vermont Law Review* 1, 32.

[186] Lin (n 185) 32.

[187] Zhang (n 36); Chen (n 121) 112.

[188] K Guo and D Hu, 'The Integration of Party Building Work of SOEs into the Article of Association' [《国企党建工作进章程——路径及机制分析》] (Zhong Lun Law Firm, 1 August 2017) at www.zhonglun.com/Content/2017/08-01/1843041618.html.

[189] Fu (n 152) 145–62; Lin (n 185) 8.

[190] See, eg, J Leng, *Corporate Governance and Financial Reform in China's Transition Economy* (Hong Kong, HKU Press, 2009) 48–49.

the impacts of investments on appreciating the value of state-owned assets.[191] In this way, the board of directors can retreat from short-term risky investments and preserve state-owned assets.[192] Therefore, the involvement of the Party branches in SOEs' decision-making can facilitate the orderly allocation of limited resources and address the inefficiencies of SOEs. As demonstrated by empirical research, the involvement of Party branches in decision-making does not necessarily reduce efficiency, especially in central SOEs.[193] Other empirical research also illustrates that the Party branches can help to mitigate potential business conflicts among directors and provide a perspective different from the economic one, thus constructing a scientific decision-making process.[194]

### *ii. Influence on Managerial Appointments*

The Party branches can also appoint top managers, who, in the case of large energy SOEs, hold the rank of vice-minister, to guide investment-making,[195] although central SOEs sometimes resist the inclusion of provisions on the Party's influence on personnel management in their Articles of Association.[196] The organisation department of the CCP appoints top executives in 52 central SOEs in strategic industries (eg, the energy industry).[197] Taking the position of top leadership of SOEs is often considered as 'one step up the career ladder in the Party'.[198] The potential promotion incentivises SOEs to comply with the instructions given by the Party branches.[199] When reviewing proposed foreign investments, directors appointed by the Party branches are expected to consider policy objectives.[200] Therefore, strategy committees under the board of directors, which are responsible for drafting investment plans, cannot draft investment plans based entirely on the need for corporate development.[201] When financial interests and state goals conflict, the career incentive regime strongly encourages SOEs to meet state

[191] See, eg, J Zhu, 'Reasons for Insisting, Strengthening and Improving the Party Leadership' [《深化国企改革为什么必须坚持、加强和改进党的领导》] (2015) 19 *Red Flag Manuscript* 9.

[192] Keay and Zhao (n 43) 212–13; Lin (n 185) 9.

[193] M Lai, 'An Analysis of the Investment Governance Effect of SOEs' Party Organization under the Situation of "Strict Administration of the Party"' [《从严治党情境下国有企业党组织的投资治理效应分析》] (2018) 4 *Business Analysis* 1.

[194] L Ma, Y Wang and X Shen, 'Research on Governance Effects of China's State-owned Companies' Party Organization – A Perspective Based on "Insiders Control"' [《中国国有企业党组织治理效应研究——基于"内部人控制"的视角》] (2012) 8 *China Industrial Economics* 82.

[195] State Council (n 78); CPC and State Council (n 176); CPC and SASAC (n 178); LW Lin and C Milhaupt, 'We Are National Champions: Understanding the Mechanisms of State Capitalism in China' (2013) 65 *Stanford Law Review* 697; Lin (n 172) 133–54.

[196] Lin (n 185) 32.

[197] Xu (n 138) 87–88; W Leutert, 'Challenges Ahead in China's Reform of State-Owned Enterprises' (2016) 21 *Asia Policy* 83; Z Chen and G Chen, 'The Changing Political Economy of Central State-Owned Oil Companies in China' [2019] *The Pacific Review* 1.

[198] Tunsjø (n 179) 41; Jiang (n 46) 393; KE Brødsgaard, 'Politics and Business Group Formation in China: The Party in Control?' (2012) 211 *The China Quarterly* 624, 637–38.

[199] Lin (n 24) 583.

[200] Zhu (n 93); Chen (n 121).

[201] Asian Corporate Governance Association (n 103) 52.

interests rather than the economic returns of private shareholders (if any).[202] However, good business performance, such as a greater say in the international energy market, is one of energy policy objectives. Therefore, top executives of energy SOEs can occasionally justify their resistance to political duties by arguing that they are helping the companies develop into 'world-class firms' now.[203]

In addition, cross-appointments between directors and members of Party branches facilitate the integration of the Party leadership into the decision-making of SOEs.[204] Members of the Party branches sit on the board of directors, the supervisory board and the management organs of energy companies.[205] Seven out of 10 directors of CNPC, for example, are members of the Party branches, as are three out of nine at Sinopec, six out of nine at State Grid, and nine out of 14 at CNOOC.[206] The chairmen of the boards are also the secretaries of the Party branches. Directors (or managers) who sit in the Party branches need to act upon the Party's instructions.[207]

Similar to the participation in decision-making, the Party involvement in appointing top executives of SOEs can also contribute to solving the problem of insider control and dealing with corruption.[208] Several empirical research studies have highlighted that the cross-appointment reduced agency costs to protect state assets.[209] They added that the board of directors performed their obligations better when the secretaries of the Party branches took the positions of deputy chairman, the chairman of the supervisory board or the general manager.[210]

## B. Political Leadership of the Party Over POEs

The Party branches have also been established in large POEs, which creates a potential channel for exerting state influence over their management and

[202] M Du, 'China's State Capitalism and World Trade Law' (2014) 64 *International and Comparative Law Quarterly* 403.

[203] CS Liou and CM Tsai, 'The Dual Role of Cadres and Entrepreneurs in China' (2017) 57 *Asian Survey* 1058; L Song, J Yang and Y Zhang, 'State-owned Enterprises' Outward Investment and the Structural Reform in China' (2011) 19 *China & World Economy* 38, 39; Y Jiang, 'Red Trojan Horses? A New Look at Chinese SOEs' Outward Investment' (2014) 2 *Journal of China and International Relations* 1.

[204] Wang (n 24); D Rosen, W Leutert and S Guo, *Missing Link: Corporate Governance in China's State Sector* (Asia Society, November 2018) 6.

[205] CPC and State Council (n 80).

[206] CNPC, 'Top Management' at www.cnpc.com.cn/cnpc/gltd/gltd_index.shtml#lyz; Sinopec, 'Leadership' at www.sinopecgroup.com/group/en/companyprofile/Leadership/; State Grid, 'Leadership' at www.sgcc.com.cn/html/sgcc_main/col2017011822/column_2017011822_1.shtml?childColumnId=2017011822; CNOOC, 'Leadership' at www.cnooc.com.cn/col/col6201/index.html.

[207] CPC and SASAC (n 178).

[208] Wang and Tan (n 40).

[209] Wang, Feng and Xu (n 38) 34–35; see also C Zhang, 'Do Party Branches of SOEs Conflict with the Modern Enterprise System?' [《国有企业党组织与现代企业制度冲突吗?》] (2019) 12 *Contemporary Economic Research* 42.

[210] Y Wang and L Ma, 'Can the Party Organization of China's State-owned Companies Reduce Agency Cost? A Perspective Based on "Insiders Control"' [《国有企业党组织能降低代理成本吗?——基于"内部人控制"的视角》] (2014) 26 *Management Review* 138.

investment decisions.[211] The secretaries of the Party branches exercise political control over POEs by participating in management meetings and communicating with top management, according to the *Improvement of Party Building Work in Non State-Owned Enterprises* (2012).[212] The secretaries of the Party branches in POEs are responsible for organising regular assemblies of Party members employed by the POEs, and providing assistance for the employees' association.[213] In practice, only a low percentage of POEs set up the Party organs.[214] Only one-quarter of the POEs examined include provisions on the involvement of the Party organs in decision making in their Articles of Association, and only around 16 per cent of POEs include provisions on the involvement of the Party organs in appointment in the Articles.[215] To secure corporate development, some POEs or joint ventures even voted against the amendment of their Articles to enable the Party branches to participate in the decision-making process or the appointment process.[216] This is possibly because, compared with SOEs, POEs' amendment of their Articles regarding the Party-building movement is more akin to a demonstration of loyalty to the CCP, rather than de facto institutionalising the role of the Party branches within the corporate governance.[217]

## VII. The Impact of the Strategic Nature of Energy on the Ownership Reform

The strategic nature of the energy sector limits the implementation of the ownership reform in energy SOEs.[218] The Chinese Government is less likely to sacrifice its control over SOEs engaged in strategic industries such as the energy industry.[219] In 2006, SASAC suggested that state capital should be invested in strategic industries, for example building infrastructure and developing mineral resources to foster international competitive champions.[220] In the same year, the former head

[211] E Francia, 'Chinese Corporate Law Developments and Go-Global Policy' (2020) 11 *Beijing Law Review* 184, 189; Lin (n 185) 4.

[212] CPC, *Improvement of Party Building Work in Non State-Owned Enterprises (Trial Implementation)* [《关于加强和改进非公有制企业党的建设工作的意见(试行)》] (2012).

[213] Asian Corporate Governance Association (n 103) 27.

[214] Q Wei and H Li, *Entities and Structures in the Embedding Process: A Sociological Analysis of Changes in the Government-enterprise Relations* (Singapore, Springer, 2019) 198.

[215] ibid.

[216] T Wei, J Clegg and L Ma, 'The Conscious and Unconscious Facilitating Role of The Chinese Government in Shaping the Internationalization of Chinese MNCs' (2015) 24 *International Business Review* 331; Lin (n 185) 24–25.

[217] Lin and Milhaupt (n 25); N Lardy, *Markets Over Mao: The Rise of Private Business in China* (Peterson Institute for International Economics, 2014) 120–21.

[218] Zhou, Gao and Bai (n 44).

[219] Yu (n 18) 344.

[220] SASAC, Promoting the Adjustment of State-owned Capital and the Reorganization of State-owned Enterprises [《国务院办公厅转发国资委关于推进国有资本调整和国有企业重组指导意见的通知》] (2006).

of SASAC emphasised that state capital should be used to acquire dominant shares of oil, gas and electricity companies and associated construction companies.[221]

In 2015, China aimed to classify SOEs in accordance with their business functions, and each set of SOEs is subject to different reform measures.[222] According to *the Guiding Opinions on Functional Definition and Classification of State-owned Enterprises* (2015), SOEs were classified as commercial SOEs and public-interest SOEs. Commercial SOEs the business of which concerns national security and economic development should focus on developing the future strategic industries, while public-interest SOEs should provide public goods and services.[223] Private investors can invest in commercial SOEs specialising in strategic business, such as petroleum, natural gas and the electricity grid, only when the state is the controlling shareholder, according to the CCP and the State Council.[224] Commercial SOEs engaging in natural monopoly business need to 'separate infrastructure networks from network operations and liberalize competitive business', and private actors can participate in the competitive business.[225] By actively attracting private capital, other commercial SOEs should advance corporate-style shareholding reform to boost the value of state-owned assets. However, the interviewees suggested that third-tier subsidiaries of group companies, rather than central energy companies themselves, were usually selected as experimental platforms for introducing private capital. State capital still has a significant influence over mixed-ownership companies after the reform. Furthermore, public-interest SOEs are allowed to remain wholly state-owned.[226]

The measure of SOEs' classification has two implications for the ownership reform of energy SOEs and thus for their global expansion. Although it has been suggested that most energy SOEs should be categorised as commercial SOEs,[227] they cannot pursue a high percentage of private capital. In other words, the ownership reform has limited salutary effects on diversifying the stakeholders of decision-making bodies of SOEs. Therefore, it is possible for the state to continue to exert an influence on energy state-controlled companies when they invest abroad. Furthermore, with both reforms, classifying SOEs and the energy industrial reform, competitive business, such as oil and gas exploration and power generation, gradually separated from business for the public good, such as the operation of grids or pipelines.[228] Investors with competitive business may be more commercially oriented in global energy expansion.

[221] 'SASAC: State-Owned Capital should Dominate Seven Key Industries' (The Central Government Website, 8 December 2006) at www.gov.cn/ztzl/2006-12/18/content_472256.htm.

[222] SASAC, MOF and NDRC, *Guiding Opinions on Functional Definition and Classification of State-owned Enterprises* [《关于国有企业功能界定与分类的指导意见》] (2015).

[223] ibid.

[224] CPC and State Council (n 80); Liu and Zhang (n 101) 10.

[225] SASAC, MOF and NDRC (n 222).

[226] ibid.

[227] H Guo, 'Adjustment Orientation and Key Points of China's Energy Policy in 2016' [《2016年中国能源政策调整方向及重点研判》] (2016) 24 *International Petroleum Economics* 1, 5.

[228] 'From Three Categories to Two Categories: Commercialization of the Petroleum and Power Sectors' [《央企分类方案终极版：三类变两类石油电力商业化》] *Finance* (17 December 2014) at www.yicai.com/news/4053368.html.

## VIII. Conclusion

A great number of scholars are of the opinion that China's companies, regardless of ownership, are instruments of the Chinese Government due to state control over corporate governance. Indeed, despite corporate reform and energy industrial reform, the Chinese state, through SASAC and the Party branches, continues to participate in the decision-making on overseas investments, and to appoint the senior management of companies. The strategic nature of energy also constrains the influence of private capital on the decision-making of state-controlled energy companies, because private shareholders are not allowed to acquire dominant shares in commercial SOEs involved in strategic business.

The internationally recommended practices governing the commercial activities of SOEs and SWFs allow the state to consolidate its ownership right in one administrative entity. In China, SASAC is a single ownership entity that exercises ownership rights and is accountable to the State Council, thus removing other ministries' claims to power over management of state-owned assets. Therefore, China's approach is consistent with the internationally recommended practices.

These internationally recommended practices governing commercial activities of SOEs and SWFs also recognise that the day-to-day operational autonomy of the board of directors should be guaranteed. However, the roles of SASAC (for SOEs only) and the Party (for both SOEs and private enterprises) limit the autonomy of the board of directors in the making of individual investment decisions. SASAC's dual roles as a regulator and the state shareholder far exceed what is provided for in the *OECD Guidelines*, despite the reform separating ownership from administration by establishing SIOCs. At the same time, the Party rules adopted by the CCP enable the Party branches to influence investment decisions in both energy SOEs and POEs. The Party influence remains a key characteristic of China's economic and political system, particularly in the strategically important energy sector. Regarding the precise extent of the Party's influence on decision-making on overseas energy investments, more research into the political bargaining between companies and the CCP is required, which is beyond the scope of a regulatory analysis.

# 7

# Case Studies of China's Foreign Energy Projects

## I. Introduction

The deregulation of outbound investments and SOE reform should in principle increase the investment-making autonomy of Chinese energy companies. Indeed, China's energy companies claim to assess the profitability of projects before making investment decisions.[1] For instance, Sinopec is obliged to make profits and increase the value of state-owned assets.[2] The Sinopec Corp, the listed subsidiary of Sinopec, needs to be accountable to its shareholders and secure business interests.[3] Similarly, CNPC has the goal of growing into 'a first-class integrated international energy company with enhanced competitiveness and profitability'.[4] PetroChina, the listed subsidiary of CNPC, aims to adapt itself to the international energy market, develop a suitable business model and 'use its best endeavours to maximise its profits'.[5] The China National Offshore Oil Corporation has also committed to internationalising its business to achieve increased oil and gas cooperation around the world.[6] In the power sector, the ultimate goal of State Grid is to develop into a first-class energy networks company with global competitiveness.[7]

Given these claims, this chapter discusses whether, in practice, China's energy companies have pursued commercial interests in the operation of their foreign projects. It presents cases of oil, gas and power projects invested in by China's SOEs

[1] Z Zhang, 'The Overseas Acquisitions and Equity Oil Shares of Chinese National Oil Companies: A Threat to The West but A Boost to China's Energy Security?' (2012) 48 *Energy Policy* 698.
[2] About Sinopec Group at www.sinopecgroup.com/group/en/companyprofile/AboutSinopecGroup/.
[3] Sinopec Corp, Articles of Association of Sinopec Corp [《中石化股份公司章程》] Art 12.
[4] CNPC, 'Our Goal' at www.cnpc.com.cn/en/ourgoal/about_common.shtml.
[5] PetroChina, Articles of Association of PetroChina Limited, Art 10 at www.petrochina.com.cn/ptr/gsgg/202006/129f0c18a231464198621cff89d9109a/files/1e74805ea9c14f168ef1bc5fe140ca54.pdf.
[6] 'Words Delivered by the Secretary of the Party Organization and the Board of Directors' [《党组书记、董事长致辞》] at www.cnooc.com.cn/col/col19761/index.html.
[7] State Grid, 'About Us' at www.sgcc.com.cn/html/sgcc_main/col2017012538/column_2017012538_1.shtml?childColumnId=2017012538; YC Xu, *Sinews of Power: Politics of the State Grid Corporation of China* (Oxford, Oxford University Press, 2016) 268.

and POEs.[8] It is necessary to distinguish oil and gas projects from power projects, because power projects play a less important role in securing China's external energy supply: electricity investments can hardly realise the energy policy goal of diversifying suppliers and routes. Will these electricity projects be more commercially oriented? To facilitate the discussion, I have mainly selected projects that were directly prioritised in energy policies (eg, cross-border pipelines), projects that the Chinese Government got directly involved in, and projects that impact the implementation of external energy strategies such as those exporting equipment, services and products. These cases are drawn from the literature on China's external energy security and media reports.

By looking at the pursuit of state interests and commercial interests in overseas energy projects, this chapter finds that it is sometimes extremely hard for the Chinese Government to influence foreign projects through the implementation of domestic regulations, even when the Government exerted tight control over outbound investments at the early stages of China's global energy expansion. Additionally, it is arguable that China's energy companies are sometimes competent enough to persuade the Government to support the operation of their foreign projects. The discussion of the interaction between energy companies and the Chinese Government in different types of energy projects has theoretical importance, since legal scholars pay little attention to the implementation of China's investment-related policies or regulations in practice.[9]

The following sections assess how the state interests interact with companies' interests in oil and gas projects (section II) and electricity projects (section III). Finally, section IV summarises and discusses the implications.

## II. Oil and Gas Investments

By examining the rationales behind oil and gas projects, this section establishes that it was possible for China's oil companies to pursue corporate development in their overseas investments. China's NOCs sometimes pursued their commercial interests in projects endorsed in energy policies, or sometimes maintained their commercial interests at the cost of state interests. The non-compliance of NOCs with state orders occurred even when the Government exercised tight control over the management of outbound energy investments. Regulatory relaxation rather played the role of enabling NOCs to adopt a streamlined process for making investments.

[8] L Corkin, 'Redefining Foreign Policy Impulses toward Africa: The Roles of the MFA, the MOFCOM and China Exim Bank' (2011) 40 *Journal of Current Chinese Affairs* 61, 75.

[9] See, eg, K Sauvant and M Nolan, 'China's Outward Foreign Direct Investment and International Investment Law' (2015) 18 *Journal of International Economic Law* 893.

## A. Projects Endorsed in Energy Policies

### *i. China–Kazakh Oil Pipeline*

An agreement was signed by CNPC and KMG to build the China–Kazakh crude oil pipeline in 2004.[10] Phase I was completed in December 2005.[11] The construction of the first stage of Phase II was completed in 2009[12] and the construction of its second stage began in 2012.[13] Later, CNPC and KMG agreed to expand the capacity of the pipeline in 2013.[14]

The China–Kazakh oil pipeline was included in energy five-year plans to realise the policy goals of diversifying oil supply routes and boosting economic development in Xinjiang, as well as the possible goal of exerting a strategic influence on Central Asia.[15] First, Kazakhstan is a crucial supplier of oil to China.[16] This pipeline represents a new oil-export corridor to China, starting from Kazakhstan's oil-rich Caspian basin.[17] Importing oil from Kazakhstan can reduce China's reliance on the Middle East, given the political instability of that region.[18] Apart from diversifying transportation routes, this pipeline also connects CNPC's previously acquired oil fields. Therefore, the Kazakh subsidiary of CNPC can transport oil back to China.[19]

Second, by leveraging this pipeline, Beijing can boost the economic development of Northwestern China.[20] Xinjiang links the energy-starved coastal cities with the oil supplier – Kazakhstan.[21] Capitalising on its position on the linking point, Xinjiang is expected to offer downstream services covering refining, chemical products, storage, engineering and technology.[22] For example, the Dushanzi

[10] CNPC, 'CNPC in Kazakhstan' at www.cnpc.com.cn/cnpc/Kazakhstan/country_index.shtml.

[11] ibid.

[12] O Auyezov, 'Kazakhstan expands China oil pipeline link' *Reuters* (1 July 2009) at www.reuters.com/article/kazakhstan-china-pipeline/kazakhstan-expands-china-oil-pipeline-link-idUSL17937520090701.

[13] KazTransOil, 'Investment Projects: Kazakh-China Project' at www.kaztransoil.kz/en/about_the_company/investment_projects/.

[14] CNPC (n 10).

[15] Ø Tunsjø, *Security and Profit in China's Energy Policy: Hedging Against Risk* (New York, Columbia University Press, 2013); B Cole, *China's Quest for Great Power: Ships, Oil, and Foreign Policy* (Annapolis, MD, Naval Institute Press, 2016).

[16] F Fazilov and X Chen, 'China and Central Asia: A Significant New Energy Nexus' [2013] (April– May) *The European Financial Review* 38.

[17] M Ögütçü, 'Kazakhstan's Expanding Cross-Border Gas Links: Implications for Europe, Russia, China and other CIS countries' (2006) 17 *Centre for Energy, Petroleum and Mineral Law and Policy Journal* 1.

[18] A Kotfis, 'China's Energy Policy towards Central Asia and Russia' in E Trojnar and Ł Gacek (eds), *China at the Beginning of the 21st Century* (Cambridge, Cambridge University Press, 2014) 87–96.

[19] F Aminjonov et al, 'BRI in Central Asia' (2019) 22 *Central Asia Regional Data Review* 1.

[20] U Suleimen, 'Energy Cooperation between Kazakhstan and China' *The Astana Times* (15 January 2014); JX Liao, 'A Silk Road for Oil: Sino-Kazakh Energy Diplomacy' (2006) 12 *Brown Journal of World Affairs* 39.

[21] S Peyrouse, 'Chinese Economic Presence in Kazakhstan' (2008) 3 *China Perspective* 34, 46.

[22] D Liu, K Yamaguchib and H Yoshikawa, 'Understanding the Motivations behind the Myanmar–China Energy Pipeline: Multiple Streams and Energy Politics in China' (2017) 107 *Energy Policy* 403.

refinery of PetroChina received the first oil flow from Kazakhstan in 2006 and transported its refined products to eastern China.[23] Transforming the economic structure of Xinjiang can reduce regional economic disparities.[24]

Finally, successfully operating the China–Kazakh oil pipeline had signal impacts on the member states of the Shanghai Cooperation Organisation (SCO), and would thus facilitate China's future energy cooperation with Central Asian states.[25] This project has enabled Kazakhstan to divert part of its oil exports from Russia to China, thus helping guarantee the export security of Kazakhstan.[26] Other Central Asian resource-rich states might welcome China's investments to diversify buyers of their oil and gas.

However, this pipeline is not just about realising government goals.[27] The realisation of this project was pushed forward by CNPC without clear policy guidance because the timeline of the project suggests that policy guidance lagged behind progress on the project. Only Phase II (the second stage) was listed as a key construction project in *The 12th Energy Development Five-Year Plan* (2013).[28] The maintenance and upgrading of pipelines started before 2016, while the guidance on maintenance and expansion was not endorsed by policymakers until *The 13th Energy Development Five-Year Plan* (2016) was issued.[29] The Corporation was concerned about profitability of this project, given the insufficient production to fill this pipeline.[30] It did not revive this project until Kazakhstan increased its oil production at the beginning of twenty-first century.[31] Subsequently, CNPC International sold part of its oil equity from Kazakhstan on the international market to make a profit.[32]

Accordingly, although projects endorsed in energy policies can help to implement the Government's external energy strategy, they are not necessarily entirely strategic investments. Given the increasing oil production, CNPC restarted the project's profit-making operation before the pipeline was endorsed in the energy development five-year plans. This implies that China's NOCs were more commercially driven than the world expected when making investment decisions.[33]

[23] CNPC, 'Crude Oil Imports Reach PetroChina Dushanzi Refinery via China-Kazakhstan Pipeline' at www.petrochina.com.cn/enpetrochina/xwxx/201404/97e1c4e34a3c49b09629bfd670c171d4.shtml.

[24] A Erickson and G Collins, 'China's Oil Security Pipe Dream' (2010) 63 *Naval War College Review* 89.

[25] Suleimen (n 20).

[26] Aminjonov et al (n 19).

[27] D Yergin et al, 'Fueling Asia's Recovery' (1998) 77 *Foreign Affairs* 34.

[28] NDRC, *The 12th Energy Development Five-Year Plan* [《能源发展"十二五"规划的通知》] (2013).

[29] NDRC and NEA, *The 13th Energy Five-Year Plan* [《十三五能源规划》] (2016).

[30] S Peyrouse, 'The Economic Aspects of the Chinese–Central Asia Rapprochement', Silk Road Paper (Central Asia–Caucasus Institute & Silk Road Studies Program, 2007); T Marketos, *China's Energy Geopolitics: The Shanghai Cooperation Organization and Central Asia* (London, Routledge, 2009) 103.

[31] E Downs, *Energy Security Series: China* (The Brookings Foreign Policy Studies, December 2006) 33.

[32] Zhang (n 1); L Yao, 'Looking into Energy Security Through The Lens Of The Belt And Road Initiative: Can China Achieve A More Secure Energy Future' in JC Liow, H Liu and X Gong (eds), *Research Handbook on the Belt and Road Initiative* (Cheltenham, Edward Elgar, 2021) 54–64, 60.

[33] Yao (n 32).

## *ii. China–Myanmar Oil and Gas Pipelines*

Oil and gas pipelines run in parallel in Myanmar. They start near Kyaukpyu, enter the border city, Ruili, in Yunnan province, and then stretch further to Chongqing and the Guangxi autonomous region.[34] Scholars at Yunnan University proposed the construction of the China–Myanmar Pipeline in 2004.[35] This proposal was later supported by the local government and came before the central Government in 2006.[36] The Chinese Government and the Government of Myanmar signed the Cooperation Agreement on China–Myanmar Oil and Gas Pipelines Projects between the People's Republic of China and the Republic of the Union of Myanmar in 2009.[37] This Agreement provided that CNPC was to be responsible for the design, construction, operation, expansion and maintenance of the pipelines.[38] Construction started in 2010.[39] The gas pipeline entered into operation in 2013.[40] The oil pipeline entered into operation in 2015.[41] However, the China–Myanmar oil and gas pipelines were not listed as key projects in five-year plans for energy development until 2013.[42]

The aims of CNPC were to reduce the cost of providing oil to the domestic market and strengthen its power in the competition with Sinopec for more shares of the refining business. Oil transportation through this overland project to south-western refineries was cheaper than sea shipping at the time when it was under consideration.[43] By realising this project, CNPC fought to expand its shares of the domestic oil and gas markets as well.[44] It has operated for many years in the oil and gas fields of Myanmar, and developed the strategy of building a refinery near Yunnan to access south-western downstream markets.[45]

In addition to CNPC's corporate interests, the construction of the China–Myanmar oil and gas pipelines illustrates how to realise the policy objectives of diversifying energy supply and minimising disparities in regional economic

[34] S Cao and J Shan, 'Sino-Myanmar Oil Pipeline Launch a Good Signal: Experts' *Global Times* (28 March 2017) at www.globaltimes.cn/content/1039861.shtml.

[35] Erickson and Collins (n 24).

[36] Tunsjø (n 15).

[37] Cooperation Agreement on China–Myanmar Oil and Gas Pipelines Projects between the People's Republic of China and the Republic of the Union of Myanmar [《中华人民共和国政府与缅甸联邦政府关于中缅油气管道项目的合作协议》] (2009).

[38] ibid.

[39] Overseas Business of CNPC, 'CNPC in Myanmar' [《中国石油在缅甸》] at www.cnpc.com.cn/cnpc/Myanmar/country_index.shtml.

[40] Cao and Shan (n 34).

[41] ibid.

[42] State Council, *The 12th Energy Development Five-Year Plan* [《国务院关于印发能源发展"十二五"规划的通知》](2013).

[43] Liu, Yamaguchib and Yoshikawa (n 22); D Zha, *Oil Pipeline from Myanmar to China: Competing Perspectives* (RSIS report, 24 July 2009) at www.rsis.edu.sg/wp-content/uploads/2014/07/CO09074.pdf; Erickson and Collins (n 24).

[44] Tunsjø (n 15).

[45] See also X Li, *China's Outward Foreign Investment: A Political Perspective* (Landham, University Press of America, 2010) 164–65.

development, as well as the possible strategic goal of influencing Southeast and South Asia. First, the potential contribution of the pipeline to China's stable energy supply persuaded the CDB to finance this project.[46] This land-based pipeline project reduces the need to transport oil and gas through the Malacca Strait,[47] and enables China to access oil and gas fields in Myanmar.[48] Second, developing the petroleum chemical industry can boost the economic development of Southwest China.[49] By operating this pipeline, the provincial government of Yunnan decided to transform the province into an 'oil refining base in Southwest China',[50] and transported refined products to other provinces and even back to Southeast Asia.[51] Third, the geographical location of Yunnan provides an opportunity for China to strengthen its economic links with South Asia and Southeast Asia.[52] Not only can Yunnan transport refined products back to South Asia and Southeast Asia,[53] but also existing cross-border gas pipelines among ASEAN states may be extended into China through the China–Myanmar gas pipeline to further link Southwest China with Southeast Asia and South Asia.[54] The consequent energy interdependence is likely to enable China to solidify its economic relations with these two regions and spread its strategic influence into them.[55]

In summary, the construction of the China–Myanmar oil and gas pipelines implies that China's NOCs were able to seek commercial interests despite the pursuit of state interests. After exchanging assets with Sinopec in the energy industrial reform, CNPC was eager to enhance their competitiveness. This driver might explain why CNPC pushed forward this project for seeking shares of the downstream market in Southwest China. In addition, to pursue commercial interests, NOCs are willing to meet state interests (eg, stable oil and gas supplies and the economic development of Southwest China) in their proposed investments in order to obtain state support. As discussed in chapters five and six, before

[46] E Downs, *China Development Bank's Oil Loans: Pursuing Policy and Profit* (Brookings, 9 December 2011) at www.brookings.edu/articles/china-development-banks-oil-loans-pursuing-policy-and-profit/.

[47] P Andrews-Speed, M Qiu and C Len, 'Chinese Engagement in Southeast Asian Energy and Mineral Resources: Motivations and Outlook' (2016) 57 *Eurasian Geography and Economics* 316, 330–31; T Ptaka and D Hommel, 'The Trans-Political Nature of Southwest China's Energy Conduit, Yunnan Province' (2016) 21 *Geopolitics* 556; see also J Jiang and J Sinton, *Overseas Investments by Chinese Multinational Oil Companies* (IEA, 2011); AR Malik, 'An Analysis of the China-Pakistan Economic Corridor (CPEC) and Its Prospects' in L Wang and J Zhao (eds), *The Belt and Road Initiative in the Global Context* (Singapore, World Scientific Publishing, 2019) 99–109.

[48] H Zhao, 'China–Myanmar Energy Cooperation and Its Regional Implications' (2011) 30 *Journal of Current Southeast Asian Affairs* 89.

[49] Y Zhu, 'Analysis of Importance of Building China-Myanmar Oil and Gas Pipelines to China' [《中缅油气管道对我国能源安全的重要意义分析》] (2017) 16 *China Management Informationization* 115; R Zhang, 'To suspend Or Not to Suspend: A Cost–Benefit Analysis of Three Chinese Mega-Projects in Myanmar' [2020] *The Pacific Review* 1, 17.

[50] Liu, Yamaguchib and Yoshikawa (n 22).

[51] Zhao (n 49).

[52] Malik (n 47); See Ptaka and Hommel (n 47).

[53] Ptaka and Hommel (n 47).

[54] Liu, Yamaguchib and Yoshikawa (n 22).

[55] Malik (n 47).

submitting an application to NDRC, NOCs usually communicate with SASAC when devising investment plans and enter into discussions with NDRC officials. On these two occasions, it is arguable that CNPC explained to the Government how the construction of the oil and gas pipelines could help the state meet national interests as identified above, to compete for state support (eg, the financing provided by CDB) and endorsement. After so much project progress, the ultimate endorsement of this project in *The 12th Energy Development Five-Year Plan* (2013) may be viewed as CNPC's continuing efforts to influence policy-making.

### *iii. China–Central Asia Gas Pipeline*

The China–Central Asia gas pipeline, construction of which was contracted for by CNPC, starts at the Turkmen–Uzbek border city of Gedaim, passes through central Uzbekistan and southern Kazakhstan, and ends at Xinjiang.[56] Lines A and B were in operation in 2009 and 2010 respectively.[57] Line C became operational in 2014.[58] The construction of the Tajikistan section of Line D started in September 2014.[59] However, the Uzbekistan section and the Kyrgyzstan section were suspended in early 2016.[60] Tajikistan resumed construction in 2018.[61] The part from Tajikistan to China was supposed to be operational in 2020.[62] However, in practice, the final completion date has not yet been disclosed.[63] The postponement of the construction of Line D is possibly due to disagreement between Uzbekistan and upstream states,[64] rather than bargaining between CNPC and the central Government.

There were debates about the commercial nature of the China–Central Asia gas pipeline. Tunsjø questioned the economic viability of this pipeline and characterised it as a more politically-oriented project, because the construction cost was extremely high[65] and the fixed import price might be higher than the import

[56] Cole (n 15) 150.

[57] CNPC, 'Central Asia–China Gas Pipeline' at www.cnpc.com.cn/en/CentralAsia/CentralAsia_index.shtml.

[58] CNPC, 'CNPC in Uzbekistan' at www.cnpc.com.cn/cnpc/Uzbekistan/country_index.shtml; see also CNPC (n 10).

[59] CNPC, 'Flow of Natural Gas from Central Asia' at www.cnpc.com.cn/en/FlowofnaturalgasfromCentralAsia/FlowofnaturalgasfromCentralAsia2.shtml.

[60] C Michel, 'Line D of the Central Asia-China Gas Pipeline Delayed' *The Diplomat* (31 May 2016) at thediplomat.com/2016/05/line-d-of-the-central-asia-china-gas-pipeline-delayed/.

[61] B Pannier, 'Tajik Claim of Pipeline Progress is Welcome News in Turkmenistan' *RadioFreeEurope* (31 January 2020) at www.rferl.org/a/tajik-claim-of-pipeline-progress-is-welcome-news-in-turkmenistan/30410670.html; 'Tajikistan Resumes Building Turkmenistan-China Pipeline' *eurasianet* (31 January 2018) at eurasianet.org/tajikistan-resumes-building-turkmenistan-china-pipeline.

[62] 'Construction of an additional line of the Central Asia-China gas pipeline completes' *Media-Turkmen* (30 January 2020) at orient.tm/en/construction-of-an-additional-line-of-the-central-asia-china-gas-pipeline-completes.

[63] F Aminjonov and O Dovgalyuk, 'Central Asia–China Gas Pipeline (Line D)' *The People's Map* (February 2023) at thepeoplesmap.net/project/central-asia-china-gas-pipeline-line-d.

[64] ibid.

[65] Tunsjø (n 15) 174–76.

price in the international petroleum spot market.[66] However, for Vermeer, CNPC considered profitability in this project, and decided to pursue the project because piped gas was cheaper than imported LNG at that time.[67]

This project met government interests. Helping to realise energy policy goals of a stable energy supply explained why China's energy policymakers prioritised the project in the five-year plans for energy development. This pipeline can directly meet the gas needs of north-western provinces[68] and transport gas to the middle and east of China.[69] Additionally, by relying on this pipeline, China can access rich gas reserves in the Caspian Basin.[70] Given this, during the construction of Line C, it was listed as a key project in *The 12th Energy Five-Year Plan* (2013).[71] In particular, Line D will allow China to minimise its reliance on gas supplies from Kazakhstan and to strengthen its bargaining power against Kazakhstan, as most of China's current oil and gas transmission routes in Central Asia bypass the Kazakh territory.[72] Therefore, Line D was listed as a key project in *The 13th Energy Development Five-Year Plan* (2016).[73]

China was also likely to realise the strategic goal of exerting a strategic influence over Central Asia.[74] Line D will connect Tajikistan and Kyrgyzstan, both of which lack oil and gas resources, to the China–Central Asia gas pipeline.[75] Therefore, China's infrastructure investments will help to alleviate the energy needs of these two states, thus providing an example of how China's energy investments will benefit the development of host states. In addition to winning political support from Central Asian states, China is likely to break the 'monopolistic power of Russia over gas exports' in Central Asia.[76] Kazakhstan, Uzbekistan and Turkmenistan are more willing to export gas to China because they sell gas

[66] ibid.

[67] E Vermeer, 'The Global Expansion of Chinese Oil Companies: Political Demands, Profitability and Risks' (2015) 29 *China Information* 3, 4.

[68] E Koolaee and M Tishehyar, 'China's Energy Security Approach in Central Asia' paper presented at *Silk Route and Eurasia: Peace & Cooperation*, Conference of Globalisation and Eurasian Peace in Kashmir (October 2011).

[69] L Zhang, 'The Great International Strategic Significance of Constructing Energy Corridor on Land in Northwest China' [《中国西北陆路能源通道构建的重大国际战略意义》] (2013) 3 *Northeast Asia Forum* 108.

[70] Cole (n 15) 150.

[71] NDRC (n 28).

[72] Aminjonov and Dovgalyuk (n 63).

[73] NDRC and NEA (n 29).

[74] T Miller, *China's Asian Dream*, 2nd edn (London, Zedbooks, 2019) 74–75; M Tukmadiyeva, 'Xinjiang in China's Foreign Policy toward Central Asia' (2013) 12 *Connections* 87; S Yilmaz and O Daksueva, 'The Energy Nexus in China– Russia Strategic Partnership' (2019) 19 *International Relations of the Asia-Pacific* 63, 74–75.

[75] Q Liu and X Wang, 'The Shaping Effect of the Belt and Road Initiative on China's International Oil and Gas Cooperation Strategy' (2020) 13 *International Relations* 20, 25.

[76] Aminjonov et al (n 19).

to Gazprom at below-market prices.[77] CNPC's increasing role in Central Asia's upstream and distribution networks may also threaten Gazprom's position in Central Asia.[78]

In sum, the China–Central Asia gas pipeline is more like a state-driven project for pursuing government interests, since the commercial viability of the project largely remained uncertain based on the little information available. This project could at least realise the energy policy objectives of diversifying gas suppliers and strengthening energy cooperation with Central Asian states. However, the construction of Line D was not completed during the implementation of *The 13th Energy Development Five-Year Plan* (2016) because of the suspension initiated by Uzbekistan. It means that the delay in realising projects endorsed in energy policies cannot always be laid at the door of NOCs' pursuit of commercial interests.

### *iv. Power of Siberia Gas Pipeline*

China and Russia achieved political consensus in 2011 on building a gas pipeline from Siberia to China.[79] In May 2014, Gazprom and CNPC finalised the 30-year gas deal for the Power of Siberia pipeline.[80] Within Russian territory, the construction of the first 80 kilometres of the pipeline began in 2015, the remaining 35 kilometres getting underway in 2016.[81] China started the construction of its domestic section in 2015. However, the construction was interrupted because of the ambiguous and changing attitudes of Russia (eg, the anti-monopoly issues in Russia),[82] which is similar to the slow progress of the construction of Line D of China–Central Asia gas pipeline (see section II.A.iii).

The construction of the Power of Siberia gas pipeline implies that commercial viability and the pursuit of state interests are not mutually exclusive. This project made economic sense because the agreed price level was on China's terms and far lower than Russia had first proposed.[83] The construction of the Power of Siberia gas pipeline, listed as a key project in both *The 12th Energy Development*

[77] Miller (n 74) 74–75.

[78] A Cooley, *The Emerging Political Economy of OBOR* (Centre for Strategic and International Studies, October 2016).

[79] A Belyi, 'Russia's Gas Export Reorientation from West to East: Economic and Political Considerations' (2015) 8 *Journal of World Energy Law & Business* 76, 79.

[80] T Røseth, 'Russia's Energy Relations with China: Passing the Strategic Threshold?' (2017) 58 *Eurasian Geography and Economics* 23, 40.

[81] ibid 40.

[82] 'China and Russia Signed the Complementary Agreement of Gas Sales: A Reshape of Global Energy Sector' [《中俄签署天然气购销补充协议，"双头鹰"向东重塑全球能源格局》] *Huaxia Energy* (8 September 2022) at www.hxny.com/nd-77047-0-8.html.

[83] Belyi (n 79) 80; M Bradshaw and A Waterworth, 'China's Dash for Gas: Local Challenges and Global Consequences' (2020) 61 *Eurasian Geography and Economics* 266, 287.

*Five-Year Plan* (2013) and *The 13th Energy Development Five-Year Plan* (2016),[84] was perceived as providing another land-based gas transportation route, in addition to LNG imports by sea.[85]

## B. Projects Involving the Chinese Government

### *i. CNPC's Early Global Expansion in Sudan*

Africa is an important investment destination in CNPC's investment plan, given Africa's rich energy resources and the long-term China–Africa relationship.[86] Representatives were delegated by CNPC to conduct geological explorations in Sudan's oil fields in 1994,[87] and to present a report on investment feasibility to NDRC and MOFCOM.[88] The then Sudanese President Bashir visited China in 1995 and invited China's oil companies to participate in oil exploration in Sudan.[89] Facilitated by both Governments, CNPC officially launched China–Sudan oil cooperation in 1995 by concluding the Products Sharing Agreement of Developing Block 6 in the Muglad Basin.[90]

Despite its facilitation by the Chinese Government, there was not sufficient endorsement of this project by the Government. First, the final official endorsement of CNPC's investments in Sudan was not made until 1997, which was three years after CNPCs' geological explorations.[91] Second, Yongkang Zhou attended the oil-production ceremony in 1999 only as a representative of the domestic petroleum sector rather than as a high-level official.[92] A possible reason for the low level of government endorsement is that the Chinese Government had little national interest in early overseas energy projects in the early 1990s.[93] The empirical research conducted by Buckley and others supports this explanation, because resource-seeking was not a significant driver of the global expansion during the

[84] NDRC (n 28); NDRC and NEA (n 29).

[85] Bradshaw and Waterworth (n 83) 286.

[86] C Zhang, 'China's Energy Diplomacy in Africa' in C Dent (ed), *China and Africa Development Relations* (London, Routledge, 2010) 143–62.

[87] L Jiang and J Xiao, 'Reflection on the Cooperative Path of CNPC and Sudan' [《中石油苏丹之路的回顾和反思》] *Aisixiang* (13 March 2014) at www.aisixiang.com/data/72966.html; The Open University, 'Timeline for China and Sudan Oil' at www.open.edu/openlearn/ocw/pluginfile.php/1421200/mod_resource/content/2/ca_1_timeline.pdf.

[88] Overseas Business of CNPC, 'Report of CNPC in Sudan' [《中国石油在苏丹》] at csr.cnpc.com.cn/cnpccsr/xhtml/PageAssets/sdbg_cn.pdf.

[89] L Jiang and J Xiao, 'China's Oil Diplomacy towards Sudan: The State-Enterprise Roles Analysis' [《中国对苏丹的石油外交:政企角色研究》] (2011) 5 *Arab World Studies* 40.

[90] Embassy of PRC in Sudan 'Important Cooperative Projects between China and Sudan' [《中国石油苏丹项目》] (3 September 2019) at sd.china-embassy.gov.cn/jmwl/201909/t20190907_6756289.htm.

[91] Jiang and Xiao (n 89).

[92] ibid.

[93] L Patey, 'Learning in Africa: China's Overseas Oil Investments in Sudan and South Sudan' (2017) 26 *Journal of Contemporary China* 756.

period from 1991 to 1998.[94] China's leadership paid more attention to oil cooperation after 2000, and visited oil projects during state visits between 2000 and 2009,[95] but the Chinese Government had little interest in CNPC's early expansion in Sudan.

The realisation of this project was mainly driven by CNPC's desire to invest abroad for the company's survival.[96] The Corporation had suffered substantial losses, as its production costs were higher than the state-set oil price.[97] Downs recorded that CNPC 'began to set its sights beyond China's borders in the late 1980s in search of reserves and profits'.[98] The Corporation was eager to sell oil in the global market at a price higher than the domestic set-oil price.[99] Therefore, in pursuing this project, CNPC was similar to other international oil companies, as it viewed internationalisation as a key solution to the problem of a slow-down in domestic production and price controls.

In view of the few state interests involved and CNPC's pursuit of corporate development, the company's early expansion to Sudan was mainly commercially oriented. In other words, to achieve corporate development, a big NOC like CNPC sometimes did not wait for the government endorsement by going through the approval procedure, despite the tight regulatory control before 2000.

### *ii. The Competition between Subsidiaries of CNPC and Sinopec in Sudan*

In 2003, the overseas engineering subsidiary of CNPC competed with Sinopec International Petroleum Service Corp (SIPSC) in the bidding for the pipeline project involving Block 3 and Block 7 in Sudan.[100] The Chinese Government aimed to reduce competition between the overseas subsidiary of CNPC and SIPSC in the overseas bidding process, to preserve state energy assets and to persuade the companies to invest in different parts of world.[101] The MFA notified MOFCOM about the competition. MOFCOM then authorised the China International

[94] P Buckley et al, 'Explaining China's Outward FDI: An Institutional Perspective' in K Sauvant, K Mendoza and I Irmak (eds), *The Rise of Transnational Corporations from Emerging Markets: Threats or Opportunities?* (Cheltenham, Edward Elgar Publishing 2008) 107–57, 132–33.

[95] Jiang and Xiao (n 87).

[96] R Li and GCK Leung, 'The Integration of China into the World Crude Oil Market Since 1998' (2011) 39 *Energy Policy* 5159, 5161–62; P Vasquez, 'China's Oil and Gas Footprint in Latin America and Africa' (2019) 11 *International Development Policy* 1; X Xu, *Chinese NOCs' Overseas Strategies: Background, Comparison and Remarks* (The James A Baker III Institute for Public Policy, 2007).

[97] E Downs, 'Who's Afraid of China's Oil Companies?' in C Pascual and J Elkind (eds), *Energy Security: Economics, Politics, Strategies, and Implications* (Washington, DC, Brookings Institution Press, 2010) 73–102, 79.

[98] Downs (n 31) 38.

[99] Zhang (n 86).

[100] J Meckling, B Kong and T Madan, 'Oil and State Capitalism: Government–Firm Cooperation in China and India' (2015) 22 *Review of International Political Economy* 1159, 1172.

[101] 'The Overseas War Between China's Two Oil Giants' [《"中国两大石油巨头海外打响遭遇战"》] *NewsSina* (28 June 2004) at news.sina.com.cn/w/2004-06-28/09422927201s.shtml.

Contractor Association (CHINCA) to establish a dialogue between the subsidiary of CNPC and SIPSC, urging them to conclude a cooperation agreement.[102] CHINCA made no progress because it did not have official standing.[103] The state coordination of this project was rejected by SIPSC, which outbid the subsidiary of CNPC in 2004.[104]

This project chiefly suggests that SOEs' pursuit of corporate development could sometimes override state coordination. Its unwillingness to accept the state coordination of the project was justified by SIPSC as being driven by the need to secure business interests in exporting construction services in the upstream sector.[105] As the investment proposals of overseas subsidiaries should be approved by the parent company, the decision made by SIPSC was assumed to be supported by Sinopec.[106] The vice-president of the parent company – Sinopec – confirmed that the subsidiary was not involved in a vicious bidding war with the subsidiary of CNPC but complied with international practice when placing its bid.[107] The top management of the parent company – Sinopec – further explained that 'the cost of dropping the bid made the senior management of Sinopec choose to stay in the project instead of conceding to the central government's interest in maximising the oil supply'.[108] By increasing SIPSC's overseas upstream shares, Sinopec aimed at breaking CNPC's monopoly on crude oil pricing and squeezing Sinochem out of the downstream business.[109]

Moreover, SOEs' pursuit of expanding their shares in foreign oil fields was not necessarily due to regulatory relaxation, but it led the Chinese Government to impose tight control over outbound investments at the early stages of implementing the 'Going Out' Policy. The central Government's failure to coordinate these two big national oil companies might explain why the 'information report system' was later initiated by NDRC in 2004 (see chapter five). The central Government aimed to impose binding obligations on energy companies to secure bids without losing state-owned assets.

### *iii. CEFC's Aggressive Overseas Expansion*

Despite the private ownership of CEFC China Energy (hereinafter 'CEFC'), the chairman of CEFC once confirmed that CEFC aimed to implement China's energy

[102] CS Liou, 'Bureaucratic Politics and Overseas Investment by Chinese State-Owned Oil Companies: Illusory Champions' (2009) 49 *Asian Survey* 670.

[103] ibid.

[104] W Wu, *Chinese Oil Enterprises in Latin America* (Cham, Springer International Publishing, 2019) 29.

[105] ibid; 'Sinopec Service' at www.sinopecgroup.com/group/gsjs/shwq/gjsygcyxgs.shtml.

[106] World Resource Institute, *Research into Promoting the Overseas Renewable Energy Investments of Chinese Companies* (《促进中国企业可再生能源海外投资研究》) (World Resource Institute, 2022) 34–35.

[107] 'The Overseas War Between China's Two Oil Giants' (n 101).

[108] Liou (n 102).

[109] Meckling, Kong and Madan (n 100) 1172.

policies, for example by acquiring overseas energy resources.[110] More specifically, the company's global energy expansion was motivated by the wish to help China rebuild connections within the Eurasian states.[111] In 2016, CEFC signed an agreement with KMG, an oil company registered in Kazakhstan, to acquire 51 per cent of shares in KMG International (KMGI).[112] By relying on the high-quality assets of KMGI in Europe,[113] CEFC could engage in the downstream business of Central and Eastern Europe.[114] Therefore, with the acquisition of KMGI, China was likely to increase its influence in the downstream European market.[115] Later, CEFC intended to acquire a 14.2 per cent stake in Rosneft.[116] It was predicted that this project would significantly contribute to Chinese–Russian energy cooperation by increasing China's participation in Russia's oil value chains, from exploration, refining, distribution and even devolved financial services.[117]

The connections of CEFC with the political leaders and the Party branch embedded in CEFC helps in understanding CEFC's concession to national energy interests.[118] The CEO of CEFC was closely linked to the central leadership, as he was once the personal advisor to the Czech President regarding Chinese inward investments.[119] Most of CEFC's deals were concluded during President Xi's official visits to the Czech Republic.[120] Establishing the Party branch in the company also led to speculation that this POE operated as a 'state-controlled organisation'.[121]

[110] J Wang, 'CEFC: The BRI and New Strategies of Oil and Gas' [《中国华信:深耕"一带一路"布局"油气新生"》] (2018) 1 *China Report* 60.
[111] See, eg, E Ng, 'Meet CEFC China, A Private Company That's Managed Like a State Organisation' *SCMP* (12 August 2017).
[112] 'CEFC Takes Controlling Shares of KMGI' *China Energy* (20 December 2016) at www.cnenergy.org/yq/sy/201612/t20161220_410162.html.
[113] 'China's CEFC to Take Control of Unit of Kazakh State-Run Oil Firm' *Reuters* (15 December 2015) at www.reuters.com/article/china-kazakhstan/chinas-cefc-to-take-control-of-unit-of-kazakh-state-run-oil-firm-idUST9N0NH05G20151215.
[114] Z Tang, 'CEFC Expands Influence in Oil and Gas' *China Daily* (14 May 2017) at www.chinadaily.com.cn/cndy/2017-05/14/content_29339582.htm.
[115] Wang (n 110).
[116] 'The Mysterious Energy Giant – CEFC is Losing Favor of the Chinese Government' [《神秘的能源巨頭華信在北京「失寵」》] *New York Times* (Chinese version) (15 March 2018) at cn.nytimes.com/business/20180315/china-cefc-investigation/zh-hant/.
[117] 'CEFC as the Third Largest Shareholder: 9 Billion for Rosneft' [《中国民企华信能源91亿美元入股俄石油成第三大股东》] *Observer* (10 September 2017) at www.guancha.cn/Neighbors/2017_09_10_426508.shtml.
[118] T Durden, 'Meet China's Biggest Oil Trader: At 39, He Generated $38 Billion in Revenue' *ZeroHedge* (24 February 2017) at www.zerohedge.com/news/2017-02-24/meet-chinas-biggest-oil-trader-39-he-generated-38-billion-revenue.
[119] J Garlick, 'Chinese Investments in the Czech Republic: Opportunity or Threat?' *China Observers in Central and Eastern Europe* (12 February 2020) at chinaobservers.eu/chinese-investments-in-the-czech-republic-opportunity-or-threat/.
[120] 'The Secretive China Energy Giant That Faces Scrutiny: QuickTake' *Bloomberg* (3 April 2018) at www.bloombergquint.com/quicktakes/the-secretive-china-energy-giant-that-faces-scrutiny-quicktake.
[121] Ng (n 111).

## C. A Commercially Viable LNG Project – Yamal LNG Project

With equity funding from the Silk Road Fund, CNPC and its Russian counterparts (eg, Novatek) began to establish the Yamal LNG project in Arctic Siberia in 2013. Construction of the gas liquefaction plant was completed in 2018.[122] The Yamal LNG Project commenced commercial operations in December 2017,[123] and distributed cash to shareholders in June 2019.[124]

In addition to receiving a cash return, CNPC invested in this LNG project in order to expand its market shares and gain advanced expertise. When CNPC started construction in 2013, the company had already been subject to a relatively relaxed investment approval system that was designed to implement the 'Going Out' strategy. The regulatory relaxation enabled CNPC to undertake a more streamlined process for investing abroad and to successfully operate the project. Due to its successful operation, CNPC was able to access Russian upstream assets.[125] This was the first time that China's NOC participated in the oil value chain in Russia.[126] In addition, CNPC gained technical skills and operational expertise whilst engaged on this project.[127] The Corporation learned from Russian companies about the expertise required for exploration in extremely cold conditions (eg, the design of sophisticated drilling equipment), which would break the technology monopoly previously enjoyed by the US, Canada and Russia.[128] Its subsidiaries also gained module operation experience in the gas fields of the North Pole.[129] In the module operation, those subsidiaries provided services ranging from upstream exploration and factory construction to natural gas storage.[130] Therefore, CNPC and its

[122] 'Yamal LNG: A Titanic Gas Project in Arctic Siberia' *Alten around the World* 12 April 2019, at www.alten.com/yamal-lng-project-gas-arctic-anotech-energy/.

[123] 'Natural Gas Weekly Update' *EIA* (21 December 2017) at www.eia.gov/naturalgas/weekly/archivenew_ngwu/2017/12_21/.

[124] 'Yamal LNG Operational and Logistical Tests Done' *Offshore Energy* (28 June 2019) at www.offshore-energy.biz/yamal-lng-operational-and-logistical-tests-done/.

[125] Q Liu, 'Investing in the Yamal LNG Project: CNPC Finally Achieves the Strategic Aim' [《入股亚马尔:中石油夙愿已偿》] (2013) 19 *China Petroleum and Chemical Products* 45; J Henderson and T Mitrova, *Energy Relations between Russia and China: Playing Chess with the Dragon* (Oxford Institute for Energy Studies, 2016) 55.

[126] Q Xu and Y Miao, 'Belt and Road Initiative and China's International Energy Cooperation' (2019) 29 *China International Relations* 66, 68.

[127] Y Xiao, 'On the Sino-Russia Co-construction of the Arctic Energy Corridor: Strategic Fulcrum and Promotion Pathway' [《中俄共建"北极能源走廊":战略支点与推进理路》] (2016) 5 *Northeast Asia Forum* 109.

[128] L You, 'Motivation, Risks and Path Selection of China-Russia Energy Cooperation' [《中俄能源产业合作动因、风险及路径选择——以亚马尔 LNG 项目为例》] (2018) 4 *International Economic Cooperation* 15.

[129] Q Jin, 'Investment and Financing Opportunities along the Silk Road and Choices of the Silk Road Fund' [《一带一路投融资机会与丝路基金的选择》] (2017) 5 *Modern Bankers* 50; J Guo, C Xia and W Yu, 'Selection of Yamal LNG as the Focus of Integrated Energy Cooperation between CNPC and Russia' [《亚马尔LNG项目开辟中俄能源合作蹊径》] (2014) 10 *International Petroleum Economics* 48.

[130] 'Opportunities of China–Russia Yamal LNG Project Financed by the Silk Road Fund' [《丝路基金入股的中俄合作亚马尔LNG项目造就了哪些机会》] Sohu Finance (26 October 2015)

subsidiaries not only obtained the experience of operating oil and gas projects in extremely cold conditions, but also explored new markets in the construction business.

At the same time, by exporting services, this commercially viable project would enable the Chinese Government to achieve its policy objective of increasing its influence in the global energy market.[131] When subsidiaries in the construction business provided services and products to support the project's operation, they exported relevant technological standards,[132] which is crucial for taking a dominant position in global energy supply chains. Therefore, the Chinese Government is likely to influence the north-east Asian gas market.

The Chinese Government may also realise the policy goal of securing a stable and affordable gas supply and promoting gas cooperation in the BRI.[133] First, the North Pole is becoming another stable LNG supply source (in addition to the Middle East and Africa) and will help to fill the gap between domestic LNG supply and demand.[134] Indeed, CNPC received the first shipment of LNG on 19 July 2018.[135] Second, China will be able to develop the northern sea route to mitigate the risk of possible interruption of supply in the Malacca Strait and South China Sea.[136] Third, Beijing included the Arctic region in the BRI, and could develop the Polar Silk Road via this project.[137] Successfully operating the Yamal LNG project had signal impacts on oil and gas cooperation in the Arctic region.[138] These impacts would boost the confidence of states along the Polar Silk Road (especially Russia) and further promote the development of the BRI.[139]

Apart from energy policy objectives, China may also have diplomatic considerations. For Hsiung and Paik, China aims to 'maintain stable and positive bilateral

at business.sohu.com/20151026/n424177115.shtml; F Lasserre and O Alexeeva, 'An Analysis on Sino-Russian Cooperation in the Arctic in the BRI Era' (2018) 29 *Advances in Polar Sciences* 269.

[131] State Council, China's Arctic Policy (January 2018). Exporting services, products and technological standards to achieve a greater influence in the global energy market is one of China's principal energy policy objectives (see chapter two). 'Foreign Media: What is China's Motivation behind Investment in the Yamal LNG Project' [《外媒:中国在北极投资俄罗斯液化天然气项目的背后动机是什么?》] *Polar Ocean* (26 January 2018) at www.polaroceanportal.com/article/1934.

[132] Liu and Wang (n 75); Lasserre and Alexeeva (n 130).

[133] TK Leng, 'China's Arctic Diplomacy: Global and Regional Aspects' in TK Leng and R Aoyama (eds), *Decoding the Rise of China: Taiwanese and Japanese Perspectives* (London, Palgrave Macmillan, 2018) 147–70.

[134] K Sun and Y Ma, 'China–Russia Arctic Energy Cooperation in the Context of the "Polar Silk Road" – A Case Study of Yamal LNG Project' [《"冰上丝绸之路"背景下的中俄北极能源合作 ——— 以亚马尔 LNG 项目为例》] (2018) 6 *Academic Journal of Ocean University of China* 1.

[135] 'Milestone Events and Key Projects in 2018' *CNPC News Release* (19 December 2018) at news.cnpc.com.cn/system/2018/12/19/001714443.shtml.

[136] KW Paik, 'The Role of Sino-Russian Gas cooperation in China's Natural Gas Expansion' in J Considine (ed), *Handbook of Energy Politics* (Cheltenham, Edward Elgar Publishing, 2018) 133–52.

[137] Lasserre and Alexeeva (n 130).

[138] 'Thoughts of China's Overseas Oil and Gas Cooperation after 5 years of Implementation of the BRI' [《"一带一路"倡议五周年中国石油海外油气合作的思考》] *CNPC News Center* (11 September 2018) at news.cnpc.com.cn/system/2018/09/11/001704337.shtml.

[139] 'Foreign Media: What is China's Motivation behind Investment in the Yamal LNG Project' (n 131).

relations with Russia' by playing the role of the main financier in this project.[140] The Yamal LNG project 'is often cited as a perfect example of successful Sino-Russian collaboration in the development of the Arctic'.[141]

In summary, although this project could facilitate the pursuit of state interests, the direct cash return and the expansion of market shares by CNPC remind us that a conventional energy project invested in by a Chinese SOE can be a commercially viable project.

# III. Power Investments

The operation of power projects is usually accompanied by the export of services, equipment and products, and by the setting up of factories for the manufacture of energy products and equipment (eg, solar photovoltaic cells).[142] This has helped China's energy companies to expand their shares of foreign markets, and meanwhile to achieve the policy objective of exporting services, equipment and products. The Chinese Government may realise additional goals, depending on different investment destinations. The electricity projects discussed in this section are located in Brazil, the UK and Pakistan. Brazil and the UK are more geographically remote from China, compared to Pakistan. Therefore, China might intend to link its power market to that in Pakistan, instead of those in Brazil and the UK. In addition, given the Chinese Government's interest in promoting energy cooperation in the BRI, the Karot Hydropower Project has helped to push forward energy cooperation in the China–Pakistan Economic Corridor (CPEC).

However, China's outbound electricity projects cannot be convincingly described as tools of the Chinese Government as long as the electricity companies can pursue their own corporate development in the operation of foreign projects. Sometimes, China's electricity SOEs, such as State Grid, have even sought state support for their expansion into foreign energy markets in their informal communications with SASAC about their annual investment plans, or with other central administrative departments about approval for a specific project.

## A. State Grid's Deal with Plena Transmissoras

State Grid International Development (SGID), a subsidiary of State Grid, invests in foreign power transmission projects and provides services relevant to the procurement of overseas electrical equipment.[143] It acquired seven Brazilian

[140] CW Hsiung, 'China and Arctic Energy: Drivers and Limitations' (2016) 6 *The Polar Journal* 243; Paik (n 136).

[141] Liu and Wang (n 75) 27.

[142] World Resource Institute (n 106) 38.

[143] 'State Grid Buys Brazilian Power Giants' *China.org* (27 August 2010) at www.china.org.cn/business/2010-08/27/content_20805031.htm.

transmission companies from Plena Transmissoras in 2010, and could thus access 3,000 kilometres of transmission lines in Brazil.[144]

State Grid's investments in Brazil have been motivated by its pursuit of profits and international competitiveness.[145] As the company has struggled with the regulated and less profitable Chinese transmission sector, an internal officer of State Grid stated that 'an overseas project is only considered if expected returns are at least twice or three times as high as can be achieved in China'.[146] These investments also constitute part of State Grid's market strategies to further increase its presence in global power generation and distribution.[147] Winning and Yap predicted that, by exporting transmission technology, equipment products and services to foreign markets through SGID's investments,[148] State Grid could forge a complete industrial chain in the global electricity market.[149]

To realise the projects, State Grid invited officials from the MFA, NDRC, NEA and SASAC to its regular business meetings and communicated with officials about the contribution of its investments in Brazil to meeting national energy interests.[150] State Grid argued that the project would enable the company to develop high-end business in the global electricity industry, and in the long term could facilitate China's participation in global power standard-setting.[151] Because standards serve the technical basis of power interconnection and interoperability,[152] a unified standard system would eliminate trade barriers and facilitate the establishment of global production chains.[153] Being at the centre of such a chain, China would be likely to lead energy research and development, create electricity inter-dependence and have a greater say in the global power market.[154] Therefore, by placing the desired project on the policy agenda, State Grid justified its investment decisions and lobbied for state support, such as the host government's support during high-level state visits or state financing.[155]

[144] ibid.

[145] J Husar and D Best, *Energy Investments and Technology Transfer Across Emerging Economies: The Case of Brazil and China* (IEA, 2013).

[146] ibid.

[147] D Becard and BV de Macedo, 'Chinese Multinational Corporations in Brazil: Strategies and Implications in Energy and Telecom Sectors' (2014) 57 *Revista Brasileira de Política Internacional* 143.

[148] D Winning and CW Yap, 'China's State Grid to Buy Brazilian Power Firms' *Wall Street Journal* (22 December 2010) at www.wsj.com/articles/SB10001424052748703581204576032841364944586; 'State Grid Buys Brazilian Power Giants' (n 144).

[149] Winning and Yap (n 148); 'State Grid Buys Brazilian Power Giants' (n 143).

[150] Xu (n 7) 278.

[151] JAG Albuquerque and LAF Lima, 'Chinese Investment in Brazil: Can it Match the Relevance of Bilateral Trade?' (2016) 40 *Asian Perspective* 579; Xu (n 7) 205 and 278–81.

[152] C Liang, H Song and X Zhang, 'Advancing Principles and Strategies of Power Grid Interconnection in the Belt and Road', International Conference on Energy, Power, Electrical and Environmental Engineering, at Wuhan (2018).

[153] ibid.

[154] P Cai, *Understanding China's Belt and Road Initiative* (Lowy Institute, March 2017).

[155] YC Xu, 'China's Giant State-Owned Enterprises as Policy Advocates: The Case of the State Grid Corporation of China' (2017) 79 *The China Journal* 21.

Accordingly, State Grid was largely commercially driven in operating its projects in Brazil. Similar to its international counterparts, State Grid has expanded into the overseas market by utilising its expertise in ultra-high voltage (UHV). State Grid has also tried to avoid domestic regulatory constraints to achieve more economic returns. The reason why the company stressed the achievement of policy goals was to gain state support. To expand its shares of foreign electricity sectors, State Grid persuaded the Government that this project could enhance China's influence over the global energy sector. The meetings between State Grid and officials from SASAC confirm that the company in practice communicated with SASAC and NDRC before investing in a new project, as discussed in chapters five and six. It implies that SOEs can seek deals favourable to them by making use of administrative procedures that are viewed as facilitating state influence over their overseas investments. However, before March 2018, power grids projects were still listed as sensitive projects. Therefore, communicating with the officials of NDRC is necessary not only for seeking state support but also for ensuring the approval of NDRC.

## B. Hinkley Point C Project

Both China General Nuclear Power Corporation (CGN) and China National Nuclear Corporation (CNNC) submitted bids for the Hinkley Point C project to the UK Government in 2012, but both of them failed.[156] The British integrated energy company EDF Energy succeeded in the bidding and concluded a basic commercial agreement with the UK Government in 2013.[157] Both CGN and CNNC then intended to place bids as minor shareholders in the project.[158] When President Xi visited the UK in 2015, CGN and EDF Energy signed an agreement to construct two nuclear reactors at Hinkley Point C.[159] Due to coordination by the Chinese Government,[160] CNNC and CGN jointly owned 30–40 per cent of the shares in the project and would build the two nuclear reactors.[161]

These two nuclear power SOEs not only sought profits, but also expanded their shares in foreign markets. To guarantee investors' revenues, the contract with the UK Government provided a strike price, which was 'more than twice its present cost'.[162] In addition, CNNC has long pursued investment opportunities

[156] L Che, *China's State-Directed Economy and the International Order* (Singapore, Springer, 2019) 176–86.

[157] 'Hinkley Point C – the Commercial Case' *Nuclear Engineering* (6 January 2014) at www.neimagazine.com/opinion/opinionhinkley-point-c---the-commercial-case-4155692/.

[158] ibid.

[159] Che (n 156).

[160] ibid.

[161] 'Hinkley Point C Nuclear Power Station' *Power Technology*, 5 May 2023, at www.power-technology.com/projects/hinkley-point-c-nuclear-power-station/.

[162] 'Hinkley Point C – the Commercial Case' (n 157); A McSmith, 'Hinkley Point: Putting the Brakes on Could be Prudent in Light of Security Concerns over China' *The Independent* (29 February 2016) at

in the UK.[163] Similarly, CGN aims to deploy its expertise on developing nuclear power and to engage with foreign supply chains for nuclear power.[164] Both companies provided services involving design, engineering and construction to this project, to fully employ their technology and products.[165] Successfully operating this project could help these two SOEs to expand their shares in the markets of other states, such as Thailand, Indonesia and Turkey, because these states view the approval of reactors by the UK Generic Design Assessment (GDA) as the industrial benchmark for assessing the potential for applying the Hualong One technology.[166]

Although CNNC and CGN realised corporate goals in this project, the Chinese Government coordinated CNNC alongside CGN to carry out its energy policies of increasing China's future presence in the global power market.[167] Andrews-Speed explained that Beijing could have more influence over the international nuclear power market through exporting China's technical standards and equipment, such as the purely Chinese-designed Hualong One technology.[168] By taking the Hinkley Point C project as a model, China would be able to enter into discussions with France, the UK and other states about cooperation in third-generation technology for nuclear power.[169] These cooperation talks would lay the foundation for China's suggestions as to how the next generation of nuclear technology should be used in the global power market, and thus strengthen its influence on the market.[170]

Accordingly, like State Grid, Chinese nuclear power SOEs are also competitive enough to expand abroad, and are willing to accept coordination to secure their deals. Prior to 1 March 2018, China's energy companies were still required to submit information reports before participating in bidding processes. This regulatory requirement provided NDRC with the opportunity to persuade CNNC and

www.independent.co.uk/news/uk/home-news/putting-the-brakes-on-hinkley-point-pcould-be-prudent-in-light-of-security-concerns-over-china-a7162786.html.

[163] B Zhang, 'State Transformation Goes Nuclear: Chinese National Nuclear Companies' Expansion into Europe' (2019) 40 *Third World Quarterly* 1459.

[164] 'Case study: Hinkley Point C – It's about the Long Game' *KWM* (25 July 2016) at www.kwm.com/en/knowledge/insights/china-general-nuclear-power-corporation-investment-in-hinkley-point-c-plant-somerset-20160725.

[165] R Sweet, 'UK Nuclear Power, with Chinese Characteristics' *Global Construction Review* (5 November 2013) at www.globalconstructionreview.com/perspectives/uk-nuclear-power-chinese-characteristics/.

[166] Oxford Analytica Daily Brief Service, *China: Nuclear Exporters Will Target Developing World* (Oxford Analytica Daily Brief Service, 21 September 2016).

[167] 'China Says Third Pakistan Nuclear Reactor Connected to Grid' *Reuters* (17 October 2016) at www.reuters.com/article/us-china-nuclear-pakistan-idUSKBN12H0AE. The Hinkley Point C project was listed in the report.

[168] P Andrews-Speed, 'Hinkley Point Boosts China's Nuclear Ambitions' (24 September 2016) at www.andrewsspeed.com/hinkley-point-boosts-chinas-nuclear-ambitions/.

[169] S Xu et al, 'Central and Eastern European Countries' in S Xu (ed), *BRI and International Cooperation in Industrial Capacity* (London, Routledge, 2020) 289–365.

[170] Sweet (n 165).

CGN to collaborate. The strategic objectives of these two nuclear power SOEs, specifically, establishing a presence in the UK nuclear power market, align with the Chinese Government's interest in exporting nuclear technology. This explains why CNNC and CGN agreed to coordinate their efforts. Consequently, the expired regulations requiring the submission of reports for the purpose of coordinating acquisitions by Chinese companies did not always impede these companies in successfully securing their deals.

## C. Karot Hydropower Project

The Karot Hydropower Project (Karot HPP) was built on the Jhelum River and developed by Karot Power Company (Private) Ltd,[171] a joint venture of China Three Gorges South Asia Investment Ltd (93 per cent) and Silk Road Venture Investment Company (7 per cent).[172] Construction commenced in December 2015, and the project entered into commercial operation by July 2022.[173] China Three Gorges Corp will own and operate this hydropower plant for 30 years by adopting the build-own-operate-transfer model.[174]

This project was expected to make economic sense. The project financing granted by EXIMB and CDB to the Karot Power Company was based on commercial terms.[175] The People's Bank of China, the Silk Road Fund and the World Bank also invested in this project through equity financing to China Three Gorges South Asia Investment Ltd, after assessing the economic viability of this project.[176]

[171] 'Karot Hydropower Plant to be Put into Commercial Operation by End of 2021' *Link News* (24 January 2020) at mettisglobal.news/karot-hydropower-plant-to-be-put-into-commercial-operation-by-end-of-2021.

[172] C Wright, 'Making Sense of Belt and Road – The Belt and Road Project Borrower: Karot Hydropower, Pakistan' *Euromoney* (26 September 2017) at www.euromoney.com/article/b14t13rsrlb4r9/making-sense-of-belt-and-road-the-belt-and-road-project-borrower-karot-hydropower-pakistan?copyrightInfo=true.

[173] CPEC, 'Karot Hydropower Station' at cpec.gov.pk/project-details/16; 'Pakistan's 720 MW Karot Hydropower Plant Starts Commercial Operation' at www.enerdata.net/publications/daily-energy-news/pakistans-720-mw-karot-hydropower-plant-starts-commercial-operation.html.

[174] A Ahmed, 'Construction Work Begins on CPEC's Karot Hydropower Project' *Business Recorder* (25 September 2018) at www.brecorder.com/2020/04/24/592081/oil-heads-for-steep-weekly-slide-after-coronavirus-turmoil/.

[175] 'China Makes Multibillion-Dollar Down-Payment on Silk Road Plans' *Wall Street Journal* (21 April 2015) at blogs.wsj.com/chinarealtime/2015/04/21/china-makes-multibillion-dollar-down-payment-on-silk-road-plans/; E Ingram, 'Karot in Pakistan to be First Hydropower Project Financed by China's Silk Road Fund' *Hydro Review* (30 April 2015) at www.hydroreview.com/2015/04/30/karot-in-pakistan-to-be-first-hydropower-project-financed-by-china-s-silk-road-fund/#gref.

[176] Z Hussain, 'The China-Pakistan Economic Corridor and the New Regional Geopolitics' (2017) 94 *Asie.Visions* 1; 'Silk Road Fund to invest in hydropower project in Pakistan' *Xinhua* (21 April 2015) at www.china.org.cn/business/2015-04/21/content_35373868.htm; 'Karot Hydropower Project, Jhelum River' *Power Technology* (10 November 2023) at www.power-technology.com/projects/karot-hydropower-project-jhelum-river/.

As disclosed by the Silk Road Fund, 'the Pakistani government promised a sound return on investment after recovering construction and operation costs'.[177] The Power Purchase Agreement would enable Karot Power to sell the power plant to the Government of Pakistan so that Karot Power might recover its costs in the event of default of payment by the Central Power Purchasing Agency (Guarantee) Limited, Pakistan.[178] In addition to profits, China Three Gorges Corp was able to explore new foreign markets through this project.[179] The company exported productivity for the construction team owing to the reduced need for dam construction in the domestic market.[180]

Despite the pursuit of commercial interests, the Chinese Government realised its policy goals in this project. First, it helped to develop the CPEC – a crucial part of the Mega Belt and Road Initiative'.[181] Insufficient energy infrastructure in Pakistan has restricted energy cooperation along the CPEC.[182] The embassy in Pakistan confirmed that successfully operating the Karot HPP would help to accelerate energy cooperation along the CPEC.[183] Second, the Chinese Government can also achieve the policy objective of deploying China's equipment and technical standards outside China.[184] For Liu, 'The Karot project has become the first hydropower plant in Pakistan that has completely adopted China's technical and environmental standards.'[185] Chinese power companies thus had the opportunity to move to the upper end of global energy value chains, equipping the Chinese Government with the ability to have a greater say in the global hydropower market.[186]

Accordingly, in the Karot HPP, China Three Gorges Corp sought economic returns and market expansion, like other international energy companies. The economic logic of this project helps to rebut the claim that China's energy projects in the BRI are strategic investments. Nevertheless, hydropower projects are still listed as sensitive projects in the current regulation on managing overseas investments. China Three Gorges Corp thus needed to secure approval by emphasising

[177] 'Why Pakistan Gets Silk Road Fund's First Investment?' *Beijing Review* (21 April 2015) at www.bjreview.com/quotes/txt/2015-04/21/content_684220.htm.

[178] E Downs, *The China–Pakistan Economic Corridor Power Projects: Insights into Environmental and Debt Sustainability* (Center on Global Energy Policy, Columbia SIPA, October 2019).

[179] ibid.

[180] Andrews-Speed, Qiu and Len (n 47).

[181] K Hassan, 'CPEC: A Win-Win for China and Pakistan' (2019) 30 *Human Affairs* 212.

[182] Y Xu, 'China–Pakistan Energy Cooperation: Background, Current Situation and Prospect' [《中巴能源合作:背景·现状·前景》] (2015) 17 *Journal of Southwest Petroleum University* 42.

[183] Embassy of the People's Republic of China in the Islamic Republic of Pakistan, 'Karot Hydropower Project' (1 October 2018) at pk.chineseembassy.org/eng/zbgx/CPEC/t1627107.htm.

[184] F Leverett and B Wu, 'The New Silk Road and China's Evolving Grand Strategy' (2016) 77 *The China Journal* 110.

[185] T Liu, 'Feature: China-Aided Hydroelectric Plant to Brighten Homes, Hearts in Pakistan' (*Xinhua News*, 22 April 2019), at www.xinhuanet.com/english/2019-04/22/c_137997677.htm.

[186] Cai (n 154).

in its application how this project could carry out energy policies, including the export of technology and relevant standards, but not hamper China's relations with Pakistan.

## IV. Conclusion

These case studies, based on the international relations literature, at least illustrate that in its foreign energy projects, the Chinese Government has endeavoured to advance its policy objectives of securing stable oil and gas supplies, having a greater say in the international oil, gas and power markets, and developing underdeveloped provinces. Despite the pursuit of these objectives, the regulatory requirements do not necessarily restrict energy companies seeking corporate development. Instead, while SOEs were aware of how their projects could address policy priorities, they intended to secure regulatory approval (in the case of sensitive energy investments) and state support by stressing the overlapping interests between them and the Chinese Government. More specifically, instead of being a state-imposed burden on energy companies, the inclusion of investments in five-year plans may be welcomed by companies, as it can ensure state support for projects that are conducive to their commercial development in challenging investment environments. Companies, regardless of ownership, therefore, have an interest in emphasising the strategic benefits of their projects and persuading the Government to endorse these investments in China's macro-economic policies. In other words, policy guidance and state support are sometimes not instruments of government instruction or control but tools to enable energy companies to pursue their own interests in overseas energy investments.

Furthermore, regulatory relaxation is not directly linked to the increasing investment autonomy of energy companies. Even when the Chinese Government exercised tight control over the management of outbound investments, China's SOEs would oppose policy guidance or regulatory requirements and pursue their corporate development. After the Government started to deregulate overseas energy investments, CNNC and CGN still accepted government coordination to acquire shares in the UK market. Meanwhile, despite regulatory relaxation, POEs have still completed the mission of investing in foreign energy markets assigned by the state to enhance their political connections. In other words, regulatory relaxation does not necessarily guarantee the disappearance of state objectives (energy policy objectives at least).

Accordingly, in practice, Chinese overseas energy projects should not be bluntly categorised as geopolitical tools, because the Government could not always effectively control energy companies to pursue diplomatic or energy interests when implementing policies and regulations on managing outbound energy investments. These case studies also imply that, as the changing attitudes of SOEs towards compliance with regulatory requirements during different periods of regulatory reform are driven by their corporate interests, it is necessary to examine individual cases when assessing China's potential policy and regulatory tools for shaping its global energy expansion. In addition, in a broader sense, commercial viability and the requirement to act as private entities, provided for in some free-trade agreements, may not be a determining factor when assessing whether the state pursues national interests, such as pursuing industrial development in overseas investments made by SOEs or companies with political connections. This is because the state's pursuit of industrial development will usually be consistent with energy companies' goals of corporate development.

# 8

# The Chinese Government's Efforts to Facilitate Companies' Access to Foreign Energy Markets

## I. Introduction

Host states' national security reviews often question whether China's energy investments are made for purely commercial reasons or in pursuit of foreign policy objectives.[1] For instance, the acquisition of Ausgrid by two Chinese companies – the State Grid and Hong Kong's Cheung Kong Infrastructure – was blocked by Australia based on national security concerns,[2] considering the strategic nature of the electricity asset.[3] Although legal scholars propose that China should consider stronger pre-investment treatment to meet companies' need to participate in global value chains,[4] they rarely look at the application of these treaties in the energy sector. Also, the discussion of energy cooperation agreements at the government level focuses more on their general non-binding nature.[5] These legal scholars have

[1] See, eg, Regulation (EU) 2019/452 of the European Parliament and of the Council of 19 March 2019 Establishing a Framework for the Screening of Foreign Direct Investments into the Union [2019] OJ L791/1; Treasury of the Commonwealth of Australia, Australia's Foreign Investment Policy (2016) 10 at firb.gov.au/files/2015/09/Australias-Foreign-Investment-Policy-2016-2017.pdf; Guidance Concerning the National Security Review Conducted by the Committee on Foreign Investment in the United States, 73 Fed Reg 74,567, 74,571 (8 December 2008) at www.treasury.gov/resource-center/international/foreign-investment/Documents/CFIUSGuidance.pdf; See also US Court of Appeals for the District of Columbia Circuit, *Ralls Corporation v Committee on Foreign Investment in the United States et al* (15 July 2014) No 13-5315 ('*Ralls v CIFUS*').

[2] 'Australia Formally Rejects Bids by State Grid and Cheung Kong Infrastructure for Ausgrid' *Reuters* (19 August 2016).

[3] Commonwealth of Australia, *Foreign Investment Review Board: Annual Report 2016–2017* (2018) 23 at cdn.tspace.gov.au/uploads/sites/79/2018/05/FIRB-16-17-Annual-Report.pdf.

[4] See, eg, H Wang, 'The RCEP and Its Investment Rules: Learning from Past Chinese FTAs' (2017) 3 *The Chinese Journal of Global Governance* 160; A Berger, 'Hesitant Embrace: China's Recent Approach to International Investment Rule-Making' (2016) 16 *Journal of World Investment & Trade* 843.

[5] See, eg, ZW Wang, *Securing Energy Flows from Central Asia to China and the Relevance of the Energy Charter Treaty to China* (Energy Charter Secretariat, 2015); H Wang, 'China's Approach to the Belt and Road Initiative: Scope, Character and Sustainability' (2019) 22 *Journal of International Economic Law* 29; H Wang, 'The Belt and Road Initiative Agreements: Characteristics, Rationale and Challenges' (2021) 20 *World Trade Review* 282, 291.

not examined the contents of these agreements,[6] nor touched upon the impact of the controversial binding force of framework agreements on access to foreign energy markets. Further, they fail to look at the application of domestic regulations on backing companies in dealing with investment barriers.

Building on the current discussion, this chapter aims to examine how the Chinese Government assists energy companies to deal with host states' bans on China's investments from the regulatory perspective. The long-established approach to investment promotion through investment treaties and investment-related trade laws provides theoretical foundation for this research. Investment treaties forbid arbitrary treatment at the ex ante stage.[7] In reaction to the approach to promoting investments in a well-established regulatory framework, does the Chinese Government rely on domestic regulatory measures, energy cooperation agreements and investment treaties to facilitate companies' access to foreign energy markets, while limiting its influence on overseas energy investments? To assess the implementation of these regulations, the legal analysis is complemented by case studies of whether China's energy companies, such as CNOOC and the Sany company, turn to legal remedies when they faced barriers to accessing foreign energy markets in practice.

This chapter argues that the Chinese Government provides both the domestic and international regulatory measures for energy investment promotion. Domestic regulatory measures act in a preventive manner and play a role in providing information about the investment environment of the host state for energy companies. While investment treaties can offer greater protection to energy companies, the Chinese Government is making efforts to achieve political agreement with host states to minimise the possibility that host states will ban China's energy investments. This conclusion contributes to the current academic discussion of the provisions on market access in China's international legal arrangements, and adds to the energy law literature on investment promotion.

Section II introduces the general approach to enhancing access to foreign markets. Section III discusses the risks to Chinese energy companies of entering foreign markets. Section IV presents the existing discussion of how the Chinese Government grants diplomatic support to energy companies to facilitate their access to foreign energy markets. Section V examines domestic regulatory mechanisms for preventing investment risks. Section VI explains China's growing interest in seeking non-discriminatory treatment at the pre-investment stage. Section VII assesses how the Chinese Government manages host states' national security concerns by fostering political acceptability between China and the host states. Section VIII concludes and suggests implications.

[6] See, however, WH Shan and P Wang, 'The International Legal Framework for Belt and Road Energy Cooperation: Progress and Prospect' (2019) 20 *Journal of World Investment and Trade* 259.

[7] JW Salacuse, *The Law of Investment Treaties* (Oxford, Oxford University Press, 2010) 201–02; K Talus, *Introduction to EU Energy Law* (Oxford, Oxford University Press, 2016) 151–52.

# II. Legal Responses to Barriers to Entry Based on Unproven Geopolitical Concerns and Investment Law

A barrier to accessing foreign energy markets refers to an obstacle or a restriction that prevents investors from entering the host state's market.[8] Such barriers include selective measures that disadvantage all foreign investors (compared to national ones) or a group of foreign investors (compared to other foreign ones).[9] Consequently, investors encounter higher transactions costs or earn less profit.[10] Since energy investments are perceived to contribute to energy security, energy investment law has been developed to lift barriers to accessing foreign energy markets. An investor's right to access these markets is defined in such a way that the investor has 'a right, conferred by law, by virtue of any licences and permits, to undertake an economic activity in the energy sector'.[11] Legal arrangements, such as pre-investment provisions in investment treaties, have been adopted to ensure the enforcement of this right. These legal arrangements are supposed to create non-discriminatory access to the energy market of a host state by domestic energy companies and foreign energy companies, or between foreign energy companies.

## A. Barriers Based on Unproven Geopolitical Concerns

The dynamics of the international political economy have a significant impact on enforcing the legal right to make energy investments.[12] Investment screening mechanisms can deviate from liberal investment policies,[13] by assessing the economic and political impacts of foreign investments[14] and forbidding investments on the grounds of protecting the national/public interest or guaranteeing fair competition.[15] Among investment-screening mechanisms, national security reviews are legalising a political issue as to whether a foreign investment can threaten the

[8] Ministry of Commerce (MOFCOM), Foreign Trade Barrier Investigation Rules [《对外贸易壁垒调查规则》] (2005) Art 3(2).

[9] G Davies, 'Understanding Market Access: Exploring the Economic Rationality of Different Conceptions of Free Movement Law' (2010) 11 *German Law Journal* 671, 677.

[10] ibid 681–82.

[11] TW Waelde, 'International Investment under the 1994 Energy Charter Treaty' (1995) 29 *Journal of World Trade* 5, 33.

[12] M Rajavuori and K Huhta, 'Investment Screening: Implications for the Energy Sector and Energy Security' (2020) 144 *Energy Policy* 111646, 111649.

[13] IFI Shihata, 'Recent Trends Relating to Entry of Foreign Direct Investment' (1994) *ICSID Review* 47, 51.

[14] ibid 50.

[15] F Wehrlé and J Pohl, 'Investment Policies Related to National Security: A Survey of Country Practices', OECD Working Papers on International Investment No 2016/02 at doi.org/10.1787/5jlwrrf038nx-en (last accessed 4 January 2018).

national security of a host state.[16] In national security reviews, the foreign government carries out a geopolitical assessment, rather than a legal assessment, although the procedures of national security reviews are provided for in laws. Whether a project will be approved by the foreign government largely depends on the political background of the investor, the sensitivity of the project and the possibility of lifting potential security threats that are posed by the project.[17] For example, when assessing the potential national security risks posed by foreign investments, the New Zealand Government seeks 'advice on international relations' given by the Ministry of Foreign Affairs and Trade.[18] In particular, state-owned investors are subject to a high level of scrutiny,[19] as their investments involve their home states and may substitute political motivations for profit-making.[20] For instance, the review by the Committee on Foreign Investment in the United States (CIFUS) differentiates privately-owned investors from state-owned ones.[21] The problem remains that concepts such as national interests, the substantive essence of national security reviews, do not have a common or precise definition, thus opening the door to discrimination against foreign investors (sovereign investors in particular).[22]

The fear of foreign state control is more obvious when states review investments in the energy sector that have strategic features.[23] Host states are afraid of control by other states over energy resources located within their territories.[24] These states are also worried about an interruption to critical infrastructure caused by investors,[25] because digitalising energy transmission systems makes these systems vulnerable to foreign cyber-attacks.[26] Therefore, the definition of investments in

[16] DG Wang, 'National Security Review: Legalizing Politics and Politicizing Laws' [《国家安全审查:法律政治化与政治法律化》] (2016) 28 *Peking University Law Journal* 1289, 1289; LW Lin, 'China's National Champions: Governance Change through Globalization' (2015) 11 *University of Pennsylvania Asian Law Review* 82, 83.

[17] Wang (n 16) 1296–97.

[18] New Zealand Government, 'Foreign Investment Policy and National Interest Guidance', Guidance Note (May 2020) at www.treasury.govt.nz/sites/default/files/2020-05/for-invest-policy-nat-interest-guidance-may20-v2.pdf.

[19] J Li, *The Clash of Capitalisms? Chinese Companies in the United States* (Cambridge, Cambridge University Press, 2018) 183.

[20] J Slawotsky, 'Sovereign Wealth Funds as Emerging Financial Superstars: How US Regulators Should Respond' (2009) 40 *Georgetown Journal of International Law* 1239; J Chaisse, 'Demystifying Public Security Exception and Limitations on Capital Movement: Hard Law, Soft Law and Sovereign Investments in the EU Internal Market' (2015) 37 *University of Pennsylvania Journal of International Law* 583, 594–95.

[21] Li (n 19) 185–87.

[22] KP Sauvant, *FDI Protectionism is on the Rise* (The World Bank, 2009) 8 and 14.

[23] M Bungenberg and A Hazarika, 'Chinese Foreign Investments in the European Union Energy Sector: The Regulation of Security Concerns' (2019) 20 *Journal of World Investment & Trade* 375, 380.

[24] KP Sauvant, LE Sachs and WS Jongbloed, 'Sovereign Investment: An Introduction' in KP Sauvant, LE Sachs and WS Jongbloed (eds), *Sovereign Investment: Concerns and Policy Reactions* (Oxford, Oxford University Press, 2012) 3–23, 11–12.

[25] G Dimitropoulos, 'National Security: The Role of Investment Screening Mechanisms' in J Chaisse et al (eds), *Handbook of International Investment Law and Policy* (Singapore, Springer, 2019) 1–37, 4.

[26] Editorial, 'Chinese Investments in Europe's Energy Sector: Risks and Opportunities?' (2017) 101 *Energy Policy* 644, 646; F Umbach, 'China's Belt and Road Initiative and Its Energy-Security Dimensions', The RSIS Working Paper Series No 320 (January 2019) 7 (last accessed 8 January 2020);

various national investment-screening regulations is becoming broad enough to cover investments ranging from energy development, to transmission and distribution.[27] For instance, the US Department of Defense views CIFUS as an instrument for keeping 'foreign adversaries' away from the US's crucial energy infrastructure.[28]

## B. Admitting Investments in the Light of International Investment Law

Host states do not have the obligation to automatically admit foreign investments within their territories,[29] but they have every right to prevent uncontrolled foreign investments from harming national security interests.[30] They can impose conditions such as performance requirements (ie, local content rules, technology transfer, local employment or export requirements) on access to their markets.[31] To advance cross-border capital flows, investment treaties and investment-related trade laws have been developed to limit part of the regulatory right of host states.

Energy service suppliers can rely on the pre-establishment disciplines of Most-Favoured Nation (MFN) treatment and National Treatment (NT) in GATS to access foreign energy markets.[32] By relying on mode 3 – the establishment of commercial presence – energy companies are able to set up a new firm or invest in a member-state firm to provide services across energy value chains.[33] Member states will grant non-discriminatory treatment to energy companies in accessing, using and even building pipelines or power grids, for the purpose of transporting energy

OECD, 'Foreign Government-Controlled Investors and Recipient Country Investment Policies – A Scoping Paper' (OECD Publishing, January 2009) 14.

[27] Rajavuori and Huhta (n 12).

[28] S Heifetz and M Gershberg, 'Why Are Foreign Investments in Domestic Energy Projects Now under CFIUS Scrutiny' (2013) 3 *Harvard Business Law Review* 203, 210.

[29] Salacuse (n 7) 213; KJ Vandevelde, 'Investment Liberalization and Economic Development: The Role of Bilateral Investment Treaties' (1998) 36 *Columbia Journal of Transnaional Law* 501, 511.

[30] UNCTAD, 'Admission and Establishment', IIA issues series paper (2002) 11; Shihata (n 13) 47; P Muchlinski and I Gómez-Palacio, 'Admission of Investment and Right of Establishment' in P Muchlinski, F Ortino, and C Schreuer (eds), *The Oxford Handbook of International Investment Law* (Oxford, Oxford University Press, 2008) 227–58, 236.

[31] UNCTAD (n 30) 7.

[32] The General Agreement on Trade in Services (entered into force in 1995), Art XVI; R Adlung, 'International Rules Governing Foreign Direct Investment in Services: Investment Treaties versus the GATS' (2016) 17 *The Journal of World Investment & Trade* 47, 52 and 65; M Cossy, 'Energy Services Under the General Agreement on Trade in Services' in Y Selivanova (ed), *Regulation of Energy in International Trade Law: WTO, NAFTA and Energy Charter* (Leiden, Kluwer Law International, 2011) 149–80, 150.

[33] S Sinclair, 'The WTO and its GATS' in J Michie (ed), *The Handbook of Globalisation*, 3rd edn (Cheltenham, Edward Elgar, 2019) 359–67, 364; I Musselli and S Zarrilli, 'Oil and Gas Services: Market Liberalization and the Ongoing GATS Negotiations' (2005) 8 *Journal of International Economic Law* 551, 554; JJ Nedumpara, 'Energy Security and the WTO Agreements' in S Mathur (ed), *Trade, the WTO and Energy Security* (Singapore, Springer, 2014) 15–71, 42.

products.[34] However, the application of GATS in broadening access to foreign energy markets gives rise to two problems. First, there is no clear definition of the term 'services'.[35] Second, energy companies cannot initiate investor–state arbitration under GATS.[36]

Compared with GATS, investment treaties are more ambitious and were created to develop a liberal investment regime that is underpinned by the principle of market facilitation.[37] Investment treaties limit host states' right to block energy investments and require contracting parties to create favourable conditions for investment-making.[38] However, such a requirement is vague and inoperable.[39] Salacuse summarised three approaches to regulating investment-making: the 'controlled entry model', the 'liberalized entry model' and the 'establishment model'.[40] Compared with the other two models, the 'establishment model' allows investors to unconditionally invest in host states.[41] The 'controlled entry model' was used in most early bilateral investment treaties (BITs) to control the entry of foreign capital and screen investments on the grounds of national security, industrial development and social benefits.[42] As admitting investments is subject to the laws and regulations of capital-importing states,[43] these states can take discriminatory measures that are allowed in national laws and regulations without providing remedies for investors.[44] Host states have growingly adopted the 'liberalized entry' model, which requires host states to include provisions on MFN and NT in investment treaties to grant non-discriminatory access to investors.[45] More specifically, host states issue negative lists and specify sectors or commercial activities that are not subject to non-discriminatory treatment.[46] Therefore, except for the specified sectors and activities, host states cannot discriminate against investors or investments only because of the worsening of diplomatic relations with that state.[47]

[34] TM Dralle, *Ownership Unbundling and Related Measures in the EU Energy Sector* (Singapore, Springer, 2018) 86–87; Cossy (n 32) 154.
[35] Dralle (n 34) 88; Musselli and Zarrilli (n 33) 555.
[36] Cossy (n 32) 150.
[37] Adlung (n 32) 67–68; KJ Vandevelde, *Bilateral Investment Treaties: History, Policy, and Interpretation* (Oxford, Oxford University Press, 2010) 75–121; Salacuse (n 7) 214.
[38] Shihata (n 13) 47; Muchlinski and Gómez-Palacio (n 30) 251; see Sauvant (n 22); UNCTAD (n 30) 11.
[39] Salacuse (n 7) 216.
[40] ibid 218; UNCTAD presented similar models – UNCTAD (n 30).
[41] Salacuse (n 7) 226.
[42] ibid 219.
[43] Muchlinski and Gómez-Palacio (n 30) 241.
[44] ibid; Shihata (n 13) 50.
[45] J Bonnitcha, L Poulsen and M Waibel, *The Political Economy of the Investment Treaty Regime* (Oxford, Oxford University Press, 2017) 173.
[46] ibid 178 and 217.
[47] See, eg, I Go´mez-Palacio and P Muchlinski, 'Admission and Establishment' in P Muchlinski, F Ortino and C Schreuer (eds), *The Oxford Handbook of International Investment Law* (Oxford, Oxford University Press, 2012) 227–257; Salacuse (n 7) 221–22; Muchlinski and Gómez-Palacio (n 30) 242.

The Energy Charter Treaty (ECT), as a sector-specific treaty, aims to 'strengthen the global rule of law on energy issues' by requiring contracting states to commit to 'open markets and non-discriminatory access for foreign investments'.[48] But it only created a 'soft' regime of 'best endeavour' obligations that encourages contracting parties to make voluntary but binding commitments to grant NT or MFN at the pre-investment stage.[49] If the commitments are made, the non-compliance of pre-investment provisions is addressed by diplomatic negotiation or the arbitration provided for in Article 27.[50] Although on November 2020 and July 2021 the negotiation rounds on the modernisation of the ECT proposed that states should pledge to progressively remove barriers to entry and declare no new barriers,[51] according to *Finalisation of the Negotiations on the Modernisation of the Energy Charter Treaty* (June 2022), the 'soft' regime of 'best endeavours' obligations will not become binding. Therefore, the ECT cannot provide strong protection for energy investors at the pre-investment stage.

## C. The Limits of Investment Law in Lifting Barriers to Entry Based on Unproven Geopolitical Concerns

International investment norms have been struggling to accommodate the strategic distrust growing in global capital flows.[52] But they play a limited role in guaranteeing access to foreign energy markets, as they need to balance the protection for investments at the pre-investment stage and the right of host states to regulate.[53] Host states can hardly give up the protection of national interests, such as energy security, in order to embrace investment liberalisation.[54] Also, the establishment of the legal agenda itself is impacted by diplomatic relations between states. For instance, the EU sanctioning of some of China's officials delays the further negotiation of the investment treaty between these two parties.

[48] 'The International Energy Charter: Consolidated Energy Charter Treaty' (Energy Charter, 1994) at www.energycharter.org/fileadmin/DocumentsMedia/Legal/ECTC-en.pdf; R Leal-Arcas, *International Energy Governance: Selected Legal Issues* (Cheltenham, Edward Elgar, 2015) 346.

[49] TW Waelde, 'International Law of Foreign Investment: Towards Regulation by Multilateral Treaties' [1999] *Business Law International* 50, 65; K Hober, 'The Energy Charter Treaty: An Overview' (2007) 8 *Journal of World Investment & Trade* 324, 325; ECT (n 48) Art 10(2)–(3); Waelde (n 11) 31; S Elshihabi, 'The Difficulty Behind Securing Sector-Specific Investment Establishment Rights: The Case of the Energy Charter Treaty' (2001) 35 *The International Lawyer* 137, 148.

[50] Waelde (n 11) 37.

[51] International Energy Charter (2015) 10 at www.energycharter.org/fileadmin/DocumentsMedia/Legal/IEC_EN.pdf.

[52] See, eg, HG Cohen, 'Nation and Markets' (2020) 23 *Journal of International Economic Law* 793, 793; M Du, 'Huawei Strikes Back: Challenging National Security Decisions Before Investment Arbitral Tribunals' (2022) 37 *Emory International Law Review* 1.

[53] Cohen (n 52).

[54] A Goldthau and N Sitter, *A Liberal Actor in a Realist World: The European Union Regulatory State and the Global Political Economy of Energy* (Oxford, Oxford University Press, 2015) 122.

Furthermore, international adjudication bodies are normally deferential to geopolitical assessments made by one party,[55] although they have tried to limit the scope of 'security interests' and build a connection between the measure in question and the security interest.[56] Adjudication bodies may not be able to discuss national security issues as they do not understand the practical complexity of the states involved.[57] For example, Russia challenged the unbundling measure of the EU under GATS, as it would cost Gazprom more to supply gas to the EU and thus adversely impact Gazprom's business of supply services.[58] The EU responded by highlighting its concerns over Russia's possible interruption of the gas supply for political purposes.[59] However, the panel was reluctant to examine whether the 'politically motivated measures of energy-exporting members' might be viewed as threats to the EU's energy security.[60] Similarly, regarding the security exception provided for in GATT, *Russia – Measures Concerning Traffic in Transit* highlights that member states are allowed to determine their perception of national security based on their own assessments.[61] Therefore, regular diplomatic dialogue among states for addressing political concerns may play a complementary role in establishing a common legal framework for promoting energy investments.[62]

## III. Chinese Energy Companies' Difficulties in Managing National Security Reviews

MOFCOM reported that it had been difficult for China's energy companies to access foreign markets because of the national security concerns of host states.[63]

[55] See, eg, J Slawotsky, 'The National Security Exception in US–China FDI and Trade: Lessons from Delaware Corporate Law' (2018) 6(2) *The Chinese Journal of Comparative Law* 228, 250; A Tomkins, National Security and the Role of the Court: A Changed Landscape? (2010) 126 *Law Quarterly Review* 543, 543–44; Du (n 52) 28.

[56] UNCTAD, *World Investment Report 2016: Investor Nationality: Policy Challenges* (UNCTAD, 2017) 97; *CMS Gas Transmission Co v Argentina*, ICSID Case No ARB/01/8, Award (12 May 2005) para 355; *Sempra Energy Int'l v Argentina*, ICSID Case No ARB/02/16, Award (28 September 2007) para 348; *Enron Corp v Argentina*, ICSID Case No ARB/01/3, Award (22 May 2007) paras 306–07.

[57] J Ma, 'International Investment and National Security' (2021) 52 *Vanderbilt Law Review* 899, 934; Cohen (n 52) 808; J Bentonheath, The New Security Challenge to the Economic Order (2020) 129 *Yale Law Journal* 1020, 1072–73.

[58] V Pogoretskyy and K Talus, 'The WTO Panel Report in EU–Energy Package and Its Implications for the EU's Gas Market and Energy Security' (2019) *World Trade Review* 1, 10.

[59] ibid 15.

[60] ibid 16.

[61] The General Agreement on Tariffs and Trade (GATT) (signed in 1947), at www.wto.org/english/docs_e/legal_e/gatt47_01_e.htm; *Russia – Measures Concerning Traffic in Transit*, Panel Report (5 April 2019) WT/DS512/R, para 7.131.

[62] N Pradel, 'The EU External Energy Policy and the Law: Does the EU Really Matter?' in L Squintani et al (eds), *Sustainable Energy United in Diversity – Challenges and Approaches in Energy Transition in the European Union* (Liepzig, EELF, 2014) 237–49, 245.

[63] MOFCOM, *The Report of Development of Overseas Investments 2018* [《对外投资合作发展报告2018》] (2018) 19–20.

Host states are alert to China's massive investments in energy infrastructure because they think China may control their energy supplies (eg, investments in power grids).[64] A empirical study highlights that three Central European states have a more negative perception of Chinese investments in the energy sector due to the strategic nature of this sector, compared with Chinese investments in other economic sectors.[65] Moreover, Chinese energy companies' increasing engagement with technology development and global energy value chains exposes them to more regulatory risks at the pre-investment stage.[66] The EU Commission encourages Member States to pay attention to energy investments that constitute part of the government-led industrial programme, such as China's *Made in China 2025*.[67] In particular, Chinese renewable energy companies have been forbidden to acquire advanced renewable energy technologies or invest in the solar- and wind-power sectors.[68] For example, a transaction by the Chinese POE, ENN was blocked by the US due to its concerns about transferring US technology back to China.[69]

Compared with POEs, managing national security reviews is more difficult for China's energy SOEs.[70] Host states are concerned about the link between Chinese energy SOEs and the Chinese Government, and attach political tags to energy investments made by Chinese SOEs.[71] For example, the EU believed that China would instruct its SOEs to delay maintenance of critical energy infrastructure in the event of a break-down in diplomatic relations.[72] The reviews carried out by the

[64] YP Duan et al, 'China's Overseas Energy Investment Overview' [《中国全球能源投资分析》] (2015) 3 *Sino-Global Energy* 9, 12–13; MA Carrai, The Rise of Screening Mechanisms in the Global North: Weaponizing the Law against China's Weaponized Investments? (2020) 8(2) *The Chinese Journal of Comparative Law* 351, 354; M Otero-Iglesias and M Weissenegger, 'Motivations, Security Threats and Geopolitical Implications of Chinese Investment in the EU Energy Sector: The Case of CDP Reti' (2020) 26 *European Journal of International Relations* 595, 597; A Okutsu, C Venzon and CK Tan, 'China's Belt and Road Power Grids Keep Security Critics Awake' *Nikkei Asian Review* (11 March 2020) at www.ft.com/content/f2b6e395-f1ee-4a6d-8839-009a35555b52.

[65] RQ Turcsanyi, 'Central European Attitudes Towards Chinese Energy Investments: The Cases of Poland, Slovakia, and the Czech Republic' (2017) 101 *Energy Policy* 711, 719.

[66] Rajavuori and Huhta (n 12) 8.

[67] See Bungenberg and Hazarika (n 23) 390; J Seaman, M Huotari and M Otero-Iglesias (eds), *Chinese Investment in Europe – A Country-Level Approach* (ETNC Report, December 2017) at www.ifri.org/en/publications/publications-ifri/ouvrages-ifri/chinese-investment-europe-country-level-approach; W Yin, 'A Comparison of the US and EU Regulatory Responses to China's State Capitalism: Implication, Issue and Direction' (2021) 19 *Asia Europe Journal* 1, 9.

[68] Seaman, Huotari and Otero-Iglesias (n 67).

[69] 'Toshiba Says Transfer of US LNG Business to China's ENN Delayed' *Hellenic Shipping News* (5 April 2019) at www.hellenicshippingnews.com/toshiba-says-transfer-of-u-s-lng-business-to-chinas-enn-delayed.

[70] Carrai (n 64) 353; Editorial (n 26) 646.

[71] C Chang and H Li, 'Political Risks and Evasion Strategies of Chinese Petroleum Corporations during Transnational Operation' [《中国石油企业跨国经营的政治风险及规避策略》] (2008) 24 *Journal of China University of Petroleum* 5; see, eg, White & Case LLP, 'FIRRMA: Proposed CFIUS Legislation Would Bring Significant Changes' (JDSUPRA, 10 November 2017) at www.jdsupra.com/legalnews/firrma-proposed-cfius-legislation-would-38940/; L Xiao, 'CFIUS with More Power: US Will Strengthen the Examination of National Security' [《CFIUS扩权：美国强化国家安全审查制度》] *Zhong Lun Law Firm* (17 October 2018) at www.zhonglun.com/content/2018/10-17/1625174332.html.

[72] Bungenberg and Hazarika (n 23) 389; 'China Raises Concern over EU Investment Screening Initiative' *Xinhuanet* (18 September 2017) at news.xinhuanet.com/english/2017-09/18/c_136618794.htm.

Commission and its Member States focus on SOEs' acquisition of control and their participation in business management.[73] Therefore, China's SOEs fear that they may be discriminated against simply due to unproven geopolitical fears.

Because of these challenges, MOFCOM and Sinosure recorded that Chinese investors suffered significant losses.[74] In the long run, Chinese energy companies' failure to access foreign energy markets will frustrate the realisation of policy goals. For instance, CNPCs' failed acquisition of Slavneft Oil & Gas Company and the Orenburg-based Stimul Company in Russia hampered the implementation of the strategy to diversify oil and gas suppliers.[75]

## IV. Current Discussion of China's Support for Facilitating Market Access

Scholars in the field of international relations have argued that, to mitigate the risk to access to foreign energy markets, the Chinese Government has provided economic incentives for resource-rich states and strengthened political connections with these states.[76] For Downs, through financial, political and even military support, the Chinese Government has cultivated good relations with the resource-rich states, and thus has secured deals on behalf of NOCs.[77] An empirical study highlights that China's diplomatic and financial support has had the significant effect of securing access to foreign energy markets.[78]

### A. Positive Diplomatic Relations

The closer the diplomatic relationship between the two states, the more energy investments that will occur between them.[79] For Lee and others, establishing good relations with resource-rich states has been China's preferred method of choice for entering their energy markets.[80] For instance, Talyor believed that 'China

[73] Yin (n 67) 9.

[74] MOFCOM, *The Report of Development of Overseas Investments 2016* [《对外投资合作发展报告2016》] (2016) 215; see also Sinosure, *Report of Investments Facilitation in Different States 2015* [《国别投资经营便利化状况报告2015》] (2015).

[75] B Kong, *China's International Petroleum Policy* (Santa Barbara, CA, ABC-CLIO, 2009) 108.

[76] See, eg, AM Jaffe and S Lewis, 'Beijing's Oil Diplomacy' (2002) 44 *Survival* 115; D O'Neill, 'Risky Business: The Political Economy of Chinese Investment in Kazakhstan' (2014) 5 *Journal of Eurasian Studies* 145.

[77] E Downs, *Energy Security Series: China* (*Brookings Foreign Policy Studies*, 1 December 2006) 41.

[78] T Wei, J Clegg and L Ma, 'The Conscious and Unconscious Facilitating Role of The Chinese Government in Shaping the Internationalization of Chinese MNCs' (2015) 24 *International Business Review* 331.

[79] P Andrews-Speed, M Qiu and C Len, 'Chinese Engagement in Southeast Asian Energy and Mineral Resources: Motivations and Outlook' (2016) 57 *Eurasian Geography and Economics* 316.

[80] CY Lee, 'China's Energy Diplomacy: Does Chinese Foreign Policy Favor Oil-Producing Countries?' (2019) 15 *Foreign Policy Analysis* 570, 580; D Sun and YH Zoubir, 'China's Economic Diplomacy

aims to establish special relationships with African countries in the hope that this will result in preferential access to oil resources for China's NOCs'.[81] Moreover, it has been argued that Chinese oil and gas investments can bypass investment approval if they are backed by political support from the government authorities of resource-rich states.[82] For instance, a positive bilateral relationship between China and Kazakhstan laid a political foundation for the bilateral energy cooperation.[83] Similarly, the close relations between China and Iran enable Chinese NOCs to maintain good relations with the Iranian local authorities who control oil and gas fields.[84]

## B. Economic Incentives

It is reported that China aimed to 'exclude competitors' interference in its access to oil resources' by taking advantage of the economic reliance of host states on it.[85] The mode of infrastructure-for-oil provides an example of how China has assisted NOCs to invest in the under-developed resource-rich states.[86] In this mode, policy banks grant loans to infrastructure investments made by Chinese companies in resource-rich states.[87] The financing agreements require exporting states to deliver

towards Arab States' [《中国对阿拉伯国家的经济外交》] (2016) 3 *Foreign Social Science* 155, 156; Ø Tunsjø, *Security and Profit in China's Energy Policy* (New York, Columbia University Press, 2013) 231–32; H Voss, PJ Buckley and AR Cross, 'An Assessment of the Effects of Institutional Change on Chinese Outward Direct Investment Activity' in I Alon et al (eds), *China Rules: Globalization and Political Transformation* (London, Palgrave Macmillan, 2009) 135–65.

[81] M Taylor, *The Chinese State, Oil and Energy Security* (Singapore, Palgrave Macmillan, 2014) 171.

[82] SS Seliverstov and VD Krivonosov, 'Structuring Chinese Energy Investments under the Russian Law on Strategic Investments' (2019) 20 *Journal of World Investment & Trade* 355, 367.

[83] S Orazgaliyev, 'The Role of Home Governments in Entry Bargaining of Multinationals: China's Investment in Central Asia's Natural Resource Sector' (2020) 62 *Thunderbird International Business Review* 249, 256.

[84] G Yu, 'China's Energy Foreign Policy towards Iran: Domestic Factors and Geopolitical Challenges' in MP Amineh and Y Guang (eds), *Secure Oil and Alternative Energy* (Leiden, Brill, 2012) 143–66, 150.

[85] M Gueldry and W Liang, 'China's Global Energy Diplomacy: Behavior Normalization Through Economic Interdependence or Resource Neo-mercantilism and Power Politics?' (2016) 21 *Journal of Chinese Political Science* 217, 227.

[86] C Zhang, *The Domestic Dynamics of China's Energy Diplomacy* (Singapore, World Scientific, 2016) 126; J Jiang and C Ding, *Update on Overseas Investments by China's National Oil Companies: Achievements and Challenges since 2011* (IEA, 2014); Ł Jureńczyk, 'Analysing China's "Angola Model": A Pattern for Chinese Involvement in Africa?' (2020) 42 *Strategic Review for Southern Africa* 1, 6 and 11; L Corkin, *Uncovering African Agency: Angola's Management of China's Credit Lines* (Abingdon, Routledge, 2013) 75–86; M Sanfilippo, 'Chinese FDI to Africa: What Is the Nexus with Foreign Economic Cooperation?' (2010) 22(1) *African Development Review* 599, 602; DM Shapiro, C Vecino and J Li, 'Exploring China's State-Led FDI Model: Evidence from the Extractive Sectors in Latin America' (2017) 35 *Asia Pacific Journal of Management* 11, 23.

[87] Tunsjø (n 80) 81; PC Evans and ES Downs, 'Untangling China's Quest for Oil through State-backed Financial Deals', *Policy Brief* 154 (The Brookings Institution, May 2006); D Braeutigam and KP Gallagher, 'Bartering Globalization: China's Commodity-backed Finance in Africa and Latin America' (2014) 5 *Global Policy* 346, 347; KP Gallagher and A Irwin, 'China's Economic Statecraft in Latin America' (2015) 88 *Pacific Affairs* 99, 117.

a certain amount of oil or gas as a repayment for the loan provided by the policy bank.[88] The policy banks finally receive the repayment generated by proceeds earned from the sale of oil to Chinese NOCs. When CDB directly financed the host government, the bank participated in drafting bilateral economic cooperation plans between China and other foreign governments,[89] and gave recommendations on investment plans.[90] Therefore, the mode of infrastructure-for-oil secured deals for Chinese energy SOEs. For instance, the CDB concluded a loan-for-gas agreement with Turkmengaz in 2009 to finance its gas exploration of the South Yolotan field. Later, the Turkmenistan Government awarded CNPC a service contract in 2009.[91]

## V. Domestic Mechanisms for Managing Pre-Investment Risks

The Chinese Government has endeavoured to provide both sufficient information about the investment environment in host states and remedies for combatting barriers to entering foreign markets. In principle, Chinese energy companies can benefit from the regulatory support to prevent risks.[92] However, in practice, it has been hard for them to rely on the general and vague administrative remedies for addressing denial of access to foreign energy markets.

### A. Information Services

MOFCOM reported that Chinese investors had suffered substantial losses (eg, from investments in Africa and Latin America) due to insufficient information on local markets, laws and labour policies.[93] In particular, POEs struggled to overcome the difficulties of information asymmetry due to their limited overseas experience and insufficient competence regarding risk management.[94] The Chinese Government

[88] Tunsjø (n 80) 82; L Corkin, 'Redefining Foreign Policy Impulses toward Africa: The Roles of the MFA, the MOFCOM and China EXIM Bank' (2011) 40 *Journal of Current Chinese Affairs* 61, 69.

[89] B Kong, *Modernization Through Globalization: Why China Finances Foreign Energy Projects Worldwide* (Singapore, Palgrave Macmillan, 2019) 39–40.

[90] B Hogenboom, 'Latin America and China's Transnationalizing Oil Industry: A Political Economy Assessment of New Relations' (2014) 13 *Perspectives on Global Development and Technology* 626, 635–36.

[91] ES Downs, *Inside China Inc: China Development Bank's Cross-Border Energy Deals* (Brookings, March 2011) 53 and 75.

[92] W Xiao and L Liu, *Internationalization of China's Privately Owned Enterprises: Determinants and Pattern Selection* (Singapore, World Scientific, 2015) 95–96.

[93] MOFCOM, *The Report on Development of Overseas Investments 2014* [《对外投资合作发展报告2014》] 70 and 75.

[94] J Qian, 'Suggestions on Overseas Energy Investments of Companies from Xin Jin' (The Institute of Economic Research of Xin Jiang Development and Reform, 15 August 2017) at xjyj.xjdrc.gov.cn/info/1027/5114.htm.

has therefore optimised information services to help Chinese energy companies to manage pre-investment risks.[95]

According to the State Council, the comprehensive information service platform updates 'information on the investment environment, industrial development and policies, market demand, and project cooperation'.[96] More specifically, MOFCOM and MFA have jointly published the *Guidelines on Investing in Different States (Regions)* annually.[97] Nearly all important resource-rich states are included in the *Guidelines*.[98] Chinese energy companies can also obtain the information from the *Report on Investment Conditions of Various Host Countries*, issued by MOFCOM.[99]

Apart from the written guidance, MOFCOM requires the Chamber of Commerce (Association), directed by the commercial offices of local embassies, to build communication platforms to enable new investors to consult with the authorities of host governments.[100] The Chinese embassies also assist domestic energy investors to conduct feasibility assessments to evaluate the likely success of the proposed project.[101] For example, the Chinese embassy in Zambia provided investment options for investors, as well as helping Chinese investors to communicate and to negotiate with local authorities.[102]

By counting on information services, energy investors should be able to develop more mature systems of risk control.[103] For instance, Chinese oil companies made use of dedicated services provided by the Ghana embassy to arrange meetings with local authorities and the NOC of Ghana.[104] In particular, being familiar with host

[95] Sanfilippo (n 86) 604.

[96] State Council, *Guiding Opinions on Promoting Cooperation on Manufacture and Productivity* [《国务院关于推进国际产能和装备制造合作的指导意见》] (2015).

[97] All *Guidelines* are available at fec.mofcom.gov.cn/article/gbdqzn/.

[98] ibid.

[99] State Council, Notice on the Instruction of Further Guiding and Regulating Overseas Investments' Direction [《国务院办公厅转发国家发展改革委、商务部、人民银行和外交部关于进一步引导和规范境外投资方向知道意见的通知》] (2017).

[100] MOFCOM, Notice on Issuing the Interim Regulation on the Establishment of Chambers of Commerce (Associations) of Overseas Sino-funded Enterprises [《关于成立境外中资企业商会（协会）的暂行规定》] (2002); MOFCOM, Notice on Issuing the Model Service Guidelines for Overseas Economic and Trade Cooperation Zones [《商务部关于印发<境外经贸合作区服务指南范本>的通知》] (2015).

[101] State Council, *Opinions on Encouraging and Regulating Overseas Investments Cooperation* [《国务院关于鼓励和规范企业对外投资合作的意见》] (2007); M Meidan, *The Structure of China's Oil Industry: Past Trends and Future Prospects* (Oxford Institute for Energy Studies, June 2016) 42 at www.oxfordenergy.org/wpcms/wp-content/uploads/2016/05/The-structure-of-Chinas-oil-industry-past-trends-and-future-prospects-WPM-66.pdf.

[102] L Kong, 'Interpreting *Decision on Reform of Investment System* (2004): The New Trend of the Reform of the Investment Management System' [《投资体制改革新动向—对<国务院关于投资体制改革的决定>》] (2005) 1 *Macro-Economics* 19, 21.

[103] Y Li and Z Tian, 'Risks and Solution of Cross-Border Operation of Chinese Oil Companies' [《中国石油企业跨国经营若干风险及对策分析》] (2007) 23 *Techno-Economics in Petrochemicals* 4, 6.

[104] S Hradus, 'Chinese National Oil Companies in Ghana: CNOOC and Sinopec' (2014) 13 *Perspectives on Global Development and Technology* 588.

states' laws and regulations enabled these companies to prepare for investment-screening mechanisms.[105] For example, by making use of the introduction to the regulatory environment, CNOOC promised to submit a compliance report every year to the Industrial Ministry of Canada when seeking to acquire shares in Nexen.[106] However, the information service system remains a problem.[107] Domestic energy companies cannot adjust investment strategies promptly, as the guidance book is issued annually.[108]

## B. Administrative Remedies for Combatting Barriers to Entry

In addition to the information service system, the Chinese Government has endeavoured to offer domestic administrative remedies to investors at the pre-investment stage.[109] MOFCOM issued the Foreign Trade Barrier Investigation Rules in 2005. These provide that 'the foreign investment barrier investigation shall be carried out by referring to the present Rules'.[110] Provided that the investigated practice is shown to be a barrier to investment, MOFCOM will pursue bilateral negotiations or initiate a settlement mechanism for multilateral disputes.[111] In practice, the following two cases demonstrate that energy companies withdrew from the transaction or brought the case before the court, instead of turning to the administrative remedies, when facing denial of access to foreign energy markets.

On 23 June 2005, CNOOC Ltd made an all-cash bid of US$18.5 billion for Unocal.[112] To alleviate the US's national security concerns, such as theft of exploration technology and the locking up of resources, CNOOC was willing to submit to a CIFUS review in early July.[113] The US regulator thought that the high bidding price

[105] X Qiao, D Chen and G Zhang, 'The Research of the International Macro-Promotion Mechanism of Chinese Outbound Resources Investments' [《中国资源类境外投资国际宏观促进机制研究》] (2009) 23 *East China Economic Management* 40.

[106] MOFCOM (n 93) 159–60.

[107] R Li, 'The Establishment of Legal Protection Mechanism of Chinese Overseas Energy Investments under the Comparative Law' [《比较法视野下中国海外能源投资保障法律机制的构建》] (2017) 6 *Law Review* 119, 124.

[108] C Pei and W Zheng, *China's Outbound Foreign Direct Investment Promotion System* (Singapore, Springer, 2015) 159–60.

[109] S Wang, 'National Treatment to Chinese Investors at the *Ex Ante* Stage from the Geopolitical Perspective' [《地缘政治视阈下的中国海外投资准入国民待遇保护》] (2012) 2 *Studies in Law and Business* 112, 119; J Zhou, 'Investment Barriers in South Asian Countries: Implications for China and Policy Recommendations' [《南亚国家投资壁垒及其对我国的影响、对策建议》] (2018) 3 *South Asian Studies* 39, 42.

[110] MOFCOM (n 8) Art 35.

[111] ibid Art 33.

[112] Wharton School, University of Pennsylvania, 'Is CNOOC's Bid for Unocal a Threat to America?' at knowledge.wharton.upenn.edu/article/is-cnoocs-bid-for-unocal-a-threat-to-america/.

[113] AT Lenihan, *Balancing Power Without Weapons* (Cambridge, Cambridge University Press, 2018) 114.

provided by CNOOC[114] was explained by the need of the Chinese Government to pursue strategic goals.[115] Because the legislative branches later issued new laws to extend the review of the deal, the company dropped the bid in August 2005 to avoid financial losses.[116]

Later, in 2012, the Sany company tried to protect its right by challenging the decision to divest itself of the assets of its subsidiary – Ralls – in the US, which was made by CIFUS.[117] Ralls purchased Lower Ridge Windfarm LLC, located within the restricted airspace of the US Navy even after relocation. CIFUS thus identified the project as a threat to national security. The US President ordered Ralls to divest itself of the project. Ralls appealed on the grounds of its due process rights.[118] The Court refused to make decisions on foreign policy matters, namely, whether the investment posed a national security threat to the US, but was able to assess how the procedure was complied with by the CIFUS and the President.[119] The Court stated that 'it is not disputed that neither CFIUS nor the President gave Ralls notice of the evidence on which they respectively relied nor an opportunity to rebut that evidence'.[120] Therefore, the Court concluded that 'the Presidential Order deprived Ralls of its constitutionally protected property interests without due process of law'.[121] Accordingly, the Sany company successfully defended its right to continue investing in the US by making use of legal remedies provided in the host state – the US – instead of pursuing China's administrative remedies. It was very likely that the Sany company realised that the involvement of domestic administrative departments could only intensify the US's political concerns. This

[114] See Wharton School (n 112); V Vivoda and G Graetz, 'Mergers and Acquisitions: The Politics of Megadeals in the Mining Industry' in T O'Callaghan and G Graetz (eds), *Mining in the Asia-Pacific* (Cham, Springer International Publishing, 2017) 121–38; see also J Kahn, 'China's Costly Quest for Energy Control' *New York Times* (27 June 2005) at www.nytimes.com/2005/06/27/business/worldbusiness/chinas-costly-quest-for-energy-control.html.

[115] P Bansal, S Kim and B Lim, 'Special Report: The US and China Start an M&A Cold War' *Reuters* (12 April 2011) at www.reuters.com/article/us-specialreport-china-merger-idUKTRE73B47V20110412.

[116] AS Campion, *The Geopolitics of Red Oil* (London, Routledge, 2016) 107; D Lee and E Douglass, 'Chinese Drop Takeover Bid for Unocal' *Los Angeles Times* (3 August 2005) at www.latimes.com/archives/la-xpm-2005-aug-03-fi-chinaoil3-story.html; Y Liang, *Legal Protection and Risk Prevention on Outbound Investment by Chinese Investors* [《中国投资者海外投资法律保障与风险防范》] (Beijing, Law Press, 2010).

[117] See *Ralls v CIFUS* (n 1).

[118] ibid 27.

[119] H Zhao, 'The Absence of Investor Protection in National Security Investigations for Foreign Investment: An Analysis of the Ralls v Obama Case' [《论外资并购国家安全审查中的投资者保护缺失—以三一集团诉奥巴马案为视角》] (2015) 37 *Modern Law Science* 139, 143; S Wang, 'Legal Research of "Transactions Controlled by Foreign Governments in International Investments: An Analysis of the Ralls v Obama Case' [《国际投资中"外国政府控制的交易"之法律问题研究-以三一集团诉奥巴马案引发的思考》] (2013) 5 *Studies in Law and Business* 102, 169; B Gong and G Tan, 'The Availability of Judicial Review over the Vetoing of Foreign Acquisition by the US President for National Security: Comments on the Case of *Ralls Corporation v Barack H Obama* as the US President' [《美国总统以国家安全为由否决外资并购令可诉性分析—兼析中国三一集团告美国总统否决并购侵权案》] (2014) 3 *International Business Research* 46.

[120] See *Ralls v CIFUS* (n 1) 11.

[121] ibid 36.

implies that turning to local remedies can be a way of defending companies' right to access foreign energy markets, if host states have a strong rule of law.

## VI. Greater Protection from Investment Treaties at the Entry Stage

Challenging the 'weaponized national security decisions' before arbitration tribunals has become the increasing choice of China's investors.[122] Given that, it is necessary to assess what protection is given by investment treaties. China's BITs are generally consistent with the practice that investment treaties are not created as 'market access treaties' but to protect investments once they are made.[123] Most of China's BITs with its energy cooperation partners allow these partners to admit investments in accordance with their laws and regulations.[124] In other words, these energy cooperation partners have the discretion to discriminate between China's energy companies and their domestic energy companies or energy companies from third states regarding the making of investments.[125] For example, China's BITs with Indonesia and Saudi Arabia provide that investors' investments are accorded fair and equitable treatment before investments are made.[126] This provision is problematic because it may only imply a 'fair and reasonable application or administration of laws and regulations'.[127] This allows the Governments of Indonesia and Saudi Arabia to employ full discretion to interpret the content of laws and regulations and possibly ban China's energy investments.

However, some of Chinese BITs grant MFN treatment at the entry stage.[128] Therefore, in national security reviews, contracting states are not allowed to discriminate against China's energy companies based only on their geopolitical tensions with China, or to favour investors from third states who have developed good diplomatic relations with them. China and Uzbekistan agreed on MFN

[122] Du (n 52).

[123] N Gallagher and W Shan, *Chinese Investment Treaties: Policies and Practice* (Oxford, Oxford University Press, 2009) para 2.100; Berger (n 4) 853–54.

[124] China–Uzbekistan BIT (2011) Art 2; China–Mongolia BIT (1991) Art 2; China–Kyrgyzstan BIT (1992) Art 2; China–Kazakhstan BIT (1992) Art 2; China–Tajikistan BIT (1993) Art 2; China–Cambodia BIT (1996) Art 2; China–Sudan BIT (1997) Art 2; China–Qatar BIT (1999) Art 2; China–Iran BIT (2000) Art 3; China–Nigeria BIT (2001) Art 2; China–Myanmar BIT (2001) Art 2; China–Russia BIT (2006) Art 2; Free Trade Agreement between the Government of the People's Republic of China and the Government of the Islamic Republic of Pakistan (2006) Art 47; China-United Republic of Tanzania BIT (2013) Art 2.

[125] GM Vaccaro-Incisa and W Giemza, 'Economic Integration via Novel Investment Agreements: CAI's Focus on Market Access vis-à-vis the Current Bilateral Investment Treaties Between China and European Union Member States' (2022) 23 *The Journal of World Investment & Trade* 521, 534.

[126] China–Indonesia BIT (1994) Art 2; China–Saudi Arabia BIT (1995) Art 2.

[127] Gallagher and Shan (n 123) para 2.105.

[128] Berger (n 4); W Shen, 'Leaning Towards a More Liberal Stance' (2010) 26 *Arbitration International* 549, 565.

treatment at the 'establishment' stage.[129] The Agreement on Investment of the Framework Agreement on Comprehensive Economic Cooperation between China and ASEAN (2010) also specifies that both China and ASEAN should liberalise investment regimes and grant MFN treatment at the 'establishment/admission' stage.[130] Likewise, the China–Canada BIT grants MFN treatment to companies from China and Canada at the ex ante stage.[131] Therefore, in the national security reviews of those contracting states, China's energy companies should be treated no less favourably than energy companies from third states.

More recently, the Chinese Government has been working on including provisions on non-discriminatory treatment for the establishment of investments in more investment treaties.[132] Through an advanced practice of admitting investments, China's energy companies are likely to have a wider access to foreign energy sectors. China signed the Regional Comprehensive Economic Partnership Agreement (RCEP) in November 2020.[133] ASEAN states grant both NT and MFN treatment to Chinese companies regarding their new establishment.[134] Relying on the non-discriminatory treatment, China's energy companies should in principle have the confidence that they will not be discriminated against regarding the making of investments in the investment-screening mechanism if an ASEAN state does not make any exceptions to access to the energy sector. More specifically, this agreement created a voluntary regime of best endeavour obligations for simplifying approval procedures and offering information services to investors.[135] Therefore, ASEAN states should aim to keep their national security review processes streamlined.

The recently signed EU–China Comprehensive Agreement on Investment (CAI) also deserves attention, because China's energy companies have aggressively invested in the renewable energy sectors of European states.[136] During the negotiation of CAI, China was concerned about domestic companies' access to the EU due to growing protectionist sentiments on the Continent.[137] To promote investments, both parties have adopted the negative-list approach with respect to

[129] China–Uzbekistan BIT (2011) Art 4.

[130] Agreement on Investment of the Framework Agreement on Comprehensive Economic Cooperation between China and ASEAN (2010) Arts 2 and 5.

[131] Canada–China Promotion and Reciprocal Protection of Investments Agreement (CCFIPPA) (entered into force in 2014) Art 5.

[132] G Shaffer and H Gao, 'A New Chinese Economic Order?' [2020] *Journal of International Economic Law* 1, 16; Wang (n 4) 167.

[133] RCEP, 'ASEAN hits historic milestone with signing of RCEP' at rcepsec.org/2020/11/26/asean-hits-historic-milestone-with-signing-of-rcep/.

[134] The Regional Comprehensive Economic Partnership (RCEP) Agreement (2020) Arts 10.3 and 10.4.

[135] ibid Art 10.17.1.

[136] See, eg, P Pareja-Alcaraz, 'Chinese Investments in Southern Europe's Energy Sectors: Similarities and Divergences in China's Strategies in Greece, Italy, Portugal and Spain' (2017) 101 *Energy Policy* 700.

[137] F Bickenbach, WH Liu and G Li, 'The EU–China Bilateral Investment Agreement in Negotiation: Motivation, Conflicts and Perspectives', *Kiel Policy Brief* No 95 (October 2015) 4.

granting NT at the entry stage in the CAI.[138] Although China's energy companies have already invested in the European energy sector, the negotiation of CAI will result in a binding commitment to open up the EU's energy sector.[139] Chinese energy companies, including energy SOEs, will thus in principle be granted non-discriminatory treatment, and will not need to comply with performance requirements when entering the EU's energy market.[140] China's investors are also granted the right to make a review or appeal regarding the 'administrative actions' relevant to 'the establishment of enterprises'.[141] Therefore, it is possible for China's energy companies to challenge the decision on banning their investments based on national security concerns.

However, there are limits to China's legal agenda for lifting barriers to entry. Investment treaties usually include a security exception, which allows host states to exempt themselves from liability if they successfully invoke the public interest exception (eg, Article 10.15 RCEP).[142] The China–Australia Free Trade Agreement also excludes the protection of security interests from Australia's treaty obligations.[143] Furthermore, national security decisions are not enforceable in some Chinese BITs. For example, a national security decision made at the ex ante stage cannot be challenged according to the Canada–China BIT.[144] Given that, the Chinese Government has made efforts to achieve political agreement with its energy cooperation partners for the promotion of investment. But it does not mean that China has given up regulatory instruments for facilitating access to foreign energy markets.

## VII. Policy Coordination for Investment Promotion

Host states' national security concerns usually derive from their mistrust of China.[145] The BRI's abstract cooperation priorities leave host states suspicious

[138] EU–China Comprehensive Agreement on Investment (CAI) (signed in 2021); H Wang and L Wang, 'China's Bilateral Investment Treaties' in Chaisse et al (eds) (n 25) 1–21, 13; Vaccaro-Incisa and Giemza (n 125) 540.

[139] 'EU agrees investment deal with China to rebalance ties' *Reuters* (30 December 2020).

[140] EU–China CAI (2021) (n 138) s 2, Arts 3, 4 and 5.

[141] ibid s 3, subs 1 (Art 1) and subs 2 (Art 6).

[142] OECD, *International Investment Perspectives: Freedom of Investment in A Changing World* (OECD 2007).

[143] China–Australia Free Trade Agreement (signed in 2015) Annex 3, Section B.

[144] China–Canada BIT (signed in 2012), Annex D.34, Can–China, 9 September 2012, providing 'A decision by Canada following a review under the Investment Canada Act, an Act respecting investment in Canada, with respect to whether or not to: (a) initially approve an investment that is subject to review; or (b) permit an investment that is subject to national security review; shall not be subject to the dispute settlement provisions under Article 15 and Part C of this Agreement.'

[145] N Morris, 'Developing a Sustainable Legal System for the Belt and Road Initiative' in W Shan, K Nuotio and K Zhang (eds), *Normative Readings of the Belt and Road Initiative* (Singapore, Springer, 2018) 43–58, 46; H Liu, Q Feng and H Zhao, 'Challenges and Counter-Measures for China's OFDI in the Context of Intensified Foreign Investment Security Review – Based on Japanese Experience of Evading US Investment Barriers' [《外资安全审查加剧背景下中国OFDI面临的挑战及对策》] (2022) 8 *International Trade* 70, 70.

of the contribution of this grand strategy to the development of their energy sectors.[146] MOFCOM and NEA realised that 'trustworthy arrangements between states for investment cooperation help to address host states' suspicion and ensure projects operation'.[147] Therefore, achieving political agreement is a prerequisite for pushing forward energy cooperation.[148] To achieve political agreement, China has coordinated energy development policies with host states by complying with the principle of common development, sought regular interstate dialogues and signed binding or non-binding energy cooperation agreements. These efforts possibly lead to the establishment of binding legal regimes for investment promotion, as this process can be viewed as a progressive approach that reaches a political consensus first and leaves to the future negotiations addressing controversial issues.[149]

## A. Policy Coordination Based on the Principle of Common Development

Common development in both China and host states can marginalise political tensions by meeting the development needs of the host state.[150] If the benefits that host states can obtain from China's energy projects outweigh the costs of rejecting China's investments,[151] these states will be eager to eliminate barriers to entry.[152]

[146] A Jiang, B Liu and J Huang, 'A Research Review of China-Central Asia Energy Cooperation in the BRI' [《"一带一路"背景下中国—中亚能源合作研究述要》] (2017) 1 *Journal of Guizhou Provincial Party School* 63, 65; W Shan, 'Introduction' in Shan, Nuotio and Zhang (eds) (n 145) 1–6, 2.

[147] MOFCOM, Initiative on Promoting Unimpeded Trade Cooperation along the Belt and Road (26 May 2017) at english.mofcom.gov.cn/article/newsrelease/counselorsoffice/westernasiaandafricareport/201705/20170502582635.shtml; Morris (n 145) 46; NEA, *Vision and Actions on Energy Cooperation in Jointly Building Silk Road Economic Belt and 21st Century Maritime Silk Road* (2017).

[148] X Chen, 'China's Energy Security and China-Russia Energy Cooperation' [《中国能源安全与中俄能源合作》] (2017) 3 *North Eastern Asia* 59, 68; X Wang, 'Sino-Pakistan Economic and Trade Relations: Status Quo and Challenges' in R Wang and C Zhu (eds), *Annual Report on the Development of International Relations in the Indian Ocean Region* (Berlin, Springer, 2014) 97–130, 111; A Vangeli, 'The Normative Foundations of the Belt and Road Initiative' in Shan, Nuotio and Zhang (eds) (n 145) 59–83, 70; C Bian, 'Foreign Direct Investment Screening and National Security: Reducing Regulatory Hurdles to Investors Through Induced Reciprocity' (2021) 22 *Journal of World Investment & Trade* 561, 593.

[149] J Chaisse, 'China's International Investment Policy: Formation, Evolution, and Transformation(s)' in J Chaisse and L Nottage (eds), *International Investment Treaties and Arbitration Across Asia* (Leiden, Brill, 2018) 544–78, 571–72.

[150] A Roberts, H Choer Moraes and V Ferguson, 'Toward a Geoeconomic Order' (2019) 22 *Journal of International Economic Law* 655, 660; Y Wang, *The Belt and Road Initiative: What Will China Offer the World in Its Rise?* (Beijing, New World Press, 2016) 57; N Nie, 'China's Risks in Overseas Investment and the Preventions in Participating in the "One Belt and One Road" Project' [《中国参与共建"一带一路"的对外投资风险来源及防范机制》] (2016) 38 *Contemporary Economic Management* 84, 88.

[151] E Koolaee and M Tisheyar, 'New Regionalism in the Shanghai Cooperation Organization (SCO)' (2014) 41 *International Studies Journal* 97, 108; D O'Neill, 'Playing Risk: Chinese Foreign Direct Investment in Cambodia' (2014) 36 *Contemporary Southeast Asia* 173, 175.

[152] Y Hu, 'Roadmap of China's Energy Security Strategy in Context of New Silk Road Initiative: Legal and Policy Implication from ECT and NAFTA' (2017) 3 *Entrepreneurship & Alliance in OBOR* 1, 5.

As confirmed by the Chinese Government, its overseas energy investments should actively contribute to local economic and social development, while achieving self-growth and guaranteeing access to oil and gas.[153] For instance, China can invite host states to invest in its domestic energy market to marginalise the political sensitivity of Chinese investments in the host states.[154]

Given the importance of common development, MOFCOM and the State Council proposed policy coordination as a major means of realising the development goals of both China and its cooperation partners,[155] and perceived that policy coordination could contribute to long-term stable cooperative relationships.[156] The *Measures for Managing Overseas Investments* (2017) also called for 'strengthening policy exchange and coordination, and creating a fair and investor-friendly environment'.[157] In the BRI, the central Government believed that there should be 'a multi-level intergovernmental macro policy exchange' that helps to boost investment cooperation.[158] Through policy coordination, China and the BRI states have worked both to open markets and to 'encourage a predictable environment for making investments'.[159] For example, Middle Eastern states such as Saudi Arabia and Iran lack knowledge of technology for renewable energy development, thus giving Chinese energy companies opportunities to expand their shares of these markets.[160]

More specifically, NDRC and NEA have advanced the harmonisation of energy infrastructure development plans.[161] The *Plan of Action to Implement the Joint Declaration on the ASEAN–China Strategic Partnership for Peace and Prosperity (2016–2020)* (2015) promoted exchanges of energy infrastructure development plans ('particularly on hydrology, hydropower, coal and clean coal technology, and gas-fired power plants').[162] Therefore, Chinese power companies can expand their

[153] State Council, China's Energy Policy 2012; MOFCOM, *The Report of Development of Overseas Investments 2015* [《对外投资合作发展报告2015》] (2015) 177; NEA (n 147).

[154] Shan and Wang (n 6); Jiang, Liu and Huang (n 146) 66.

[155] MOFCOM (n 63) 17.

[156] State Council, *Opinions on Encouraging and Promoting Wholesome Development of Private Investment* [《国务院关于鼓励和引导民间投资健康发展的若干意见》] (2010).

[157] NDRC, Measures for the Administration of Overseas Investment of Enterprises [《企业境外投资管理办法》] (2017) Art 11.

[158] NDRC, MFA and MOFCOM, *Vision and Proposed Actions Outlined on Jointly Building Silk Road Economic Belt and 21st-Century Maritime Silk Road* (2015).

[159] 'Joint Communique of the Leaders' Roundtable of the Belt and Road Forum for International Cooperation' (2019) at www.fmprc.gov.cn/mfa_eng/zxxx_662805/t1658766.shtml; S Lain, 'The Potential and Pitfalls of Connectivity along the Silk Road Economic Belt in China's Belt and Road Initiative and Its Impact in Central Asia' in M Laruelle (ed), *China's Belt and Road Initiative and Its Impact in Central Asia* (Washington, DC, The George Washington University, Central Asia Program, 2018) 1–10, 1.

[160] Y Zhang and X Jiang, 'The Influence of Trump's New Energy Policy and China's Countermeasures' [《特朗普能源新政的影响及我国应对策略》] (2018) 20 *Journal of Southwest Petroleum University* 12.

[161] NDRC, *The Revolutionary Strategy of Energy Production and Consumption (2016–2030)* [《能源生产和消费革命战略（2016–2030)》] (2016).

[162] Plan of Action to Implement the Joint Declaration on ASEAN–China Strategic Partnership for Peace and Prosperity (2016–2020) (2015) section 2.10 at asean.org/storage/2012/05/ASEAN-China-POA-2021-2025.pdf.

business in ASEAN states by meeting the important energy infrastructure needs of BRI states.[163]

However, China did not to 'transplant Chinese law into host states or direct intervention in the legal systems of recipient economies'.[164] NEA explained that China's energy cooperation partners could interpret collaboration principles in accordance with their interests, influence the cooperation agenda and play a role in building the regional energy order.[165] Energy policymakers of those partners can propose concrete cooperative measures by considering the current state of their energy development.[166] Therefore, these states can take advantage of their competitiveness and meet the development needs of their energy industries.[167]

Accordingly, coordinating energy policies can boost energy interdependence, alleviate concerns of host states and offer Chinese energy companies easy access to the energy markets of host states. Achieving harmonisation usually starts with interstate dialogue, then comes the negotiation of MOUs or framework agreements, and finally the presentation of joint development programmes or binding agreements for specific projects.[168]

## B. Contribution of Interstate Dialogue to Policy Coordination

Interstate dialogue has helped the Chinese Government to coordinate development policies with its energy cooperation partners and thus to promote investments, as explained by the State Council, NDRC and MOFCOM.[169] The

[163] C Gao, 'The Strategic Importance of the Belt and Road Initiative from the Perspective of Transformation of China's Economic Diplomacy' [《从中国经济外交转型的视角看"一带一路"的战略性》] (2015) 4 *International Review* 35, 43; G Desarnaud and J Seaman, 'OBOR and Energy: China's Evolving Internationalization Strategy in Three Years of China's New Silk Roads from Words to (Re)action?' in A Ekman (ed), *Three Years of China's New Silk Roads from Words to (Re)action* (Paris, Ifri, 2017) 29–40, 29.

[164] MS Erie, 'Chinese Law and Development' (2020) 62(1) *Harvard International Law Journal.*

[165] NEA (n 147); M Kaczmarski, 'Non-Western Visions of Regionalism: China's New Silk Road and Russia's Eurasian Economic Union' (2017) 93 *International Affairs* 1357, 1366.

[166] S Wu, 'Current Status of Prospects of China-Central Asia Oil and Gas Cooperation' [《浅析中国－中亚油气合作现状与前景》] (2018) 10 *China Chemical Trade* 1, 3; Jiang, Liu and Huang (n 146) 66; C Bao and H Wang, 'The Contribution of Developing Central Asia's Natural Gas Resources to China's Security of Interests and Related Advice' [《"丝绸之路经济带"中亚天然气资源开发利用对中国的保障效益及对策建议》] (2018) 33 *Chinese Academy of Science* 585, 590.

[167] NEA, Cooperation Principles and Concrete Actions of the Belt and Road Energy Partnership [《"一带一路"能源合作原则与行动》] (2019); Office of the Leading Group for the Belt and Road Initiative, *Building the Belt and Road: Concept, Practice and China's Contribution* (May 2017) 49–52.

[168] Wang, 'China's Approach to the Belt and Road Initiative' (n 5) 42.

[169] MOFCOM (n 63) 72; MOFCOM (n 93) 206; NDRC, *The 12th Five-Year Plan of Capitalizing Foreign Capital and Overseas Investments* [《"十二五"利用外资和境外投资规划》] (2012); State Council (n 96). See also Office of the Leading Group for the Belt and Road Initiative (n 167) 49–52; NDRC et al, 'The Instruction of Encouraging and Guiding Overseas Investment of Private Owned Enterprises' [《关于鼓励和引导民营企业积极开展外投资的实施意见》] (2012); C Pei, Chinese Companies' Overseas Investments and Opportunities in the Belt and Road Initiative' [《中国企业对外投资与"一带一路"建设机遇》] (2017) 3 *Financial Supervision* 16, 19.

top leaders of China and its cooperative partners have explored the economic competitive advantages in bilateral or multilateral dialogues, respectively.[170] For instance, given the important status of Russia, Central Asian states and the Middle East as oil and gas suppliers, the Chinese leadership had meetings with the leaders of these states to reach consensus on energy package deals or specific energy projects.[171] By relying on the consensus, China's energy companies can identify the sovereign choices of the BRI states (eg, the extent of their commitment to projects).[172]

To formalise interstate dialogues, NDRC suggested the establishment of intergovernmental working mechanisms.[173] The *Vision and Actions on Energy Cooperation in Jointly Building Silk Road Economic Belt and 21st-Century Maritime Silk Road* (2017) proposed regular bilateral joint working mechanisms for realising energy investments.[174] By exchanging government expectations of investments, formulating implementation plans, fixing implementation problems and offering policy support,[175] these mechanisms have helped to carry out projects step by step, and have left room for future adjustments in accordance with the other state's development needs and any change in its political economy.[176] For instance, according to NDRC, the China–Kazakhstan Energy Committee and the China–Turkmenistan Energy Committee have played a strong role in deepening investment cooperation.[177] MOFCOM also reported that the Chinese Government established the Sino-African Cooperation Forum to increase domestic energy companies' access to African states.[178]

[170] Wang (n 150) 136; M Johec and JJ Kyzy, 'China's BRI Investments, Risks, and Opportunities in Kazakhstan and Kyrgyzstan' in Laruelle (ed) (n 159) 67–76, 71.

[171] J Henderson and T Mitrova, *Energy Relations between Russia and China: Playing Chess with the Dragon* (Oxford Institute for Energy Studies, August 2016) 37; H Sun, 'Energy Cooperation between China and Latin America' in Amineh and Guang (eds) (n 84) 213–43, 227.

[172] Vangeli (n 148) 69; G Cao and J Xie, 'State Visits and the Large-scale Overseas Investment of China's Enterprises: A Case Study of Transportation Infrastructure Industry' [《国事访问的海外大型投资促进效应 —以交通基础设施行业为例》] (2022) 38 *International Economics and Trade Research* 87.

[173] NDRC (n 169).

[174] NEA (n 147).

[175] Wang (n 150) 169; D Zhou, 'An Analysis of Controllability of Chinese Enterprises' Energy Investment Risk in Pakistan' (2018) 248 *Advances in Social Science, Education and Humanities Research* 31, 35.

[176] Shaffer and Gao (n 132) 27; Wang (n 150) 159; Q Xu, 'The Strategically Important Core of China's International Energy Cooperation: Energy Technology, Energy Networks and Green Development' [《中国国际能源合作战略重点之— 能源技术、能源网络共享与绿色发展》] (2018) 4 *Petroleum Technology Forum* 8, 9; 'Why the Ambiguity of China's Belt and Road Initiative is Perhaps its Biggest Strength' *Forbes* (19 October 2017) at www.forbes.com/sites/wadeshepard/2017/10/19/what-chinas-belt-and-road-initiative-is-really-all-about/#6307ff38e4de; see also Q Yuan and Y Yu, 'The Research of Political Risks of Overseas Merger and Acquisition of Chinese Resource-Based Enterprises in the Period of Post Financial Crisis' [《后金融危机时期中国资源型企业海外并购政治风险研究》] (2017) 40 *Journal of Liaoning Normal University* 93.

[177] NDRC (n 169).

[178] MOFCOM (n 93) 68.

## C. The Achievement of Policy Coordination

Memorandums of Understanding (MOUs) and framework agreements signed by China, together with bilateral energy cooperation plans, may be viewed as the achievement of policy communication for facilitating access to foreign energy markets.[179] The agreements are usually signed in summit meetings between Chinese leaders and the leaders of resource-rich states.[180] After signing MOUs or framework agreements, 'China will work with the state in outlining bilateral cooperation plans'.[181] The tables in Appendix 3 to this book list the contents of energy investment cooperation set out in MOUs, framework agreements and joint development programmes.

MOUs and framework agreements specify cooperation areas and institutions that are responsible for the promotion of investment, and thus provide a policy guarantee for Chinese energy investors.[182] By deploying these energy cooperation agreements, Chinese NOCs can press for investment opportunities.[183] These companies negotiate with local governments for land, tax and labour issues, and will later invite other domestic companies to jointly operate projects.[184] The Leading Group for the Belt and Road Initiative confirmed that these agreements enabled Chinese energy companies to invest, at least, in transmission networks.[185] For example, the *Guidelines on the Construction of China-Mongolia-Russia Economic Corridor* stimulated investment in oil and gas pipelines.[186]

Since MOUs, framework agreements and joint development agendas (see Appendix 3 to this book) provide similar content, this section discusses their

[179] MR Sanchez-Badin and F Morosini, 'International Economic Law By Other Means: A Three-Level Matrix of Chinese Investments In Brazil's Electric Power Sector' (2021) 62 *Harvard International Law Journal* 105, 113; J Zeng and C Wang, 'Legal Issues of Energy Cooperation under the Belt and Road Initiative' [《"一带一路"能源合作法律问题探析》] (2016) 3 *Journal of the Party School of Qindao Municipal Committee* 88, 90; Shan and Wang (n 6); Wang, 'China's Approach to the Belt and Road Initiative' (n 5) 35–36; Standard Chartered, 'China – Belt and Road Is Taking Shape' *Global Research* (8 November 2017) 2 at av.sc.com/corp-en/content/docs/China-Belt-and-Road-is-taking-shape.pdf; Vangeli (n 148) 69–70.

[180] Downs (n 77) 42.

[181] See Office of the Leading Group for the Belt and Road Initiative (n 167) 9; Plan of Action to Implement the Joint Declaration on ASEAN–China Strategic Partnership for Peace and Prosperity (2016–2020) stated that it implemented the joint declaration. China Chamber of Commerce for Petroleum Industry, 'Increase Oil and Gas Cooperation Mechanism in the B&R Initiative' [《加快"一带一路"油气合作机制建设》] (2018) at www.cccpi.org/first/firstAction_showJiChuXinXiSanJi?kid=bfd7f776-48fe-4158-be3d-0b30dda82224&id=251.

[182] C Sun and Y Liu, 'Can China's Diplomatic Partnership Strategy Benefit Outward Foreign Direct Investment?' (2019) 27 *China & World Economy* 108, 131; Wang, 'Securing Energy Flows from Central Asia to China' (n 5) 30; Sanchez-Badin and Morosini (n 179) 135; J Yuan et al, 'Electric Power Investment Risk Assessment for Belt and Road Initiative Nations' (2018) 10 *Sustainability* 3119, 3132.

[183] Downs (n 77) 42; Wang, 'The Belt and Road Initiative Agreements' (n 5) 230.

[184] Pei (n 169) 20.

[185] See Office of the Leading Group for the Belt and Road Initiative (n 167) 22.

[186] S Yan and G Xu, 'Discussion on Deepening Energy Cooperation between China and Neighbouring States' [《"一带一路"下深化中国与周边国家能源合作策略探讨》] (2017) 11 *Practice in Foreign Economic Relations and Trade* 8, 11.

contribution to Chinese energy companies' access to foreign markets in general. First, Chinese energy companies can invest not only in conventional oil and gas sectors, but also in the renewable energy sector (eg, the arrangement with Kazakhstan). Second, Chinese energy companies have the opportunity to engage in different segments of energy value chains of host states, from oil and gas exploration to the construction of pipelines and power grids (eg, the arrangement with Pakistan). These companies can expand their market share across energy value chains of other states by offering construction services and exporting their technology (eg, the arrangement with ASEAN countries). Third, China attached loans to energy infrastructure construction in intergovernmental agreements,[187] such as the ones signed with Russia and with Kazakhstan. Energy-backed loans have certainly played a role in increasing access to foreign energy markets.

Whether these agreements have binding force or not is crucial, because it determines whether China's energy cooperation partners are obliged to grant Chinese energy companies the right to make investments within their territories.[188] NDRC and NEA often 'take a soft law approach' to motivating energy cooperation.[189] Non-binding energy MOUs provide quasi-legal obligations,[190] which means that the cooperation provided for in the MOUs cannot be implemented with 'judicial coercion', merely indicating the possibility of obtaining the right to invest in host states' energy value chains.[191] Therefore, Chinese energy companies cannot pursue remedies for denial of access to the energy markets of China's energy cooperation partners based on the MOUs.[192]

Unlike MOUs, whether framework agreements are binding remains uncertain. If the contents of the framework agreements overlap with the provisions of other international treaties, China's investors are able to enforce their rights to make investments based on those treaties.[193] Otherwise, the agreements vary case by case. The China–Russia Agreement (2009) and the China–United Arab Emirates Agreement (2017) provided that both parties needed to complete domestic legal procedures for concluding government agreements.[194] *The Law*

[187] Braeutigam and Gallagher (n 87) 348; AV Belyi, 'North Asian Hydrocarbon Markets Regionalised' (2019) 20 *Journal of World Investment & Trade* 221, 226. The cooperative MOU in oil industries between Russia and China follows the supply agreement between Rosneft and CNPC.

[188] The existence of an obligation is a distinction between hard law and soft law. See F Terpan, 'Soft Law in the European Union – The Changing Nature of EU Law' (2015) 21 *European Law Journal* 68, 73.

[189] NDRC, MFA and MOFCOM (n 158); Shan and Wang (n 6) 270; see Erie (n 164).

[190] Shan and Wang (n 6) 279; H Zhao and H Wu, 'China's Energy Foreign Policy towards the Caspian Region: The Case of Kazakhstan' in Amineh and Guang (eds) (n 84) 167–95, 184; Yan and Xu (n 186) 11; Wang, 'The Belt and Road Initiative Agreements' (n 5) 284 and 297.

[191] For the non-binding forces of MOUs and joint declaration, see Terpan (n 188) 75–76.

[192] Wang, 'The Belt and Road Initiative Agreements' (n 5) 305.

[193] Part of the contents of framework agreements are governed by other international treaties. See, eg, Y Zhu, Z Mu and Y Mu, 'A Jurisprudence Analysis on the Nature and Effect of "the Framework Agreement on Hong Kong and Guangdong", with Suggestion for Legislation' [《粤港合作框架协议>的性质、效力分析及立法建议》] (2011) 6 *Academic Research* 38.

[194] Agreement on Cooperation in the Oil Sector between the People's Republic of China and the Russian Federation [《中华人民共和国政府和俄罗斯联邦政府关于石油领域合作的协议》] (2009);

*of the People's Republic of China on the Procedure for the Conclusion of Treaties* (1990) provides that central administrative departments are required to go through domestic procedures for entering into treaties to confirm the binding force.[195] If the conclusion of framework agreements requires the completion of domestic procedures then the framework agreements can be viewed as binding treaties.[196] Therefore, the China–Russia Agreement (2009) and the China–United Arab Emirates Agreement (2006) could have become binding after completion of the domestic procedure. The China–Pakistan Agreement (2006) was silent on the binding force of the Agreement.[197] The China–Uzbekistan Agreement (2009) only provided that there should be no obstacles to complying with other international obligations of both states.[198] It implies that this Agreement may create obligations and rights and thus be binding.[199] Accordingly, framework agreements for energy cooperation do not necessarily provide a stronger guarantee for accessing foreign energy markets.

To realise the projects for transmission networks provided in MOUs and framework agreements in practice, there are binding agreements for the construction of pipelines.[200] China's pipeline agreements with Turkmenistan and Myanmar (listed in Appendix 4 to this book) prescribed how the NOCs of China and the other state should construct the pipeline, and allowed for the negotiation of associated agreements. By guaranteeing the right to provide services for building oil and gas pipelines, China's NOCs have accessed the development of the upstream sectors of Turkmenistan and Myanmar. Nevertheless, these specific pipeline agreements do not have significant practical effects because of the lack of a model agreement and vague operating terms, such as pricing and a political disputes settlement mechanism (ie negotiation or consultation).[201]

Framework Agreement on Strengthening Cooperation on Production Capacity and Investment Between the NDRC and the Ministry of Economy of the United Arab Emirates [《中华人民共和国国家发展和改革委员会与阿拉伯联合酋长国经济部关于加强产能与投资合作的框架协议》] (2017).

[195] Law of the People's Republic of China on the Procedure for the Conclusion of Treaties [《中华人民共和国缔结条约程序法》] (1990) Art 7.

[196] ibid Art 7; G Jiang, 'Several Issues of International Law and International Treaties' [《国际法与国际条约的几个问题》] Talks of National People Congress (29 April 2000) at www.npc.gov.cn/npc/c12434/c541/201905/t20190522_7285.html.

[197] Framework Agreement on Energy Cooperation between the People's Republic of China and Pakistan [《中华人民共和国国家发展和改革委员会和巴基斯坦伊斯兰共和国石油和自然资源部关于能源领域合作框架协议》] (2006).

[198] Framework Agreement on Expand Cooperation Areas in Oil and Gas between the People's Republic of China and Uzbekistan [《中华人民共和国政府与乌兹别克斯坦共和国政府关于扩大油气领域合作的框架协议》] (2009).

[199] Wang, 'The Belt and Road Initiative Agreements' (n 5) 10.

[200] L Xie and X Fang, 'Legal Issues of China-Kazakhstan Energy Cooperation along the Silk Economic Belt' [《丝绸之路经济带建设背景下中国与哈萨克斯坦能源合作的法律问题研究》] (2016) 6 *Russian Studies* 181, 183–90; Wang, 'The Belt and Road Initiative Agreements' (n 5) 290 and 295; Wang, *Securing Energy Flows from Central Asia to China* (n 5) 30.

[201] Shan and Wang (n 6) 277; Wang, *Securing Energy Flows from Central Asia to China* (n 5) 30.

## D. Towards a Binding Agreement: Policy Coordination within the Shanghai Cooperation Organisation?

China may employ policy coordination to create an energy investment liberalisation regime.[202] Although MOUs, framework agreements and pipeline agreements do not represent a systematic approach to facilitating access to foreign energy markets, they have helped China to promote overseas energy investments.[203] By accommodating the interests of China's energy cooperation partners, the achievement of cooperation agreements and joint development programmes has helped them to attain a high level of mutual state understanding.[204] In the long term, less political sensitivity is likely to enable China to negotiate investment treaties for increasing Chinese companies' access to foreign energy markets.[205] The MOUs, framework agreements and pipeline agreements may be developed into a systematic and binding document (eg, an influential regional energy investment agreement).[206] For instance, MOFCOM recorded that the Agreement on Trade and Economic Cooperation between China and the Eurasian Economic Union (EAEU) 'started with the coordination of policies and rules between China and the EAEU'.[207] The conclusion of this Agreement implies that policy coordination helps to form an institution-led mode.[208]

[202] Hu (n 152) 4–5.

[203] Y Wang, 'Belt and Road Initiative: Mutual Connectivity of the World' (2018) 1 *China and the World: Ancient and Modern Silk Road* 1, 12–13; S Zhang, 'Developing China's Investor–State Arbitration Clause' in Shan, Nuotio and Zhang (eds) (n 145) 147–81, 172; K Yu, 'Energy Cooperation and Regional Order in the Belt and Road Initiative: A Case Study of China's Investment in the China–Pakistan Economic Corridor', London Asia Pacific Centre for Social Science Working Paper (October 2018) 11 (last accessed 20 February 2020).

[204] Sanchez-Badin and Morosini (n 179) 135; C Bian, 'Foreign Direct Investment Screening and National Security: Reducing Regulatory Hurdles to Investors Through Induced Reciprocity' (2021) 22 *Journal of World Investment & Trade* 561, 595; J Zhou, 'A New Multilateralism? A Case Study of the Belt and Road Initiative' [2020] *The Chinese Journal of Comparative Law* 1, 25.

[205] M Manfredi, 'Foreign Direct Investments in African Lands: The Chinese and EU Different Approaches' (2017) 30 *DPCE Online* 193, 199; Z Shi, 'Energy Cooperation: The Pillar of the Belt and Road Initiative' [《能源资源合作：共建"一带一路"的着力点》] (2015) 1 *Academic Journal of Xinjiang Normal University* 68; W Zhou and M Esteban, 'Beyond Balancing: China's Approach Towards the Belt and Road Initiative' (2018) 27 *Journal of Contemporary China* 487, 496–97.

[206] S Zhang, 'China's Approach in Drafting the Investor-State Arbitration Clause: A Review from the "Belt and Road" Regions' Perspective' (2017) 5 *The Chinese Journal of Comparative Law* 79, 106; Wang, 'China's Approach to the Belt and Road Initiative' (n 5) 40; W Zeng and S Dang, 'International Economic Rules Innovation on the Belt and Road Initiative' [《"一带一路"战略下的国际经济规则创新》] (2016) 3 *International Business Research* 25, 27.

[207] MOFCOM, 'Premiers of Six States Jointly Announced Agreement on Trade and Economic Cooperation is in Effect: A Significant Step of Building the EAEU and the Silk Road Economic Belt' [《六国总理共同宣布经贸合作协定生效 ——"一带一路"与欧亚经济联盟对接合作迈出坚实一步》] (25 October 2019) at www.mofcom.gov.cn/article/i/jyjl/e/201910/20191002908338.shtml. However, the main text of the agreement is not available online.

[208] H Lu, 'Striving for Coordinated Development of SCO and BRI' (2019) 77 *China International Studies* 82, 87.

This subsection focuses on the potential establishment of an energy investment liberalisation regime within the Shanghai Cooperation Organisation (SCO). The SCO is an important platform for strengthening energy cooperation between China and the member states of the EAEU, mainly Russia and Central Asian states.[209] Based on the previous experience of concluding the Agreement on Trade and Economic Cooperation between China and the EAEU, it is possible to build a common energy legal framework that will coordinate their energy policies and harmonise their energy regulations and standards within the SCO.[210]

Policy coordination within the SCO should progressively enhance mutual political trust between China and other member states,[211] and lay the institutional foundation for energy investment-making.[212] The Charter of the Shanghai Cooperation Organisation (2002) provides that member states 'shall facilitate the exchange of legal information in the interests of developing cooperation within the SCO'.[213] More specifically, the SCO member states should advance 'mutually beneficial' energy cooperation and create favourable conditions for investment-making by 'developing common approaches', according to the *Development Strategy of the Shanghai Cooperation Organisation until 2025* (2015).[214] With policy coordination, China and Central Asian states can 'share their energy information and deepen political trust to ensure the practicability and stability of multilateral cooperation'.[215] The Central Asian states and other member states (Russia in particular) need to make sure that they can carry out their development strategies and benefit from energy cooperation within the SCO.[216] The common benefits will enable member states of the SCO to increasingly endorse and nurture 'the

[209] Shanghai Cooperation Organisation, *Development Strategy of the Shanghai Cooperation Organisation until 2025* (2015) at eng.sco-russia2020.ru/images/00/44/004418.pdf; NEA (n 147); Joint Statement of the Russian Federation and the People's Republic of China on Cooperation in Coordinating the Building of the Eurasian Economic Union and the Silk Road Economic Belt [《中华人民共和国与俄罗斯联邦关于丝绸之路经济带建设和欧亚经济联盟建设对接合作的联合声明》] (2015); Yan and Xu (n 186) 9.

[210] Z Kembayev, 'The Emerging Eurasian Common Energy Market: What is Its Potential Impact on China's Belt and Road Initiative?' (2019) 20 *Journal of World Investment & Trade* 401, 401.

[211] P Guang, 'A Chinese Perspective on the Shanghai Cooperation Organization' in AJK Bailes et al (eds), *The Shanghai Cooperation Organization* (Stockholm International Peace Research Institute, 2007) 45–58, 45; T Pradt, *The Prequel to China's New Silk Road: Preparing the Ground in Central Asia* (Singapore, Springer, 2020) 71; R Alimov, 'The Shanghai Cooperation Organisation and the Development of Eurasia' in Alexander Lukin (ed), *The 'Roads' and 'Belts' of Eurasia* (Singapore, Springer, 2020) 261–300, 269.

[212] Zeng and Wang (n 179) 89.

[213] Charter of the Shanghai Cooperation Organisation (adopted in 2002) Art 3 at eng.sectsco.org/load/203013/.

[214] *Development Strategy* (n 209).

[215] Q Zhou, Z He and Y Yang, 'Energy Geopolitics in Central Asia: China's Involvement and Responses' (2020) 30 *Journal of Geographical Sciences* 1871, 1891; Koolaee and Tisheyar (n 151) 109.

[216] Charter of SCO (2002) (n 213) Art 16; X Chen and R Ma, 'The Role of and Options for the Shanghai Cooperation Organization vis-à-vis the Silk Road Economic Belt' [《上合组织在丝绸之路经济带中的作用与路径选择》] (2015) 6 *Journal of Contemporary Asia-Pacific Studies* 63, 76–77.

collective identity' – accepting other member states as partners.[217] It is thus possible for China to 'reduce the negative perceptions of China's appetite for Central Asian energy'.[218] Ultimately, energy policy coordination within the SCO should create an investment environment favourable to Chinese energy investors.[219]

In the long run, institutionalising energy interdependence among exporting states, importing states and transit states through policy coordination within the SCO will facilitate the negotiation of a binding agreement.[220] As suggested by the Treaty on Long-Term Good-Neighbourliness, Friendship and Cooperation between the Member States of the Shanghai Cooperation Organisation (2007), the contracting parties should cooperate in making international legal documents.[221] For Lanteigne, the exchange of legal information 'constitutes a shift towards a more integrated and comprehensive energy policy in the region'.[222] Despite these efforts to merge rules, seeking common policies/rules cannot be insulated from interstate relations. Kembayev has said that 'economic cooperation within the SCO is closely related with the (geo-)political interests of its members, which support each other on the international scene'.[223] Since Russia is a leading actor in the EAEU, China might make use of Russian–European tensions (especially after the issue of REPower EU 2022) to accelerate the coordination of energy policies with the member states of EAEU and ultimately facilitate energy investment cooperation in the BRI.[224]

## VIII. Conclusion

The international relations literature has summarised that the Chinese Government secured domestic companies' access to foreign energy markets through building diplomatic relations with resource-rich states and making use of the economic reliance (ie, energy-backed loans) of these states on China. China's energy policy

[217] GA Movkebaeva, 'Energy Cooperation Among Kazakhstan, Russia, and China Within the Shanghai Cooperation Organization' (2013) 51 *Russian Politics and Law* 80, 81.

[218] EM Pron, 'China's Energy Diplomacy via the Shanghai Cooperation Organisation' in S Yao et al, (eds), *Energy Security and Sustainable Economic Growth in China* (London, Palgrave Macmillan, 2014) 52–73, 66.

[219] Alimov (n 211) 261–300, 270.

[220] M Fredholm, 'Understanding China's Policy and Intentions Towards the SCO' (2013) 17 *Himalayan and Central Asian Studies* 38, 51; Pradt (n 211) 71.

[221] Treaty on Long-Term Good-Neighbourliness, Friendship and Cooperation Between the Member States of the Shanghai Cooperation Organization [《上海合作组织成员国长期睦邻友好合作》] (2007) Art 16.

[222] M Lanteigne, 'China, Energy Security and Central Asian Diplomacy – Bilateral and Multilateral Approaches' in I Overland et al (eds), *Caspian Energy Politics: Azerbaijan, Kazakhstan and Turkmenistan* (London, Routledge, 2010) 101–15, 101.

[223] Z Kembayev, 'Implementing the Silk Road Economic Belt: From the Shanghai Cooperation Organisation to the Silk Road Union?' (2018) 16 *Asia Europe Journal* 37, 46.

[224] ibid 49; JL Wilson, 'The Eurasian Economic Union and China's Silk Road: Implications for the Russian–Chinese Relationship' (2016) 17 *European Politics and Society* 113, 127.

documents indeed emphasise the importance of interstate communication for alleviating the unproven geopolitical fears of host states. Interstate dialogue has helped to coordinate energy policies between China and resource-rich states. Through policy coordination, those host states can capitalise on their competitive economic, institutional or even cultural advantages to shape their energy cooperation with China. Chinese energy companies may thus face fewer risks of being banned from investing in energy projects because of the national security concerns of the host states. China's efforts in policy coordination can therefore fix the limits of the strict approach to negotiating binding treaties for investment promotion. China does not ignore the political factors but aims to achieve political agreement with host states through policy coordination. China also undeniably has provided the economic incentives discussed in the international relations literature on Chinese overseas energy investments. However, loans and access to China's downstream sector are included in most MOUs or framework agreements. Therefore, economic incentives granted to host states are transparent.

Meanwhile, China has provided both domestic and international legal remedies for addressing barriers to access to foreign energy markets. Domestically, MOFCOM and MFA are chiefly responsible for providing information about the investment environment. Chinese investors have the right to request MOFCOM to initiate interstate negotiations to eliminate barriers to investments. However, encouraging energy companies to rely on legal domestic remedies requires more specific measures for implementing the regulation on lifting barriers to investments. Also, the involvement of domestic departments may intensify host states' beliefs that the Chinese Government stands behind Chinese energy companies, and strengthen their geopolitical fears. Internationally, China's progressive approach to energy policy coordination to realise potential binding agreements and its growing commitment to pre-investment obligations in investment treaties reflect the state's inclination towards promoting energy investments through legal agendas. Therefore, China is adopting a flexible approach to promoting investments by combining the use of legal agendas and intergovernmental coordination.

# 9

# Energy Investment Protection: Depoliticisation or a Strong Role of the Chinese Government?

## I. Introduction

China's energy companies have been struggling to manage political instability in certain host states, and to respond to various government interventions in the operation of their foreign energy projects.[1] It has been argued that to minimise threats to the operation of Chinese energy projects, the Chinese Government has established good diplomatic relations with host states and granted financial aid to those states,[2] rather than relying on host governments' binding commitments to protect property rights.[3] Building on this, this chapter aims to question whether China's domestic and international institutional arrangements for managing *ex post* investment risks enable the Government to play a leading role in energy investment protection and thus maintain an influence on energy companies. Although legal scholars regularly discuss how China's investment treaties protect overseas investments in general,[4] they pay less attention to investment protection specifically in the energy sector.[5] Therefore, it is hoped that answering this question will

[1] MOFCOM, 'Interpretation of *Interim Measures of Recordation or Confirmation of Overseas Investments*' [商务部合作司负责人解读《对外投资备案（核准）报告暂行办法》] (25 January 2018) at swt.xizang.gov.cn/xxgk/zcfg/201905/t20190517_72948.html (last accessed 18 October 2020).

[2] J Jiang and C Ding, *Update on Overseas Investments by China's National Oil Companies: Achievements and Challenges since 2011* (Paris, IEA, 2014) 8–9; DG Victor and L Yueh, 'The New Energy Order' (2010) 89(1) *Foreign Affairs* 61, 62.

[3] See, eg, D O'Neill, 'Playing Risk: Chinese Foreign Direct Investment in Cambodia' (2014) 36(2) *Contemporary Southeast Asia* 173, 185.

[4] See, eg, N Gallagher and W Shan, *Chinese Investment Treaties: Policies and Practice* (Oxford, Oxford University Press, 2009). For China's increasingly liberal approach to treaty-making, see V Bath, 'China's Role in the Development of International Investment Law – From Bystander to Participant' (2020) 15 *Asian Journal of WTO and International Health Law and Policy* 359.

[5] However, some Chinese scholars pay attention to domestic regulations, eg, L Cheng and S Li, 'Chinese Enterprises' Overseas Mergers and Acquisitions: Political Risk and Protection Strategies' [《我国企业海外并购的政治风险及防范策略研究》] (2013) 5 *Academic Journal of Foreign Economic and Trade University* 1; see also, eg, R Li, 'The Establishment of Legal Protection Mechanism of Chinese Overseas Energy Investments under the Comparative Law' [《比较法视野下中国海外能源投资保障法律机制的构建》] (2017) 6 *Law Review* 119, 126; S Ling, 'Protecting Chinese Overseas Interests in China's Neighbourhood' [《中国周边地区海外利益维护探讨》] (2018)10(1)

enrich the legal discussion of China's energy investment protection and add to the energy law literature on investment protection.

The regulatory analysis of China's efforts to protect overseas energy investments is framed within the historical development of energy investment protection, namely from diplomatic protection to depoliticisation. Diplomatic protection means the leading role of home states in seeking compensation. By contrast, depoliticisation marginalises the role of home states in pursuing investors' interests. Investor–state arbitration and investment insurance are major mechanisms for facilitating depoliticisation, by helping investors to seek compensation without relying on their home states. In reaction to the historical development of energy investment protection, this chapter discusses China's domestic regulations for managing *ex post* investment risks and its investment treaties. Do domestic regulations, which include the improvement of the risk-management systems of companies, and the management of emergencies as well as insurance regimes, provide a channel for the Government to replace investors in seeking compensation? This chapter also looks at the development of investor–state disputes settlement, provided for in China's BITs and FTAs.

It is argued that the Chinese Government has used domestic and international regulatory measures to help energy companies to manage *ex post* investment risks of security threats and regulatory instability, instead of playing a leading role in seeking compensation from host states. In particular, the Chinese Government has been reluctant to get directly involved in the political crises of host states in order to protect domestic energy companies, because such protection through the diplomatic agenda can be a burden in the implementation of China's diplomatic strategy.

Section II of this chapter introduces the historical development of energy investment protection. Section III discusses the political risks to China's overseas energy investments. Section IV then looks at China's domestic and international measures for reducing threats to the safe operation of energy projects. Section V discusses China's domestic and international remedies against government interference. Section VI concludes and suggests the implications for China's energy investment protection.

## II. The Historical Development of Energy Investment Protection

This section introduces the way in which the role of home states in managing *ex post* investment risks has gradually been marginalised, with the transition from diplomatic protection to depoliticisation.

*Global Review* 31, 45. For the implications of Chinese investment treaties for energy investments, see, eg, W Shan and P Wang, 'The International Legal Framework for Belt and Road Energy Cooperation: Progress and Prospect' (2019) 20 *Journal of World Investment & Trade* 259.

## A. Home States' Right to Diplomatic Protection

The principle of diplomatic protection gives states the right to protect their nationals.[6] Home states play a leading role in seeking compensation and can choose whether to exercise this right. A possible problem remains whether investors' rights can be guaranteed.

### *i. The Meaning of Diplomatic Protection*

According to the *UN Draft Articles on Diplomatic Protection* (2006), it is the state of nationality that takes diplomatic action or other peaceful means (eg, judicial proceedings) to complain that another state has caused harm to an injured national, and to seek reparation on behalf of that injured national.[7] Diplomatic protection is a right granted to the state of nationality, rather than an obligation of that state.[8] The *Mavrommatis Palestine Concessions Case* confirmed that home states have the right to 'protect their subjects, when injured by acts contrary to international law committed by another State … by resorting to diplomatic action or international judicial proceedings on its behalf'.[9] In *Barcelona Traction*, the International Court of Justice (ICJ) decided that 'the state must be viewed as the sole judge to decide whether its protection will be granted, to what extent it is granted and when it will cease'.[10] Therefore, nationals (eg, legal persons) do not have a say in the process of seeking reparation.

At the same time, the *Draft Articles on Diplomatic Protection with Commentaries* (2006) differentiate diplomatic protection from consular assistance.[11] Diplomatic protection represents state interests, but it may not concern investors' rights.[12] The protection is usually granted in the form of legal action or diplomatic efforts, such as protests and explicit requests to settle the dispute.[13] In contrast, consular assistance may be defined as the way in which home states assist their investors to do business in foreign states.[14] Consular assistance represents individual interests and

[6] K Miles, *The Origins of International Investment Law* (Cambridge, Cambridge University Press, 2013) 47.

[7] United Nations, Draft Articles on Diplomatic Protection (2006), Art 1; United Nations, Draft Articles on Diplomatic Protection with Commentaries (2006) 26–27.

[8] See Draft Articles on Diplomatic Protection (n 7) Art 2; see Draft Articles on Diplomatic Protection with Commentaries (n 7) 28.

[9] *Mavrommatis Palestine Concessions Case*, PCIJ Series A, No 2, Judgment of 30 August 1924, at 12; E Denza, 'Nationality and Diplomatic Protection' (2018) 65 *Netherlands International Law Review* 463, 466.

[10] *Barcelona Traction, Light and Power Company, Limited (Belgium v Spain)*, Second Phase, Judgement [1970] ICJ reports 3, 44.

[11] Draft Articles on Diplomatic Protection with Commentaries (n 7) 27–28.

[12] R Polanco, *The Return of the Home State to Investor-State Disputes: Bringing Back Diplomatic Protection?* (Cambridge, Cambridge University Press, 2018) 291.

[13] ibid.

[14] ibid.

aims to minimise the harm to the individuals outside judicial proceedings.[15] It is usually effected using weaker forms of action, including meetings, letters and telephone calls.[16]

### *ii. The Impact of Diplomatic Protection on Energy Investment Protection*

With diplomatic protection, in investor–state disputes, it is the home states, rather than investors, that assert legal rights to seek compensation for losses caused by host states.[17] Investors' interests may not be fully protected if home states prioritise their political considerations.[18] To maintain diplomatic relations and economic cooperation, home states and host states usually draft written or oral statements without mentioning compensation to investors.[19] Or host states and home states negotiate a lump-sum settlement comprising a single payment for expropriation of different investments.[20]

However, the difference between diplomatic protection and consular assistance suggests that the involvement of the state does not necessarily imply state influence on settling disputes. With consular assistance, the home state may only aid energy companies to bring claims against the host state without stressing state interests. Therefore, any analysis of the government efforts to protect overseas energy investments should assess whether the efforts prioritise the pursuit of national interests or assistance to energy companies in seeking compensation.

## B. Marginalising the Role of Home States in Investment Protection

To reduce home states' political influence, the approach to investment protection has evolved from diplomatic protection to depoliticisation. Depoliticisation enables energy investors to make claims themselves without being influenced by the national interests of their home states. However, given the complexity of energy geopolitics, depoliticisation has limits in settling investor–state disputes.

[15] Draft Articles on Diplomatic Protection with Commentaries (n 7) 27–28; Polanco (n 12) 223.

[16] Polanco (n 12) 230.

[17] M Potestà, 'Towards a Greater Role for State-to-State Arbitration in the Architecture of Investment Treaties?' in S Lalani and RP Lazo (eds), *The Role of the State in Investor-State Arbitration* (Leiden, Brill Nijhoff, 2015) 241–73, 255–56.

[18] R Dolzer and CH Schreuer, *Principles of International Investment Law* (Oxford, Oxford University Press, 2012) 233.

[19] JW Salacuse, *The Law of Investment Treaties* (Oxford, Oxford University Press, 2010) 312.

[20] KJ Vandevelde, *Bilateral Investment Treaties: History, Policy, and Interpretation* (Oxford, Oxford University Press, 2010) 41–42.

## *i. The Definition of Depoliticisation*

Depoliticisation is defined as the way of 'removing the need for an investor to rely on the exercise of diplomatic protection to recover any losses'.[21] For Vandevelde, 'the attempt to depoliticize investment policy is embodied most visibly in the investor-to-state arbitration provision of the BITs'.[22] Investor–state arbitration corrects the deficiency that investors need to rely on their home states to claim rights and has shifted investor–state dispute resolution from the political realm to the legal realm.[23] For example, the ICSID Convention aimed to remove home states' intervention by creating an investor–state dispute settlement regime.[24] According to *The History of the ICSID Convention*:

> An investor's national state would no longer be able to espouse a claim of its national. The Convention would therefore offer a means of settling directly, on the legal plane, investment disputes between the State and the foreign investor and insulate such disputes from the realm of politics and diplomacy.[25]

The ICSID Convention adds that 'No Contracting State shall give diplomatic protection, or bring an international claim.'[26] Therefore, contracting states are not allowed to seek diplomatic protection for claims involving its nationals and the other signatory party.

Similarly, the insurance regime is designed to directly recover investors' losses and reduce the home states' influence on investors' pursuit of compensation. Salacuse has defined political risk insurance as an agreement between an investor and an insurer to compensate the investor wholly or partially for financial loss caused by political risks.[27] Therefore, investors can receive compensation without turning to their home states.[28] For instance, the Multilateral Investment Guarantee

[21] G Gertz, S Jandhyala and LNS Poulsen, 'Legalization, Diplomacy, and Development: Do Investment Treaties Depoliticize Investment Disputes?' (2018) 107 *World Development* 239, 242; Miles (n 6) 85.

[22] KJ Vandevelde, 'Of Politics and Markets: The Shifting Ideology of the BITs' (1993) 11 *International Tax and Business Law* 159, 163.

[23] Vandevelde (n 20) 431; TW Waelde, 'International Law of Foreign Investment: Towards Regulation by Multilateral Treaties' (1999) 1 *Business Law International* 50, 67; M Paparinskis, 'The Limits of Depoliticisation in Contemporary Investor–State Arbitration' (2012) 3 *Select Proceedings of the European Society of International Law* 271, 276; RO Keohane, A Moravcsik, and AM Slaughter, 'Legalized Dispute Resolution: Interstate and Transnational' (2000) 54 *International Organization* 457, 457–58.

[24] International Centre for Settlement of Investment Disputes, Convention on the Settlement of Investment Disputes between States and Nationals of Other States (opened for signature 18 March 1965, entered into force 14 October 1966) (ICSID Convention). See PD Cameron, *International Energy Investment Law: The Pursuit of Stability*, 1st edn (Oxford, Oxford University Press, 2010) 174; A Broches, 'The Convention on the Settlement of Investment Disputes between States and Nationals of Other States' (1972) 136 *Recueil des Cours* 331, 344.

[25] *The History of the ICSID Convention* (ICSID, 1970) 241–42 at icsid.worldbank.org/en/Documents/resources/History%20of%20ICSID%20Convention%20-%20VOLUME%20II-1.pdf.

[26] ICSID Convention (n 24) Art 27(1).

[27] Salacuse (n 19) 247.

[28] X Liu, 'China's Overseas Insurance Legal System' [《中国海外投资保险法律制度研究—基于一带一路倡议和全球治理理论视角》] (2018) 4 *Research on Financial and Economic Issues* 71, 72.

Agency (MIGA), as an international insurance regime, facilitates amicable settlements between investors and host states, and ensures that compensation for losses is examined only against the legal and economic background.[29]

### *ii. The Impact of Depoliticisation on Energy Investment Protection*

Depoliticising the settlement of disputes between energy investors and host states can remove the uncertainty of whether investors' rights will be protected,[30] and thus promote energy investments to ensure global energy security.[31] Unlike the calculation of strategic interests by home states in diplomatic protection, investor–state arbitration and the insurance regime prioritise role of binding rules in managing political risks.[32] These two regimes for depoliticisation also increases energy investors' bargaining power in their negotiations with host governments, by guaranteeing the original risk allocation and the pursuit of compensation.[33] Furthermore, the investor–state dispute settlement regime creates a general deterrence, in that 'host states will not get away with breaches of investment treaties'.[34] In the event of a breach of legal obligations, the host state will either pay a huge amount of compensation or find itself with a bad international image.[35] In either case, it is hard for the state to attract future investments. Therefore, the stabilised enforcement regime guaranteed by depoliticisation will enhance the confidence of energy companies. Energy companies will require lower risk premiums in their future negotiations with host states, which will help to stabilise energy prices.

Nevertheless, establishing international investment rules and institutions cannot overshadow the political, economic and social interests that help to shape those rules and institutions.[36] For Anghie, powerful states tried to institutionalise their interests in international investment law.[37] The investor–state arbitration

[29] N Maurer, *The Empire Trap: The Rise and Fall of US Intervention to Protect American Property Overseas, 1893–2013* (Princeton, NJ, Princeton University Press, 2013); I Shihatal, 'Towards A Greater Depoliticization of Investment Disputes: The Roles of ICSID and MIGA' (1986) 1 *ICSID Review* 1, 24–26.

[30] W Alschner, 'The Return of the Home State and the Rise of "Embedded" Investor–State Arbitration' in Lalani and Lazo (eds) (n 17) 293–333, 300–01.

[31] GJ Garcia-Sanchez, 'The Footprint of the Chinese Petro-Dragon: The Future of Investment Law in Transboundary Resources' (2020) 94 *Tulane Law Review* 314, 321.

[32] SW Schill, 'In Defense of International Investment Law' in M Bungenberg et al (eds), *European Yearbook of International Economic Law 2016* (Cham, Springer, 2016) 309–41, 314.

[33] Cameron (n 24) 7; Salacuse (n 19) 28.

[34] SW Schill, *The Multilateralization of International Investment Law* (New York, Cambridge University Press, 2009) 260–61.

[35] S Puig, 'Emergence and Dynamism in International Organizations: ICSID, Investor–State Arbitration, and International Investment Law' (2013) 44 *Georgetown Journal of International Law* 531.

[36] S Miroudot and A Ragoussis, 'Actors in the International Investment Scenario' in R Echandi and P Sauvé (eds), *Prospects in International Investment Law and Policy* (Cambridge, Cambridge University Press, 2013) 51–72, 59–62; M Sornarajah, *The International Law on Foreign Investment*, 3rd edn (Cambridge, Cambridge University Press, 2010) 9; HG Cohen, 'Nation and Markets' (2020) 23 *Journal of International Economic Law* 793, 803.

[37] A Anghie, 'Imperialism and International Legal Theory' in A Orford and F Hoffmann (eds), *The Oxford Handbook of the Theory of International Law* (Oxford, Oxford University Press, 2016) 156–72.

regime enforces rules that benefit powerful states and imposes heavy burdens on host states by subjecting the laws of host states to international adjudication.[38] In addition, home states have the ability to influence the arbitral process,[39] as the right enforced by investors under investments treaties is usually viewed as the right of home states provided for in treaties.[40] In practice, investors usually first turn to the officials of the home state to complain about the host state.[41]

Furthermore, depoliticisation may not be able to settle disputes with political features.[42] Host states may unilaterally interfere with energy investments based on national security concerns,[43] and justify their breach of the investment treaty by referring to exception clauses. In the case of self-judged security exception clauses, arbitration tribunals are not allowed to examine the national security issue in question.[44] The core of investor–state disputes, namely whether investments pose a threat to national security, cannot be addressed by a legal analysis by the tribunal. Therefore, the strong state involvement in the energy sector implies that the settlement of energy investment disputes must take political factors into account, especially in a geopolitically hostile environment.

## III. Political Risks to China's Overseas Energy Investments

This section focuses on what political risks China's energy companies need to deal with after making their investments. Political risks in resource-rich states usually relate to the political instability of these states and the change of host governments' behaviour and regulations.[45] MOFCOM identifies political instability as 'the changes of political situation, wars, armed conflicts, terrorist attacks or kidnappings, social turmoil, ethnic and religious conflicts, public security crimes, etc'.[46] Regulatory risks include the adjustment of financial, monetary, foreign exchange, tax, environmental protection, labour and resources policies of the governments of the countries of residence and nationalisation of enterprises'.[47]

[38] Paparinskis (n 23) 277.
[39] Polanco (n 12) 19.
[40] Sornarajah (n 36) 254.
[41] Paparinskis (n 23) 276.
[42] C Titi, 'Are Investment Tribunals Adjudicating Political Disputes?' (2015) 32 *Journal of International Arbitration* 261, 266.
[43] ibid.
[44] L Wang, 'Chinese SOE Investments and the National Security Protection under IIAs' in J Chaisse (ed), *China's International Investment Strategy: Bilateral, Regional, and Global Law and Policy* (Oxford, Oxford University Press, 2019) 67–86.
[45] F Duan et al, 'Energy Investment Risk Assessment for Nations along China's Belt & Road Initiative' (2018) 170 *Journal of Cleaner Production* 535, 537.
[46] MOFCOM, *The Risk Warning and Information Regime for Outward Investment* [《对外投资合作境外安全风险预警和信息通报制度》] (2010).
[47] ibid.

## A. Political Instability

China's overseas energy projects easily fall victim to political instability, such as civil wars, ethnic tensions and terrorist attacks.[48] Damage to equipment, facilities and the production chain may interrupt the daily operation of projects, and thus result in insufficient energy supply.[49] For instance, Chinese NOCs' production output in Syria dropped because of the civil war.[50] China's oil and gas production in Angola was destroyed in the two-decade-long civil war as well.[51] Furthermore, the BRI – China's great plan for international energy cooperation – includes the 'so-called arc of instable regions' (ie, Central Asia and the Middle East).[52] The East Turkistan Islamic Movement (ETIM) terrorist forces once attacked Chinese personnel and property.[53]

In particular, fixed energy infrastructure, such as power grids and oil and gas pipelines, are susceptible to physical attacks.[54] The attacks on China's cross-border oil and gas pipelines posed a big threat to reliable supplies, because the pipelines could not be repaired overnight or replaced with another pipeline.[55] For example, the unrest resulting from Islamic fundamentalism once jeopardised the pipelines built by China, and impeded oil and gas supplies to China.[56] Similarly, the Chinese Government has been nervous about the safe operation of the China–Myanmar oil and gas pipelines and the projects involving electricity transmission networks because of the ethnic tensions in Myanmar.[57]

[48] MOFCOM et al, *Provisions on the Safety Management of Overseas Chinese-Funded Enterprises, Institutions and Personnel* [《境外中资企业机构和人员安全管理规定》] (2010); Y Duan et al, 'China's Overseas Energy Investment Overview' [《中国全球能源投资分析》] (2015) 3 *Sino-Global Energy* 9, 13; F He and B Wang, 'Chinese Interests in the Global Investment Regime' (2014) 7 *China Economic Journal* 4, 11; HN Huang and TC Tian, 'Turning Current Scepticism into Future Success: Observations on the Cooperation between China and Pakistan' in LC W and C Xi (eds), *Legal Dimension of China's Belt and Road Initiative* (Hong Kong, Wolters Kluwer, 2016) 55–72, 60–62.

[49] W Liu et al, 'Practices of Safety Culture in CNPC's Overseas Projects' [《中国石油海外作业安全文化实践》] (2014) 34 *Natural Gas Industry* 135, 136–37.

[50] X Qian, 'Protecting China's Energy Interests in the Middle East' (2014) 8 *Journal of Middle Eastern and Islamic Studies (in Asia)* 48, 55.

[51] The Eurasia Group, 'China's Overseas Investments in Oil and Gas Production', Prepared for the US–China Economic and Security Review Commission (16 October 2006) 23.

[52] M Dian and S Menegazzi, *New Regional Initiatives in China's Foreign Policy* (Cham, Springer International Publishing, 2018) 85.

[53] H Liu, 'The Security Challenges of the "One Belt, One Road" Initiative and China's Choices' (2017) 23 *Croatian International Relations Review* 129, 139.

[54] See, eg, G Li, 'New Challenge and Solution of Chinese Energy Diplomacy' [《中国能源外交的新问题及其对策》] (2008) 3 *Contemporary World* 56.

[55] H Zhao, *The Economics and Politics of China's Energy Security Transition* (San Diego, CA, Elsevier Science & Technology, 2018) 211.

[56] H Lee and DA Shalmon, *Searching for Oil: China's Oil Initiatives in the Middle East* (Belfer Center for Science and International Affairs, January 2007) 13.

[57] H Zhao, 'China–Myanmar Energy Cooperation and Its Regional Implications' (2011) 30 *Journal of Current Southeast Asian Affairs* 89, 102; J Yuan et al, 'Electric Power Investment Risk Assessment for Belt and Road Initiative Nations' (2018) 10 *Sustainability* 3119, 3131.

## B. Regulatory Risks

A MOFCOM report recorded that China's overseas energy investments had to cope with the frequent policy changes in host states.[58] Chinese energy companies' investment-related rights were amended or even revoked.[59] The reason for the policy changes could be weak legal governance in the host states, or national security concerns of host states.[60]

### *i. Weak Legal Institutions*

In resource-rich states with powerful leaders, the personal interests of the political elites in these states determine the revision of laws and the renegotiation of contracts.[61] The reshuffling of host governments can challenge policy contingency.[62] The new government may not enforce the legal commitment made by the old one[63] but may categorise the already existing energy projects as 'politically discredited foreign-owned projects' and discriminate against them through the enforcement of new laws and regulations.[64] Chinese energy companies may thus suffer substantial losses or divest themselves of the projects.[65] For instance, it is suggested that China's energy investors should be careful about the protection offered by the current leadership of Kazakhstan, given the constant political changes in Central Asian states.[66]

Weak legal institutions also mean non-transparent legislation, imperfect legislative procedures and inadequate enforcement.[67] For instance, the Middle-Eastern

[58] MOFCOM, *The Report of Development of Overseas Investments 2014* [《对外投资合作发展报告2014》] (2014) 74–75.

[59] SCIO, 'NDRC's Press Conference on "Guiding Opinions on Promoting Cooperation on Manufacture and Productivity"' [《发改委就〈关于推进国际产能和装备制造合作的指导意见〉举行发布会》] (21 May 2015) at www.scio.gov.cn/xwfbh/gbwxwfbh/xwfbh/fzggw/Document/1434465/1434465.htm.

[60] W Shan and P Wang, 'Balanced Liberalism and China's Position on International Arbitration Reform' [《均衡自由主义与国际投资仲裁改革的中国立场分析》] (2019) 39 *Journal of Xi'an Jiaotong University (Social Science)* 20, 24.

[61] S Moreira, 'Learning from Failure: China's Overseas Oil Investments' (2013) 1 *Journal of Current Chinese Affairs* 131, 151; D O'Neill, 'Risky Business: The Political Economy of Chinese Investment in Kazakhstan' (2014) 5 *Journal of Eurasian Studies* 145, 148.

[62] A Jiang, B Liu and J Huang, 'China–Central Asia Energy Cooperation under the Belt and Road Initiative' [《"一带一路"背景下中国—中亚能源合作研究述要》] (2017) 1 *Journal of Guizhou Provincial Party School* 63, 66.

[63] O'Neill (n 3) 189.

[64] T Waelde, 'Treaties and Regulatory Risk in Infrastructure Investment' (2000) 34 *Journal of World Trade* 1, 8.

[65] D Wei and J Wang, 'Perfection of the Legal System of Oil and Gas International Cooperation in the Context of "the Belt and Road"' [《"一带一路"背景下油气国际合作法律制度的完善》] (2019) 21 *Journal of Southwest Petroleum University* 1.

[66] O'Neill (n 61) 149.

[67] G Wang, 'Risk Management of China's Overseas Energy Investment in Mongolia' [《中国对蒙古国海外能源投资风险控制研究》] (2016) 33 *Journal of Political Science and Law* 43, 44.

states frequently change their laws and regulations, 'due to the shortage of the legal mechanism or frequent socio-economic changes'.[68] China's energy investments are thus highly likely to be disrupted by political changes in the Middle-Eastern states.[69] Also, the investment environment in Cambodia is characterised by the weak rule of law.[70] A policy change by the Cambodian Government once negatively affected China's hydropower assets, but its judicial system failed to 'protect property rights or enforce contracts'.[71]

## *ii. Host States' National Security Concerns*

Both western states and emerging economies 'tend to politicise the overseas investment of Chinese companies for political and economic interests', and intervene with China's investments (eg, cancelling licences or restricting capital transfers) based on national security concerns.[72] Western states are worried about China's control over global energy resources and thus aim to interrupt the operation of China's energy projects.[73] Developing resource-rich states (eg, Russia and Kazakhstan) are also alert to their economic reliance on China's energy companies.[74] For example, in 2007, together with two local companies, State Grid won the bid for a 25-year licence to maintain, expand and operate the national transmission networks in the Philippines.[75] In early 2015, the Government of the Philippines decided to end the technical involvement of State Grid.[76] It is reported that 'the politicians in Manila felt that the country's electricity grid was too crucial to the national economy and security to allow the Chinese to operate the system'.[77] Senator Miriam Defensor-Santiago claimed that 'Chinese Government invaded the Philippine power sector

[68] J Chang, 'Assessment of the Key Political Risks of China's Overseas Direct Investment' [2014] *International Conference on Economic Management and Trade Cooperation* 295, 297.

[69] ibid.

[70] O'Neill (n 3) 174.

[71] ibid 175 and 184.

[72] Q Yuan and Y Yu, 'The Research of Political Risks of Overseas Merger and Acquisition of Chinese Resource-Based Enterprises in the Period of Post Financial Crisis' [《后金融危机时期中国资源型企业海外并购政治风险研究》] (2017) 40 *Journal of Liaoning Normal University* 93; C Chang and H Li, 'Political Risk and Evasion Strategy of Chinese Petroleum Corporations during Transnational operation' [《中国石油企业跨国经营的政治风险及规避策略》] (2008) 24 *Journal of China University of Petroleum* 5; L Cheng and S Li, 'Chinese Enterprises' Overseas Mergers and Acquisitions: Political Risk and Protection Strategies' [《我国企业海外并购的政治风险及防范策略研究》] (2013) 5 *Academic Journal of Foreign Economic and Trade University* 1; Wang (n 46) 70.

[73] B Lai, 'A Study on the Political Risk of Overseas M&A of Chinese Enterprises and the Countermeasures' [《中国企业海外并购的政治风险与对策研究》] (2013) 3 *Journal of Zhangzhou Normal University* 44, 45–46.

[74] Wang (n 44) 45; G Bahgat, *Energy Security: An Interdisciplinary Approach* (New York, Wiley, 2011) 75.

[75] YC Xu, *Sinews of Power: Politics of the State Grid Corporation of China* (Oxford, Oxford University Press, 2017) 270–76.

[76] TK Stern, 'Chinese Investments in the Philippines' (2016) 4 *Journal of Political Risk* 1.

[77] Xu (n 75) 275; 'Philippines Announces "Repatriation" of Chinese SOE Employees Operating Power Grid over National Security Concerns' (RWR Advisory Group, 25 February 2015) at www.rwradvisory.com/philippines-announces-repatriation-of-chinese-soe-employees-operating-power-grid-over-national-security-concerns/.

through its 40% stake in the NGCP'.[78] As a result, State Grid lost the right to operate the system and could not participate in the management of NGCP, although it could still receive dividends.[79]

# IV. Domestic and International Remedies for Political Instability

## A. Domestic Measures

Most of the Chinese investors lack awareness of safety management and have not yet established well-functioning response mechanisms.[80] To facilitate the implementation of the 'Going Out policy', the central Government issued regulations for improving companies' capacities to pursue the operation of safe projects.[81]

### *i. Improving Energy Companies' Capacities to Manage Political Instability*

Domestic administrative departments seek to play a role in assisting investors in addressing security threats.[82] Since 2010, MOFCOM has required its overseas commercial institutions affiliated with embassies, with the assistance of MFA, to give foreign subsidiaries of domestic investors concrete guidance on dealing with security threats.[83] From 2012 on, domestic investors should report their safety management regimes to MOFCOM, in accordance with the *Guidance on Safety Management of Chinese Enterprises and Personnel* (2012).[84] In addition to guidance and report mechanisms, the MOFCOM requires all embassies and consulates to supervise the safety training work of foreign subsidiaries of domestic investors.[85]

[78] Stern (n 76). 'NGCP' is the National Grid Corporation of the Philippines.

[79] Xu (n 75) 276.

[80] MOFCOM, *Introduction of Suggestions on Protecting Overseas Chinse-Funded Enterprises and Personnel* [《对<关于加强境外中资企业机构与人员安全保护工作的意见>的解读》] (2005).

[81] See, eg, State Council, Suggestions on Protecting Overseas Chinse-Funded Enterprises and Personnel [《关于加强境外中资企业机构与人员安全保护工作的意见》] (2005); MOFCOM et al (n 48); MOFCOM, MFA et al, *Responses to Safety Accidents in Overseas Investments Cooperation* [《对外投资合作境外安全事件应急响应和处置规定》] (2013).

[82] MOFCOM, Notice on Issuing the System of Signing in and Registration of Overseas Chinese-funded Enterprises or Institutions [《境外中资企业（机构）报到登记制度》] (2005) Art 2; NDRC et al, Issuing the Code of Conduct for the Operation of Overseas Investments by Private Enterprises [《国家发展改革委、商务部、人民银行等关于发布<民营企业境外投资经营行为规范>的通知》] (2017); D Freeman, 'China's Outward Investment Institutions, Constraints, and Challenges' (2013) 7 *Asia Paper* 2, 13; H Liu, 'Research on Chinese Overseas Investment Risk and Guarding of It' [《中国境外投资风险及其防范研究》] (2006) 3 *Central University of Economics and Finance* 63, 65.

[83] MOFCOM et al (n 48) Art 13; MOFCOM (n 46); See MOFCOM, MFA et al (n 81).

[84] MOFCOM, Notice on Issuing Guidance on Safety Management of Chinese Enterprises and Personnel [《境外中资企业机构和人员安全管理指南的通知》] (2012).

[85] MOFCOM et al (n 48) Art 7.

MOFCOM is also responsible for carrying out a general review of the progress of companies' safety management mechanisms.[86] In the case of emergencies, such as terrorist attacks, since 2019, MOFCOM has required domestic investors to report to it directly within 24 hours.[87]

Compared with MOFCOM, NDRC focuses more on assisting Chinese energy companies to manage emergencies. Investors must submit a Report of Major Adverse Conditions to NDRC when there are serious occurrences such as casualties or the major loss of overseas assets,[88] and can list what kind of state support they need.[89] Particularly in the event of 'wars or incidents endangering personal or property safety', central SOEs need to report to SASAC within 24 hours.[90]

Apart from their respective guidance on dealing with political instability, MOFCOM, MFA, NDRC and SASAC have since 2010 collaborated with each other to establish a working group for overseeing the safe operation of China's overseas investments, in accordance with the *Provisions on the Safety Management of Overseas Chinese-Funded Enterprises, Institutions and Personnel* (2010).[91] This working group assesses the feasibility of the emergency plans for key overseas projects, including energy projects.[92] For example, since 2010, SASAC has required central SOEs to submit a report on how they would deal with a political incident, and copy the report to the NDRC, MFA, MOFCOM and other relevant ministries.[93] Based on the report, the working group will oversee the safe operation of China's overseas investments to give frontline guidance.[94] To avoid conflicts among ministries, the *Interim Measures of Record-Keeping or Confirmation of Overseas Investments* (2018) authorised MOFCOM to play a coordinating role through establishing an information-sharing platform for managing *ex post* investment risks.[95] In 2018, MOFCOM updated *Guidance on Safety Management of Chinese Enterprises and Personnel*.[96] The new document emphasised again that government departments

[86] MOFCOM (n 84).

[87] MOFCOM, Notice on Implementation Procedures of Overseas Investments Recordation (Approval) [《对外投资备案（核准）报告实施规程》] (2019).

[88] NDRC, The Measures for Managing Outbound Investment of Enterprises [《企业境外投资管理办法》] (2017) Art 43.

[89] NDRC, The Format of the Report of Major Adverse Conditions [《境外投资重大不利情况报告表格式文本》] at www.ndrc.gov.cn/xxgk/zcfb/tz/201802/W020190905503714361032.doc.

[90] SASAC, Interim Measures for the Supervision and Administration of Overseas State-owned Assets of Central Enterprises [《中央企业境外国有资产监督管理暂行办法》] (2011) Art 31.

[91] MOFCOM et al (n 48).

[92] For the definition of 'key overseas projects', refer to the definition given in the *Notice on Giving Credit Support to the Key Overseas Investments Encouraged by the State* (2004). Energy investments have been listed as key overseas projects.

[93] MOFCOM et al (n 48) Art 17.

[94] ibid.

[95] MOFCOM et.al, Interim Measures of Record-Keeping or Confirmation of Overseas Investments [《商务部 人民银行 国资委 银监会 证监会 保监会 外汇局关于印发<对外投资备案（核准）报告暂行办法>的通知》] (2018) Art 4.

[96] MOFCOM, *Guidance on Safety Management of Chinese Enterprises and Personnel* [《境外中资企业机构和人员安全管理指南》] (2018).

should systematise guidance on daily safety management and share relevant information with investors to promote investment cooperation in the BRI.[97]

### *ii. Consular Support*

The CPC and the State Council have stated that 'we should perfect the mechanism of consular protection for domestic investors' legal rights'.[98] Consular protection refers to the way in which local embassies communicate with host-state authorities to urge them to deal fairly with harms to Chinese citizens and legal persons.[99] The MFA established the Centre for Consular Assistance and Protection to coordinate consular actions.[100] The local embassies are responsible for implementing the actions and assisting Chinese investors to seek compensation for losses caused by accidents in host states.[101] They provided the 'on-site assistance' for China's investors, for example the establishment of ad hoc work groups during the Libyan and Sudanese crises.[102]

However, in practice, China's NOCs prefer to cultivate close relations with host states to protect their business.[103] They have even occasionally refused to follow the guidance given by domestic administrative departments in emergencies. In the Myitsone hydropower dam project in Myanmar, MOFCOM warned China Power Investment Corporation (CPI) that the rising societal opposition could negatively affect the safe operation of the project.[104] However, CPI ignored the warning and finally suffered losses.[105] Given that, Chinese scholars such as Qi suggested that the Chinese Government needed to play a better role in improving its services to help companies to manage security risks.[106]

## B. Bilateral and Multilateral Security Cooperation

In addition to domestic mechanisms for helping investors to manage political instability, the Chinese Government also disclosed its objective of strengthening

[97] ibid.

[98] CPC, Decisions on Deepening a Comprehensive Reform [《关于全面深化改革若干问题的决定》] (2013); CPC and State Council, Opinions on Developing a New System of Open Economy [《中共中央、国务院关于构建开放型经济新体制的若干意见》] (2015).

[99] J Chen, 'The Current Situation of China's Overseas Interests Protection and the Corresponding Strategies' [《论中国海外投资利益保护的现状与对策》] (2014) 16 *International Forum* 35.

[100] Centre for Consular Assistance and Protection at www.fmprc.gov.cn/mfa_eng/wjb_663304/zzjg_663340/lss_665290/; Chen (n 99) 37.

[101] State Council (n 81).

[102] 'CNPC's Working Personnel Coming back to China', The Central People's Government of People's Republic of China, 1 March 2011 at www.gov.cn/gzdt/2011-03/01/content_1813694.htm.

[103] Moreira (n 61) 142.

[104] L Jones and Y Zou, 'Rethinking the Role of State-owned Enterprises in China's Rise' (2017) *New Political Economy* 1, 11.

[105] ibid.

[106] T Qi, 'Chinese Investors Make Use of International Investment Arbitration' [《论中国海外投资者对国际投资仲裁机制的利用》] (2014) 3 *Oriental Law* 89, 95–96.

security cooperation with its energy cooperation partners to guarantee the safe operation of China's energy projects, particularly the projects for energy transmission networks.[107] By seeking bilateral security cooperation with these states (eg, personnel training and the exchange of security information), China can rely on the host states' forces to protect its economic interests.[108] For example, China granted military aid to Central Asian states and launched joint military exercises for border control.[109] In their joint statement, China and Tajikistan aimed to 'ensure the safety of construction, maintenance and operation of the Line D of the China–Central Asia Gas Pipeline' to guarantee an uninterrupted gas supply.[110] China and Pakistan have strengthened their cooperation on anti-terrorism and anti-piracy as well, to ensure the overall security of the CPEC projects and the safety of Chinese workers.[111]

Further, China has aimed to initiate multilateral security cooperation to protect energy interests.[112] Although China can work with each transit state for the safe operation of pipelines, multilateral security cooperation with exporting and various transit states is more efficient.[113] *The 13th Natural Gas Development Five-Year Plan* (2016) suggested that China and transit states should join together to establish a multi-dimensional coordinating mechanism to shelter gas pipelines from attacks and ensure reliable gas supplies.[114] The coordinating mechanism requires China and its energy cooperation partners to produce coherent policy responses and actions (eg, cutting financing to terrorist forces).[115]

The Shanghai Cooperation Organisation (SCO) is an example of how China has sought multilateral security cooperation to protect its energy projects in Central Asia.[116] The SCO was established for regional security and stability.[117] Given the

[107] State Council, *China's Military Strategy* [《中国的军事战略》] (2015); NEA, Cooperation Principles and Concrete Actions of the Belt and Road Energy Partnership (2019).

[108] MOFCOM (n 96).

[109] X Zhao, *The Shanghai Cooperation Organisation and Counter-Terrorism Cooperation* (Institute for Security and Development Policy, 2012).

[110] The Joint Declaration of Partnership and Promoting Win-Win Cooperation between China and Tajikistan [《中华人民共和国和塔吉克斯坦共和国关于进一步发展和深化战略伙伴关系的联合宣言》] (2014).

[111] D Zhou, 'An Analysis of Controllability of Chinese Enterprises' Energy Investment Risk in Pakistan' (2018) 248 *Advances in Social Science, Education and Humanities Research* 31, 35; F Boni, 'Protecting the Belt and Road Initiative: China's Cooperation with Pakistan to Secure CPEC' (2019) 14 *Asia Policy* 5, 6; SH Basit, 'Terrorizing the CPEC: Managing Transnational Militancy in China–Pakistan Relations' (2019) 32 *The Pacific Review* 694, 706.

[112] Jiang and Ding (n 2) 26.

[113] Y Ling, 'Legal Protection against the Political Risk on Overseas Infrastructure Investments along "One Belt One Road"' [《"一带一路"境外基础设施投资政治风险防范的法律路径》] (2018) 34 *Journal of Lanzhou University of Finance and Economics* 110, 111.

[114] NDRC, *The 13th Natural Gas Development Five-year Plan* (《天然气发展"十三五"规划》) (2016).

[115] S Aris, *Eurasian Regionalism – The Shanghai Cooperation Organization* (London, Palgrave Macmillan, 2011) 109.

[116] The Eurasia Group (n 51) 8; Jiang and Ding (n 2) 26; NEA (n 107); NEA, *Vision and Actions on Energy Cooperation in Jointly Building Silk Road Economic Belt and 21st-Century Maritime Silk Road* (2017).

[117] S Handke, *Securing and Fuelling China's Ascent to Power* (CIEP, August 2006) 65–66 at www.clingendaelenergy.com/inc/upload/files/Chinese-Kazakh_Oil_Pipeline.pdf.

transnational nature of terrorist activities or military exercises, member states regularly exchange information about the security situation and anti-terrorism training programmes through the high-level meetings.[118] More specifically, the Regional Anti-Terrorist Structure of the SCO (RATS) coordinates the high-level meetings among the security organs of member states and disseminates security information (eg, suspected or known extremists and terrorists).[119] Through the information exchange, China and other member states are able to develop a common method for combatting security threats and responding to emergency situations.[120] Indeed, to ensure the safe operation of pipelines and the development of overseas energy value chains, China has actively participated in the military exercises of the SCO.[121] For example, in 2008, the special forces of the SCO members combatted a terrorist attack on an oil tanker with the organisation of RATS.[122]

## C. State Assistance as a Way of Exercising Influence?

The Chinese Government has actively helped Chinese energy companies to deal with the political instability of host states to promote overseas energy investments – a key objective of its external energy strategy.[123] However, domestic regulatory efforts to reduce security threats do not automatically indicate the replacement of home states with investors in investment management. These efforts represent consular assistance, because the main rationale behind the relevant regulations is to improve China's energy companies' internal safety management systems. The central Government grants support as required by investors in reports, instead of asserting the rights of domestic energy companies.

Aiding domestic energy companies to enhance their capacity to reduce security threats could relieve China's diplomatic dilemma.[124] China has so far abided by the diplomatic principle of non-interference when launching bilateral and multilateral security cooperation to protect its energy interests. However, as China's global

[118] Development Strategy of The Shanghai Cooperation Organization until 2025 (2015) at eng.sco-russia2020.ru/images/00/44/004418.pdf.

[119] S Aris, 'The Shanghai Cooperation Organisation: "Tackling the Three Evils" – A Regional Response to Non-traditional Security Challenges or an Anti-Western Bloc?' (2009) 61 *Europe-Asia Studies* 457, 469–70; F Indeo, 'China as Security Provider in Central Asia Post 2014: A Realistic Perspective?', *Central Asia Security Policy Briefs* (January 2015) 15.

[120] T Pradt, *The Prequel to China's New Silk Road: Preparing the Ground in Central Asia* (Singapore, Springer, 2020) 91.

[121] H Zhao, 'China's View of and Expectations from the Shanghai Cooperation Organization' (2013) 53 *Asian Survey* 436, 442; P Guang, 'A Chinese Perspective on the Shanghai Cooperation Organization' in AJK Bailes et al (eds), *The Shanghai Cooperation Organization* (Stockholm International Peace Research Institute, 2007) 45–58, 46.

[122] Pradt (n 120) 91.

[123] N Zhang, 'Safeguarding Overseas Interests in China's Rise' [《崛起过程中的海外利益维护》] (2014) 6 Social Science in Ningxia 10, 11.

[124] M Duchatel, O Brauner and Z Hang, 'Protecting China's Overseas Interests', SIPRI Policy Paper No. 41 (Stockholm International Peace Research Institute, June 2014) 34.

energy expansion continues, it is becoming increasingly difficult for the state to stay in line with this principle.[125] As discussed above, China has massive energy interests in rogue states such as Iran and Sudan. The principle of non-interference would restrict China's ability to get involved in a political crisis resulting from the internal tensions of the host state.[126] Owing to this, the Chinese Government has doubts about whether or not it should get directly involved in the political conflicts of host states to protect Chinese energy companies.[127] This dilemma may explain the revision of the provision on international energy cooperation in the draft of the PRC Energy Law. *The PRC Energy Law (2008 Draft)* prescribed that the state needs to deal with political risks such as internal conflicts of host states.[128] However, the 2020 draft deleted this provision.[129]

# V. Domestic and International Remedies against Regulatory Risks

Similar to managing political instability, the Chinese Government has given regulatory support to investors to deal with host states' political interference. Internationally, China has marginalised its role by embracing the mechanism of investor–state arbitration, but has tried to imbue this system with its own values.

## A. Domestic Measures

The report mechanism initiated by MOFCOM and SASAC aims to guide energy investors as to how they can deal with political interference by host states. At the same time, Sinosure, as a state-owned insurance company, helps energy investors to mitigate investment risks.

[125] M Hirono, Y Jiang and M Lanteigne, 'China's New Roles and Behaviour in Conflict-Affected Regions: Reconsidering Non-Interference and Non-Intervention' (2019) 239 *The China Quarterly* 573, 583.

[126] Duchatel, Brauner and Hang (n 124) 34; D Large, 'China & the Contradictions of "Non-Interference" in Sudan' (2008) 35 *Review of African Political Economy* 93, 105.

[127] International Crisis Group, *China's Thirst for Oil* (2008) 30–31; L Jakobson, 'Does China Have an "Energy Diplomacy"? Reflections on China's Energy Security and its International Dimensions' in A Marquina (ed), *Energy Security: Visions from Asia and Europe* (London, Palgrave Macmillan, 2008) 121–34, 128–29; Y Zou and L Jones, 'China's Response to Threats to Its Overseas Economic Interests: Softening Non-Interference and Cultivating Hegemony' (2020) 29 *Journal of Contemporary China* 92, 101–02.

[128] The Energy Law of the PRC (Draft) (2008) Art 110.

[129] The Energy Law of the PRC (Draft) (2020); Jun He Law Firm, 'Comments on *The Energy Law of the PRC (Draft, 2020)*' [简评《能源法征求意见稿》] (12 May 2020) at www.junhe.com/law-reviews/1196; BJX Electricity, 'The Declarative Energy Law Draft' [《宣言式的能源法草案》] (14 April 2020) at shoudian.bjx.com.cn/html/20200415/1063503-3.shtml.

### *i. Domestic Report Mechanism*

The report mechanism has helped domestic investors to seek support and suggestions from the Chinese Government in investment crises.[130] Since 2010, Chambers of Commerce (Associations) of Overseas Sino-funded Enterprises, guided by the economic and commercial counsellors' offices of the embassies, have been responsible for analysing the impact of regulatory change on the operation of existing energy investments, and notifying Chinese investors.[131] The companies should report to the Chambers and the economic and commercial counsellors' offices of the embassies on how they have dealt with policy inconsistencies.[132] More specifically, since 2011, in the event of emergencies such as 'frozen bank accounts', a sudden political coup or a breach of contract by the host government, central SOEs need to report to SASAC and MOFCOM, respectively, within 24 hours.[133] In practice, CNPC sought support and suggestions from the Chinese Government when the company felt threatened by a political change in the host state.[134]

### *ii. Domestic Insurance Services*

To promote energy investments that export production capacity, the central Government established a national insurance mechanism in 2005 for mitigating political risks.[135] SASAC requires central SOEs to buy overseas investment insurance.[136] Overseas investment insurance will compensate investors for risks such as expropriation, currency transfer, wars and breach of contract by host governments.[137] Under the *Guiding Opinions of the China Insurance Regulatory Commission on Insurance Service's Contribution to the Belt and Road Initiative* (2017), insurance institutions provide serial insurance services, ranging from consultation, to insurance arrangements to loss evaluation.[138]

[130] S Kang and J Mu, 'Risk Analysis and Prevention of Foreign Direct Investment by Chinese State-owned Enterprises' [《中国国有企业境外投资风险分析与防范》] (2020) 40 *Hebei Academic Journal* 122, 129.
[131] MOFCOM (n 46).
[132] ibid.
[133] SASAC (n 90) Art 31; MOFCOM (n 87).
[134] EB Vermeer, 'The Global Expansion of Chinese Oil Companies: Political Demands, Profitability and Risks' (2015) 29 *China Information* 3, 11.
[135] NDRC and China Export & Credit Insurance Corporation, 'Relevant Issues on Setting up A Risk Prevention Mechanism for Key Overseas Investment Projects' [《国家发展和改革委员会、中国出口信用保险公司关于建立境外投资重点项目风险保障机制有关问题的通知》] (2005); CIRC, Guiding Opinions of the China Insurance Regulatory Commission on Insurance Service's Contribution to the Belt and Road Initiative [《中国保监会关于保险业服务"一带一路"建设的指导意见》] (2017) 2; State Council, *The 12th Five-Year Plan of Energy Development* [《能源发展"十二五"规划》] (2013).
[136] SASAC, Measures for the Supervision and Administration of Overseas Investments by Central Enterprises [《中央企业境外投资监督管理办法》] (2017) Art 27.
[137] China Export & Credit Insurance Corporation, 'Corporate File' at www.sinosure.com.cn/en/Sinosure/Profile/index.shtml; MOFCOM, Notice on Enhancement of Risks Mitigation and Prevention in Overseas Economic Trade and Investment Cooperation Zones [《关于加强境外经济贸易合作区风险防范有关问题的通知》] (17 August 2010).
[138] CIRC (n 135).

Sinosure was established in 2001 as a state-owned insurance company to facilitate the implementation of the 'Going Out' policy.[139] Its overseas investment insurance recovers investors' losses resulting from expropriation, exchange restrictions, war and political riots, and breach of contract.[140] Sinosure also has to monitor changes in the investment environment during a project's operation to make necessary adjustments to relevant insurance services.[141] Since 2021, Sinosure has provided insurance services for more than 150 projects for clean energy development.[142] It is argued that Sinosure's investment insurance services are more appealing to Chinese investors, compared to initiating expensive and time-consuming arbitration for legal protection.[143] However, there are three problems with providing insurance services. First, Sinosure prefers to insure SOEs that are backed by the Government,[144] which limits the possibility of POEs' involvement in risky energy investments. Second, Sinosure's insurance policies do not automatically include the subrogation rights found in BITs.[145] Therefore, Sinosure needs to ensure its subrogation rights by adding relevant provisions in individual insurance policies.[146] Finally, there should be more domestic insurance institutions, because Sinosure may not have the capacity to provide insurance policies for every energy company.[147]

## B. China's Approach to Investor–State Dispute Settlement

To promote global energy expansion, China has gradually liberalised its investment regime[148] by negotiating or renegotiating strict clauses for investor–state dispute settlement.[149] China's companies thus have a strong legal basis to initiate

[139] China Export & Credit Insurance Corporation (n 137).

[140] Sinosure, 'Overseas Investment Insurance' at www.sinosure.com.cn/en/Insurance/oii/index.shtml.

[141] China Export & Credit Insurance Corporation (n 137).

[142] 'The Insurance Coverage for China Export & Credit Insurance Corporation's Green Projects Is Approximately 7.7 billion US Dollars.' [中国信保绿色项目保额约77亿美元] *China Banking and Insurance News* (20 April 2022) at www.cbimc.cn/content/2022-04/20/content_460111.html.

[143] KP Sauvant and MD Nolan, 'China's Rising Outward FDI, Its Reception in Host Countries and Implications for International Investment Law and Policy' in BL Liebman and CJ Milhaupt (eds), *Regulating the Visible Hand?: The Institutional Implications of Chinese State Capitalism* (Oxford, Oxford University Press, 2015) 285–311.

[144] X Gong, 'Time for Action: Chinese Companies and "One Belt One Road"' *IPP Review* (10 June 2016).

[145] ibid.

[146] X Wu, 'China's Political Risk Insurance for Outward FDI Within the Context of Belt and Road Initiative' in G Martinico and X Wu (eds), *A Legal Analysis of the Belt and Road Initiative* (Cham, Palgrave Macmillan, 2020) 185–97, 187.

[147] X Li, 'A Study on the Legal Protection of China's Overseas Energy Investment from the Perspective of "One Belt One Road"' [《"一带一路"视域下我国海外能源投资保护的法律问题研究》] (2015) 15 *Journal of Nanjing Institute of Technology* 40, 42.

[148] LE Trakman, 'Geopolitics, China and Investor-State Arbitration' in L Toohey, CB Picker and J Greenacre (eds), *China in the International Economic Order* (Cambridge, Cambridge University Press, 2015) 268–92, 287.

[149] See Sanchez (n 31) 340.

arbitration against host states. For instance, based on the China–Sweden BIT, Huawei brought its dispute with the Swedish Government to ICSID to seek compensation.[150] At the same time, China has developed clauses for investor–state dispute settlement in a diversified and flexible manner. The settlement of investor–state disputes should not be limited to submitting claims to arbitration. Negotiating treaties with states with a weak rule of law requires a step-by-step approach and leaves room for future progress.

### *i. Early Clauses in Investor–State Arbitration*

China had a conservative attitude towards investor–state arbitration, because early BITs signed by China with developing states chiefly aimed at developing diplomatic alliances and defending China's interest in being a capital-importing state.[151] For instance, the China–Pakistan BIT grants Chinese investors the right to request an international arbitration tribunal to review the amount of compensation only if the court of Pakistan cannot resolve it.[152] The list below demonstrates treaties negotiated with resource-rich states that only allow Chinese energy companies to submit disputes concerning the amount of compensation to international arbitration:

- China-Mongolia BIT (1991).
- China-Kyrgyzstan BIT (1992).
- China-Kazakhstan BIT (1992).
- China-Tajikistan BIT (1993).
- China-Indonesia BIT (1994).
- China-Saudi Arabia BIT (1995).
- China-Cambodia BIT (1996).
- China-Sudan BIT (1997).
- China-Qatar BIT (1999).

Similarly, the China–Turkmenistan BIT only leaves the possibility of negotiating complementary agreements on submitting disputes to ICSID.[153] The China–Philippines BIT also provides that whether disputes other than the amount of compensation can be submitted to international arbitration depends on the complementary agreement between the two states.[154]

[150] D Charlotin and L Bohmer, 'Chinese Network Companies Notifies Sweden of Alleged BIT Breaches', *Investment Arbitration Reporter* (latest update 12 March 2021).
[151] M Du, 'Huawei Strikes Back: Challenging National Security Decisions Before Investment Arbitral Tribunals' (2022) 37 *Emory International Law Review* 1, 32; L Trakman, 'China's Regulation of Foreign Direct Investment' in J Chaisse, T Ishikawa and S Jusoh (eds), *Asia's Changing International Investment Regime* (Singapore, Springer, 2017) 67–95, 69.
[152] China–Pakistan BIT (signed in 1989, in effect in 1990).
[153] China–Turkmenistan BIT (signed in 1992, came into effect in 1994) Art 8.
[154] China–Philippines BIT (1992) Art 10(2).

The narrowly defined clauses for investor–state arbitration in these early BITs placed Chinese energy investors at a disadvantage.[155] For example, State Grid almost lost equity control of the investee in the Philippines, as discussed in section III. According to the China–Philippines BIT (1992), except for disputes relating to compensation for expropriation, submission of other disputes to international arbitration required the consent of the host state. It means that State Grid might not be able to bring the case before investor–state arbitration as it was naïve to confirm the existence of expropriation in the dispute settlement regimes of Philippines.

Since these treaties grant only limited access to investor–state arbitration, Chinese energy companies may try to apply MFN treatment to dispute resolution mechanisms.[156] In principle, they can bring the case against host states by relying on advanced dispute resolution clauses in other investment treaties concluded by the host states. However, an increasing number of host states decided to forbid the application of MFN in dispute resolution. For example, MFN treatment is not allowed to include international dispute resolution under the China–Uzbekistan BIT (2011), Agreement on Investment of the Framework Agreement on Comprehensive Economic Cooperation between China and ASEAN (2010) and RCEP Agreement (2020).[157]

### *ii. Wider Access to Investor–State Arbitration*

To promote global energy expansion, the Chinese Government aims to progressively enhance the treatment of Chinese investors during the negotiation of investment treaties.[158] Because a wider access to investor–state arbitration can help to enforce obligations imposed on host states,[159] the Chinese Government now

[155] N Eliasson, 'The Chinese Investment Treaty Programme, Jurisdictional Challenges and Investment Planning' in W Shan and J Su (eds), *China and International Investment Law: Twenty Years of ICSID Membership* (Leiden, Brill, 2015) 235–59, 239–40.

[156] H Lai and GM Lentner, 'Paving the Silk Road BIT by BIT: An Analysis of Investment Protection for Chinese Infrastructure/Projects under the Belt & Road Initiative' in J Chaisse and J Górski (eds), *The Belt and Road Initiative: Law, Economics, and Politics* (Leiden, Brill, 2018) 250–83, 270.

[157] China–Uzbekistan BIT (2011) Art 4(3); Agreement on Investment of the Framework Agreement on Comprehensive Economic Cooperation between China and ASEAN (2010) Art 5(4); The Regional Comprehensive Economic Partnership (RCEP) Agreement (2020) Art 10.4.

[158] MOFCOM's Interpretation of *Measures for the Administration of Overseas Investment* [《商务部解读<境外投资管理办法>》] (2014); State Council, Several Opinions of the State Council on Accelerating the Implementation of the Strategies for Free Trade Areas [《国务院关于加快实施自由贸易区战略的若干意见》] (2015); Supreme People's Court, Several Opinions on the Provision by the People's Court of Judicial Services and Safeguards for the Construction of the BRI [《最高人民法院关于人民法院为"一带一路"建设提供司法服务和保障的若干意见》] (2015); State Council, China to Fast-Track FTA Strategy (17 December 2015) at english.www.gov.cn/policies/latest_releases/2015/12/17/content_281475255618346.htm; H Wang, 'The RCEP and Its Investment Rules: Learning from Past Chinese FTAs' (2017) 3 *The Chinese Journal of Global Governance* 160.

[159] S Liedtke, 'Chinese Energy Investments in Europe: An Analysis of Policy Drivers and Approaches' (2017) 101 *Energy Policy* 659, 667.

has a more positive attitude towards such arbitration.[160] The investment report published by MOFCOM in 2017 recorded that wider access to investor–state arbitration incentivised Chinese energy investors to continue their global energy expansion.[161]

The investment treaties with China's key energy cooperation partners grant investors the right to bring claims before arbitration tribunals:

- China-Iran BIT (2000).
- China-Nigeria BIT (2001).
- China-Myanmar BIT (2001).
- China-Russia BIT (2006).
- Free Trade Agreement between the Government of the People's Republic of China and the Government of the Islamic Republic of Pakistan (2006).
- Agreement on Investment of the Framework Agreement on Comprehensive Economic Co-operation between China and ASEAN (2010).
- China-Uzbekistan BIT (2011).
- China-United Republic of Tanzania BIT (2013).

It remains to be seen how the EU–China Comprehensive Agreement on Investment (CAI) provides investor–state dispute settlement,[162] because China's renewable energy companies operate many projects in the EU. Furthermore, regarding multilateral regimes, it is possible for China to join the ECT because it signed the International Energy Charter Declaration.[163]

More specifically, China has a strong interest in guaranteeing SOEs' access to investor–state arbitration as they are leading players in the global energy expansion (especially in energy infrastructure investments).[164] Therefore, MOFCOM made an explicit statement that China firmly opposes discriminatory measures against SOEs (eg, blocking their access to investor–state arbitration) and calls for respect

[160] Recommendations of China regarding Investor–State Dispute Settlement Reform, Annex of Possible Reform of Investor-State Dispute Settlement (ISDS) Submission from the Government of China (19 July 2019) at undocs.org/en/A/CN.9/WG.III/WP.177. See, eg, A Berger, 'Hesitant Embrace: China's Recent Approach to International Investment Rule-Making' (2015) 16 *Journal of World Investment and Trade* 843; N Gallagher, 'Role of China in Investment: BITs, SOEs, Private Enterprises, and Evolution of Policy' (2016) 31 *ICSID Review* 88; JJ Huang, 'Silk Road Economic Belt: Can Old BITs Fulfil China's New Initiative? (2016) 50 *Journal of World Trade* 733.

[161] MOFCOM, *Report of Development of Overseas Investments 2017* [《对外投资合作发展报告2017》] (2017) 128; W Shan, *International Law Protection for China's Overseas Energy Investment: The Research of Regulations Based on Field Research and Research in Different Regions* [《中国对外能源投资的国际法保护一基于实证和区域的制度研究》] (Beijing, Qinghua University Press, 2014).

[162] EU–China Comprehensive Agreement on Investment (CAI) (signed in 2021) section V.

[163] M Hodgson and A Bryan, 'Investment Treaty Arbitration in Asia' in Chaisse (ed) (n 44) 430–43, 440–41.

[164] Lai and Lentner (n 156) 264; X Liu, 'Protection for Investors of Stated-Owned Enterprises under the "Theory of State Capitalism" – Based on the Angle of Investment Treaty Reform' [《"国家资本主义论"下的国企投资者保护—基于投资协定革新的视角》] (2018) 5 *Law Science* 15.

for development models in different states.[165] To promote SOEs' access to investor–state arbitration, scholars have proposed that China should explicitly include SOEs or state entities within the scope of the investor.[166] China can even specify the standards for assessing whether SOEs are instruments of the Government in treaties.[167]

### *iii. Development-Oriented Clauses for Investor–State Dispute Settlement*

The Chinese Government has endorsed the 'development-oriented' treaty-making practice, under which China's investment treaties should help host states to develop economies and pursue public interests.[168] It implies that China oscillates between the romantic vision of facilitating under-developed states' development and the realist vision of hard-treaty protection, to balance Chinese investors' interests and resource-rich states' development needs.[169] Relatively weak treaty partners need to have leeway to change their domestic policies and regulations.[170] Derogating from advanced practice can also avoid a drawn-out negotiating process.[171] In the BRI, most resource-rich states are developing Asian and African states with weak rule of law. They are reluctant to renegotiate BITs with China or embrace a stricter liability.[172] Therefore, China has taken the 'Early-Harvest' approach by institutionalising what stakeholders currently agree with.[173] Through ongoing

[165] MOFCOM, 'China's Position Paper on WTO Reform' (20 December 2018) at english.mofcom.gov.cn/sys/print.shtml?/newsrelease/counselorsoffice/westernasiaandafricareport/201812/20181202818679.

[166] See, eg, L Wang, 'State Controlled Entities as Qualified "Investors": Implications for the Pacific Region Investment Treaty Making' (2015) 12 *Transnational Disputes Management* 1; M McLaughlin, 'Defining a State-Owned Enterprise in International Investment Agreements' (2019) 34 *ICSID Review* 595; Liu (n 164) 21.

[167] Liu (n 164) 22.

[168] MOFCOM (n 165); NEA (n 116); J Yang, 'China's Competitive FTA Strategy: Realism on a Liberal Slide' in M Solís, B Stallings and SN Katada (eds), *Competitive Regionalism: FTA Diffusion in the Pacific Rim* (London, Palgrave Macmillan, 2009) 216–35, 224.

[169] K Zeng, 'China's Free Trade Agreement Diplomacy' (2016) 9 *The Chinese Journal of International Politics* 277; H Wang, 'China's Approach to the Belt and Road Initiative: Scope, Character and Sustainability' (2019) 22 *Journal of International Economic Law* 29, 49; Dian and Menegazzi (n 52).

[170] AC Dai, 'The International Investment Agreement Network under the "Belt and Road" Initiative' in Chaisse and Górski (eds) (n 156) 241–42.

[171] P Xiong and R Tomasic, 'Soft Law, State-Owned Enterprises and Dispute Resolution on PRC's Belt and Road: Towards an Emerging Legal Order' (2019) 49 *Hong Kong Law Journal* 1025; Q Kong, 'Bilateral Investment Rule-Making: BITs or FTAs with Investment Rules?' (2013) 14 *The Journal of World Investment & Trade* 638, 640.

[172] V Bath, '"One Belt, One Road" and Chinese Investment' in L-C Wolff and C Xi (eds), *Legal Dimension of China's Belt and Road Initiative* (Hong Kong, Wolters Kluwer, 2016) 165–217, 186; L Zhang, 'Research on Improvement of the International Investment Disputes Settlement Mechanism under "One Belt One Road" Initiative' [《"一带一路"国际投资争端解决机制完善研究》] (2018) 8 *Law Science Magazine* 32, 39.

[173] W Shan, 'Investment Treaty Regime of the Silk Road Economic Belt and Its Improvement' [《丝绸之路经济带国家投资条约体制的现状与完善》] (2018) 5 *China Law Review* 33, 43; Berger (n 161) 865; J Chaisse, 'China's International Investment Policy: Formation, Evolution, and Transformation(s)' in J Chaisse and L Nottage (eds), *International Investment Treaties and Arbitration Across Asia* (Leiden, Brill, 2018) 544–78, 563. Berger (n 160) 849.

communication, China is likely to update treaties, such as by including higher-standard clauses for investor–state arbitration.[174]

With the 'development-oriented' treaty-making practice, host states can impose admissibility requirements on wider access to investor–state arbitration.[175] In the agreement with ASEAN states, Indonesia, the Philippines, Thailand and Vietnam made reservations and did not allow investors to submit disputes already submitted to domestic legal or administrative institutions to tribunals for investor–state arbitration.[176] Also, in the China–Pakistan FTA, China–Uzbekistan BIT and China–Tanzania BIT, the responding state has the right to require Chinese investors to exhaust domestic administrative reviews prior to investor–state arbitration.[177] In the China–Myanmar BIT, submitting claims to ICSID does not require recourse to domestic administrative reviews but submitting claims to ad hoc arbitration does.[178] Similarly, the RCEP Agreement has so far only included dispute settlement resolution in the future work programme.[179] However, this Agreement created a soft regime of best-endeavour obligations regarding the settlement of disputes between investors and host states.[180] ASEAN states thus voluntarily assist Chinese companies to resolve complaints with administrative agencies.

## C. The Marginalised Role of the Chinese Government in Managing Regulatory Risks

By offering assistance to investors and covering investors' losses through insurance, the domestic report system and insurance services have placed energy investors in a leading position to manage investment risks. Internationally, China has tried to be consistent in the practice of depoliticising investor–state disputes by providing Chinese energy investors with the choice of bringing cases to investor–state arbitration.[181] Moreover, by pursuing its own values of win-win/harmonious world, China can contribute to the reform of the mechanism of investor–state

[174] ibid 849.

[175] M Chi and X Wang, 'The Evolution of ISA Clauses in Chinese IIAs and Its Practical Implications – The Admissibility of Disputes for Investor–State Arbitration' (2015) 16 *Journal of World Investment & Trade* 869, 888; Dian and Menegazzi (n 52) 113.

[176] Agreement on Investment of the Framework Agreement (n 157) Art 14(5).

[177] M Sornarajah, 'Chinese Investment Treaties in the Belt and Road Initiative Area' (2020) 8 *The Chinese Journal of Comparative Law* 55, 71; Free Trade Agreement between the Government of the People's Republic of China and the Government of the Islamic Republic of Pakistan (2006) Art 54; China–Uzbekistan BIT (n 157) Art 12; China–United Republic of Tanzania BIT (2013) Art 13.

[178] China–Myanmar BIT (2001) Art 9(3).

[179] RCEP (n 157) Art 10.18.

[180] ibid Art 10.17.2.

[181] Shaffer and Gao (n 182) 17; M Zhang, 'Comprehensively Promote Cooperation on BRI Framework Mechanism', State Council (2017) at www.scio.gov.cn/xwfbh/xwbfbh/wqfbh/35861/36637/xgbd36644/Document/1551139/1551139.htm (the BRI should envisage major normative and rule innovations in the trade and investment system).

dispute settlement.[182] By adopting the flexible approach to disputes settlement resolution,[183] China and its energy cooperation partners are likely to shape the investor–state arbitration scheme to suit their needs.[184]

## VI. Conclusion

Most of the scholars in the field of international relations have argued that the Chinese Government has played a leading role in energy investment protection by taking advantage of good relations with its energy cooperation partners.[185] However, the analysis of domestic regulations on outbound investments and investment treaties provides a more nuanced perspective.

China has strengthened investment protection against regulatory risks by providing domestic energy companies with wider access to investor–state arbitration and, moreover, has actively adopted a 'development-oriented' practice to negotiate treaties with under-developed resource-rich states. These efforts align with the process of depoliticisation. Furthermore, welcoming China's state-owned investors to investor–state arbitration does not necessarily bring the Chinese Government before tribunals, nor does it politicise this dispute settlement regime.[186] Instead, granting legal protection to SOEs can prevent them from turning to the Chinese Government for diplomatic protection.

However, the principle of depoliticisation cannot help Chinese energy companies to manage the political instability of host states given security threats obviously riven with geopolitical complexities. Therefore, to manage political instability, the understanding of depoliticisation should be broadened to allow home states to assist their investors to ensure the safety of foreign property and workers. As demonstrated in the case of China, in addition to the measures for improving the risk management of energy companies and consular support, the Chinese Government has sought security cooperation to ensure the safe operation of foreign energy projects, without replacing the leading role of investors in managing their projects. However, because of the complexity of energy geopolitics and the dynamics of relations among global powers, the Chinese Government remains very cautious about its direct involvement in dealing with political crises in host states.

[182] C Cai, *The Rise of China and International Law* (Oxford, Oxford University Press, 2019) 37. The author argues that China 'seeks international law to better accommodate it'.

[183] G Shaffer and H Gao, 'A New Chinese Economic Order?' [2020] *Journal of International Economic Law* 1, 19 and 21. Although there may be political considerations behind the negotiation of treaties: Sornarajah (n 177); T Cohen and D Schneiderman, 'The Political Economy of Chinese Bilateral Investment Treaty Policy' (2017) 5 *The Chinese Journal of Comparative Law* 110.

[184] S Zhang, 'China's Approach in Drafting the Investor-State Arbitration Clause: A Review from the "Belt and Road" Regions" Perspective' (2017) 5 *The Chinese Journal of Comparative Law* 79, 103; Wang (n 169) 55.

[185] Moreira (n 61) 147.

[186] See, eg, J Li, 'State-Owned Enterprises in the Current Regime of Investor-State Arbitration' in S Lalani and R Polanco Lazo (eds), *The Role of the State in Investor-State Arbitration* (Leiden, Brill Nijhoff, 2015) 380–404, 400.

# 10

# Conclusion

A substantial body of international relations literature characterises China's energy companies as the tools of the Chinese Government for achieving its strategic objectives. This book provides a nuanced analysis by discussing whether China's domestic regulatory framework for overseas investments, investment treaties and energy cooperation agreements provides official channels for the Chinese Government to exercise the perceived state influence over energy companies. The deregulation of management of outbound energy investments has helped to reduce potential avenues through which the Government can exert an influence over the investment-making of energy companies. Internationally, the Chinese Government has attempted to include treaty protection for securing access to foreign energy markets, and has displayed a positive attitude towards investor–state arbitration as well, to place energy companies in a good position to pursue compensation in the light of regulatory risks. However, China's political economy and the existing hostile international environment prevent the state from fully stepping back from its global energy expansion. The approval of sensitive investments and the integration of Party branches in both SOEs and POEs can at least help the Government to achieve energy policy objectives. At the same time, the Chinese Government has pursued policy coordination with its energy cooperation partners to build mutual trust, to alleviate national security concerns and thus to remove barriers to foreign energy markets. It has also launched security cooperation with its energy cooperation partners, to ensure the safe operation of China's energy projects.

More specifically, by broadening the application of the simpler and less time-consuming record-keeping procedure, the reform of investment approval procedures has restricted state involvement in the decision-making of energy investments. China's outbound energy investments are usually subject to the record-keeping system, with the exception of those in the hydropower sector. This reform aligns with the legal expectation that companies will operate free from government influence. However, the Chinese Government has not relinquished all forms of administrative control over the decision-making of overseas energy investments. Investments in sensitive destinations and areas that risk damaging China's diplomatic image, or its industrial development remain subject to approval, and can thus be stopped by the Government. In practice, case studies demonstrate how difficult it sometimes was for the Chinese Government to rein in companies whose financial interests were at stake.

To meet its external energy interests in the global energy expansion of energy companies, instead of straightforwardly managing investments through administrative orders, the Chinese Government now prefers to be seen as a provider of services that aid companies to make overseas investments. In this new role, the Government continues to influence investment decisions through policy guidance and support. However, policy guidance is not necessarily a measure for viewing China's energy investments as strategic investments. The influence required for achieving energy policy objectives is exercised in a relatively transparent manner, because energy investments that help the Chinese Government to achieve energy policy objectives are categorised in 'encouraged' lists, which is similar to the programme concerning 'projects of common interest' initiated by the EU. Disclosing how states achieve energy policies through domestic companies is in line with the requirement for disclosure and transparency when making commercial investments. Furthermore, most of the energy investments that are endorsed in the five-year plans still pursue commercial interests. As demonstrated in the State Grid case study, the company tried to align its interest in expanding its share of foreign markets with the policy goal of integrating global energy value chains. Therefore, it remains possible that companies will have an interest in lobbying the Government to recognise their projects, thus facilitating their access to policy support.

Similar to state guidance and support, the integration of Party branches into SOEs and POEs remains a very important channel for exercising state control over their corporate governance. The Party branches can exercise influence over the drafting of investment plans and management of these companies by participating in decision-making on corporate issues and influencing the appointment of energy companies. It is possible for the Party branches to pursue strategic interests and restrict China's energy companies from pursuing commercial interests or acting independently. The Party's influence over the investment-making of energy companies largely aims to implement energy policies. It is difficult to determine whether the Party interferes with decisions on investing abroad beyond the projects endorsed in the five-year plans. This requires analysis in a 'fact-specific' context, because the corporate structure of China's SOEs does not itself indicate state control over outbound investments, according to the tribunal in *Beijing Urban Construction Group v Yemen*.[1]

Internationally, to help companies access foreign energy markets, MOFCOM has played a leading role in providing information on the investment environment of host states and a remedy to assist in breaking down barriers to foreign market access, although the remedy has rarely been used by domestic investors. After investments are made, the Chinese Government sets up the consular support scheme, report mechanism and the regime for insurance services to help

[1] *Beijing Urban Construction Group Co Ltd v Republic of Yemen*, ICSID Case No ARB/14/30, Decision on Jurisdiction, 31 May 2017, para 39.

energy companies manage political risks. Also, it has tried to marginalise its role in investor–state dispute settlement by offering companies the choice of utilising investor–state arbitration. Apart from embracing strict investor–state arbitration clauses in investment treaties, the Government has devised flexible mechanisms for settling investor–state disputes to help China's energy companies to seek compensation from host states in which there is weak application of the rule of law.

Given the complex political economy in the global energy sector, China has adopted extra-legal means to cope with geopolitical threats to its global energy expansion. To alleviate host states' national security concerns, China has taken a progressive approach to seeking political acceptability. This approach includes providing economic incentives for resource-rich states to boost energy investment cooperation, and the gradual coordination of energy development strategies of both states for common development. This approach can build mutual political trust, as host states will be more familiar with the energy policy objectives of China and more willing to attract China's energy investments, which can also help to develop their own energy sectors. By pushing forward the policy coordination, China's current energy cooperation MOUs and framework agreements are likely to be developed into bilateral or multilateral binding treaties that grant China's energy companies the enforceable right to make investments in host states. Also, the state collaborates with its energy cooperation partners to minimise the adverse effects of security threats on the operation of energy projects, as demonstrated by China–Central Asia security cooperation.

The regulatory analysis of the role of the Chinese Government in China's overseas energy investments adds to the energy law literature on maintaining the liberal investment climate in the global energy sector with the emergence of security considerations. The reform of China's domestic regulatory framework governing overseas investments, and specifically its application to energy companies, provides an important nuance in the debate on the purpose of China's outbound energy investments. This nuanced discussion of China's domestic regulations offers a method of assessing Chinese investments under national security reviews and protecting their standing before investor–state arbitration. Moreover, as China and other emerging economies are major capital exporters in the energy sector, safeguarding the economic interests of state-owned investors from China and other emerging economies will contribute to a reliable global energy supply.

# APPENDIX 1: PREFERRED FOREIGN ENERGY PROJECTS AND INVESTMENT DESTINATIONS

| Official documents | Key investment destinations | Key energy projects |
|---|---|---|
| The *10th Petroleum Development Five-year Plan* (2001)[1] | ☙ Oil production in Russia, Kazakhstan, Turkmenistan, Iran, Iraq, Sudan, Venezuela and Indonesia | ☙ Irkutsk-Manchuria-Daqing oil pipeline |
| Directions of Industries in Different Host States (I) (2004)[2] | ☙ Oil and gas investments in Myanmar, Indonesia, Brunei, Uzbekistan, Iran, Saudi Arabia, the United Arab Emirates and Sudan<br>☙ Power investments in Pakistan | N.A. |
| Directions of Industries in Different Host States (II) (2005)[3] | ☙ Oil and gas investments in Yemen, the Republic of Congo, Turkmenistan, Syria, the Gabonese Republic and Angola<br>☙ Power investments in Nepal and Albania<br>☙ Water resource development in Tajikistan | N.A. |

*(continued)*

[1] State Commission for Economics and Trade, The 10th Petroleum Development Five-year Plan [《石油工业"十五"规划》] (2001).

[2] MOFCOM and MFA, Directions of Industries in Different Host States (I) [《对外投资国别产业导向目录（一）》] (2004).

[3] MOFCOM and MFA, Directions of Industries in Different Host States (II) [《对外投资国别产业导向目录（二）》] (2005).

*(Continued)*

| Official documents | Key investment destinations | Key energy projects |
|---|---|---|
| Directions of Industries in Different Host States (III) (2007)[4] | ☙ Oil and gas investments in Kuwait, Qatar, Oman, Morocco, Libya, Niger, Norway, Ecuador and Bolivia<br>☙ Power investments in Bolivia | N.A. |
| The *12th Energy Five-Year Plan* (2013)[5] | N.A. | ☙ North-western pipeline (China-Kazakhstan), north-eastern pipeline (China-Russia) and south-western pipeline (China-Myanmar) for oil and gas imports |
| The *13th Petroleum Development Five-year Plan* (2016)[6] | N.A. | ☙ Line 2 of the China-Russia oil pipeline<br>☙ Expanding China-Kazakhstan oil pipeline<br>☙ The Chinese section of the China-Myanmar oil pipeline |
| The *13th Natural Gas Development Five-year Plan* (2016)[7] | N.A. | ☙ Complete the construction of the east line of China-Russia gas pipeline<br>☙ Line D of China-Central Asia pipeline<br>☙ The Chinese section of China-Myanmar gas pipeline |
| Notice on the Guidance of the National Energy Administration's Working Plan in 2016 (2016)[8] | ☙ Pakistan (energy cooperation in the CPEC) | ☙ Start the construction of the west line of China-Russia gas pipeline |

*(continued)*

[4] MOFCOM and MFA, Directions of Industries in Different Host States (III) [《对外投资国别产业导向目录（三）》] (2007).
[5] NDRC, The 12th Energy Five-Year Plan [《能源发展 " 十二五 " 重点专项规划》] (2013).
[6] NDRC, The 13th Petroleum Development Five-year Plan [《石油发展"十三五"规划》] (2016).
[7] NDRC, The 13th Natural Gas Development Five-year Plan [《天然气发展"十三五"规划》] (2016).
[8] NEA, Notice on Guidance of the National Energy Administration's Working Plan in 2016 [《2016年能源工作指导意见》] (2016).

***(Continued)***

| Official documents | Key investment destinations | Key energy projects |
|---|---|---|
| Notice on the Guidance of the National Energy Administration's Working Plan in 2017 (2017)[9] | ☙ Oil and gas cooperation in Central Asia, Russia, the Middle East, Africa, America and Asia Pacific<br>☙ Nuclear power cooperation with Pakistan, UK, Russia, US, Argentina, Turkey and Romania | ☙ Karachi nuclear power project in Pakistan<br>☙ Construction of the 'Hualong One' in the UK |
| China's Arctic Policy (2018)[10] | ☙ Oil and gas exploration in the Arctic region<br>☙ Renewable energy development in the Arctic region | N.A. |

[9] NEA, Notice on Guidance of the National Energy Administration's Working Plan in 2017 [《2017年能源工作指导意见》] (2017).

[10] State Council, China's Arctic Policy [《中国的北极政策》] (2018).

# APPENDIX 2: TYPOLOGY OF CHINA'S OVERSEAS ENERGY INVESTMENTS

| | State objectives | | | | Corporate objectives | |
|---|---|---|---|---|---|---|
| **Projects** | **External energy security** | **Strategic influence** | **Stability and development of domestic underdeveloped regions** | **Internationalisation of the domestic energy industry** | **Profits** | **Market expansion or technology management** |
| Early expansion by CNPC (early 1990s) | N/A | | | | Sold oil in the global market at a price higher than the domestic set price;[1] | Accessed foreign reserves due to slowdown of domestic production;[2] |
| Competition in Sudan between the subsidiaries of CNPC and Sinopec (2003) | CHINCA's coordination for preserving state energy assets;[3] | N/A | | | Sinopec could suffer huge economic losses in the case of dropping the bid.[4] | N/A |

*(continued)*

[1] See, eg, C Zhang, 'China's Energy Diplomacy in Africa' in C Dent (ed), *China and Africa Development Relations* (London, Routledge, 2010) 143–62.
[2] See, eg, L Patey, 'Learning in Africa: China's Overseas Oil Investments in Sudan and South Sudan' (2017) 26 *Journal of Contemporary China* 756.
[3] CS Liou, 'Bureaucratic Politics and Overseas Investment by Chinese State-Owned Oil Companies: Illusory Champions' (2009) 49 *Asian Survey* 670.
[4] ibid.

*(Continued)*

| | State objectives | | | | Corporate objectives | |
|---|---|---|---|---|---|---|
| **Projects** | **External energy security** | **Strategic influence** | **Stability and development of domestic underdeveloped regions** | **Internationalisation of the domestic energy industry** | **Profits** | **Market expansion or technology management** |
| China-Kazakh oil pipeline (2004) (endorsed in the 12th & 13th Energy Five-Year Plans) | Diversification of oil supply;[5] | Signal impacts on other SCO member states;[6] | • The transformation of industrial structure in Xinjiang[7] • Xinjiang's stability | N/A | Sold oil in the global oil market[8] | N/A |
| China-Myanmar pipeline (2004) (endorsed in the 12th Energy Five-Year Plan) | Diversification of transmission routes;[9] | Regional economic development via infrastructure connection;[10] | Develop the petroleum chemistry industry of Yunnan;[11] | N/A | N/A | In competition with Sinopec, CNPC aimed to penetrate the downstream markets in the southwest.[12] |

[5] Ø Tunsjø, *Security and Profit in China's Energy Policy: Hedging Against Risk* (New York, Columbia University Press, 2013).
[6] U Suleimen, 'Energy Cooperation between Kazakhstan and China' (*The Astana Times*, 15 January 2014).
[7] See, eg, L Zhang, 'The Great International Strategic Significance of Constructing Energy Corridor on Land in Northwest China' [《中国西北陆路能源通道构建的重大国际战略意义》] (2013) 3 *Northeast Asia Forum* 108.
[8] Z Zhang, 'The Overseas Acquisitions and Equity Oil Shares of Chinese National Oil Companies: A Threat to the West But a Boost to China's Energy Security?' (2012) 48 *Energy Policy* 698.
[9] See, eg, J Jiang and J Sinton, 'Overseas Investments by Chinese Multinational Oil Companies: Addressing the Drivers and Impacts' (IEA, 2011).
[10] D Liu, K Yamaguchib and H Yoshikawa, 'Understanding the Motivations Behind the Myanmar-China Energy Pipeline: Multiple Streams and Energy Politics in China' (2017) 107 *Energy Policy* 403.
[11] See, eg, H Zhao, 'China–Myanmar Energy Cooperation and Its Regional Implications' (2011) 30 *Journal of Current Southeast Asian Affairs* 89.
[12] See, eg, X Li, *China's Outward Foreign Investment: A Political Perspective* (Lanham, University Press of America, 2010) 164–65.

| | | | | | | |
|---|---|---|---|---|---|---|
| China-Central Asia gas pipeline (2007) (endorsed in the12th Energy Five-Year Plan & the 13th Energy Five-Year Plan) | Break Russia's monopoly on gas export;[13] | Seek regional energy interdependence;[14] | Prosperity and peace of Xinjiang;[15] | N/A | CNPC compared the prices of importing LNG gas with importing pipeline gas.[16] | N/A |
| State Grid's deal with Plena Transmissoras (2010) | N/A | N/A | N/A | Latin America as an encouraged investment destination & deeper integration into the global energy market;[17] | Higher investment returns in overseas projects;[18] | Market expansion due to domestic competitive but less profitable environment;[19] |
| Power of Siberia gas pipeline (2011) | Stable gas supply | N/A | | | Lower prices for gas sales than those previously set by the Russian company | N/A |

*(continued)*

[13] F Aminjonov et.al, 'BRI in Central Asia: Energy Connectivity Projects' (2019) 22 *Central Asia Regional Data Review* 1.
[14] ibid.
[15] Tunsjø (n 5).
[16] E Vermeer, 'The Global Expansion of Chinese Oil Companies: Political Demands, Profitability and Risks' (2015) 29 *China Information* 3.
[17] NDRC, NDRC's Interpretation on *Guiding Opinions on Promotion of International Production Capacity and Equipment Manufacturing Cooperation* [《发改委解读推进国际产能和装备制造合作指导意见》] (2015); YC Xu, *Sinews of Power* (Oxford, Oxford University Press, 2016).
[18] J Husar and D Best, Energy Investments and Technology Transfer Across Emerging Economies: The Case of Brazil and China (IEA, 2013).
[19] ibid.

***(Continued)***

| | State objectives | | | | Corporate objectives | |
|---|---|---|---|---|---|---|
| **Projects** | **External energy security** | **Strategic influence** | **Stability and development of domestic underdeveloped regions** | **Internationalisation of the domestic energy industry** | **Profits** | **Market expansion or technology management** |
| Yamal LNG project (2013) | Stable and affordable energy supply[20] | • Maintain stable relations with Russia;[21]<br>• Develop the Polar Silk Road;[22] | N/A | Export equipment and technology;[23] | CNPC received profits distribution in 2019.[24] | • Gained Russian upstream assets<br>• Learned technology and operational expertise in the North Pole[25] |

[20] KW Paik, 'The Role of Sino-Russian Gas cooperation in China's Natural Gas Expansion' in J Considine (ed), *Handbook of Energy Politics* (Cheltenham, Edward Elgar Publishing, 2018).

[21] CW Hsiung, 'China and Arctic Energy: Drivers and Limitations' (2016) 6 *The Polar Journal* 243; F Lasserre and O Alexeeva, 'An Analysis on Sino-Russian Cooperation in the Arctic in the BRI Era' (2018) 29 *Advances in Polar Sciences* 269.

[22] ibid.

[23] NDRC and NEA, Vision and Actions on Energy Cooperation in Jointly Building Silk Road Economic Belt and 21st-Century Maritime Silk Road [《推动丝绸之路经济带和21世纪海上丝绸之路能源合作愿景与行动》] (2017).

[24] 'Yamal LNG Operational and Logistical Tests Done', (*Offshore Energy*, 28 June 2019), www.offshore-energy.biz/yamal-lng-operational-and-logistical-tests-done/.

[25] Q Liu, 'Investing in the Yamal LNG Project: CNPC Finally Achieves the Strategic Aim' [《入股亚马尔:中石油夙愿已偿》] (2013) 19 *China Petroleum and Chemical Products* 45; Y Xiao, 'On the Sino-Russia Co-construction of the Arctic Energy Corridor: Strategic Fulcrum and Promotion Pathway' [《中俄共建"北极能源走廊":战略支点与推进理路》] (2016) 5 *Northeast Asia Forum* 109.

| | | | | | | |
|---|---|---|---|---|---|---|
| Hinkley Point C project (2015) | State coordination for preserving energy assets[26] | N/A | N/A | Internationalising the nuclear industry[27] | Made profits due to host government's strike price[28] | Market expansion in the UK[29] |
| Karot hydropower project (2015) | N/A | Promote the development of China-Pakistan Economic Corridor[30] | Stability and economic prosperity of China's northwest flank[31] | Export China's equipment and technical standards[32] | • Guarantee profits through the BOT model<br>• State financing on a commercial basis[33] | Export productivity[34] |
| CEFC's failed acquisition of Rosneft (2017) | Increase China's presence in Russia's whole oil value chain[35] | N/A | N/A | | N/A | N/A |

[26] L Che, *China's State-Directed Economy and the International Order* (Singapore, Springer, 2019).

[27] State Administration of Science Technology and Industry for National Defense, the 13th Five-Year Plan of Nuclear Industrial Development [《核工业"十三五"规划》] (2017); 'China: Nuclear Exporters Will Target Developing World', Oxford Analytica Daily Brief Service, 21 September 2016.

[28] A McSmith, 'Hinkley Point: Putting the Brakes on Could be Prudent in Light of Security Concerns over China' (*UK Independent*, 29 February 2016), www.independent.co.uk/news/uk/home-news/putting-the-brakes-on-hinkley-point-pcould-be-prudent-in-light-of-security-concerns-over-china-a7162786.html.

[29] B Zhang, 'State Transformation Goes Nuclear: Chinese National Nuclear Companies' Expansion into Europe' (2019) 40 *Third World Quarterly* 1459.

[30] 'Karot Hydropower Project', Embassy of the People's Republic of China in the Islamic Republic of Pakistan, 1 October 2018, pk.chineseembassy.org/eng/zbgx/CPEC/t1627107.htm.

[31] S Rahman and S Zhao, 'Analysis of Chinese Economic and National Security Interests in China- Pakistan Economic Corridor (CPEC) under the Framework of One Belt One Road (OBOR) Initiative' (2017) 8 *Arts and Social Sciences Journal* 284.

[32] F Leverett and B Wu, 'The New Silk Road and China's Evolving Grand Strategy' (2016) 77 *The China Journal* 110.

[33] D Bhattacharjee, 'China Pakistan Economic Corridor (CPEC)' (*ICWA Issue Brief*, 12 May 2015); 'Project Progress', Karot Power, karotpower.com/Projects/Project-Progress.

[34] P Andrews-Speed, M Qiu and C Len, 'Chinese Engagement in Southeast Asian Energy and Mineral Resources: Motivations and Outlook' (2016) 57 *Eurasian Geography and Economics* 316.

[35] J Wang, 'CEFC: The BRI and New Strategies of Oil and Gas' [《中国华信:深耕"一带一路"布局"油气新生"》] (2018) 1 *China Report* 60.

# APPENDIX 3: MEMORANDUM OF UNDERSTANDINGS (MOUs), FRAMEWORK AGREEMENTS AND JOINT DEVELOPMENT PROGRAMMES FOR ENERGY COOPERATION

| Framework Agreements/MOUs | Investment-related objectives | Cooperative areas | Coordinating mechanisms | Future associated agreements |
|---|---|---|---|---|
| The MOU of the Cooperation between NDRC of the People's Republic of China and the Ministry of Petroleum of Iran (2004)[1] | ￬ Promote bilateral oil and gas investments by leveraging the synergies in the development of the oil-and-gas sector and the petrochemical industry | ￬ Promote investments in oil and gas exploration, oil refineries, petrochemical products, LNG, pipelines and other engineering services | ￬ Regular meetings of the oil and gas cooperation committee<br>￬ Establish oil and gas policy communication<br>￬ Suggestions to both governments on implementing important oil and gas projects<br>￬ Study the possibility of making joint investments in the petrochemical industry and the LNG industry | ￬ Project details negotiated by NOCs of both states |

[1] The MOU of Cooperation between NDRC of the People's Republic of China and the Ministry of Petroleum of Iran [《中华人民共和国国家发展和改革委员会与伊朗伊斯兰共和国石油部合作谅解备忘录》] (2004).

| | | | | |
|---|---|---|---|---|
| The Framework Agreement on Energy Cooperation between NDRC of the People's Republic of China and the Ministry of Petroleum and Natural Resources of Pakistan (2006)[2] | ☙ Energy cooperation for guaranteeing a reliable, safe and economical energy supply | ☙ Investments in the generation of nuclear power, hydropower, coal power and renewable energy power such as wind and solar<br>☙ Investments in the construction of power grids<br>☙ Investments in the exploration of coal, oil and gas<br>☙ Investments in the construction of refineries, LNG terminals, storage facilities and pipelines | ☙ Establish an energy working team<br>☙ Coordinate energy policies<br>☙ Study the feasibility of establishing the China-Pakistan Energy Corridor | N.A. |

*(continued)*

[2] Framework Agreement on Energy Cooperation between the People's Republic of China and Pakistan [《中华人民共和国国家发展和改革委员会和巴基斯坦伊斯兰共和国石油和自然资源部关于能源领域合作框架协议》] (2006).

*(Continued)*

| Framework Agreements/MOUs | Investment-related objectives | Cooperative areas | Coordinating mechanisms | Future associated agreements |
|---|---|---|---|---|
| The Framework Agreement on Expanding Cooperation Areas in Oil and Gas between the People's Republic of China and Uzbekistan (2009)[3] | • Expand cooperation in exploration, transmission and processing of oil and gas<br>• The training of talents in the oil and gas sectors of Uzbekistan | • Establish a joint venture between CNPC and the NOC of Uzbekistan<br>• Upstream exploration by the joint venture<br>• Expand the capacity of China-Uzbekistan gas pipeline | N.A. | • Gas Sales Agreement |
| The MOU of A Package of Cooperation on Energy and Loans between the People's Republic of China and Kazakhstan (2009)[4] | • Strengthen cooperation on energy development and the construction of pipelines in Kazakhstan<br>• Use Chinese commercial loans to expand energy cooperation | • Joint efforts by CNPC and the NOC of Kazakhstan to provide oil for China-Kazakh oil pipeline<br>• Half of the loan provided by CNPC will be allocated to support the realisation of projects that it negotiated with NOC of Kazakhstan | • Coordination between the NEA and the Ministry of Energy and Mineral Resources of Kazakhstan to solve problems relevant to energy projects or loans | N.A. |

[3] Framework Agreement on Expand Cooperation Areas in Oil and Gas between the People's Republic of China and Uzbekistan [《中华人民共和国政府与乌兹别克斯坦共和国政府关于扩大油气领域合作的框架协议》] (2009).

[4] The MOU of A Package of Cooperation on Energy and Loans between the People's Republic of China and Kazakhstan [《中华人民共和国政府与哈萨克斯坦共和国政府关于能源和贷款领域一揽子合作的备忘录》] (2009).

| | | | | |
|---|---|---|---|---|
| The Agreement on the Cooperation on the Oil Sector between the People's Republic of China and the Russian Federation (2009)[5] | ☙ Strengthen the strategic partnership between China and Russia | ☙ Design, build and operate the oil pipeline from oil terminus in Skovorodino to Mohe (CNPC and Transneft)<br>☙ Chinese companies as contractors of the pipeline | ☙ A joint working team consisting of NEA and the Ministry of Energy of Russia<br>☙ The possible participation of state banks and oil companies in both states | ☙ The loan agreement between CDB and Transneft<br>☙ The loan agreement between CDB and Rosneft<br>☙ The pipeline agreement<br>☙ Oil sales agreement |
| The Framework Agreement on Strengthening Cooperation on the Production Capacity and Investments Between the NDRC and the Ministry of Economy of the United Arab Emirates (2017)[6] | ☙ Strengthen cooperation on production capacity and investments | ☙ Investments in oil-and-gas processing<br>☙ Investments in the development of renewable energy | ☙ Establish a bilateral working group<br>☙ Figure out policy recommendations on promoting investments and proposing projects in listed cooperative areas<br>☙ Review project progress<br>☙ Solve problems relevant to cooperation | N.A. |

[5] The Agreement on the Cooperation on the Oil Sector between the People's Republic of China and the Russian Federation [《中华人民共和国政府和俄罗斯联邦政府关于石油领域合作的协议》] (2009).

[6] Framework Agreement on Strengthening Cooperation on Production Capacity and Investment Between the NDRC and the Ministry of Economy of the United Arab Emirates [《中华人民共和国国家发展和改革委员会与阿拉伯联合酋长国经济部关于加强产能与投资合作的框架协议》] (2017).

| Joint development programmes | Investment-related objectives | Cooperative areas | Coordinating mechanisms |
|---|---|---|---|
| China-Russia Investment Cooperation Program (2009)[7] | ☙ Promote bilateral investments in accordance with national investment policies and the principle of MFN<br>☙ Improve the international competitiveness of the companies of both states | ☙ Establish joint ventures to invest in upstream, in the construction of transmission infrastructure (eg, LNG terminals) and in projects for oil-and-gas processing<br>☙ Investments in the manufacture of energy equipment (especially the power sector) | ☙ Establish a bilateral working group<br>☙ Discuss investment policies of both states<br>☙ Discuss and carry out key/preferred projects |
| Joint Declaration on Further Developing and Deepening Comprehensive Strategic Partnership and Promoting Win-Win Cooperation between China and Tajikistan (2014)[8] | ☙ Promote investments through creating a favourable institutional environment | ☙ Promote investments in the exploration and processing of oil and gas<br>☙ Guarantee the construction and operation of Line D (in the territory of Tajikistan) of China-Central Asia gas pipeline<br>☙ Renewable energy cooperation | ☙ China-Tajikistan economic and trade cooperation committee |
| Joint Declaration on Deepening Comprehensive the Strategic Partnership and Promoting Win-Win Cooperation between China and the Russian Federation (2015)[9] | ☙ Solidify the comprehensive energy cooperation partnership between China and Russia | ☙ Push forward the construction of the east line of China-Russia gas pipeline<br>☙ Continue the negotiation of building the west line of China-Russia gas pipeline<br>☙ Technology cooperation on energy equipment | N.A. |

[7] China-Russia Investment Cooperation Program [《中俄投资合作规划纲要》] (2009).

[8] Joint Declaration on Further Developing and Deepening Comprehensive Strategic Partnership and Promoting Win-Win Cooperation between China and Tajikistan [《中华人民共和国和塔吉克斯坦共和国关于进一步发展和深化战略伙伴关系的联合宣言》] (2014).

[9] Joint Declaration on Deepening Comprehensive the Strategic Partnership and Promoting Win-Win Cooperation between China and the Russian Federation [《中华人民共和国和俄罗斯联邦关于深化全面战略协作伙伴关系、倡导合作共赢的联合声明》] (2015).

| | | | |
|---|---|---|---|
| Joint Declaration on Establishing the Strategic Partnership Between the People's Republic of China and the Republic of Iraq (2015)[10] | ☙ A long-term comprehensive energy (oil and gas in particular) cooperation partnership | ☙ Investments in oil and gas exploration, engineering services, storage facilities, refineries, energy equipment, etc. | N.A. |
| Joint Declaration on A New Stage of the Comprehensive Strategic Partnership Between the People's Republic of China and the Republic of Kazakhstan (2015)[11] | ☙ Expand and deepen China-Kazakhstan comprehensive energy partnership | ☙ Develop the upstream of oil, gas and coal<br>☙ Expand the capacity of China-Kazakhstan crude oil pipeline, accelerate the construction of Phase-II of China-Kazakhstan Gas Pipeline<br>☙ Crude oil processing and refinery (eg, Kazakhstan's investments in Northwestern China) | N.A. |
| Plan of Actions to Implement the Joint Declaration on ASEAN-China Strategic Partnership for Peace and Prosperity (2016–2020) (2015)[12] | ☙ Promote mutually beneficial investment cooperation | ☙ Encourage energy investments in resource exploration, power generation, and power interconnection<br>☙ Enhance technology cooperation on renewable energy | N.A. |

*(continued)*

[10] Joint Declaration on Establishing the Strategic Partnership Between the People's Republic of China and the Republic of Iraq [《中华人民共和国和伊拉克共和国关于建立战略伙伴关系的联合声明》] (2015).

[11] Joint Declaration on A New Stage of the Comprehensive Strategic Partnership Between the People's Republic of China and the Republic of Kazakhstan [《中华人民共和国和哈萨克斯坦共和国关于全面战略伙伴关系新阶段的联合宣言》] (2015).

[12] Plan of Actions to Implement the Joint Declaration on ASEAN-China Strategic Partnership for Peace and Prosperity (2016–2020) (2015) section 2.10.

***(Continued)***

| Joint development programmes | Investment-related objectives | Cooperative areas | Coordinating mechanisms |
|---|---|---|---|
| The Joint Cooperative Plan for Implementing the Silk Economic Road Policy and the Bright Road New Economic Policy between the People's Republic of China and the Republic of Kazakhstan (2016)[13] | ☙ Provide a great potential for investment cooperation in different economic sectors including the energy one | ☙ Connect cross-border energy infrastructure<br>☙ Renewable energy cooperation | ☙ The role of bilateral working groups in coordinating projects operation |
| China's Arab Policy Paper (2016)[14] | ☙ Promote investment collaboration with Arab countries in the oil and gas sectors | ☙ Oil prospecting, extraction, transportation and refining<br>☙ Synergise the technology service for the oilfield engineering technology, and industrial standards<br>☙ Promote the trade for energy equipment | N.A. |
| Guidelines on the Construction of China-Mongolia-Russia Economic Corridor (2016)[15] | ☙ Connect the Silk Road Economic Belt with the regional development programs respectively initiated by Russia and Mongolia | ☙ Mongolia will facilitate the oil and gas transmission through the China-Russia oil and gas pipeline, by acting as a transit state.<br>☙ Develop new electricity networks and electricity generation facilities<br>☙ Promote cooperation in the development of nuclear power, hydropower, wind power and solar power | ☙ Have meetings among NDRC, Ministry of Foreign Affairs of Mongolia and Ministry of Economic Development of Russia<br>☙ Review project progress<br>☙ Do research on establishing a centre for investment management |

[13] Joint Cooperative Plan for Implementing the Silk Economic Road Policy and the Bright Road New Economic Policy between the People's Republic of China and the Republic of Kazakhstan (《中华人民共和国政府和哈萨克斯坦共和国政府关于"丝绸之路经济带"建设与"光明之路"新经济政策对接合作规划》) (2016).
[14] China's Arab Policy Paper (2016).
[15] Guidelines on the Construction of China-Mongolia-Russia Economic Corridor [《建设中蒙俄经济走廊规划纲要》] (2016).

| | | | |
|---|---|---|---|
| Long Term Plan for China-Pakistan Economic Corridor (2017–2030) (2017)[16] | ☙ Give play to China's advantages in capital, technology, production capacity and providing engineering services<br>☙ Activate regional economic integration through the construction of transport infrastructure | ☙ Exploration of oil and gas, oil refineries and oil storage<br>☙ The development of renewable energy such as solar and wind<br>☙ Build electricity grids<br>☙ Chinese experts will help the Pakistan to train technical professionals | ☙ 'Synergize development strategies' through the Joint Committee of the China-Pakistan Economic Corridor<br>☙ Regular meetings to facilitate project operation and conclude specific cooperation agreements<br>☙ Every two-year review of the implementation of this Long-Term Plan |
| The Development Plan of China and Russia in the Far East (2018–2024) (2018)[17] | ☙ Contribution of Chinese investments to developing the Far Eastern region of Russia<br>☙ Eliminate investment barriers | ☙ The oil and gas industry as a prioritised cooperation area<br>☙ Identify key energy projects such as the Yamal LNG project, the manufacture of LNG equipment at the Vladivostok Free Port | ☙ Establish the intergovernmental cooperative committee (MOFCOM and the Ministry of Far Eastern Development of Russia)<br>☙ Collect suggestions from entrepreneurs from both China and Russia |

*(continued)*

[16] Long Term Plan for China-Pakistan Economic Corridor (2017–2030) (2017).
[17] The Development Plan of China and Russia in the Far East (2018–2024) [《中俄远东地区合作发展规划(2018–2024)》] (2018).

***(Continued)***

| **Joint development programmes** | **Investment-related objectives** | **Cooperative areas** | **Coordinating mechanisms** |
|---|---|---|---|
| The Joint Declaration on the Comprehensive Strategic Partnership Between the People's Republic of China and the Republic of Kyrgyzstan (2018)[18] | ☙ Promote investments by leveraging economic complementarities | ☙ Guarantee the operation and maintenance of China-Kyrgyzstan gas pipeline | ☙ Establish the China-Kyrgyzstan bilateral working committee for economic and trade cooperation |
| The Joint Communique on the Strategic Partnership between China and the United Arab Emirates (2018)[19] | ☙ Comprehensive cooperation in the energy sector (the oil and gas sectors in particular) | ☙ Oil and gas exploration<br>☙ Engineering services in oil fields<br>☙ Establish oil strategic storage<br>☙ The trade for petrochemical products | N.A. |
| Africa-China Cooperation Forum: Beijing's Action Plan (2019–2021) (2018)[20] | ☙ Develop the BRI<br>☙ Meet African states' needs of attracting foreign investments<br>☙ Reduce barriers to entry | ☙ Renewable energy investments (solar power in particular)<br>☙ Upgrade power grids<br>☙ Provide training for governmental officials and staff of energy companies and enhance their capacities of governing the energy sector | ☙ Coordinate energy development strategies to jointly make practical working plans<br>☙ Establish the China-Africa energy cooperation centre |

[18] The Joint Declaration on the Comprehensive Strategic Partnership Between the People's Republic of China and the Republic of Kyrgyzstan [《中华人民共和国和吉尔吉斯共和国关于建立全面战略伙伴关系的联合声明》] (2018).

[19] The Joint Communique on the Strategic Partnership between China and the United Arab Emirates [《中华人民共和国和阿拉伯联合酋长国关于建立全面战略伙伴关系的联合声明》] (2018).

[20] Africa-China Cooperation Forum: Beijing's Action Plan (2019–2021) [《中非合作论坛 – 北京行动计划（2019–2021年）》] (2018).

# APPENDIX 4: CONTENTS OF PIPELINE AGREEMENTS CONCLUDED AT THE GOVERNMENTAL LEVEL

| Agreement | Key issues | Intergovernmental coordination | Market access |
|---|---|---|---|
| General Agreement on Carrying out the Project of China-Turkmenistan Gas Pipeline and Distributing Gas to China (2006)[1] | ☙ The design, construction and operation of the pipeline<br>☙ Future negotiation of associated agreements for gas exploration, for details of the construction of the pipeline and gas sales | ☙ Instant communication regarding regulatory changes affecting this pipeline project<br>☙ A bilateral working mechanism to conduct feasibility studies and draft intergovernmental agreements/contracts<br>☙ Regular meetings within the mechanism | ☙ CNPC's involvement in the gas sector of Turkmenistan by putting associated agreements into practice |
| Cooperation Agreement on China-Myanmar Oil and Gas Pipelines Project between the People's Republic of China and the Republic of the Union of Myanmar (2009)[2] | ☙ CNPC's responsibility for designing, building, operating the pipeline<br>☙ The possible expansion of the capacity of China-Myanmar oil and gas pipelines | ☙ Coordination between NEA and the Ministry of Energy of Myanmar to promote project operation | ☙ Broaden cooperation in oil and gas fields<br>☙ More investments in Myanmar's onshore or offshore oil and gas fields |

[1] General Agreement on Carrying out the Project of the China-Turkmenistan Gas Pipeline and Distributing Gas to China [《中华人民共和国政府和土库曼斯坦政府关于实施中土天然气管道项目和土库曼斯坦向中国出售天然气的总协议》] (2006).

[2] Cooperation Agreement on the China- Myanmar Oil and Gas Pipeline Project between the People's Republic of China and the Republic of the Union of Myanmar [《中华人民共和国政府与缅甸联邦政府关于中缅油气管道项目的合作协议》] (2009).

# APPENDIX 5: TYPICAL INTERVIEW QUESTIONS

## 1. The Administrative Management of Outbound Energy Investments

a) Is MOFCOM's management system different from NDRC's management system?
b) What is the difference between the approval system and the record-keeping system?
c) Is record-keeping a kind of administrative licence?
d) For 7-days limit for record-keeping, do you think it gives the department sufficient time to review the project so as to avoid some problems?
e) What is the purpose of the investment approval system?
f) What is the purpose of the record-keeping system? What does the government aim to avoid or achieve?
g) Do you think the procedures are clear and the implementation of these procedures are transparent?
h) What is the role of NEA in approving/keeping records of outbound energy investments?
i) Could you please provide more details of the communication of energy companies with NDRC? What do they exactly do in the communication?
j) Are the approval system and the record-keeping system equally applied to SOEs and POEs in practice?
k) Is there any preferential treatment granted by NDRC and MOFCOM to SOEs in practice?
l) What are the consequences of failing to comply with the approval system or the record-keeping system in practice?
m) Can the *ex post* supervision help NDRC and MOFCOM to influence investments operation?

## 2. Policy Guidance on Outbound Energy Investments

a) How important are projects recognised in the five-year plans or other policies for energy companies when they invest abroad?
b) Will energy SOEs charge all projects, eg, pipelines construction, provided in energy policies?

c) Are energy-related five-year plans and policies legally-binding? If they are not legally-binding, then how can the government ensure their implementation?
d) Will NDRC or MOFCOM look at those policies when reviewing energy projects?
e) What does SASAC's approval system mean?
f) Will SASAC look at the implementation of energy policies in its approval system?
g) To what extent state support is important for outbound energy investments?
h) What kind of support is the most important one?
i) Can projects be supported if they are not recognised in policies?
j) Are POEs financially supported by policy banks in practice?

## 3. Corporate Governance of Energy Companies

a) Does SASAC view itself as a shareholder or an administrative agency?
b) How do the Party branches participate in the decision-making of energy companies and influence the appointment?
c) How does the domestic energy industrial reform impact POEs' global energy expansion?

# BIBLIOGRAPHY

## Books


Andrews-Speed P, *Energy Policy and Regulation in the People's Republic of China* (London, Kluwer Law International, 2004)

Andrews-Speed P and Dannreuther R, *China, Oil and Global Politics* (London, Routledge, 2011)

Andrews-Speed P, Liao X and Dannreuther R, *The Strategic Implication of China's Energy Needs* (London, Routledge, 2009)

Aris S, *Eurasian Regionalism – The Shanghai Cooperation Organization* (London, Palgrave Macmillan, 2011)

AS Campion, *The Geopolitics of Red Oil* (London, Routledge, 2016)

Bahgat G, *Energy Security: An Interdisciplinary Approach* (New York, Wiley, 2011)

Barton B et al, 'Introduction' in B Barton et al (eds), *Energy Security Managing Risk in A Dynamic Legal and Regulatory Environment* (Oxford, Oxford University Press, 2004)

Bedeski R and Swanström N (eds), *Eurasia's Ascent in Energy and Geopolitics: Rivalry or Partnership for China, Russia and Central Asia?* (London, Routledge, 2012)

Belyi A, 'EU External Energy Policies: A Paradox of Integration' in J Orbie (ed), *Europe's Global Role: External Policies of the European Union* (Surrey, Ashgate, 2008)

Blackwill R and Harris J, *War by Other Means: Geoeconomics and Statecraft* (Cambridge, MA, Harvard University Press, 2016)

Bonnitcha J, Poulsen L and Waibel M, *The Political Economy of the Investment Treaty Regime* (Oxford, Oxford University Press, 2017)

Brautigam D, *The Dragon's Gift: The Real Story of China in Africa* (Oxford, Oxford University Press, 2009)

Brink T, *China's Capitalism – A Paradoxical Route to Economic Prosperity*, tr C Welch (Philadelphia, PA, University of Pennsylvania Press, 2019)

Broches A, *Selected Essays, World Bank, ICSID, and other Subjects of Public and Private International Law* (Boston, MA, Martinus Nijhoff Publishers, 1995)

Cáceres SB, *The Hungry Dragon: How China's Quest for Resources is Reshaping the World* (London, Taylor & Francis Group, 2013)

Cai C, *The Rise of China and International Law* (Oxford, Oxford University Press, 2019)

Cameron P, *International Energy Investment Law: The Pursuit of Stability*, 1st edn (Oxford, Oxford University Press, 2010)

Che L, *China's State-Directed Economy and the International Order* (Singapore, Springer, 2019)

Chen J, *Chinese Law: Context and Transformation* (Leiden, Brill, 2015)

Chen M, *Official Aid or Export Credit: China's Policy Banks and the Reshaping of Development Finance* (Boston, MA, Global Development Policy Center, Boston University, 2018)

Cole B, *China's Quest for Great Power: Ships, Oil, and Foreign Policy* (Annapolis, MD, Naval Institute Press, 2016)

Collier A, *China Buys the World: Analyzing China's Overseas Investments* (Singapore, Springer, 2018)

Corkin L, *Uncovering African Agency: Angola's Management of China's Credit Lines* (London, Routledge, 2013)

Crawford J, *The International Law Commission's Articles on State Responsibility: Introduction, Text and Commentaries* (Cambridge, Cambridge University Press, 2002)

Dian M and Menegazzi S, *New Regional Initiatives in China's Foreign Policy* (Cham, Springer International Publishing, 2018)
Dolzer R and Schreuer C, *Principles of International Investment Law*, 2nd edn (Oxford, Oxford University Press, 2012)
Dralle TM, *Ownership Unbundling and Related Measures in the EU Energy Sector* (Singapore, Springer, 2018)
Eaton S, *The Advance of the State in Contemporary China* (Cambridge, Cambridge University Press 2015)
Gallagher N and Shan W, *Chinese Investment Treaties: Policies and Practice* (Oxford, Oxford University Press, 2009)
Goldthau A and Sitter N, *A Liberal Actor in a Realist World: The European Union Regulatory State and the Global Political Economy of Energy* (Oxford, Oxford University Press, 2015)
Haghighi S, *Energy Security: The External Legal Relations of the European Union with Major Oil-and Gas-Supplying Countries* (Oxford, Hart Publishing, 2007)
Hanemann T and Rosen D, *Chinese Invests in Europe: Patterns, Impacts and Policy Implications* (New York, Rhodium Group 2012)
Heffron RJ, *Energy Law: An Introduction* (Singapore, Springer, 2015)
Högselius P, *Energy and Geopolitics* (London, Routledge, 2019)
Hsueh R, *China's Regulatory State: A New Strategy for Globalization* (Ithaca, NY, Cornell University Press, 2011)
Hu L and Song Y (eds), *Research on SOEs Reform and Development: Take CNOOC as the Example* [《国有企业改革发展研究：以中海油为例》] (Beijing, Economic & Management Publishing House, 2012)
Kong B, *China's International Petroleum Policy* (Santa Barbara, CA, ABC-CLIO, 2009)
Kong B, *Modernization Through Globalization: Why China Finances Foreign Energy Projects Worldwide* (Singapore, Palgrave Macmillan, 2019)
Kurlantzick J, *State Capitalism: How the Return of Statism Is Transforming the World* (Oxford, Oxford University Press, 2016)
Laruelle M and Peyrouse S, *The Chinese Question in Central Asia* (London, Hurst Publishers, 2012)
Leal-Arcas R, *International Energy Governance: Selected Legal Issues* (Cheltenham, Edward Elgar, 2015)
Leng J, *Corporate Governance and Financial Reform in China's Transition Economy* (Hong Kong, HKU Press, 2009)
Lenihan AT, *Balancing Power Without Weapons* (Cambridge, Cambridge University Press, 2018)
Li J, *The Clash of Capitalisms? Chinese Companies in the United States* (Cambridge, Cambridge University Press, 2018)
Li R and Cheong KC, *China's State Enterprises: Changing Role in a Rapidly Transforming Economy* (Singapore, Palgrave Macmillan, 2018)
Li X, *China's Outward Foreign Investment: A Political Perspective* (Landham, University Press of America, 2010)
Liang Y, *Legal Protection and Risk Prevention on Outbound Investment by Chinese Investors* [《中国投资者海外投资法律保障与风险防范》] (Beijing, Law Press, 2010)
Marketos T, *China's Energy Geopolitics* (London, Routledge, 2009)
Maurer N, *The Empire Trap: The Rise and Fall of US Intervention to Protect American Property Overseas, 1893–2013* (Princeton, NJ, Princeton University Press, 2013)
Miles K, *The Origins of International Investment Law* (Cambridge, Cambridge University Press, 2013)
Miller T, *China's Asian Dream*, 2nd edn (London, Zedbooks, 2019)
Moran T, *China's Strategy to Secure Natural Resources: Risks, Dangers and Opportunities* (New York, Columbia University Press, 2010)
Norris W, *Chinese Economic Statecraft* (Ithaca, NY, Cornell University Press, 2016)
Pei C, Yang C and Yang X, *The Basic Economic System of China* (Singapore, Springer, 2019)
Pei C and Zheng W, *China's Outbound Foreign Direct Investment Promotion System* (Singapore, Springer, 2015)
Polanco R, *The Return of the Home State to Investor–State Disputes: Bringing Back Diplomatic Protection?* (Cambridge, Cambridge University Press, 2018)

Pradt T, *The Prequel to China's New Silk Road: Preparing the Ground in Central Asia* (Singapore, Springer, 2020)
Sanderson H and Forsythe M, *China's Superbank: Debt, Oil and Influence* (Hoboken, NJ, Bloomberg Press, 2012)
Schill SW, *The Multilateralization of International Investment Law* (New York, Cambridge University Press, 2009)
Shan W (ed), *International Law Protection of China's Outward Energy Investment* [《中国对外能源投资的国际法保护》] (Beijing, Tsinghua University Press, 2014)
Sornarajah M, *The International Law on Foreign Investment*, 3rd edn (Cambridge, Cambridge University Press, 2010)
Sornarajah M, *The International Law on Foreign Investment*, 4th edn (Cambridge, Cambridge University Press, 2017)
Stefano C, *Attribution in International Law and Arbitration* (Oxford, Oxford University Press, 2020)
Steinfeld E, *Playing Our Game: Why China's Economic Rise Doesn't Threaten the West* (Oxford, Oxford University Press, 2010)
Talus K, *Introduction to EU Energy Law* (Oxford, Oxford University Press, 2016)
Taylor M, *The Chinese State, Oil and Energy Security* (London, Palgrave Macmillan, 2014)
Tricker B and Li G, *Understanding Corporate Governance in China* (Hong Kong, HKU Press, 2019)
Tunsjø Ø, *Security and Profit in China's Energy Policy* (New York, Columbia University Press, 2013)
Vandevelde KJ, *Bilateral Investment Treaties: History, Policy, and Interpretation* (Oxford, Oxford University Press, 2010)
Wang J, *Company Law in China: Regulation of Business Organizations in A Social Market Economy* (Cheltenham, Edward Elgar Publishing, 2014)
Wang Y, *The Belt and Road Initiative: What Will China Offer the World in Its Rise?* (Beijing, New World Press, 2016)
Wei Q and Li H, *Entities and Structures in the Embedding Process: A Sociological Analysis of Changes in the Government-enterprise Relations* (Singapore, Springer, 2019)
Woodard K, *The International Energy Relations of China* (Stanford, CA, Stanford University Press, 1980)
Wu W, *Chinese Oil Enterprises in Latin America* (Singapore, Springer, 2019)
Xiao W and Liu L, *Internationalization of China's Privately Owned Enterprises: Determinants and Pattern Selection* (Singapore, World Scientific, 2015)
Xu YC, *Powering China: Reforming the Electric Power Industry in China* (Hants and Burlington, Ashgate Publishing, 2002)
Xu YC, *Sinews of Power* (Oxford, Oxford University Press, 2016)
Ye M, *The Belt Road and Beyond – State-Mobilized Globalization in China: 1998–2018* (Cambridge, Cambridge University Press, 2020)
Zhang C, *The Domestic Dynamics of China's Energy Diplomacy* (Singapore, World Scientific, 2015)
Zhang X and Corrie B, *Investing in China and Chinese Investment Abroad* (Singapore, Springer, 2018)
Zhao H, *The Economics and Politics of China's Energy Security Transition* (San Diego, CA, Elsevier Science & Technology, 2018)
Zheng X, *China's 40 Years of Economic Reform and Development: How the Miracle Was Created* (Singapore, Springer, 2018)
Zheng Y and Huang Y, *Market in State: The Political Economy of Domination in China* (Cambridge, Cambridge University Press, 2018)

## Book Chapters

Alimov R, 'The Shanghai Cooperation Organisation and the Development of Eurasia' in A Lukin (ed), *The 'Roads' and 'Belts' of Eurasia* (Singapore, Springer, 2020) 261–300
Alschner W, 'The Return of the Home State and the Rise of "Embedded" Investor–State Arbitration' in S Lalani and RP Lazo (eds), *The Role of the State in Investor-State Arbitration* (Leiden, Brill Nijhoff, 2015) 293–333

Andrews-Speed P and Zhang S, 'China's Evolving Energy Policy: The Case of Electricity' in J Considine and KW Paik (eds), *Handbook of Energy Politics* (Cheltenham, Edward Elgar, 2018) 179–212

Andrews-Speed P, 'China's Energy Needs and Energy Security' in D Zweig and Y Hao (eds), *Sino-US Energy Triangles: Resource Diplomacy under Hegemony* (London, Routledge, 2016) 38–54

Andrews-Speed P, 'China's International Energy Engagement' in K Zeng (ed), *Handbook on the International Political Economy of China* (Cheltenham, Edward Elgar Publishing, 2019) 132–50

Andrews-Speed P, 'China's Oil and Gas Industry: Stranded Between the Plan and the Market' in A Belyi and K Talus (eds), *States and Markets in Hydrocarbon Sectors* (Singapore, Palgrave Macmillan, 2015) 214–39

Anghie A, 'Imperialism and International Legal Theory' in A Orford and F Hoffmann (eds), *The Oxford Handbook of the Theory of International Law* (Oxford, Oxford University Press, 2016) 156–71

Bath V, '"One Belt, One Road" and Chinese Investment' in Wolff L-C and Xi C (eds), *Legal Dimension of China's Belt and Road Initiative* (Hong Kong, Wolters Kluwer, 2016) 165–217

Buckley P et al, 'Explaining China's Outward FDI: An Institutional Perspective' in K Sauvant, K Mendoza and I Irmak (eds), *The Rise of Transnational Corporations from Emerging Markets: Threats or Opportunities?* (Cheltenham, Edward Elgar Publishing, 2008) 107–43

Casaburi I and Broggi CB, 'The Internationalization of Chinese Companies and Their Presence in Europe' in J Solana and A Saz-Carranza (eds), *The Global Context: How Politics, Investment, and Institutions Impact European Businesses* (ESADEgeo – Center for Global Economy and Geopolitics, 2015)

Chaisse J, 'China's International Investment Policy: Formation, Evolution, and Transformation(s)' in J Chaisse and L Nottage (eds), *International Investment Treaties and Arbitration Across Asia* (Leiden, Brill, 2018) 544–78

Clarke D, 'How China's Efforts to Bring Private-Sector Standards into the Public Sector Backfired' in B Liebman and C Milhaupt (eds), *Regulating the Visible Hand?* (Oxford, Oxford University Press, 2016) 29–47

Cossy M, 'Energy Services Under the General Agreement on Trade in Services' in Y Selivanova (ed), *Regulation of Energy in International Trade Law: WTO, NAFTA and Energy Charter* (Leiden, Kluwer Law International, 2011) 149–80

Dai AC, 'The International Investment Agreement Network under the "Belt and Road" Initiative' in J Chaisse and J Górski (eds), *The Belt and Road Initiative: Law, Economics and Politics* (Leiden, Brill | Nijhoff, 2018) 220–49

DeLuca A, 'The EU and Member States: FDI Portfolios Investments, Golden Powers and SWFs' in F Bassan (ed), *Research Handbook on Sovereign Wealth Funds and International Investment* (Cheltenham, Edward Elgar, 2015) 178–205

Desarnaud G and Seaman J, 'OBOR and Energy: China's Evolving Internationalization Strategy in Three Years of China's New Silk Roads from Words to (Re)action?' in A Ekman (ed), *Three Years of China's New Silk Roads from Words to (Re)action* (Paris, Ifri, 2017) 29–40

Dimitropoulos G, 'National Security: The Role of Investment Screening Mechanisms' in J Chaisse et al (eds), *Handbook of International Investment Law and Policy* (Singapore, Springer, 2019) 1–37

Downs E, 'Business Interest Groups in Chinese Politics: The Case of the Oil Companies' in L Cheng (ed), *China's Changing Political Landscape* (Brookings Institution, 2008) 121–41

Downs E, 'Who's Afraid of China's Oil Companies?' in C Pascual and J Elkind (eds), *Energy Security* (Washington, DC, Brookings Institution Press, 2010)

Eliasson N, 'The Chinese Investment Treaty Programme, Jurisdictional Challenges and Investment Planning' in W Shan and J Su (eds), *China and International Investment Law: Twenty Years of ICSID Membership* (Leiden, Brill, 2015) 235–59

Feinerman J, 'New Hope for Corporate Governance in China?' in P Keller (ed), *Law and the Market Economy in China* (Burlington, Ashgate, 2011) 97–119

Feldman M, 'The Standing of State-Owned Entities under Investment Treaties' in K Sauvant (ed), *Yearbook on International Investment Law and Policy 2010-2011* (Oxford, Oxford University Press, 2012) 615–38

Fu J, 'State Capitalism and Corporate Law: The Governance of State-Owned Enterprises in China' in R Tomasic (ed), *Routledge Handbook of Corporate Law* (London, Routledge, 2017)

Gao N and Schaaper J, 'Chinese Companies Go Global: The Case of Chinese Investments in France' in R Taylor and J Jaussaud (eds), *China's Global Political Economy: Managerial Perspectives* (London, Routledge, 2018) 125–46

Go´mez-Palacio I and Muchlinski P, 'Admission and Establishment' in P Muchlinski, F Ortino and C Schreuer (eds), *The Oxford Handbook of International Investment Law* (Oxford, Oxford University Press, 2012) 227–257

Goldthau A, 'Energy Diplomacy in Trade and Investment of Oil and Gas' in A Goldthau and JM Witte (eds), *Global Energy Governance: The New Rules of the Game* (Berlin, Global Public Policy Institute; Brookings Institution Press 2010) 25–47

Guang P, 'A Chinese Perspective on the Shanghai Cooperation Organization' in AJK Bailes et al (eds), *The Shanghai Cooperation Organization* (Stockholm International Peace Research Institute, 2007) 45–58

Hobér K, 'State Responsibility and Attribution' in P Muchlinski, F Ortino and C Schreuer (eds), *The Oxford Handbook of International Investment Law* (Oxford, Oxford University Press, 2008) 549–83

Hodgson M and Bryan A, 'Investment Treaty Arbitration in Asia' in J Chaisse (ed), *China's International Investment Strategy: Bilateral, Regional, and Global Law and Policy* (Oxford, Oxford University Press, 2019) 430–43

Holtbrügge D and Berning SC, 'The National Government's Role in Chinese Outward FDI' in C Julian, Z Ahmed and J Xu (eds), *Research Handbook on the Globalization of Chinese Firms* (Cheltenham, Edward Elgar Publishing, 2014) 94–134

Hu Z, 'Recent Changes in China's Outbound Investment Policies and Their Implications' in X Ding and C Meng (eds), *From World Factory to Global Investor: A Multi-perspective Analysis on China's Outward Direct Investment* (London, Routledge, 2018) 70–98

Huang HN and Tian TC, 'Turning Current Scepticism into Future Success: Observations on the Cooperation between China and Pakistan' in LC W and C Xi (eds), *Legal Dimension of China's Belt and Road Initiative* (Hong Kong, Wolters Kluwer, 2016) 55–72

Jaffe AM and Soligo R, 'State-Backed Financing in Oil and Gas Projects' in A Goldthau and JM Witte (eds), *Global Energy Governance: The New Rules of the Game* (Berlin, Global Public Policy Institute, 2010) 107–32

Jakobson L, 'Does China Have an "Energy Diplomacy"? Reflections on China's Energy Security and its International Dimensions' in A Marquina (ed), *Energy Security: Visions from Asia and Europe* (London, Palgrave Macmillan 2008) 121–34

Jiang B, 'China National Petroleum Corporation (CNPC): A Balancing Act between Enterprises and Government' in D Victor, D Hults and M Thurber (eds), *Oil and Governance: State-Owned Enterprises and the World Energy Supply* (Cambridge, Cambridge University Press, 2012) 379–417

Johec M and Kyzy JJ, 'China's BRI Investments, Risks, and Opportunities in Kazakhstan and Kyrgyzstan' in M Laruelle (ed), *China's Belt and Road Initiative and Its Impact in Central Asia* (Washington, DC, The George Washington University, Central Asia Program, 2018) 67–76

Kar BB and Eğri T, 'The China Model in the Global Economy' in BB Kar and T Eğri (eds), *The Belt and Road Strategy in International Business and Administration* (IGI Global, 2020) 1–27

Karl J, 'FDI in the Energy Sector: Recent Trends and Policy Issues' in ED Brabandere and T Gazzini (eds), *Foreign Investment in the Energy Sector: Balancing Private and Public Interests* (Leiden, Brill, 2014) 7–28

Khatib H, 'Energy Security' in MM Brown, N Desai and G Doucet (eds), *World Energy Assessment: Energy and the Challenges of Sustainability* (UNDP, 2000) 112–31

Konoplyanik A, 'Energy Security and International Energy Market Development' in B Barton et al (eds), *Energy Security Managing Risk in A Dynamic Legal and Regulatory Environment* (Oxford, Oxford University Press, 2004) 47–84

Kotfis A, 'China's Energy Policy towards Central Asia and Russia' in E Trojnar and Ł Gacek (eds), *China at the Beginning of the 21st Century* (Cambridge, Cambridge University Press, 2014) 87–96

Lai H and Lentner GM, 'Paving the Silk Road BIT by BIT: An Analysis of Investment Protection for Chinese Infrastructure/Projects under the Belt & Road Initiative' in J Chaisse and J Górski (eds), *The Belt and Road Initiative: Law, Economics, and Politics* (Leiden, Brill, 2018) 250–83

Lai H, O'Hara S and Wyscozanska K, 'Rationale of Internationalization of China's National Oil Companies: Seeking Natural Resources, Strategic Assets or Sectoral Specialization?' in H Lai and M Warner (eds), *Managing China's Energy Sector: Between the Market and the State* (London, Routledge, 2016) 77–98

Lain S, 'The Potential and Pitfalls of Connectivity along the Silk Road Economic Belt in China's Belt and Road Initiative and Its Impact in Central Asia' in M Laruelle (ed), *China's Belt and Road Initiative and Its Impact in Central Asia* (Washington, DC, The George Washington University, Central Asia Program, 2018) 1–10

Lanteigne M, 'China, Energy Security and Central Asian Diplomacy – Bilateral and Multilateral Approaches' in I Overland et al (eds), *Caspian Energy Politics: Azerbaijan, Kazakhstan and Turkmenistan* (London, Routledge, 2010) 101–15

Leng TK, 'China's Arctic Diplomacy: Global and Regional Aspects' in TK Leng and R Aoyama (eds), *Decoding the Rise of China: Taiwanese and Japanese Perspectives* (London, Palgrave Macmillan, 2018)

Leutert W, 'State-Owned Enterprises in Contemporary China' in L Bernier, M Florio and P Bance (eds), *The Routledge Handbook of State-Owned Enterprises* (London, Routledge, 2020) 201–12

Li J, 'State-Owned Enterprises in the Current Regime of Investor-State Arbitration' in S Lalani and R Polanco Lazo (eds), *The Role of the State in Investor-State Arbitration* (Leiden, Brill Nijhoff, 2015) 380–404

Liang G, 'China Goes Global: Outward Investment' in H Wang and L Miao (eds), *Handbook on China and Globalization* (Cheltenham, Edward Elgar, 2019) 115–38

LW Lin, 'Balancing Closure and Openness: The Challenge of Leadership Reform in China's State-Owned Enterprises' in B Liebman and C Milhaupt (eds), *Regulating the Visible Hand?* (Oxford, Oxford University Press, 2016) 133–54

Malik AR, 'An Analysis of the China-Pakistan Economic Corridor (CPEC) and Its Prospects' in L Wang and J Zhao (eds), *The Belt and Road Initiative in the Global Context* (Singapore, World Scientific Publishing, 2019) 99–109

McPherson C, 'National Oil Companies: Ensuring Benefits and Avoiding Systemic Risks' in A Goldthau (ed), *The Handbook of Global Energy Policy* (New York, John Wiley & Sons, 2013) 146–56

Meidan M, 'Perceptions and Misperceptions of Energy Supply Security in Europe and the "China Factor"' in A Marquina (ed), *Energy Security: Visions from Asia and Europe* (London, Palgrave Macmillan, 2008) 34–53

Meunier S, 'China's Investment Political Challenges in Europe and US' in J Chaisse (ed), *China's International Investment Strategy* (Oxford, Oxford University Press, 2019) 345–59

Milhaupt C, 'Chinese Corporate Capitalism in Comparative Context' in W Chen (ed), *The Beijing Consensus? How China Has Changed Western Ideas of Law and Economic Development* (Cambridge, Cambridge University Press, 2017)

Miroudot S and Ragoussis A, 'Actors in the International Investment Scenario' in R Echandi and P Sauvé (eds), *Prospects in International Investment Law and Policy* (Cambridge, Cambridge University Press, 2013) 51–72

Morris N, 'Developing a Sustainable Legal System for the Belt and Road Initiative' in W Shan, K Nuotio and K Zhang (eds), *Normative Readings of the Belt and Road Initiative* (Singapore, Springer, 2018) 43–58

Muchlinski P and Gómez-Palacio I, 'Admission of Investment and Right of Establishment' in P Muchlinski, F Ortino, and C Schreuer (eds), *The Oxford Handbook of International Investment Law* (Oxford, Oxford University Press, 2008) 227–58

Naughton B, 'The Transformation of the State Sector: SASAC, the Market Economy, and the New National Champions' in KS Tsai and B Naughton (eds), *State Capitalism, Institutional Adaptation, and the Chinese Miracle* (Cambridge, Cambridge University Press 2015) 46–72

Nedumpara JJ, 'Energy Security and the WTO Agreements' in S Mathur (ed), *Trade, the WTO and Energy Security* (Singapore, Springer, 2014) 15–71

Paik KW, 'The Role of Sino-Russian Gas cooperation in China's Natural Gas Expansion' in J Considine (ed), *Handbook of Energy Politics* (Cheltenham, Edward Elgar Publishing, 2018) 133–52

Petrochilos G, 'Attribution: State Organs and Entities Exercising Elements of Governmental Authority' in K Yannaca-Small (ed), *Arbitration under International Investment Agreements: A Guide to the Key Issues*, 2nd edn (Oxford, Oxford University Press, 2018) 328–73

Potestà M, 'Towards a Greater Role for State-to-State Arbitration in the Architecture of Investment Treaties?' in S Lalani and RP Lazo (eds), *The Role of the State in Investor-State Arbitration* (Leiden, Brill Nijhoff, 2015) 241–73

Poulsen LS, 'Investment Treaties and Globalization of State Capitalism: Opportunities and Constraints for Host States' in R Echandi and P Sauvé (eds), *Prospects in International Investment Law and Policy: World Trade Forum* (Cambridge, Cambridge University Press, 2013) 73–90

Pradel N, 'The EU External Energy Policy and the Law: Does the EU Really Matter?' in L Squintani et al (eds), *Sustainable Energy United in Diversity – Challenges and Approaches in Energy Transition in the European Union* (Liepzig, EELF, 2014)

Pron EM, 'China's Energy Diplomacy via the Shanghai Cooperation Organisation' in S Yao et al, (eds), *Energy Security and Sustainable Economic Growth in China* (London, Palgrave Macmillan, 2014) 52–73

Qian X, 'China's Outward Direct Investments and Its Oil Request' in YW Cheung, J Haan and C Fuest (eds), *The Evolving Role of China in the Global Economy* (Cambridge, MIT Press, 2014) 375–417

Rosen D, 'The CCP and Free-Market Principles' in S Kennedy (ed), *State and Market in Contemporary China: Toward the 13th Five-Year Plan* (Centre for Strategic & International Studies, 2016) 2–5

Salacuse JW, *The Law of Investment Treaties* (Oxford, Oxford University Press, 2010)

Sauvant K et al, 'Trends in FDI, Home Country Measures and Competitive Neutrality' in A Bjorklund (ed), *Yearbook on International Investment Law & Policy 2012–2013* (Oxford, Oxford University Press, 2014)

Sauvant K, Sachs L and Jongbloed W, 'Sovereign Investment: An Introduction' in K Sauvant, L Sachs and W Jongbloed (eds), *Sovereign Investment: Concerns and Policy Reactions* (Oxford, Oxford University Press, 2012) 3–26

Sauvant KP and Nolan MD, 'China's Rising Outward FDI, Its Reception in Host Countries and Implications for International Investment Law and Policy' in BL Liebman and CJ Milhaupt (eds), *Regulating the Visible Hand?: The Institutional Implications of Chinese State Capitalism* (Oxford, Oxford University Press, 2015)

Schill SW, 'In Defense of International Investment Law' in M Bungenberg et al (eds), *European Yearbook of International Economic Law 2016* (Cham, Springer, 2016) 309–41

Sinclair S, 'The WTO and its GATS' in J Michie (ed), *The Handbook of Globalisation*, 3rd edn (Cheltenham, Edward Elgar, 2019) 359–67

Song L, 'State-Owned Enterprise Reform in China: Past, Present and Prospects' in R Garnaut, L Song and C Fang (eds), *China's 40 Years of Reform and Development: 1978–2018* (Canberra, ANU Press, 2018) 345–74

Sun H, 'Energy Cooperation between China and Latin America' in MP Amineh and Y Guang (eds), *Secure Oil and Alternative Energy* (Leiden, Brill, 2012)

Svetlicinii A, 'The Interactions of Competition Law and Investment Law: The Case of Chinese State-Owned Enterprises and EU Merger Control Regime' in J Chaisse et al (eds), *Handbook of International Investment Law and Policy* (Singapore, Springer, 2019) 1–21

Talus K, *Introduction to EU Energy Law* (Oxford, Oxford University Press, 2016)

Tan-Mullins M, Urban F and Mang G, 'The Political Ecology of Rising China: Case Study of Chinese Hydropower Dams in Africa and Asia' in G Siciliano and F Urban (eds), *Chinese Hydropower Development in Africa and Asia* (London, Routledge, 2018) 80–99

Trakman L, 'China's Regulation of Foreign Direct Investment' in J Chaisse, T Ishikawa and S Jusoh (eds), *Asia's Changing International Investment Regime* (Singapore, Springer, 2017) 67–95

Trakman L, 'Geopolitics, China, and Investor-State Arbitration' in L Toohey, C Picker and J Greenacre (eds), *China in the International Economic Order* (Cambridge, Cambridge University Press, 2015) 268–92

Tsai K and Naughton B, 'Introduction: State Capitalism and the Chinese Economic Miracle' in KS Tsai and B Naughton (eds), *State Capitalism, Institutional Adaptation, and the Chinese Miracle* (Cambridge, Cambridge University Press 2015) 1–24

Vangeli A, 'The Normative Foundations of the Belt and Road Initiative' in W Shan, K Nuotio and K Zhang (eds), *Normative Readings of the Belt and Road Initiative* (Singapore, Springer, 2018)

Vivoda V and Graetz G, 'Mergers and Acquisitions: The Politics of Megadeals in the Mining Industry' in T O'Callaghan and G Graetz (eds), *Mining in the Asia-Pacific* (Cham, Springer International Publishing, 2017) 121–38

Voss H, Buckley P and Cross A, 'An Assessment of the Effects of Institutional Change on Chinese Outward Direct Investment Activity' in I Alon et al (eds), *China Rules: Globalization and Political Transformation* (London, Palgrave Macmillan, 2009) 135–65

Wang H and Wang L, 'China's Bilateral Investment Treaties' in J Chaisse et al (eds), *Handbook of International Investment Law and Policy* (Singapore, Springer, 2019) 1–21

Wang L, 'Chinese SOE Investments and the National Security Protection under IIAs' in J Chaisse (ed), *China's International Investment Strategy: Bilateral, Regional, and Global Law and Policy* (Oxford, Oxford University Press, 2019)

Wang X, 'Sino-Pakistan Economic and Trade Relations: Status Quo and Challenges' in R Wang and C Zhu (eds), *Annual Report on the Development of International Relations in the Indian Ocean Region* (Berlin, Springer, 2014) 97–130

Whitsitt E and Weiler T, 'Sovereign Wealth Funds and Bilateral Investment Treaties' New Models: Issues, New Trends and State Practice' in F Bassan (ed), *Research Handbook on Sovereign Wealth Funds and International Investment Law* (Cheltenham, Edward Elgar, 2015) 273–318

Wu J et al, 'The Failure of State-Owned Enterprise Reforms Under Market Socialism' in J Wu and G Ma (eds), *Whither China?: Restarting the Reform Agenda* (Oxford, Oxford University Press 2016) 59–73

Wu X, 'China's Political Risk Insurance for Outward FDI Within the Context of Belt and Road Initiative' in G Martinico and X Wu (eds), *A Legal Analysis of the Belt and Road Initiative* (Cham, Palgrave Macmillan, 2020) 185–97

Xi C, 'Shareholder Voting and Corporate Sustainability in China' in B Sjåfjell and C Bruner (eds), *The Cambridge Handbook of Corporate Law, Corporate Governance and Sustainability* (Cambridge, Cambridge University Press, 2019) 431–45

Xi C, 'Transforming Chinese Enterprises: Ideology, Efficiency and Instrumentalism in the Process of Reform' in J Gillespie and P Nicholson (eds), *Asian Socialism and Legal Change: The Dynamics of Vietnamese and Chinese Reform* (Canberra, ANU Press, 2005) 91–119

Xu S et al, 'Central and Eastern European Countries' in S Xu (ed), *BRI and International Cooperation in Industrial Capacity* (London, Routledge, 2020) 289–365

Yang J, 'China's Competitive FTA Strategy: Realism on a Liberal Slide' in M Solís, B Stallings and SN Katada (eds), *Competitive Regionalism: FTA Diffusion in the Pacific Rim* (London, Palgrave Macmillan, 2009) 216–35

Yao L, 'Looking into Energy Security Through The Lens Of The Belt And Road Initiative: Can China Achieve A More Secure Energy Future' in JC Liow, H Liu and X Gong (eds), *Research Handbook on the Belt and Road Initiative* (Cheltenham, Edward Elgar, 2021) 54–64

Yeophantong P and Maurin C, 'China and the Regulation of Outbound Investment: Toward A "Responsible Investment" Policy Framework' in A Bjorklund (ed), *Yearbook on International Investment Law and Policy 2014–2015* (Oxford, Oxford University Press, 2016) 349–73

Yeophantong P, 'China's Hydropower Expansion and Influence over Environmental Governance in Mainland Southeast Asia' in E Goh (ed), *Rising China's Influence in Developing Asia* (Oxford, Oxford University Press, 2016) 174–92

Yin W, 'China's Approach Towards Investment Agreements and Its Interests Involved in International Investment Rule Making' in J Nakagawa (ed), *Asian Perspectives on International Investment Law* (London, Routledge, 2019) 10–29

Yu G, 'China's Energy Foreign Policy towards Iran: Domestic Factors and Geopolitical Challenges' in MP Amineh and Y Guang (eds), *Secure Oil and Alternative Energy* (Leiden, Brill, 2012) 143–66

Zhang C, 'China's Energy Diplomacy in Africa' in C Dent (ed), *China and Africa Development Relations* (London, Routledge, 2010) 143–62
Zhang J, 'State Structures, Business–State Relations, and Multinational Corporate Behaviours' in X Zhang and T Zhu (eds), *Business, Government and Economic Institutions in China* (Singapore, Springer, 2018) 281–311
Zhang S, 'Developing China's Investor–State Arbitration Clause' in W Shan, K Nuotio and K Zhang (eds), *Normative Readings of the Belt and Road Initiative* (Singapore, Springer, 2018) 147–181
Zhao H, 'Central Asia in Chinese Strategic Thinking' in T Fingar (ed), The New Great Game (Stanford, CA, Stanford University Press, 2016) 171–86
Zhao H and Wu H, 'China's Energy Foreign Policy towards the Caspian Region: The Case of Kazakhstan' in MP Amineh and Y Guang (eds), *Secure Oil and Alternative Energy* (Leiden, Brill, 2012) 167–95
Zhu X, 'Performance Evaluation of State-Owned Enterprise in China: A Case of Petroleum Industry' in R Dou (ed), *Proceedings of 2012 3rd International Asia Conference on Industrial Engineering and Management Innovation* (Singapore, Springer, 2013) 843–50

## Articles

Adlung R, 'International Rules Governing Foreign Direct Investment in Services: Investment Treaties versus the GATS' (2016) 17 *The Journal of World Investment & Trade* 47
Ai H, 'Reforming the Investment Management System and Increase Returns of Investments' [《改革现行投资体制，提高政府投资效益》] (2004) 5 *Guangdong Accountancy* 19
Akram Q and Fareed M, 'China's Malacca Dilemma: Power Politics in Indian Ocean' (2019) 5 *Journal of Politics and International Studies* 29
Albuquerque JAG and Lima LAF, 'Chinese Investment in Brazil: Can it Match the Relevance of Bilateral Trade?' (2016) 40 *Asian Perspective* 579
Amighini A, Rabellotti R and Sanfilippo M, 'Do Chinese State-Owned and Private Enterprises Differ in Their Internationalization Strategies?' (2013) 27 *China Economic Review* 312
Aminjono F, et al, 'BRI in Central Asia' (2019) 22 *Central Asia Regional Data Review* 1
Andrews-Speed P, Qiu M and Len C, 'Chinese Engagement in Southeast Asian Energy and Mineral Resources: Motivations and Outlook' (2016) 57 *Eurasian Geography and Economics* 316
Aris S, 'The Shanghai Cooperation Organisation: "Tackling the Three Evils" – A Regional Response to Non-traditional Security Challenges or an Anti-Western Bloc?' (2009) 61 *Europe-Asia Studies* 457
Bai T, Chen S and Xu Y, 'Formal and Informal Influences of the State on OFDI of Hybrid State-Owned Enterprises in China' (2021) *International Business Review* 1
Bai Z, 'Dispute Settlement Mechanisms Under the Energy Charter Treaty' [《能源宪章条约的争端解决机制研究》] (2011) 3 *Foreign Affairs Review* 88
Bambawale MJ and Sovacool B, 'China's Energy Security: The Perspective of Energy Users' (2011) 88 *Applied Energy* 1949
Bao C and Wang H, 'The Contribution of Developing Central Asia's Natural Gas Resources to China's Security of Interests and Related Advice' [《"丝绸之路经济带"中亚天然气资源开发利用对中国的保障效益及对策建议》] (2018) 33 *Chinese Academy of Science* 585
Basit SH, 'Terrorizing the CPEC: Managing Transnational Militancy in China–Pakistan Relations' (2019) 32 *The Pacific Review* 694
Bath V, 'China's Role in the Development of International Investment Law – From Bystander to Participant' (2020) 15 *Asian Journal of WTO and International Health Law and Policy* 359
Becard D and de Macedo BV, 'Chinese Multinational Corporations in Brazil: Strategies and Implications in Energy and Telecom Sectors' (2014) 57 *Revista Brasileira de Política Internacional* 143
Belyi A, 'Russia's Gas Export Reorientation from West to East: Economic and Political Considerations' (2015) 8 *Journal of World Energy Law & Business* 76
Belyi AV, 'North Asian Hydrocarbon Markets Regionalised' (2019) 20 *Journal of World Investment & Trade* 221

Bentonheath J, The New Security Challenge to the Economic Order (2020) 129 *Yale Law Journal* 1020
Berger A, 'Hesitant Embrace: China's Recent Approach to International Investment Rule-Making' (2016) 16 *Journal of World Investment & Trade* 843
Beus C, 'Sovereign Wealth Funds in the ICSID' (2014) 1 *The Indonesian Journal of International & Comparative Law* 543
Bhala R, 'Exposing the Forgotten TPP Chapter: Chapter 17 as a Model for Future International Trade Disciplines on SOEs' (2017) 14 *Manchester Journal of International Economic Law* 2
Bian C, 'Foreign Direct Investment Screening and National Security: Reducing Regulatory Hurdles to Investors Through Induced Reciprocity' (2021) 22 *Journal of World Investment & Trade* 561
Bismuth R, 'The "Santiago Principles" for Sovereign Wealth Funds' (2017) 28 *European Business Law Review* 69
Blyschak P, 'State-Owned Enterprises and International Investment Treaties: When are State-Owned Entities and Their Investments Protected?' (2011) 6 *Journal of International Law and International Relations* 1
Bompard E et al, 'National Energy Security Assessment in A Geopolitical Perspective' (2017) 130 *Energy* 144
Boni F, 'Protecting the Belt and Road Initiative: China's Cooperation with Pakistan to Secure CPEC' (2019) 14 *Asia Policy* 5
Borlini L, 'When the Leviathan Goes to the Market: A Critical Evaluation of the Rules Governing State-Owned Enterprises in Trade Agreements' (2020) 33 *Leiden Journal of International Law* 313
Bouchez L, 'The Prospects for International Arbitration: Disputes Between States and Private Enterprises' (1991) 8 *Journal of International Arbitration* 81
Boute A, 'China's External Energy Security: Energy Trade and Investment Along the "Belt and Road": An Introduction' (2019) 20 *Journal of World Investment and Trade* 195
Bradshaw M and Waterworth A, 'China's Dash for Gas: Local Challenges and Global Consequences' (2020) 61 *Eurasian Geography and Economics* 266
Braeutigam D and Gallagher KP, 'Bartering Globalization: China's Commodity-backed Finance in Africa and Latin America' (2014) 5 *Global Policy* 346
Bremmer I, 'The Return of State Capitalism' (2008) 50 *Survival: Global Politics and Strategy* 55
Brink T, 'The Challenges of China's Non-Liberal Capitalism for the Liberal Global Economic Order' (2014) 16 *Harvard Asia Quarterly* 36
Broches A, 'The Convention on the Settlement of Investment Disputes between States and Nationals of Other States' (1972) 136 *Recueil des Cours* 331
Brødsgaard KE, 'Politics and Business Group Formation in China: The Party in Control?' (2012) 211 *The China Quarterly* 624
Bungenberg M and Hazarika A, 'Chinese Foreign Investments in the European Union Energy Sector: The Regulation of Security Concerns' (2019) 20 *Journal of World Investment & Trade* 375
Cao G and Xie J, 'State Visits and the Large-scale Overseas Investment of China's Enterprises: A Case Study of Transportation Infrastructure Industry' [《国事访问的海外大型投资促进效应——以交通基础设施行业为例》] (2022) 38 *International Economics and Trade Research* 87
Carrai MA, 'The Rise of Screening Mechanisms in the Global North: Weaponizing the Law against China' s Weaponized Investments?' (2020) 8 *The Chinese Journal of Comparative Law* 351
Chaisse J, 'Demystifying Public Security Exception and Limitations on Capital Movement: Hard Law, Soft Law and Sovereign Investments in the EU Internal Market' (2015) 37 *University of Pennsylvania Journal of International Law* 583
Chalmers AW and Mocker ST, 'The End of Exceptionalism? Explaining Chinese National Oil Companies' Overseas Investments' (2017) 24 *Review of International Political Economy* 119
Chang C and Li H, 'Political Risks and Evasion Strategies of Chinese Petroleum Corporations during Transnational Operation' [《中国石油企业跨国经营的政治风险及规避策略》] (2008) 24 *Journal of China University of Petroleum* 5
Chang J, 'Assessment of the Key Political Risks of China's Overseas Direct Investment' [2014] *International Conference on Economic Management and Trade Cooperation* 295

Chen D, 'China's State-Owned Enterprises: How Much Do We Know? From CNOOC to Its Siblings' (2019) 6 *The School of Public Policy Research Papers* 1

Chen H et al, 'Analysis of Chinese Overseas Oil and Gas Investments' [《中国海外油气投资现状分析与对策》] (2015) 37 *China Energy* 38

Chen J, 'The Current Situation of China's Overseas Interests Protection and the Corresponding Strategies' [《论中国海外投资利益保护的现状与对策》] (2014) 16 *International Forum* 35

Chen J, 'Thoughts about Improving the Overseas Investments Management System' [《完善中国企业"走出去"政策措施体系之思考》] (2013) 10 *International Trade* 25

Chen J and Yang C, 'SOEs' Standing in International Investment Arbitration: Structure, Trend and Responses' [《国际投资仲裁中的国有企业投资者地位认定：构造、趋势与因应》] (2018) 6 Modern Economic Research 119

Chen S, 'Has China's Foreign Energy Quest Enhanced Its Energy Security?' (2011) 207 *The China Quarterly* 600

Chen S, 'Motivations behind China's Foreign Oil Quest: A Perspective from the Chinese Government and the Oil Companies' (2008) 13 *Journal of Chinese Political Science* 79

Chen SY, 'Positioning SWFs as Claimants in Investment Arbitration' (2013) 6 *Contemporary Asia Arbitration Journal* 299

Chen X, 'China's Energy Security and China-Russia Energy Cooperation' [《中国能源安全与中俄能源合作》] (2017) 3 *North Eastern Asia* 59

Chen X, 'Legal Regulation and Political Regulation of SOEs: From Competition to Convergence' [《国有企业法律规制与政治规制：从竞争到融合》] (2019) 6 *Law Review* 111

Chen X, 'On the Record-Keeping System and Its Legal Nature' [《论备案制度及其法律性质》] (2005) 2 *Journal of Wuyi University* 72

Chen X and Ma R, 'The Role of and Options for the Shanghai Cooperation Organization vis-à-vis the Silk Road Economic Belt' [《上合组织在丝绸之路经济带中的作用与路径选择》] (2015) 6 Journal of Contemporary Asia-Pacific Studies 63

Chen Z, 'The Historical Development and Current Status of the Domestic Investment Approval System' [《我国投资审批制度的沿革和现状浅述》] (2017) 5 *Modern Business* 41

Chen Z and Chen G, 'The Changing Political Economy of Central State-Owned Oil Companies in China' [2019] *The Pacific Review* 1

Cheng JYS, 'A Chinese View of China's Energy Security' (2008) 17 *Journal of Contemporary China* 297

Cheng L and Li S, 'Chinese Enterprises' Overseas Mergers and Acquisitions: Political Risk and Protection Strategies' [《我国企业海外并购的政治风险及防范策略研究》] (2013) 5 *Academic Journal of Foreign Economic and Trade University* 1

Chi M and Wang X, 'The Evolution of ISA Clauses in Chinese IIAs and Its Practical Implications – The Admissibility of Disputes for Investor–State Arbitration' (2015) 16 *Journal of World Investment & Trade* 869

Chow D, 'Why China Established the Asia Infrastructure Investment Bank' (2016) 49 *Vanderbilt Journal of Transnational Law* 1255

Cohen HG, 'Nation and Markets' (2020) 23 *Journal of International Economic Law* 793

Cohen T and Schneiderman D, 'The Political Economy of Chinese Bilateral Investment Treaty Policy' (2017) 5 *The Chinese Journal of Comparative Law* 110

Conrad B and Kostka G, 'Chinese Investments in Europe's Energy Sector: Risks and Opportunities?' (2017) 101 *Energy Policy* 644

Corkin L, 'Redefining Foreign Policy Impulses toward Africa: The Roles of the MFA, the MOFCOM and China Exim Bank' (2011) 40 *Journal of Current Chinese Affairs* 61

Dannreuther R, 'China and Global Oil: Vulnerability and Opportunity' (2011) 87 *International Affairs* 1345

Davies G, 'Understanding Market Access: Exploring the Economic Rationality of Different Conceptions of Free Movement Law' (2010) 11 *German Law Journal* 671

Denza E, 'Nationality and Diplomatic Protection' (2018) 65 *Netherlands International Law Review* 463

Dollar D, 'Is China's Development Finance a Challenge to the International Order?' (2018) 13 *Asian Economic Policy Review* 283

Dong X, 'Legal Guarantee for the Implementation of the Development Plan' [《论发展规划法中的实施机制》] (2018) 1 *Economic Law Review* 225
Dong Y, 'The Analysis on Evolvement of Institutions of China's Overseas Investment Promotion: 1979–2009' [《我国境外投资促进体系的制度演进分析: 1979–2009》] (2012) 3 *Research on Theoretical Economy* 34
Downs E, 'The Chinese Energy Security Debate' (2004) 177 *The China Quarterly* 21
Du M, 'China's State Capitalism and World Trade Law' (2014) 64 *International and Comparative Law Quarterly* 403
Du M, 'Huawei Strikes Back: Challenging National Security Decisions Before Investment Arbitral Tribunals' (2022) 37 *Emory International Law Review* 1
Du M, 'When China's National Champions Go Global' (2014) 48 *Journal of World Trade* 1127
Duan F et al, 'Energy Investment Risk Assessment for Nations along China's Belt & Road Initiative' (2018) 170 *Journal of Cleaner Production* 535
Duan YP et al, 'China's Overseas Energy Investment Overview' [《中国全球能源投资分析》] (2015) 3 *Sino-Global Energy* 9
Eaton S and Kostka G, 'Central Protectionism in China: The Central SOE Problem in Environmental Governance' (2017) 231 *The China Quarterly* 685
Elshihabi S, 'The Difficulty Behind Securing Sector-Specific Investment Establishment Rights: The Case of the Energy Charter Treaty' (2001) 35 *The International Lawyer* 137
Erickson A and Collins G, 'China's Oil Security Pipe Dream' (2010) 63 *Naval War College Review* 89
Erie M, 'Chinese Law and Development' (2020) 62 *Harvard International Law Journal* 51
Evans P and Downs E, 'Untangling China's Quest for Oil through State-Backed Financial Deals' (2006) 154 *Brookings Policy Brief* 1
Fazilov F and Chen X, 'China and Central Asia: A Significant New Energy Nexus' [2013] (April– May) *The European Financial Review* 38
Fleury S and Marcoux JM, 'US Shaping of SOE Disciplines in TPP' (2016) 19 *Journal of International Economic Law* 445
Francia E, 'Chinese Corporate Law Developments and Go-Global Policy' (2020) 11 *Beijing Law Review* 184
Fredholm M, 'Understanding China's Policy and Intentions Towards the SCO' (2013) 17 *Himalayan and Central Asian Studies* 38
Freeman D, 'China's Outward Investment Institutions, Constraints, and Challenges' (2013) 7 *Asia Paper* 2
Gallagher K and Irwin A, 'China's Economic Statecraft in Latin America' (2015) 88 *Pacific Affairs* 1
Gallagher K et al, 'Fueling Global Energy Finance: The Emergence of China in Global Energy Investment' (2018) 11 *Energies* 2804
Gallagher N, 'Role of China in Investment: BITs, SOEs, Private Enterprises, and Evolution of Policy' (2016) 31 *ICSID Review* 88
Gao C, 'The Strategic Importance of the Belt and Road Initiative from the Perspective of Transformation of China's Economic Diplomacy' [《从中国经济外交转型的视角看"一带一路"的战略性》] (2015) 4 *International Review* 35
García-Herrero A and Xu J, 'How to Handle State-Owned Enterprises in EU-China Investment Talks' (2017) 18 *Policy Contribution* 1
Garcia-Sanchez GJ, 'The Footprint of the Chinese Petro-Dragon: The Future of Investment Law in Transboundary Resources' (2020) 94 *Tulane Law Review* 314
Garlick J, 'China's Principal–Agent Problem in the Czech Republic' (2019) 17 *Asia Europe Journal* 437
Geng JB and Ji Q, 'Multi-Perspective Analysis of China's Energy Supply Security' (2014) 64 *Energy* 541
Gertz G, Jandhyala S and Poulsen LNS, 'Legalization, Diplomacy, and Development: Do Investment Treaties Depoliticize Investment Disputes?' (2018) 107 *World Development* 239
Gippner O and Torney D, 'Shifting Policy Priorities in EU–China Energy Relations: Implications for Chinese Energy Investments in Europe' (2017) 101 *Energy Policy* 649

Gong B and Tan G, 'The Availability of Judicial Review over the Vetoing of Foreign Acquisition by the US President for National Security: Comments on the Case of *Ralls Corporation v Barack H Obama* as the US President' [《美国总统以国家安全为由否决外资并购令可诉性分析——兼析中国三一集团告美国总统否决并购侵权案》] (2014) 3 *International Business Research* 46
Gong X, 'China's Belt and Road Initiative Financing in Southeast Asia' (2020) *Southeast Asian Affairs* 77
Gong X, 'Economic Statecraft' (2017) 22 国際公共政策研究 1
Gong X, 'The Role of Chinese Corporate Players in China's South China Sea Policy' (2018) 40 *Contemporary Southeast Asia: A Journal of International and Strategic Affairs* 301
Gong X, 'Time for Action: Chinese Companies and "One Belt One Road"', *IPP Review* (10 June 2016)
Gordon J and Milhaupt C, 'China as A National Strategic Buyer' (2019) 1 *Columbia Law Review* 192
Gransow B, 'Chinese Infrastructure Investment in Latin America – an Assessment of Strategies, Actors and Risks' (2015) 20 *Journal of Chinese Political Science* 267
Gu B, 'Chinese Multilateralism in the AIIB' (2017) 20 *Journal of International Economic Law* 137
Gu G, 'The Discussion of Policy Targets and Legal Direction of the Reform of State Capital and SOEs' [《论国资国企深化改革的政策目标和法治走向》] (2014) 11 *Politics and Law* 80
Gueldry M and Liang W, 'China's Global Energy Diplomacy: Behavior Normalization Through Economic Interdependence or Resource Neo-mercantilism and Power Politics?' (2016) 21 *Journal of Chinese Political Science* 217
Guo C, 'Analysis of the Legal Nature of Plans' [《规划纲要的法律性质探析》] (2018) 3 *Academic Journal of Shanghai University of Political Science and Law* 57
Guo H, 'Adjustment Orientation and Key Points of China's Energy Policy in 2016' [《2016年中国能源政策调整方向及重点研判》] (2016) 24 *International Petroleum Economics* 1
Guo J and Chen X, 'Political Linkages, Government Subsidies and Overseas Direct Investment of Private Enterprises' [《民营企业政治关联、政府补助与境外直接投资》] (2019) 21 *Communication of Finance and Accounting* 61
Guo J, Xia C and Yu W, 'Selection of Yamal LNG as the Focus of Integrated Energy Cooperation between CNPC and Russia' [《亚马尔LNG项目开辟中俄能源合作蹊径》] (2014) 10 *International Petroleum Economics* 48
Hameiri S and Jones L, 'China Challenges Global Governance? Chinese International Development Finance and the AIIB' (2018) 94 *International Affairs* 573
Hamida WB, 'Sovereign FDI and International Investment Agreements: Questions Relating to the Qualification of Sovereign Entities and the Admission of their Investments under Investment Agreements' (2010) 9 *The Law and Practice of International Courts and Tribunals* 17
Hao T, 'Does National Economic and Social Plans Have Legal Forces?' [《我国国民经济和社会发展规划具有法律约束力吗?》] (2007) 2 *Learning and Discovery* 99
Hassan K, 'CPEC: A Win-Win for China and Pakistan' (2019) 30 *Human Affairs* 212
He F and Wang B, 'Chinese Interests in the Global Investment Regime' (2014) 7 *China Economic Journal* 4
Heath JB, 'The New National Security Challenge to the Economic Order' (2020) 129 *Yale Law Journal* 1020
Heifetz S and Gershberg M, 'Why Are Foreign Investments in Domestic Energy Projects Now under CFIUS Scrutiny' (2013) 3 *Harvard Business Law Review* 203
Hirono M, Jiang Y and Lanteigne M, 'China's New Roles and Behaviour in Conflict-Affected Regions: Reconsidering Non-Interference and Non-Intervention' (2019) 239 *The China Quarterly* 573
Ho D and Young A, 'China's Experience in Reforming Its State-Owned Enterprises: Something New, Something Old and Something Chinese?' (2013) 2 *International Journal of Economy, Management and Social Sciences* 84
Hober K, 'The Energy Charter Treaty: An Overview' (2007) 8 *Journal of World Investment & Trade* 324
Hogenboom B, 'Latin America and China's Transnationalizing Oil Industry: A Political Economy Assessment of New Relations' (2014) 13 *Perspectives on Global Development and Technology* 626
Hove A, 'Renewable Energy: Is China's Innovation System Adequate to Enable a Low-Carbon Transition?' (2021) 1 *GREEN* 72

Howson NC, 'Protecting the State from Itself?' in Liebman and Milhaupt (eds) (n 44) 49–67; Z Tang, 'Corporate Governance of China' [《论我国公司法人治理结构》] (2002) 17 *Journal of Tsing Hua University* 58

Hradus S, 'Chinese National Oil Companies in Ghana: CNOOC and Sinopec' (2014) 13 *Perspectives on Global Development and Technology* 588

Hsiung CW, 'China and Arctic Energy: Drivers and Limitations' (2016) 6 *The Polar Journal* 243

Hu AG, 'The Five-Year Plan: A New Tool for Energy Saving and Emissions Reduction in China' (2016) 7 *Advances in Climate Change Research* 222

Hu B, 'Oil and Gas Cooperation between China and Central Asia in An Environment of Political and Resource Competition' (2014) 11 *Petroleum Science* 596

Hu G, 'Analysis and Reconstruction of the Delegated Management of State-Owned Property' [《"国有资产授权经营"制度的剖析及其重构》] (2009) 2 *West Law Review* 84

Hu S, 'Clash of Identifications: State Enterprises in International Law' (2019) 19 *UC Davis Business Law Journal* 171

Hu S, 'State Enterprises in International Investment Disputes: Focus on Actor or Action?' (2020) 51 *Georgetown Journal of International Law* 323

Hu Y, 'Roadmap of China's Energy Security Strategy in Context of New Silk Road Initiative: Legal and Policy Implication from ECT and NAFTA' (2017) 3 *Entrepreneurship & Alliance in OBOR* 1

Huang JJ, 'Silk Road Economic Belt: Can Old BITs Fulfil China's New Initiative? (2016) 50 *Journal of World Trade* 733

Huang P, 'The Research on Legal Problems of the "Information Reports" Mechanism' [《境外投资"路条"的法律问题研究》] (2015) 9 *Law and Society* 92

Hughes L, 'The Four 'R's of Energy Security' (2009) 37 *Energy Policy* 2459

Hussain Z, 'The China-Pakistan Economic Corridor and the New Regional Geopolitics' (2017) 94 *Asie.Visions* 1

Jaffe AM and Lewis S, 'Beijing's Oil Diplomacy' (2002) 44 *Survival* 115

Jiang A, Liu B and Huang J, 'A Research Review of China-Central Asia Energy Cooperation in the BRI' [《"一带一路"背景下中国—中亚能源合作研究述要》] (2017) 1 *Journal of Guizhou Provincial Party School* 63

Jiang D, 'Politics/Party and Enterprises – Civilized Structure of Participation of Political Power in Resources Allocation' [《政治/政党与企业 ———政治权力参与资源分配的文明结构》] (2018) 1 *Contemporary Law Review* 11

Jiang J, 'State-owned Corporation's Ownership Structure and Its Legal Reform: A View from Corporation Governance Efficiency' [《我国国有公司股权结构及其法律改革——以公司治理效率为主要视角》] (2012) 6 *Journal of Northwest University of Political Science and Law* 131

Jiang J, 'The Research of the Implementation Mechanisms of National Five Year Plans: Implementation Paths, Implementation Difficulties and Solutions' [《国家五年规划的实施机制研究: 实施路径、困境及其破解》] (2017) 3 *North Western Normal University (Social Science)* 1

Jiang L and Xiao J, 'China's Oil Diplomacy towards Sudan' [《中国对苏丹的石油外交》] (2011) 5 *Arab World Studies* 40

Jiang Y, 'Red Trojan Horses? A New Look at Chinese SOEs' Outward Investment' (2014) 2 *Journal of China and International Relations* 1

Jiang Z, 'Thinking China's Energy Security' [《对中国能源问题的思考》] (2008) 30 *China Energy* 5

Jin Q, 'Investment and Financing Opportunities along the Silk Road and Choices of the Silk Road Fund' [《一带一路投融资机会与丝路基金的选择》] (2017) 5 *Modern Bankers* 50

Jones L and Zou Y, 'Rethinking the Role of State-owned Enterprises in China's Rise' (2017) 22 *New Political Economy* 743

Jureńczyk Ł, 'Analysing China's "Angola Model": A Pattern for Chinese Involvement in Africa?' (2020) 42 *Strategic Review for Southern Africa* 1

Kaczmarski M, 'Non-Western Visions of Regionalism: China's New Silk Road and Russia's Eurasian Economic Union' (2017) 93 *International Affairs* 1357

Kang S and Mu J, 'Risk Analysis and Prevention of Foreign Direct Investment by Chinese State-owned Enterprises' [《中国国有企业境外投资风险分析与防范》] (2020) 40 *Hebei Academic Journal* 122

Kärkkäinen A, 'Does China Have a Geoeconomic Strategy Towards Zimbabwe? The Case of the Zimbabwean Natural Resource Sector' (2016) 14 *Asia Europe Journal* 185

Keay A and Zhao J, 'Transforming Corporate Governance in Chinese Corporations: A Journey, Not a Destination' (2018) 38 *Northwestern Journal of International Law & Business* 187

Kembayev Z, 'Implementing the Silk Road Economic Belt: From the Shanghai Cooperation Organisation to the Silk Road Union?' (2018) 16 *Asia Europe Journal* 37

Kembayev Z, 'The Emerging Eurasian Common Energy Market: What is Its Potential Impact on China's Belt and Road Initiative?' (2019) 20 *Journal of World Investment & Trade* 401

Kenderdine T and Lan P, 'China's Middle East Investment Policy' (2018) 59 *Eurasian Geography and Economics* 557

Keohane RO, A Moravcsik, and AM Slaughter, 'Legalized Dispute Resolution: Interstate and Transnational' (2000) 54 *International Organization* 457

Khan SA and Marwat Z, 'CPEC: Role in Regional Integration and Peace' (2016) 31 *South Asian Studies* 499

Kim M, 'Regulating the Visible Hands: Development of Rules on State-Owned Enterprises in Trade Agreements' (2017) 58 *Harvard International Law Journal* 225

Kon M, Hsu SM and Kung LS, 'Why did China Take the One Belt and One Road (OBOR) Strategy and Initiate the Asian Infrastructure Investment Bank (AIIB)?' (2016) 6 *International Journal of Economics, Commerce and Research* 39

Kong B, 'Governing China's Energy in the Context of Global Governance' (2011) 2 *Global Policy* 51

Kong B and Gallagher K, 'Globalizing Chinese Energy Finance: The Role of Policy Banks' (2017) 26 Journal of Contemporary China 834

Kong L, 'Interpreting *Decision on Reform of Investment System* (2004): The New Trend of the Reform of the Investment Management System' [《投资体制改革新动向—对<国务院关于投资体制改革的决定>》] (2005) 1 *Macro-Economic Management (under NDRC)* 19

Kong Q, 'Bilateral Investment Rule-Making: BITs or FTAs with Investment Rules?' (2013) 14 *The Journal of World Investment & Trade* 638

Kong Q, 'Emerging Rules in International Investment Instruments and China's Reform of State-owned Enterprises' (2017) 3 *The Chinese Journal of Global Governance* 57

Koolaee E and Tisheyar M, 'New Regionalism in the Shanghai Cooperation Organization (SCO)' (2014) 41 *International Studies Journal* 97

Kung JK and Ma C, 'Friends with Benefits: How Political Connections Help to Sustain Private Enterprise Growth in China' (2018) 85 *Economica* 41

Lai B, 'A Study on the Political Risk of Overseas M&A of Chinese Enterprises and the Countermeasures' [《中国企业海外并购的政治风险与对策研究》] (2013) 3 *Journal of Zhangzhou Normal University* 44

Lai M, 'An Analysis of the Investment Governance Effect of SOEs' Party Organization under the Situation of "Strict Administration of the Party"' [《从严治党情境下国有企业党组织的投资治理效应分析》] (2018) *4 Business Analysis* 1

Large D, 'China & the Contradictions of "Non-Interference" in Sudan' (2008) 35 *Review of African Political Economy* 93

Lasserre F and Alexeeva O, 'An Analysis on Sino-Russian Cooperation in the Arctic in the BRI Era' (2018) 29 *Advances in Polar Sciences* 269

Lee CY, 'China's Energy Diplomacy: Does Chinese Foreign Policy Favor Oil-Producing Countries?' (2019) 15 *Foreign Policy Analysis* 570

Lee J, 'China's Geo-strategic Search for Oil' (2012) 35 *The Washington Quarterly* 75

Lee J, 'Trade Agreements' New Frontier – Regulation of State-Owned Enterprises and Outstanding Systemic Challenges' (2019) 14 *Asian Journal of WTO and International Health Law and Policy* 33

Len C, 'China's 21st Century Maritime Silk Road Initiative, Energy Security and SLOC Access' (2015) 11 *Maritime Affairs* 1

Leung GCK, 'China's Energy Security: Perception and Reality' (2011) 39 *Energy Policy* 1330

Leung GCK, Li R and Low M, 'Transitions in China's Oil Economy, 1990–2010' (2011) 52 *Eurasian Geography and Economics* 483

Leutert W, 'Challenges Ahead in China's Reform of State-Owned Enterprises' (2016) 21 *Asia Policy* 83
Leverett F and Wu B, 'The New Silk Road and China's Evolving Grand Strategy' (2016) 77 *The China Journal* 110
Li B, 'China's Energy Development and Energy Security' [《中国能源发展与能源安全》] (2004) 10 *Development* 2
Li C, 'Holding "China Inc" Together: The CCP and The Rise of China's Yang Qi' (2016) 228 *The China Quarterly* 927
Li G, 'New Challenge and Solution of Chinese Energy Diplomacy' [《中国能源外交的新问题及其对策》] (2008) 3 *Contemporary World* 56
Li H, Xu M and Zhang Q, 'Review of Energy Policies in the 40 Years of Reform and Opening in China: from Structure to Logic' [《改革开放 40 年中国能源政策回顾：从结构到逻辑》] (2019) 29 *China Population,Resources and Environment* 167
Li J, 'Managing Capital Still Requires SASAC's Regulation and Supervision' [《"管资本为主"不是不管企业》] (2017) 10 *State Capital Report* 71
Li L, 'Viewing the "Going Out" Strategy from the Perspective of the Government' [《从政府角度看"走出去"战略》] (2014) 6 *Commercial Research* 134
Li Q and Wang D, 'The Analysis of the Position and Corporate Governance Mechanism of SOEs' [《浅析国有企业定位与治理机制》] (2011) *Corporate Management* 17
Li R, 'The Establishment of Legal Protection Mechanism of Chinese Overseas Energy Investments under the Comparative Law' [《比较法视野下中国海外能源投资保障法律机制的构建》] (2017) 6 *Law Review* 119
Li R and Leung GCK, 'The Integration of China into the World Crude Oil Market Since 1998' (2011) 39 Energy Policy 5159
Li S and Gao Y, 'A Small Discussion on the Main Content of Decision of the State Council on Reforming the Investment System' [《浅谈投资体制改革的主要内容》] (2004) 10 *Finance and Accounting for Foreign Economic Relations and Trade* 9
Li W and Hendrischke H, 'Chinese Outbound Investment in Australia: From State Control to Entrepreneurship' [2019] *The China Quarterly* 1
Li X, 'A Study on the Legal Protection of China's Overseas Energy Investment from the Perspective of "One Belt One Road"' [《"一带一路"视域下我国海外能源投资保护的法律问题研究》] (2015) 15 *Journal of Nanjing Institute of Technology* 40
Li X and Brødsgaard KE, 'SOE Reform in China: Past, Present and Future' (2013) 31 Copenhagen Journal of Asian Studies 54
Li Y and Tian Z, 'Risks and Solution of Cross-Border Operation of Chinese Oil Companies' [《中国石油企业跨国经营若干风险及对策分析》] (2007) 23 *Techno-Economics in Petrochemicals* 4
Li Z, 'SOEs Reform: Energy SOEs at the Head' [《国企改革，能源企业站潮头》] (2015) *China Petroleum* 61
Liang X, 'The Reform of the Corporate Governance Structure of the Mixed Ownership and Improvement of Law' [《混合所有制公司治理结构的改革与法律完善》] (2015) 35 *Hebei Academic Journal* 171
Liao JX, 'A Silk Road for Oil: Sino-Kazakh Energy Diplomacy' (2006) 12 *Brown Journal of World Affairs* 39
Liao JX, 'The Chinese Government and the National Oil Companies (NOCs): Who is the Principal?' (2015) 21 *Asia Pacific Business Review* 44
Liedtke S, 'Chinese Energy Investments in Europe: An Analysis of Policy Drivers and Approaches' (2017) 101 *Energy Policy* 659
Lin C, 'Corporatisation and Corporate Governance in China's Economic Transition' (2001) 34 *Economics of Planning* 5
Lin LW, 'A Network Anatomy of Chinese State-Owned Enterprises' (2017) 16 *World Trade Review* 583
Lin LW, 'China's National Champions: Governance Change through Globalization' (2015) 11 *University of Pennsylvania Asian Law Review* 82
Lin LW and Milhaupt C, 'We Are the (National) Champions: Understanding the Mechanisms of State Capitalism in China' (2013) 65 Stanford Law Review 697

Lin LYH, 'Institutionalizing Political Influence in Business: Party-Building and Insider Control in Chinese State-Owned Enterprises' (2021) 45 *Vermont Law Review* 1

Lin LYH and Milhaupt C, 'Party Building or Noisy Signalling? The Contours of Political Conformity in Chinese Corporate Governance' (2021) 50 Journal of Legal Studies 1

Ling S, 'Protecting Chinese Overseas Interests in China's Neighbourhood' [《中国周边地区海外利益维护探讨》] (2018)10(1) *Global Review* 31

Ling Y, 'Legal Protection against the Political Risk on Overseas Infrastructure Investments along "One Belt One Road"' [《"一带一路"境外基础设施投资政治风险防范的法律路径》] (2018) 34 *Journal of Lanzhou University of Finance and Economics* 110

Liou CS, 'Bureaucratic Politics and Overseas Investment by Chinese State-Owned Oil Companies: Illusory Champions' (2009) 49 *Asian Survey* 670

Liou CS, 'Rent-Seeking at Home, Capturing Market Share Abroad: The Domestic Determinants of the Transnationalization of China State Construction Engineering Corporation' (2014) 54 *World Development* 220

Liou CS and Tsai CM, 'The Dual Role of Cadres and Entrepreneurs in China' (2017) 57 Asian Survey 1058

Liou CS and Tsai CM, 'The Governing Paradox in a Transition Economy: Repeated Institutional Reforms and Increasing Regulatory Capture in China's Energy Sector' [2019] Problems of Post-Communism 4

Liu D and Xu D, 'The Approaches and Implementation Mechanism of The Party's Participation in Administering the State-Owned Enterprises Under the Circumstances of Classification Reform' [《党组织参与国企公司治理的路径与法律保障研究——以国企分类改革为视角》] (2017) 23 *Journal of Zhongnan University (Social Science)* 31

Liu D and Yang H, 'Deeply Reforming the Investment Management System, Interpreting the New Approval and Management Rules' [《深化投资体制改革，解读新修核准管理制度》] (2014) 8 *Consultation of China's Projects* 29

Liu D, Yamaguchib K and Yoshikawa H, 'Understanding the Motivations Behind the Myanmar-China Energy Pipeline' (2017) 107 *Energy Policy* 403

Liu H, 'Research on Chinese Overseas Investment Risk and Guarding of It' [《中国境外投资风险及其防范研究》] (2006) 3 *Central University of Economics and Finance* 63

Liu H, 'The Security Challenges of the "One Belt, One Road" Initiative and China's Choices' (2017) 23 *Croatian International Relations Review* 129

Liu H, Q Feng and H Zhao, 'Challenges and Counter-Measures for China's OFDI in the Context of Intensified Foreign Investment Security Review – Based on Japanese Experience of Evading US Investment Barriers' [《外资安全审查加剧背景下中国OFDI面临的挑战及对策》] (2022) 8 *International Trade* 70

Liu J, 'China's Renewable Energy Law and Policy: A Critical Review' (2019) 99 *Renewable and Sustainable Energy Reviews* 212

Liu JZ and Zhang AH, 'Ownership and Political Control: Evidence from Charter Amendments' (2019) 60 *International Review of Law and Economics* 1

Liu Q and Wang X, 'The Shaping Effect of the Belt and Road Initiative on China's International Oil and Gas Cooperation Strategy' (2020) 13 *International Relations* 20

Liu Q, 'Investing in the Yamal LNG Project' [《入股亚马尔:中石油夙愿已偿》] (2013) 19 *China Petroleum and Chemical Products* 45

Liu W et al, 'Practices of Safety Culture in CNPC's Overseas Projects' [《中国石油海外作业安全文化实践》] (2014) 34 *Natural Gas Industry* 135

Liu X, 'China's Overseas Insurance Legal System' [《中国海外投资保险法律制度研究—— 基于一带一路倡议和全球治理理论视角》] (2018) 4 *Research on Financial and Economic Issues* 71

Liu X, 'Protection for Investors of Stated-Owned Enterprises under the "Theory of State Capitalism" – Based on the Angle of Investment Treaty Reform' [《"国家资本主义论"下的国企投资者保护——基于投资协定革新的视角》] (2018) 5 *Law Science* 15

Liu Y, 'An Analysis of the 'Going Out' Strategy of China's Energy Development' [《中国能源发展"走出去"战略探析》] (2010) 1 *Journal of University of International Relations* 69

Lo K, 'A Critical Review of China's Rapidly Developing Renewable Energy and Energy Efficiency Policies' (2019) 29 *Renewable and Sustainable Energy Reviews* 508

Lu H, 'Striving for Coordinated Development of SCO and BRI' (2019) 77 *China International Studies* 82

Luo P, 'The Power Structure of Shareholders' Meeting and the Board of Directors' [《股东会与董事会权力构造论:以合同为进路的分析》] (2016) 2 *Political Science and Law* 122

Luo Y, Xue Q and Han B, 'How Emerging Market Governments Promote Outward FDI: Experience from China' (2010) 45 *Journal of World Business* 68

Ma J, 'International Investment and National Security' (2021) 52 *Vanderbilt Law Review* 899

Ma K, 'Deepening the Reform of the Investment Management System' [《深化投资体制改革》] (2003) 12 *Macro-Economic Management* 9

Ma L, Wang Y and Shen X, 'Research on Governance Effects of China's State-owned Companies' Party Organization – A Perspective Based on "Insiders Control"' [《中国国有企业党组织治理效应研究 —— 基于"内部人控制"的视角》] (2012) 8 *China Industrial Economics* 82

Ma X and Andrews-Speed P, 'The Overseas Activities of China's National Oil Companies: Rationale and Outlook' (2006) 21 *Minerals & Energy* 17

Manfredi M, 'Foreign Direct Investments in African Lands: The Chinese and EU Different Approaches' (2017) 30 *DPCE Online* 193

Mathews J and Tan H, 'China's New Silk Road: Will It Contribute to Export of the Black Fossil-Fuelled Economy?' (2017) 15 *The Asia-Pacific Journal* 1

Matsushita M and Lim CL, 'Taming Leviathan as Merchant' (2020) 19 *World Trade Review* 402

McLaughlin M, 'Defining a State-Owned Enterprise in International Investment Agreements' (2019) 34 *ICSID Review* 595

McLaughlin M, 'State-Owned Enterprises and Threats to National Security Under Investment Treaties' (2020) 19 *Chinese Journal of International Law* 283

McNally C, 'Sino Capitalism: China's Re-emergence and the International Political Economy' (2012) 64 *World Politics* 741

Meckling J, Kong B and Madan T, 'Oil and State Capitalism: Government-Firm Coopetition in China and India' (2015) 22 *Review of International Political Economy* 1159

Mendenhall JE, 'Assessing Security Risks Posed by State-Owned Enterprises in the Context of International Investment Agreements' (2016) 31 *ICSID Review* 36

Milhaupt C and Pargendler M, 'Governance Challenges of Listed State-Owned Enterprises Around the World: National Experiences and a Framework for Reform' (2017) 50 *Cornell International Law Journal* 473

Milhaupt C, 'The State as Owner – China's Experience' (2020) 36 *Oxford Review of Economic Policy* 1

Milhaupt C and Zheng W, 'Beyond Ownership: State Capitalism and the Chinese Firm' (2015) 103 *The Georgetown Law Journal* 665

Moreira S, 'Learning from Failure: China's Overseas Oil Investments' (2013) 1 *Journal of Current Chinese Affairs* 131

Movkebaeva GA, 'Energy Cooperation Among Kazakhstan, Russia, and China Within the Shanghai Cooperation Organization' (2013) 51 *Russian Politics and Law* 80

Musselli I and Zarrilli S, 'Oil and Gas Services: Market Liberalization and the Ongoing GATS Negotiations' (2005) 8 *Journal of International Economic Law* 551

Naughton B, 'The Current Wave of State Enterprise Reform in China: A Preliminary Appraisal' (2017) 12 *Asian Economic Policy Review* 282

Nie N, 'China's Risks in Overseas Investment and the Preventions in Participating in the "One Belt and One Road" Project' [《中国参与共建 "一带一路" 的对外投资风险来源及防范机制》] (2016) 38 *Contemporary Economic Management* 84

Norton J, 'The "Santiago Principles" for Sovereign Wealth Funds' (2010) 13 *Journal of International Economic Law* 645

O'Neill D, 'Playing Risk: Chinese Foreign Direct Investment in Cambodia' (2014) 36 *Contemporary Southeast Asia* 173

O'Neill D, 'Risky Business: The Political Economy of Chinese Investment in Kazakhstan' (2014) 5 *Journal of Eurasian Studies* 145

Odgaard O and Delman J, 'China's Energy Security and Its Challenges Towards 2035' (2014) 71 *Energy Policy* 104

Ögütçü M, 'Kazakhstan's Expanding Cross-Border Gas Links: Implications for Europe, Russia, China and other CIS countries' (2006) 17 *Centre for Energy, Petroleum and Mineral Law and Policy Journal* 1

Orazgaliyev S, 'The Role of Home Governments in Entry Bargaining of Multinationals: China's Investment in Central Asia's Natural Resource Sector' (2020) 62 *Thunderbird International Business Review* 249

Otero-Iglesias M and Weissenegger M, 'Motivations, Security Threats and Geopolitical Implications of Chinese Investment in the EU Energy Sector: The Case of CDP Reti' (2020) 26 *European Journal of International Relations* 595

Paparinskis M, 'The Limits of Depoliticisation in Contemporary Investor–State Arbitration' (2012) 3 *Select Proceedings of the European Society of International Law* 271

Pareja-Alcaraz P, 'Chinese Investments in Southern Europe's Energy Sectors: Similarities and Divergences in China's Strategies in Greece, Italy, Portugal and Spain' (2017) 101 *Energy Policy* 700

Park D and Estrada G, 'Developing Asia's Sovereign Wealth Funds: The Santiago Principles and the Case for Self-Regulation' (2011) 1 *Asian Journal of International Law* 383

Patey L, 'Learning in Africa: China's Overseas Oil Investments in Sudan and South Sudan' (2017) 26 *Journal of Contemporary China* 756

Pei C, Chinese Companies' Overseas Investments and Opportunities in the Belt and Road Initiative' [《中国企业对外投资与"一带一路"建设机遇》] (2017) 3 *Financial Supervision* 16

Peng M and Luo Y, 'Managerial Ties and Firm Performance in A Transition Economy: The Nature of a Micro-Macro Link' (2000) 43 *The Academy of Management Journal* 486

Peyrouse S, 'Chinese Economic Presence in Kazakhstan' (2008) 3 *China Perspective* 34

Pogoretskyy V and Talus K, 'The WTO Panel Report in EU–Energy Package and Its Implications for the EU's Gas Market and Energy Security' (2019) *World Trade Review* 1

Ptaka T and Hommel D, 'The Trans-Political Nature of Southwest China's Energy Conduit, Yunnan Province' (2016) 21 *Geopolitics* 556

Puig S, 'Emergence and Dynamism in International Organizations: ICSID, Investor–State Arbitration, and International Investment Law' (2013) 44 *Georgetown Journal of International Law* 531

Qi T, 'Chinese Investors Make Use of International Investment Arbitration' [《论中国海外投资者对国际投资仲裁机制的利用》] (2014) 3 *Oriental Law* 89

Qian X, 'Protecting China's Energy Interests in the Middle East' (2014) 8 *Journal of Middle Eastern and Islamic Studies (in Asia)* 48

Qiao H, 'The Role of the Government in China's Outbound Investments' [《中国企业海外投资中政府的角色定位》] (2002) 1 *Asia Pacific Economic Review* 57

Qiao X, Chen D and Zhang G, 'The Research of the International Macro-Promotion Mechanism of Chinese Outbound Resources Investments' [《中国资源类境外投资国际宏观促进机制研究》] (2009) 23 *East China Economic Management* 40

Qiu Y, Lai H and Ye H, 'Institution, Marketization and Domestic Investment Management System Reform' [《制度、市场化与我国投资体制改革》] (2000) 1 *Economic System Reform* 216

Rajavuori M, 'Governing the Good State Shareholder: The Case of the OECD Guidelines on Corporate Governance of State-Owned Enterprises' (2018) 29 *European Business Law Review* 103

Rajavuori M and Huhta K, 'Investment Screening: Implications for the Energy Sector and Energy Security' (2020) 144 *Energy Policy* 111646

Rao H, 'The Transformation of the Regulatory Role after the Issuance of the New Regulation on Central SOEs' investments' [《新版央企投资监管办法背后的监管职能转变》] [2017] *State-Owned Assets Report* 29

Roberts A, Moraes HC and Ferguson V, 'Toward a Geoeconomic Order in International Trade and Investment' (2019) 22 *Journal of International Economic Law* 655

Robins F, 'The Uniqueness of Chinese Outward Foreign Direct Investment' (2013) 12 *Asian Business & Management* 525

Røseth T, 'Russia's Energy Relations with China: Passing the Strategic Threshold?' (2017) 58 *Eurasian Geography and Economics* 23

Sanchez-Badin MR and Morosini F, 'International Economic Law By Other Means: A Three-Level Matrix of Chinese Investments In Brazil's Electric Power Sector' (2021) 62 *Harvard International Law Journal* 105

Sanfilippo M, 'Chinese FDI to Africa: What Is the Nexus with Foreign Economic Cooperation?' (2010) 22(1) *African Development Review* 599

Sauvant K and Chen VZ, 'China's Regulatory Framework for Outward Foreign Direct Investment' (2014) 7 *China Economic Journal* 141

Sauvant K and Nolan M, 'China's Outward Foreign Direct Investment and International Investment Law' (2015) 18 *Journal of International Economic Law* 893

Seliverstov SS and Krivonosov VD, 'Structuring Chinese Energy Investments under the Russian Law on Strategic Investments' (2019) 20 *Journal of World Investment & Trade* 355

Shaffer G and Gao H, 'A New Chinese Economic Order?' [2020] *Journal of International Economic Law* 1

Shan W, 'Investment Treaty Regime of the Silk Road Economic Belt and Its Improvement' [《丝绸之路经济带国家投资条约体制的现状与完善》] (2018) 5 *China Law Review* 33

Shan W and Wang P, 'Balanced Liberalism and China's Position on International Arbitration Reform' [《均衡自由主义与国际投资仲裁改革的中国立场分析》] (2019) 39 *Journal of Xi'an Jiaotong University (Social Science)* 20

Shan WH and Wang P, 'The International Legal Framework for Belt and Road Energy Cooperation: Progress and Prospect' (2019) 20 *Journal of World Investment and Trade* 259

Shapiro DM, Vecino C and Li J, 'Exploring China's State-Led FDI Model: Evidence from the Extractive Sectors in Latin America' (2017) 35 *Asia Pacific Journal of Management* 11

Shen W, 'Leaning Towards a More Liberal Stance' (2010) 26 *Arbitration International* 549

Shi Z, 'Energy Cooperation: The Pillar of the Belt and Road Initiative' [《能源资源合作：共建"一带一路"的着力点》] (2015) 1 *Academic Journal of Xinjiang Normal University* 68

Shihata IFI, 'Recent Trends Relating to Entry of Foreign Direct Investment' (1994) *ICSID Review* 47

Shihatal I, 'Towards A Greater Depoliticization of Investment Disputes: The Roles of ICSID and MIGA' (1986) 1 *ICSID Review* 1

Shu X and Yan G, 'Petroleum: The Core of Chinese Energy Sources Security and the International Strategy' [《中国能源安全的核心与国际战略》] (2004) 20 *Petrochemical Technology and Economics* 12

Slawotsky J, 'Sovereign Wealth Funds as Emerging Financial Superstars: How US Regulators Should Respond' (2009) 40 *Georgetown Journal of International Law* 1239

Slawotsky J, 'The National Security Exception in US–China FDI and Trade: Lessons from Delaware Corporate Law' (2018) 6(2) *The Chinese Journal of Comparative Law* 228

Song L, Yang J and Zhang Y, 'State-owned Enterprises' Outward Investment and the Structural Reform in China' (2011) 19 *China & World Economy* 38

Sornarajah M, 'Chinese Investment Treaties in the Belt and Road Initiative Area' (2020) 8 *The Chinese Journal of Comparative Law* 55

Special Issue: China's External Energy Security – Energy Trade and Investment Along the 'Belt and Road', (2019) 20 *Journal of World Investment and Trade* 1

Stern TK, 'Chinese Investments in the Philippines' (2016) 4 *Journal of Political Risk* 1

Sun C and Liu Y, 'Can China's Diplomatic Partnership Strategy Benefit Outward Foreign Direct Investment?' (2019) 27 *China & World Economy* 108

Sun D and Zoubir YH, 'China's Economic Diplomacy towards Arab States', [《中国对阿拉伯国家的经济外交》] (2016) 3 *Foreign Social Science* 155

Sun K and Ma Y, 'China–Russia Arctic Energy Cooperation in the Context of the "Polar Silk Road" – A Case Study of Yamal LNG Project' [《"冰上丝绸之路"背景下的中俄北极能源合作 ——以亚马尔 LNG 项目为例》] (2018) 6 *Academic Journal of Ocean University of China* 1

Tan X, 'China's Overseas Investment in the Energy/Resources Sector' (2013) 36 *Energy Economics* 750

Taylor M, 'Fuelling China's Rise: Building Oil State Capacity' (2018) 16 *China: An International Journal* 107

Terpan F, 'Soft Law in the European Union – The Changing Nature of EU Law' (2015) 21 *European Law Journal* 68

Tessman B and Wolfe W, 'Great Powers and Strategic Hedging: The Case of Chinese Energy Security Strategy' (2011) 13 *International Studies Review* 214

The Research Team of State Planning Commission, 'China's Investment Management Reform: Transforming to the Socialist Market Economy' [《转向市场经济的中国投资体制改革》] (1993) 11 *Economic Discovery* 23

Tian C, 'China's 2016 Oil Import/Export' [《2016年中国石油进出口状况分析》] (2017) 25 *International Petroleum Economics* 15

Tian J, 'The Retrospects and Prospects of the Reform of the Investment Management System' [《我国投资体制改革回顾与展望》] (2008) 7 *China Technology Investment* 35

Titi C, 'Are Investment Tribunals Adjudicating Political Disputes?' (2015) 32 *Journal of International Arbitration* 261

Tomasic R, 'Company Law Implementation in the PRC' (2015) 15 *Journal of Corporate Law Studies* 285

Tomkins A, National Security and the Role of the Court: A Changed Landscape? (2010) 126 *Law Quarterly Review* 543

Tong S, 'China's New Push to Reform the State Sector: Progress and Drawbacks' (2018) 16 *China: An International Journal* 35

Tukmadiyeva M, 'Xinjiang in China's Foreign Policy toward Central Asia' (2013) 12 *Connections* 87

Turcsanyi RQ, 'Central European Attitudes Towards Chinese Energy Investments: The Cases of Poland, Slovakia, and the Czech Republic' (2017) 101 *Energy Policy* 711

Turnbull S, 'Corporate Governance: Its Scope, Concerns and Theories' (1997) 5 *Corporate Governance: An International Review* 180

Ussama M, 'Sovereign Wealth Funds and Investor-State Dispute Settlement: Examining Questions of ICSID's Jurisdiction and the Impact of Investment-Treaty Arbitration' (2021) 7(1) *Washington College Law Journals & Law Reviews* 11

Vaccaro-Incisa GM and Giemza W, 'Economic Integration via Novel Investment Agreements: CAI's Focus on Market Access vis-à-vis the Current Bilateral Investment Treaties Between China and European Union Member States' (2022) 23 *The Journal of World Investment & Trade* 521

Vandevelde KJ, 'Investment Liberalization and Economic Development: The Role of Bilateral Investment Treaties' (1998) 36 *Columbia Journal of Transnational Law* 501

Vandevelde KJ, 'Of Politics and Markets: The Shifting Ideology of the BITs' (1993) 11 *International Tax and. Business Law* 159

Vandevelde KJ, 'Sustainable Liberalism and the International Investment Regime' (1998) 19 *Michigan Journal of International Law* 373

Vasquez P, 'China's Oil and Gas Footprint in Latin America and Africa' (2019) 11 *International Development Policy* 1

Vermeer E, 'The Global Expansion of Chinese Oil Companies: Political Demands, Profitability and Risks' (2015) 29 *China Information* 3

Victor DG and Yueh L, 'The New Energy Order' (2010) 89 *Foreign Affairs* 61

Vivoda V and Manicom J, 'Oil Import Diversification in Northeast Asia: A Comparison Between China and Japan' (2011) 11 *Journal of East Asian Studies* 223

Waelde T, 'International Law of Foreign Investment: Towards Regulation by Multilateral Treaties' (1999) *Business Law International* 1

Waelde T, 'Treaties and Regulatory Risk in Infrastructure Investment' (2000) 34 *Journal of World Trade* 1

Waelde TW, 'International Investment under the 1994 Energy Charter Treaty' (1995) 29 *Journal of World Trade* 5

Wang B and Gao K, 'Forty Years Development of China's Outward Foreign Direct Investment' (2019) 27 *China & World Economy* 1

Wang C et al, 'What Drives Outward FDI of Chinese Firms? Testing the Explanatory Power of Three Theoretical Frameworks' (2012) 21 *International Business Review* 425

Wang DG, 'National Security Review: Legalizing Politics and Politicizing Laws' [《国家安全审查:法律政治化与政治法律化》] (2016) 28 *Peking University Law Journal* 1289

Wang G, 'Risk Management of China's Overseas Energy Investment in Mongolia' [《中国对蒙古国海外能源投资风险控制研究》] (2016) 33 *Journal of Political Science and Law* 43
Wang H, 'China's Approach to the Belt and Road Initiative: Scope, Character and Sustainability' (2019) 22 *Journal of International Economic Law* 29
Wang H, 'The Belt and Road Initiative Agreements: Characteristics, Rationale and Challenges' (2021) 20 *World Trade Review* 282
Wang H, 'The RCEP and Its Investment Rules: Learning from Past Chinese FTAs' (2017) 3 *The Chinese Journal of Global Governance* 160
Wang J, 'CEFC in the BRI for New Production of Oil and Gas' [《中国华信:深耕"一带一路"布局"油气新生"》] (2018) 1 *China Report* 60
Wang J, 'The Political Logic of Corporate Governance in China's State-Owned Enterprises' (2014) 47 *Cornell International Law Journal* 634
Wang J and Tan C, 'Mixed Ownership Reform and Corporate Governance in China's State-Owned Enterprises' (2020) 53 *Vanderbilt Journal of Transnational Law* 1055
Wang L, 'Comparing the Approval System and the Record-Keeping System' [《浅论行政审批与备案之比较》] (2009) 6 *South-North Bridge* 16
Wang L, 'State Controlled Entities as Qualified "Investors": Implications for the Pacific Region Investment Treaty Making' (2015) 12 *Transnational Dispute Management* 1
Wang S, 'Legal Research of "Transactions Controlled by Foreign Governments in International Investments: An Analysis of the Ralls v Obama Case' [《国际投资中"外国政府控制的交易"之法律问题研究--以三一集团诉奥巴马案引发的思考》] (2013) 5 *Studies in Law and Business* 102
Wang S, 'National Treatment to Chinese Investors at the *Ex Ante* Stage from the Geopolitical Perspective' [《地缘政治视阈下的中国海外投资准入国民待遇保护》] (2012) 2 *Studies in Law and Business* 112
Wang S, Feng L and Xu Y, 'State-owned Equity, Party Organization and Corporate Governance on the Perspective of Mixed Ownership Reform' [《混合所有制改革视野的国有股权、党组织与公司治理》] (2019) 7 *Reform* 27
Wang Y, 'Belt and Road Initiative: Mutual Connectivity of the World' (2018) 1 *China and the World: Ancient and Modern Silk Road* 1
Wang Y, 'Beyond Local Protectionism: China's State–Business Relations in the Last Two Decades' (2016) 226 *The China Quarterly* 319
Wang Y and Gu A, 'Recent Development of Energy Supply and Demand in China, and Energy Sector Prospects Through 2030' (2011) 39 *Energy Policy* 6745
Wang Y and Ma L, 'Can the Party Organization of China's State-owned Companies Reduce Agency Cost? A Perspective Based on "Insiders Control"' [《国有企业党组织能降低代理成本吗? ———基 于"内 部 人 控 制"的 视 角》] (2014) 26 *Management Review* 138
Wang Z, 'Corporate Governance under State Control: The Chinese Experience' (2012) 13 *Theoretical Inquiries in Law* 487
Wang Z, Qin H and Lewis J, 'China's Wind Power Industry: Policy Support, Technological Achievements, and Emerging Challenges' (2012) 51 *Energy Policy* 80
Wei D and Wang J, 'Perfection of the Legal System of Oil and Gas International Cooperation in the Context of "the Belt and Road"' [《"一带一路"背景下油气国际合作法律制度的完善》] (2019) 21 *Journal of Southwest Petroleum University* 1
Wei G, 'New Landscapes for Investments and Financing in the BRI – Interviews with Qi Jin' [《开创"一带一路"投融资合作新格局--访丝路基金董事长金琦》] (2017) 9 *China Finance* 20
Wei T, Clegg J and Ma L, 'The Conscious and Unconscious Facilitating Role of the Chinese Government in Shaping the Internationalization of Chinese MNCs' (2015) 24 *International Business Review* 331
Wen Z and Song S, 'Reform Logic in Divestiture of Operational Function of State-owned Capital from SOEs and Reconstruction of Performance Appraisal System' [《国有资本运营职能从国有企业剥离的改革逻辑及绩效评价体系》] (2018) 33 *Journal of Beijing Technology and Business University* 10
Willemyns I, 'Disciplines on SOEs in International Economic Law' (2016) 19 *Journal of International Economic Law* 657

Wilson JL, 'The Eurasian Economic Union and China's Silk Road: Implications for the Russian–Chinese Relationship' (2016) 17 *European Politics and Society* 113

Wu J, 'The Discovery of the Reform of the Investment Management System' [《投资体制改革探索》] (2005) 8 *Inquiry into Economic Issues* 37

Wu K, 'China's Energy Security: Oil and Gas' (2014) 73 *Energy Policy* 4

Wu M, 'The "China, Inc." Challenge to Global Trade Governance' (2016) 57 *Harvard International Law Journal* 261

Wu S, 'Current Status of Prospects of China-Central Asia Oil and Gas Cooperation' [《浅析中国 – 中亚油气合作现状与前景》] (2018) 10 *China Chemical Trade* 1

Wu Y, 'Encouraging the National Oil Companies to Go Out' [《鼓励国家石油企业走出去》] (2000) 11 *China Investment* 35

Xi C, 'The Political Economy of Cumulative Voting: The Case of China' (2014) 14 *Asian Business Law* 61

Xiao Y, 'On the Sino-Russia Co-construction of the Arctic Energy Corridor: Strategic Fulcrum and Promotion Pathway' [《中俄共建"北极能源走廊":战略支点与推进理路》] (2016) 5 *Northeast Asia Forum* 109

Xie L and Fang X, 'Legal Issues of China-Kazakhstan Energy Cooperation along the Silk Economic Belt' [《丝绸之路经济带建设背景下中国与哈萨克斯坦能源合作的法律问题研究》] (2016) 6 *Russian Studies* 181

Xiong P and Tomasic R, 'Soft Law, State-Owned Enterprises and Dispute Resolution on PRC's Belt and Road: Towards an Emerging Legal Order' (2019) 49 *Hong Kong Law Journal* 1025

Xu M, 'Development Plans of Economy and Society and the Legal Development of Plans' [《论经济社会发展规划与规划法制建设》] (2012) 2 *The Jurist* 43

Xu Q, 'The Strategically Important Core of China's International Energy Cooperation: Energy Technology, Energy Networks and Green Development' [《中国国际能源合作战略重点之——能源技术、能源网络共享与绿色发展》] (2018) 4 *Petroleum Technology Forum* 8

Xu Q and Miao Y, 'Belt and Road Initiative and China's International Energy Cooperation' (2019) 29(4) *Modern International Relations* 66

Xu X, Plans as A Governance Tool: Essence, Reasons and Paths [《作为治理工具的规划:内涵、缘起与路径》] (2017) 2 *South East Academic* 1

Xu Y, 'China–Pakistan Energy Cooperation: Background, Current Situation and Prospect' [《中巴能源合作:背景·现状·前景》] (2015) 17 *Journal of Southwest Petroleum University* 42

Xu YC, 'China's Giant State-Owned Enterprises as Policy Advocates: The Case of the State Grid Corporation of China' (2017) 79 *The China Journal* 21

Xu YC, 'Chinese State-owned Enterprises in Africa: Ambassadors or Freebooters' (2014) 23 *Journal of Contemporary China* 822

Yan S and Xu G, 'Discussion on Deepening Energy Cooperation between China and Neighbouring States' [《"一带一路"下深化中国与周边国家能源合作策略探讨》] (2017) 11 *Practice in Foreign Economic Relations and Trade* 8

Ye, M, 'China Invests Overseas: Regulation and Representation' (2014) 21 *Modern China Studies* 173, 182.

Yeo Y, 'Contextualizing Corporate Governance: The Case of China's Central State Enterprise Groups' (2013) 22 *Journal of Contemporary China* 460

Yergin D, 'Ensuring Energy Security' (2006) 85 *Foreign Affairs* 69

Yergin D et al, 'Fueling Asia's Recovery' (1998) 77 *Foreign Affairs* 34

Yilmaz S and Daksueva O, 'The Energy Nexus in China–Russia Strategic Partnership' (2019) 19 *International Relations of the Asia-Pacific* 63

Yin W, 'A Comparison of the US and EU Regulatory Responses to China's State Capitalism: Implication, Issue and Direction' (2021) 19 *Asia Europe Journal* 1

Yin W, 'Challenges, Issues in China–EU Investment Agreement and the Implication on China's Domestic Reform' (2018) 26 *Asia Pacific Law Review* 170

Yin X, 'Energy Security: China's Choices against the Complex and Changing Background' [《能源安全:复杂多变形势下的中国政策选择》] (2020) 01 *Energy* 87

You L, 'China-Russia Energy Cooperation' [《中俄能源产业合作动因、风险及路径选择——以亚马尔 LNG 项目为例》] (2018) 4 *International Economic Cooperation* 15

Yu H, 'Reform of State-owned Enterprises in China: The Chinese Communist Party Strikes Back' (2019) 43 *Asian Studies Review* 332

Yu H, 'System Equilibrium in Geo-Security: Challenges and Responses to China's Energy Security in the New Era' [《地缘安全中的体系均衡：新时期中国能源安全的挑战与应对》] (2019) 4 *West Asia and Africa* 143

Yu J and Chen Z, 'The Discussion of China's Overseas Investments Approval Procedure' [《中国境外投资核准制度改革自议》] (2013) 2 *The Jurist* 43

Yu K, 'Energy Cooperation Under the Belt and Road Initiative: Implications for Global Energy Governance' (2019) 20 *Journal of World Investment & Trade* 243

Yuan J et al, 'Electric Power Investment Risk Assessment for Belt and Road Initiative Nations' (2018) 10 *Sustainability* 3119

Yuan Q and Yu Y, 'The Research of Political Risks of Overseas Merger and Acquisition of Chinese Resource-Based Enterprises in the Period of Post Financial Crisis' [《后金融危机时期中国资源型企业海外并购政治风险研究》] (2017) 40 *Journal of Liaoning Normal University* 93

Yuan X and Zuo J, 'Transition to Low Carbon Energy Policies in China – from the Five-Year Plan Perspective' (2011) 39 *Energy Policy* 3855

Zeng J and Wang C, 'Legal Issues of Energy Cooperation under the Belt and Road Initiative' [《"一带一路"能源合作法律问题探析》] (2016) 3 *Journal of the Party School of Qindao Municipal Committee* 88

Zeng K, 'China's Free Trade Agreement Diplomacy' (2016) 9 *The Chinese Journal of International Politics* 277

Zeng W and Dang S, 'International Economic Rules Innovation on the Belt and Road Initiative' [《"一带一路"战略下的国际经济规则创新》] (2016) 3 *International Business Research* 25

Zha D, 'China's Energy Security and its International Relations' (2005) 3 *The China and Eurasia Forum Quarterly* 39

Zhang A, 'The Standing of Chinese State-Owned Enterprises in Investor–State Arbitration: The First Two Cases' (2018) 17 *Chinese Journal of International Law* 1147

Zhang AH, 'The Antitrust Paradox of China, Inc' (2017) 50 *New York University Journal of International Law and Politics* 159

Zhang B, 'State Transformation Goes Nuclear: Chinese National Nuclear Companies' Expansion into Europe' (2019) 40 *Third World Quarterly* 1459

Zhang B, 'The Record-Keeping System in The Governance by Legal Rules: Features, Origins and Drawbacks' [《法治政府视野下的行政许可式备案: 特征、成因与弊端》] (2017) 4 *The South China Sea Law Journal* 33

Zhang C, 'Do Party Branches of SOEs Conflict with the Modern Enterprise System?' [《国有企业党组织与现代企业制度冲突吗?》] (2019) 12 *Contemporary Economic Research* 42

Zhang H, 'China's Privately-owned Companies Face Financing Risks in Overseas Investments and Control them' [《中国民营企业"走出去"面临的融资风险及其控制》] (2017) 7 *Practice in Foreign Trade* 81

Zhang H, 'Where Is the future: China's SOEs Reform' (2006) 1 *Journal of the Washington Institute of China Studies* 105

Zhang J and Zhou X, 'Thoughts on Policy-Making of China's Overseas Investments against the Background of the "Going Out" Strategy' [《"走出去"战略背景下中国对外直接投资政策体系的思考》] (2007) 4 *International Trade* 27

Zhang L, 'Research on Improvement of the International Investment Disputes Settlement Mechanism under "One Belt One Road" Initiative' [《"一带一路"国际投资争端解决机制完善研究》] (2018) 8 *Law Science Magazine* 32

Zhang L, 'The Great International Strategic Significance of Constructing Energy Corridor on Land in Northwest China' [《中国西北陆路能源通道构建的重大国际战略意义》] (2013) 3 *Northeast Asia Forum* 108

Zhang M, 'Research on SOEs' Corporate Governance: Improving State-Owned Assets Regulation and Management System and SOEs' Corporate Governance' [《国有企业公司治理之研究———完善国有资产监管机制和优化国有企业公司治理结构》] (2013) 6 *Reform of Economic System* 88

Zhang N, 'Safeguarding Overseas Interests in China's Rise' [《崛起过程中的海外利益维护》] (2014) 6 Social Science in Ningxia 10

Zhang R, 'To suspend Or Not to Suspend: A Cost–Benefit Analysis of Three Chinese Mega-Projects in Myanmar' [2020] *The Pacific Review* 1

Zhang S, 'China's Approach in Drafting the Investor-State Arbitration Clause: A Review from the "Belt and Road" Regions" Perspective' (2017) 5 *The Chinese Journal of Comparative Law* 79

Zhang S et al, 'Review of China's Wind Power Firms Internationalization: Status Quo, Determinants, Prospects and Policy Implications' (2015) 43 Renewable and Sustainable Energy Reviews 1333

Zhang W, 'The Impacts of the Reform of the Investment Management System on Enterprises' [《投资体制改革对企业的影响》] (1995) 7 *Academic Journal of Central University of Finance and Economics* 29

Zhang X, 'Chinese Capitalism and the Maritime Silk Road' (2017) 22 *Geopolitics* 310

Zhang X, 'Integration of CCP Leadership with Corporate Governance' (2019) 1 *China Perspectives* 55

Zhang X, 'The Justification of the Mandatory Nature of Administrative Record – Also on the Distinction between Administrative Record and Administrative License' [《行政备案具有强制性之证成—兼论行政备案与行政许可的区分》] (2018) 4 *Graduate Law Review* 62

Zhang Y and Jiang X, 'The Influence of Trump's New Energy Policy and China's Countermeasures' [《特朗普能源新政的影响及我国应对策略》] (2018) 20 *Journal of Southwest Petroleum University* 12

Zhang Z, 'An Analysis of China's Energy Demand and Supply Policy Framework' (2013) 2 *WIREs Energy and Environment* 422

Zhang Z, 'The Overseas Acquisitions and Equity Oil Shares of Chinese National Oil Companies: A Threat to the West but a Boost to China's Energy Security?' (2012) 48 *Energy Policy* 698

Zhao C and Chen B, 'China's Oil Security from the Supply Chain Perspective: A Review' (2014) 136 *Applied Energy* 269

Zhao H, 'China's Overseas Energy Investments: Myth and Reality' (2009) 19 *Contemporary International Relations* 89

Zhao H, 'China's View of and Expectations from the Shanghai Cooperation Organization' (2013) 53 *Asian Survey* 436

Zhao H, 'China–Myanmar Energy Cooperation and Its Regional Implications' (2011) 30 *Journal of Current Southeast Asian Affairs* 89

Zhao H, 'The Absence of Investor Protection in National Security Investigations for Foreign Investment: An Analysis of the Ralls v Obama Case' [《论外资并购国家安全审查中的投资者保护缺失———以三一集团诉奥巴马案为视角》] (2015) 37 *Modern Law Science* 139

Zhao X et al, 'China's Wind, Biomass and Solar Power Generation: What the Situation Tells Us?' (2012) 16 *Renewable and Sustainable Energy Reviews* 6173

Zhao X, Shen J and Long L, 'China's Energy Security and International Energy Cooperation in the BRI' [《"一带一路"战略下中国能源安全与国际合作》] (2017) 37 *Journal of Chifeng University* 76

Zhao Y, Shi X and Song F, 'Has Chinese Outward Foreign Direct Investment in Energy Enhanced China's Energy Security?' (2020) 146 *Energy Policy* 1

Zhou D, 'An Analysis of Controllability of Chinese Enterprises' Energy Investment Risk in Pakistan' (2018) 248 *Advances in Social Science, Education and Humanities Research* 31

Zhou J, 'A New Multilateralism? A Case Study of the Belt and Road Initiative' [2020] *The Chinese Journal of Comparative Law* 1

Zhou J, 'Investment Barriers in South Asian Countries: Implications for China and Policy Recommendations' [《南亚国家投资壁垒及其对我国的影响、对策建议》] (2018) 3 *South Asian Studies* 39

Zhou L and Hang J, 'High Reliance on External Oil Supply and China's Energy Security' [《石油对外依存度高企与中国能源安全》] (2014) 68 *Review of Economic Research* 34

Zhou Q, He Z and Yang Y, 'Energy Geopolitics in Central Asia: China's Involvement and Responses' (2020) 30 *Journal of Geographical Sciences* 1871

Zhou W and Esteban M, 'Beyond Balancing: China's Approach Towards the Belt and Road Initiative' (2018) 27 *Journal of Contemporary China* 487

Zhou W, Gao H and Bai X, 'Building A Market Economy through WTO-Inspired Reform of State-Owned Enterprises in China' (2019) 68 *International and Comparative Law Quarterly* 977

Zhu C, 'The Chinese Corporate Law in Domestic and International Fusion' [《论中国公司法本土化与国际化的融合——改革开放以来的历史沿革、最新发展与未来走向》] (2020) 2 *Oriental Law* 91

Zhu C, 'The Shareholder Status of the State Contributor and the Party Leadership from the Perspective of PRC Company Law' [《公司法视角下国有出资人的股东职责与党的领导》] (2017) 2 *Economic Law Review* 47

Zhu J, 'Reasons for Insisting, Strengthening and Improving the Party Leadership' [《深化国企改革为什么必须坚持、加强和改进党的领导》] (2015) 19 *Red Flag Manuscript* 9

Zhu W, 'Research on Separating SOEs from Government in Mechanism of State-Owned Assets Management' [《国有资产管理体制中的政企分开探析》] (2005) 16 *Journal of Zhongyuan Institute of Technology* 54

Zhu Y, 'Analysis of Importance of Building China-Myanmar Oil and Gas Pipelines to China' [《中缅油气管道对我国能源安全的重要意义分析》] (2017) 16 *China Management Informationization* 115

Zhu Y, Mu Z and Mu Y, 'A Jurisprudence Analysis on the Nature and Effect of "the Framework Agreement on Hong Kong and Guangdong", with Suggestion for Legislation' [《粤港合作框架协议>的性质、效力分析及立法建议》] (2011) 6 *Academic Research* 38

Zou Y and Jones L, 'China's Response to Threats to Its Overseas Economic Interests: Softening Non-Interference and Cultivating Hegemony' (2020) 29 *Journal of Contemporary China* 92

# Reports

Alano J et al, *Foreign Case Study Report: China Petroleum & Chemical Corporation (Sinopec Corp)* (University of the Philippines Diliman, 2019)

Asian Corporate Governance Association, *The Development History of Chinese Corporate Governance* [《中国公司治理进化史》] (2018)

Bickenbach F, Liu WH and Li G, 'The EU–China Bilateral Investment Agreement in Negotiation: Motivation, Conflicts and Perspectives', *Kiel Policy Brief* No 95 (October 2015)

Brefort L, Valtchev Tenev S and Zhang C, *Corporate Governance and Enterprise Reform in China* (The World Bank, 2002)

Cai P, *Understanding China's Belt and Road Initiative* (Lowy Institute, March 2017)

CDB, *The Annual Report 2017 of CDB* [《国开行2017年度报告》] (2017)

Charlotin D and Bohmer L, 'Chinese Network Companies Notifies Sweden of Alleged BIT Breaches', *Investment Arbitration Reporter* (latest update 12 March 2021)

Cooley A, *The Emerging Political Economy of OBOR* (Centre for Strategic and International Studies, October 2016)

Downs E, *Energy Security Series: China* (The Brookings Foreign Policy Studies, 2006)

Downs E, *Inside China Inc: China Development Bank's Cross-Border Energy Deals* (Brookings, March 2011)

Downs E, *The China–Pakistan Economic Corridor Power Projects: Insights into Environmental and Debt Sustainability* (Center on Global Energy Policy, Columbia SIPA, October 2019)

Duchatel M, Brauner O and Hang Z, 'Protecting China's Overseas Interests', SIPRI Policy Paper No. 41 (Stockholm International Peace Research Institute, June 2014)

Ebel R, *Energy and Geopolitics in China: Mixing Oil and Politics* (Washing, DC, Centre for Strategic & International Studies, 2009)

Energy Charter Secretariat, *China Investment Report* (2017)

Evans PC and Downs ES, 'Untangling China's Quest for Oil through State-backed Financial Deals', *Policy Brief* 154 (The Brookings Institution, May 2006)

EXIMB, 'Annual Report 2016' [《2016年度报告》] (2016)
Ferriggi K, *Security of Oil Supply in China* (Clingendael International Energy Programme, 2020)
Galkin P, Chen D and Ke J, *China's Energy Investment Through the Lens of the Belt and Road Initiative* (King Abdullah Petroleum Studies and Research Centre, 2019)
Guang P, 'A Chinese Perspective on the Shanghai Cooperation Organization' in AJK Bailes et al (eds), *The Shanghai Cooperation Organization* (Stockholm International Peace Research Institute, 2007) 45–58
Handke S, 'Securing and Fuelling China's Ascent to Power' (Clingendael International Energy Programme, August 2006)
Handke S, *Securing and Fuelling China's Ascent to Power* (CIEP, August 2006)
Henderson J and Mitrova T, *Energy Relations between Russia and China: Playing Chess with the Dragon* (Oxford Institute for Energy Studies, 2016)
Henderson J and Moe A, *The Globalization of Russian Gas* (Cheltenham, Edward Elgar 2019)
Husar J and Best D, *Energy Investments and Technology Transfer Across Emerging Economies: The Case of Brazil and China* (IEA, 2013)
IEA, *Energy Supply Security: Emergency Response of IEA Countries* (OECD Publishing, 2014)
IEA, *Gas 2019: Analysis and forecast to 2024* (IEA, June 2019)
IEA, *World Energy Outlook 2017* (OECD Publshing, 2017)
Indeo F, 'China as Security Provider in Central Asia Post 2014: A Realistic Perspective?', *Central Asia Security Policy Briefs* (January 2015)
International Crisis Group, *China's Thirst for Oil* (2008)
Jiang J and Ding C, *Update on Overseas Investments by China's National Oil Companies: Achievements and Challenges since 2011* (IEA, 2014)
Jiang J and Sinton J, *Overseas Investments by Chinese National Oil Companies* (IEA, 2011)
Keppler JH, *International Relations and Security of Energy Supply: Risks to Continuity and Geopolitical Risks* (European Parliament's Committee on Foreign Affairs, 2007)
Kong B, *An Anatomy of China's Insecurity and Its Strategies* (Pacific Northwest National Laboratory, December 2005)
Kowalski P and Rabaioli D, 'Bringing Together International Trade and Investment Perspectives on State Enterprises', OECD Trade Policy Papers, No 201 (OECD Publishing, 2017)
Kreft H, *China's Quest for Energy* (Hoover Institution of Stanford University, October 2006)
Lardy N, *Markets Over Mao: The Rise of Private Business in China* (Peterson Institute for International Economics, 2014)
Lee H and Shalmon D, *Searching for Oil: China's Oil Initiatives in the Middle East* (Belfer Center for Science and International Affairs, January 2007)
Liu X, Zhou F and Li J, 'Adjustment and Optimization of Energy Supply Structure in China' in *China National Energy Strategy and Policy 2020* (Energy Research Institute of NDRC, 2004)
Lv G, *Historical Development of the Overseas Investment Approval Procedure* [《我国境外投资行政审批制度的历史沿革》] (Development Research Center of the State Council, 2002)
Ma D, *Rebalancing China's Energy Strategy* (Paulson Papers on Energy and Environment, January 2015)
Ma K, *China's Current Energy Situation and the '11th Five-Year Plan' for Energy Development* [《我国当前的能源形势与"十一五"能源发展》] (a Report at the Conference on the Current Situation jointly sponsored by six ministries in the Central Propaganda Department of PRC, 2006)
Meidan M, *China's 13th Five-Year Plan: Implications for Oil Markets* (Oxford Institute for Energy Studies, June 2016)
Meidan M, *The Structure of China's Oil Industry: Past Trends and Future Prospects* (Oxford Institute for Energy Studies, May 2016)
Melton O, *China's Five-Year Planning System: Implications for the Reform Agenda* (Testimony for the US–China Economic and Security Review Commission, 22 April 2015)
Milhaupt C and Zheng W, *Why Mixed-Ownership Reforms Cannot Fix China's State Sector* (Paulson Policy Memorandum, January 2016)

MOFCOM, *1992–2001: Adjustment and Development of Foreign Direct Investments* [《1992–2001：对外直接投资调整发展》] (MOFCOM, 2002)
MOFCOM, *The Report of Development of Overseas Investments 2014* [《对外投资合作发展报告2014》] (2014)
MOFCOM, *The Report of Development of Overseas Investments 2016* [《对外投资合作发展报告2016》] (2016)
MOFCOM, Report of Development of Overseas Investments 2017 [《对外投资合作发展报告2017》] (2017)
MOFCOM, *The Report of Development of Overseas Investments 2018* [《对外投资合作发展报告2018》] (2018)
OECD, *Corporate Governance of Listed Companies in China* (OECD Publishing, 2011)
OECD, 'Foreign Government-Controlled Investors and Recipient Country Investment Policies – A Scoping Paper' (OECD Publishing, January 2009)
OECD, *International Investment Perspectives: Freedom of Investment in A Changing World* (OECD 2007)
OECD, Secretariat, Assessing Foreign State-Owned Enterprises: Guidance for Regulators Based on the OECD Guidelines on Corporate Governance of SOEs (OECD Publishing, 2016)
Oxford Analytica Daily Brief Service, *China: Nuclear Exporters Will Target Developing World* (Oxford Analytica Daily Brief Service, 21 September 2016)
Peyrouse S, 'The Economic Aspects of the Chinese–Central Asia Rapprochement', Silk Road Paper (Central Asia–Caucasus Institute & Silk Road Studies Program, 2007)
Rosen D, Leutert W and Guo S, *Missing Link: Corporate Governance in China's State Sector* (Asia Society, November 2018)
Salidjanova N, *Going Out: An Overview of China's Outward Foreign Direct Investment* (USCC Staff Research Report, 30 March 2011)
SASAC, *SASAC Yearbook* [《中国国有资产监督管理年鉴》] (2012–13)
Sauvant KP, *FDI Protectionism is on the Rise* (The World Bank, 2009)
Sinosure, *Report of Investments Facilitation in Different States 2015* [《国别投资经营便利化状况报告2015》] (2015)
State Council, China's Energy Policy 2012; MOFCOM, *The Report of Development of Overseas Investments 2015* [《对外投资合作发展报告2015》] (2015)
Szamosszegi A and Kyle C, *An Analysis of State-owned Enterprises and State Capitalism in China* (US–China Economic and Security Review Commission, 26 October 2011)
The China Institute of University of Alberta, *State-Owned Enterprises in the Chinese Economy Today: Role, Reform, and Evolution* (2018)
The Eurasia Group, 'China's Overseas Investments in Oil and Gas Production', Prepared for the US–China Economic and Security Review Commission (16 October 2006)
The World Bank Group, *Energy Security Issues* (5 December 2005)
UNCTAD, *World Investment Report 2016: Investor Nationality: Policy Challenges* (UNCTAD, 2017)
United Nation, *World Investment Report 2012: Towards a New Generation of Investment Policies* (United Nation, New York and Geneva, 2012)
Wang ZW, *Securing Energy Flows from Central Asia to China and the Relevance of the Energy Charter Treaty to China* (Energy Charter Secretariat, 2015)
White House Office of Trade and Manufacturing Policy, *How China's Economic Aggression Threatens the Technologies and Intellectual Property of the United States and the World* (White House Office of Trade and Manufacturing Policy, June 2018)
World Resource Institute, *Research into Promoting the Overseas Renewable Energy Investments of Chinese Companies* (《促进中国企业可再生能源海外投资研究》) (World Resource Institute, 2022)
Xu X, *Chinese NOC's Overseas Strategies: Background, Comparison and Remarks* (James A Baker III Institute for Public Policy, 2007)
Zha D, *Oil Pipeline from Myanmar to China: Competing Perspectives* (RSIS report, 24 July 2009)

Zhang C, *The World Bank in China's State-Owned Enterprise Reform Since the 1980s* (The World Bank, 2019)
Zhao X, *The Shanghai Cooperation Organisation and Counter-Terrorism Cooperation* (Institute for Security and Development Policy, 2012)

## Working Papers

Andrews-Speed P, 'Energy Security in East Asia: a European View', paper presented at the Symposium on Pacific Energy Cooperation 2003 (12–13 February 2003)
Balding C and Clarke D, 'Who Owns Huawei?' (2019) at ssrn.com/abstract=3372669
Bustelo P, 'China and the Geopolitics of Oil in the Asian Pacific Region' (2005) Elcano Royal Institute Working Paper 38/2005
Callaghan M and Hubbard P, 'The Asian Infrastructure Investment Bank: Multilateralism on the Silk Road', EABER Working Paper Series Paper No 116 (East Asian Bureau of Economic Research, 2016)
Capobianco A and Christiansen H, 'Competitive Neutrality and State-Owned Enterprises: Challenges and Policy Options', OECD Corporate Governance Working Paper No 1 (2011)
Forstater M et al, 'Corporate Responsibility in African Development: Insights from an Emerging Dialogue', Corporate Social Responsibility Initiative Working Paper No 60 (2010)
Holz C, The Unfinished Business of State-owned Enterprise Reform in the People's Republic of China', CESifo Working Paper No 7688 (CESifo, 2019)
Kawase T and Ambashi M, 'Disciplines on State-Owned Enterprises under the Trans-Pacific Partnership Agreement: Overview and Assessment', ERIA Discussion Paper Series (February 2018)
Kong B and Gallagher K, 'Chinese Development Finance for Solar and Wind Power Abroad', GCI Working Paper 01 (2020)
Koolaee E and Tishehyar M, 'China's Energy Security Approach in Central Asia' paper presented at *Silk Route and Eurasia: Peace & Cooperation*, Conference of Globalisation and Eurasian Peace in Kashmir (October 2011)
Liang C, Song H and Zhang X, 'Advancing Principles and Strategies of Power Grid Interconnection in the Belt and Road', International Conference on Energy, Power, Electrical and Environmental Engineering, at Wuhan (2018)
Lin YH and Chang YC, 'Do State-Owned Enterprises Have Worse Corporate Governance? An Empirical Study of Corporate Practices in China', NYU Center for Law, Economics and Organization, Law & Economic Research Paper Series, Working Paper No 19-28 (December 2019)
OECD, 'State-Owned Enterprises and the Low-Carbon Transition' (2018) OECD Environment Working Papers, 18 April 2018
Tan X et al, *China's Overseas Investments in the Wind and Solar Industries: Trends and Drivers*, Working Paper Series (World Resources Institute, 2013)
Umbach F, 'China's Belt and Road Initiative and Its Energy-Security Dimensions', RSIS Working Paper Series No 320 (January 2019)
UNCTAD, 'Admission and Establishment', IIA issues series paper (2002)
Wehrlé F and Pohl J, 'Investment Policies Related to National Security: A Survey of Country Practices', OECD Working Papers on International Investment No 2016/02
Yu K, 'Energy Cooperation and Regional Order in the Belt and Road Initiative: A Case Study of China's Investment in the China–Pakistan Economic Corridor', London Asia Pacific Centre for Social Science Working Paper (October 2018)

# INDEX

www.ingramcontent.com/pod-product-compliance
Ingram Content Group UK Ltd.
Pitfield, Milton Keynes, MK11 3LW, UK
UKHW020805290926
15470UKWH00003B/962